THIRD EDITION

# *Developing and Training Human Resources in Organizations*

## Kenneth N. Wexley

*President, Wexley Consulting • Human Resources Decisions*
Annapolis, Maryland
*Affiliate Professor, George Mason University*
Fairfax, Virginia

## Gary P. Latham

*Secretary of State Professor of Organizational Effectiveness*
*Rotman School of Management*
*University of Toronto*
Toronto, Ontario

Upper Saddle River, New Jersey 07458

**Library of Congress Cataloging-in-Publication Data**

Wexley, Kenneth N., 1943–
  Developing and training human resources in organizations / Kenneth N. Wexley, Gary
P. Latham.—3rd ed.
    p. cm.
  Includes bibliographical references and index.
  ISBN 0-13-089497-4
    1. Employees—Training of.  I. Latham, Gary P.  II. Title.

  HF5549.5.T7 W46 2002
  658.3'124—dc21

2001036425

**Editor-in-Chief:** Jeff Shelstad
**Acquisitions Editor:** Melissa Steffens
**Assistant Editor:** Jessica Sabloff
**Editorial Assistant:** Kevin Glynn
**Media Project Manager:** Michele Faranda
**Senior Marketing Manager:** Shannon Moore
**Marketing Assistant:** Christine Genneken
**Managing Editor (Production):** Judy Leale
**Production Editor:** Cindy Spreder
**Production Assistant:** Diane Falcone
**Permissions Supervisor:** Suzanne Grappi
**Associate Director, Manufacturing:** Vincent Scelta
**Production Manager:** Arnold Vila
**Manufacturing Buyer:** Diane Peirano
**Cover Manager:** Jayne Conte
**Cover Design:** Bruce Kenselaar
**Cover Illustration/Photo:** Warren Gebert, Stock Illustration Source, Inc.
**Illustrator (Interior):** Rainbow Graphics
**Assoc. Dir. Multimedia Production:** Karen Goldsmith
**Manager, Print Production:** Christy Mahon
**Page Formatter:** Ashley Scattergood
**Composition:** Rainbow Graphics
**Printer/Binder:** Phoenix

Credits and acknowledgments borrowed from other sources and reproduced, with
permission, in this textbook appear on the appropriate page within the text.

10  9  8  7  6  5  4  3  2  1
ISBN 0-13-089497-4

**To the best and most loving trainers we know:**

*Ruth Wexley and Soosan Latham*

**To our wonderful children:**

*David and Matthew Wexley*
*Bryan and Brandon Latham*

**And in memory of three people who greatly influenced our lives in our formative years:**

*Ruth Sherman, Helen Wexley, and Louise Margaret Marshall*

# Contents

# *Preface*

Since we published the second edition of *Developing Human Resources in Organizations* in 1991, we've seen two major trends in training and development activities in both the private and public sectors in North America. First, more organizations are providing training and development for their employees at all levels. Second, training expenditures are increasing steadily. Today, a typical organization devotes as much as 1.8 percent of their total payroll toward training employees.

There are many societal changes responsible for increasing the popularity of training and development activities. First, with the low unemployment rate causing a very tight labor market, organizations are competing with one another to attract and retain talented people. One important way of doing this is by providing better training and career development opportunities than one's competitors. Second, as the workforce becomes more diverse demographically, organizations have a great deal of pressure on them to hire, promote, and train women, minorities, individuals over 40, and people with disabilities. Third, as a result of the rapid changes in technology, employees need to be retrained on new equipment, so that they do not become technically obsolescent. Fourth, this new era of globalization and the increase of multinational organizations put pressure on companies to provide training to employees who will have overseas assignments or who work in the United States or Canada but have to interact with individuals from other countries. Finally, through numberous mergers and acquisitions, North American employees are finding that their jobs are changing and, consequently, they have to learn new things.

With all of this in mind, the third edition of *Developing and Training Human Resources in Organizations* is intended for teachers and students as well as for human resource generalists and specialists in the private and public business sectors. Thus, we tried to make our language and writing style as straightforward as possible. We also tried to provide our readers with real-world examples, while, at the same time, making certain that we are not falling into the trap of advertising a particular consulting firm's products or services. References are provided throughout the book to substantiate key findings and to provide an exhaustive resource base for those readers who want to study a topic in greater detail.

# CONTENT CHANGES IN THE THIRD EDITION

Since the second edition, we continue to work in this field as practitioners, researchers, and teachers. If we had to choose the major development that has impacted human resources in the past 10 years, it would definitely be the impact of computer technology on the delivery of training and development programs. The onset of technology-based training (i.e., Internet, intranet, CD-ROMs, DVD-ROMs) has revolutionized this field!

We organized this third edition similar to the second edition. We continue to use our nine-cell scheme (i.e., three goals × three strategies) for categorizing the training and development methods that are currently being used by organizations. Although there are times when this model is frustrating because a particular training or development method could be placed in more than one category, it is still the best method for conceptualizing and differentiating various employee training and management development approaches.

Chapter 1 provides an overview of training and development. We revised and updated the statistics to reflect their current increase in popularity. We feel that it's important for readers to appreciate the fact that training and development can't be implemented successfully without taking into consideration their relationship with other human resource management activities such as staffing, performance appraisal, and organization development. The title of Chapter 2 has upgraded from "Organizational Factors Affecting Training and Development" to "The Organizational Role of the Training Specialist." Included in this chapter are what to consider when organizing a training department, the role of the training specialist in organizations, factors that need to be considered when organizing a training function, the importance of taking a financial approach to training, and the challenges of creating a first-rate training staff through proper selection and training. Two of the important topics covered in this chapter are how to maintain ongoing managerial support and how to ensure that all training and development activities are legal. An important new section in this chapter focuses on the impact of the Americans with Disabilities Act on the field of training and development.

Chapter 3 describes various ways of identifying training needs. Specifically, it teaches the training specialist how to find the answer to three key questions: (1) *where* is training and development needed within our organization? (2) *what* should the content of each of these training programs be? and (3) *which* of our employees would benefit from participating in one or more of these programs. Only by performing the various analyses discussed in this chapter, will organizations avoid wasting time and money on delivering training and development programs to employees and organizational units where they are not needed.

In Chapter 4, we shift our attention to ways of maximizing trainees' learning of skills and abilities needed for success not only today, but throughout their careers. We added a lot of new research to this chapter. Much of this new research derives from cognitive psychology where researchers have been examining the fundamentals of short- and long-term memory, perception, thinking, reasoning, and problem solving. We tried to create a good balance between the contributions of "behaviorists" and "cognitivists" to maximizing employee learning. One of the biggest problems faced by training specialists is finding ways to encourage trainees to apply what they learned to their jobs. In light of this, we devote a lot of time in this chapter to discussing what can be done before, during, and after training to facilitate positive transfer from the training environment to the job environment.

Once the training strategies for maximizing learning have been implemented, it is incumbent on training specialists to determine whether the strategies are effective or whether they need to be modified or even discarded prior to any large-scale implementation. Hence, Chapter 5 focuses on evaluation. It discusses various ways of measuring a training program's effectiveness. New to this chapter are the results of meta-analytical research that examines the interrelationships among these various types of criterion measures. This chapter then provides a discussion of the most applicable measurement designs that are available today to human resource specialists for determining the true effectiveness of training programs. For the reader interested and knowledgeable about statistics, we include a brief discussion of their use in assessing change. The "Final Comments" section discusses four major organizational barriers to training evaluation and how to overcome them.

With an understanding of the organizational factors affecting training and development systems, ways of identifying training needs in an organization, strategies for maximizing each trainee's learning, and methods of measuring training effectiveness so as to "tweak" and thereby ensure its success, we shift our attention to an examination of the various training approaches available today to training specialists. These training approaches can bring substantial and permanent improvements in a trainee's self-awareness, job skills, and motivation.

Chapter 6 describes on-site training methods. We changed and updated this chapter, as well as Chapter 7, more than any other chapter in this third addition. Here is where we discuss the impact of technology-based training. In Chapter 6, we describe such timely topics as the Internet, intranets, electronic performance support systems, ROMs, and the use of virtual reality. Some of the new topics covered in Chapter 7 are video conferencing, as well as equipment and virtual reality simulators. On the other hand, we don't ignore some of the popular off-site methods such as instructor-led classrooms and the use of various audiovisual training techniques.

Theoretical advances in developing and training leaders resulted in the expansion of Chapter 8. We needed to describe in detail how each of these theoretical approaches is being used today for training corporate leaders. Our goal was to provide readers with a clear understanding of each approach to leadership development so that they can judge, through discussions with other students or practitioners, the strengths and limitations of each approach. Chapter 9 focuses on different management and executive development approaches now being implemented by organizations in both the private and public sectors. We organized these approaches into categories depending on their goals of self-awareness, job skills, and motivation. Some of the approaches are totally new and have not been covered before in either the first or second editions of our book, such as outdoor experiential training, action learning, and real-time coaching.

Finally, we changed and updated Chapter 10 completely. This chapter examines various societal concerns that impact the field of training and development. We discuss the impact of certain important societal trends that evolved since the second edition of this book. Examples of these topics include basic skills training; English as a second language; the disabled, dislocated workers and youth; telecommuting training; wellness training; and team skills training.

The goal of revising this edition was straightforward: To make students and human resource professionals aware of the advances in the field of training and development that can be used to increase the effectiveness of an organization's workforce. It was our intention to bring all of our experiences, as well as the experiences of the colleagues we interviewed for this book, to our readers. It is also our intention to convey our thoughts in an interesting and informative manner through the use of concrete examples.

In closing, we would like to thank Lee Kietchel, who was a doctoral student in Industrial and Organizational Psychology at George Mason University, for all of her help in reviewing the training and development literature. We applaud Lee's thoroughness, patience, and dedication to this project. We also want to thank Dr. David Grove from Procter & Gamble for his valuable insights. Several members of David's training staff gave us so much of their time and provided such wonderful input, we would like to thank them here: Lisa Owens, Heidi Weber, Fran Sheperd, and Larry Green. Last, but not least, we would like to thank Ruth Wexley for her help in giving sagely advice on the rewriting of this edition, as well as her patience, love, and support.

**K.N.W.**
**G.P.L.**

# CHAPTER

## *Introduction*

1

- Wayne Starr has been a research chemist for the past 10 years. Both Wayne and his supervisor know all too well that Wayne has not kept up with new developments in the field. His professional obsolescence is beginning to seriously affect his performance in the company.
- Roy Davis, a 19-year-old African American mechanic's helper in a North Carolina pulp mill, desires to become a first-class maintenance mechanic or machinist.
- Pat Baker is 55 years old and has been out of the workforce for 20 years while raising her children. She was once a bookkeeper. She would like to work in an organization for the next 15 years.
- Gene Harvest is a military officer and is looking forward to retiring in two years. He would like to start a new career in the construction trade but is unsure how exactly to go about it.
- Bryan Marshall is a white electrician who is upset because he has not been admitted to a training program that would have led directly to a higher paying job. He is threatening his employer with a lawsuit because he believes he has evidence that African Americans and women who are less qualified than he have been admitted into the program.

All these people have one thing in common: They are all in need of ways to increase their knowledge and skills. Currently, they are experiencing feelings ranging from frustration due to professional obsolescence and alleged discrimination to anxiety over how to reenter the labor market and to increase their levels of expertise. They have the motivation to change their behavior, but they lack the knowledge and skill to do it. All of them are in need of training and development. Let us look at a few more examples:

- George Hancock, the executive director of a medium-sized midwestern medical center, is concerned because the department heads and supervisors at his hospital not only exhibit poor interpersonal skills with their employees but seem to have little idea what their roles should be as managers. This problem has been increasing recently as the medical center has been growing rapidly in size.

1

- Mason Smith, vice president of manufacturing of a large U.S. electronics company, plans on starting foreign plant operations in several underdeveloped nations in Central America and Africa. One of the major challenges ahead for him will be the training and development of the local labor force.
- Claire Obreza is training director of a medium-sized factory that manufactures two brands of soap using an extrusion process. Recently, a decision was made to put three additional soap products on board that require another kind of manufacturing process called milling. In addition, corporate headquarters decided to begin production of a liquid detergent product. Claire and her training staff are currently developing new hires and upgrading present employees so that they will be able to handle these technological changes.
- A diesel engine company and a large farm-equipment company have recently merged. The diesel company has had a long tradition of manufacturing engines for trucks, commercial fishing boats, and construction machinery. With the new merger, the engine company will also be involved with the production of diesel engines for tractors, combines, and self-propelled sprayers.

These four training needs sketches illustrate the need for training from a systems rather than an individual perspective. Whenever organizations grow in size, anticipate a merger, adjust to new plants coming on board, introduce new products and services, and so on, an organizationwide training effort is often needed.

Our purpose here is to describe how training and development can provide solutions to such problems. Before providing answers to these issues, a brief review of the role of training and development in organizations is in order. Accordingly, we begin with a discussion of the purpose served by training and development in organizations, and then progress to a consideration of the popularity of this approach for increasing both the individual's and the organization's effectiveness. Next, we consider how training and development is related to other human resource systems such as job analysis, personnel selection, performance appraisals, and organization development. When you complete this chapter, you should understand what constitutes training and development. You will then be ready to learn the technical aspects of this field.

## PURPOSES OF TRAINING AND DEVELOPMENT

We used the phrase *training and development* several times in the preceding section. *Training and development* refers to a planned effort by an organization to facilitate the learning of job-related behavior on the part of its employees. The term *behavior* is used in the broad sense to include any knowledge and skill acquired by an employee through practice. Four examples of acquiring knowledge and skill are discussed here.

- Margaret Knopf has been working as a salesperson in a large housewares store for six months. Her dollar sales volume has been evaluated by the store's sales manager as only "adequate" despite the fact that Margaret has been repeatedly told by the sales manager that customers find her pleasant, vivacious, and knowledgeable about store products and services. Unfortunately, Margaret has been told by the sales manager that she has a problem with her spoken grammar. Margaret was raised in a rural area and tends to use such phrases as "when we was talking" and "I'm goin' to find me a customer." Although her friends have become accustomed to Margaret's way of speaking, some of the store's customers have complained that her speech is unprofessional. This has affected Margaret's sales performance negatively because many customers approach other salespeople rather than her. It hurts Margaret to learn of her deficiency at this point in her life. Nevertheless, she wants to be a successful salesperson in this store and realizes that she needs training in grammar. Moreover, the sales manager does not want to lose Margaret. Consequently, the company has hired a trainer to teach Margaret the essentials of correct grammar.

- Bob Anderson sells life insurance for a small independent insurance firm. As an independent agent, Bob is free to sell different kinds of life insurance for various nationally known life insurance companies. Unfortunately, with the current rate of inflation, Bob's business has been declining. It seems to him that fewer and fewer people want to invest their excess capital (if they have any) in life insurance. Bob has suddenly had to compete with alternative sources of investments such as cash funds, stocks, bonds, and home mortgages. He and his colleagues must learn about the relative advantages and disadvantages of different types of life insurance (e.g., whole versus term) compared to other avenues of investment. Only in this way can Bob answer the questions and deal with the objections of potential customers. Thus, Bob has decided to enroll in a company-sponsored six-week investment course.

- Ivan Blum is attending a three-week floral arranging course stressing skills acquisition. During the course, Ivan will be learning how to take telephone orders, work with dry flowers, and care for and handle live flowers. In addition, he will be trained to create bouquets, baskets, corsages, and set pieces for weddings, graduations, funerals, and everyday work.

- Jayne Long is a middle-level manager at a large midwestern insurance company. During Jayne's yearly performance review meeting with her boss, Jayne learned that she needs to work on improving her managerial skills, especially delegating work to her employees and managing her own time better. Consequently, Jayne and her boss have agreed that she will attend several management development workshops during the upcoming year that focus on improving her weak areas.

As you can see, the general purpose of training and development involves knowledge and skill acquisition. Any training and development effort can have one or more of the following three goals: (1) to improve an individual's level of self-awareness; (2) to increase an individual's skill in one or more areas of expertise; and/or (3) to increase an individual's motivation to perform his or her job well.

Self-awareness involves learning about oneself. It includes understanding one's roles and responsibilities in the organization, recognizing differences between one's actual and espoused managerial philosophy, understanding how one is viewed by others, and learning how one's actions affect other people's actions. Later in this book, you will see that certain training and development techniques have as their objective giving trainees increased self-awareness.

Most of what is traditionally considered to be training and development deals with increasing an individual's skill. This skill may involve electrical wiring, painting, blueprint reading, using a computerized cash register, following safety procedures, setting priorities, delegating or handling employee grievances, or increasing one's effectiveness as a leader. Obviously, these are just a few of the many different kinds of skills that can be learned during training and development programs. Regardless of the type of knowledge and skill involved, the training program is based on the assumption that it will increase an employee's ability to perform effectively on the job. You will see in Chapters 6 through 9 that many training and development methods have as their goal improving an employee's knowledge and skill in the areas of decision making and problem solving.

Often, people possess the skill and knowledge to perform the job, but they lack the motivation to exhibit their abilities. For this reason, the goal of some training and development programs is to maximize the employee's desire to perform the job well. These programs, admittedly, are relatively few in number. Also, most of these programs do not have employee motivation as their sole objective. For example, job rotation (see Chapter 6) involves giving trainees an opportunity to work on a series of jobs in various parts of the organization in order to sharpen their career aspirations and commitment to the organization and, in addition, help them to develop their managerial skills in the process. On the other hand, there are training and development methods wherein the sole objective is to increase a person's managerial motivation. These programs are discussed in Chapter 8, where the focus is on the developing and training of leaders who will be able to cope effectively with the demands of the twenty-first century. Chapter 9 broadens this emphasis to a discussion of executive and management development.

These three broad goals—increasing employee self-awareness, skill (including decision making/problem solving), and motivation—are attained by using one or more training strategies. At least three basic strategies are available to a training specialist: The specialist can try to improve an employee's performance by directing his or her efforts toward (1) cognition (i.e., thoughts and ideas), (2) behavior, or (3) the environment in which the person is working. A few examples might help us to distinguish between these three strategies.

Company orientation programs (see Chapter 6) provide new hires with information about work schedules, vacations, grievance procedures, pay scales, overtime, holidays, benefits, and so on. The intervention strategy used here is one that focuses on the individual's thoughts and ideas. Chapter 8 describes a leadership program that teaches managers how to ask themselves a prescribed series of questions before deciding on how much participation they should allow their employees to have in the decision-making process. Once again, the strategy is cognitive in nature in determining an appropriate leadership style.

Behavioral modeling (see Chapter 8) has its roots in cognitive psychology, but focuses primarily on the trainee's overt behavior. With this training approach, trainees view videotapes showing models who behave appropriately in a particular situation. Supervisors, for instance, might be taught how to take effective discipline action, delegate responsibility to employees, motivate the average performer, and handle customer complaints. Prior to and after viewing each videotape, the trainees review a list of learning points (e.g., greet the irate customer in a friendly manner, listen to the customer's complaints without interrupting him or her) that specifically spell out the effective behaviors that are to be learned. The trainees are also given an opportunity to practice their newly acquired behaviors during role-play exercises, and they receive feedback from both the trainer and fellow trainees on the effectiveness with which they demonstrate these behaviors. As you can see, this training method uses a behavioral strategy in that it focuses primarily on modifying the trainee's behaviors rather than transmitting a large amount of cognitive or factual information.

Sometimes the improvement in an employee's job performance can be brought about by means of planned environmental changes. As noted earlier, job rotation involves training people by moving them systematically from department to department. During the course of training, the trainees are exposed to a well-planned sequence of environmental changes (i.e., jobs, supervisors, coworkers). Another way of effecting environmental change is to change the consequences that take place immediately after the behavior has occurred. For example, a tire manufacturing company reduced excessive employee tardiness in several of its plants. For years, it mattered little if employees came to work as much as 15 minutes late because supervisors ignored all but excessive cases. Recently, the company decided to change this behavior by instituting a program that rewarded punctual behavior. The training and development staff developed a lottery sytem whereby employees who had not been tardy for an entire month would be eligible to enter their name in a lottery drawing for cash prizes. In addition, supervisors were instructed to praise an employee periodically for continued punctual behavior. In this situation, the tire company changed its employees' tardiness record by making the consequences for punctuality positive.

At this point, we have described three goals and three strategies for training and development. Figure 1.1 presents a nine-cell scheme that is useful for categorizing the training and development methods that are currently being used by organizations. It is important to note that these nine categories are not discrete entities because some training methods can be classified properly into more than one cell. This classification was made for convenience and clarity of discussion purposes only. This figure is referred to again in Chapters 6, 7, 8, and 9, where the specific training approaches are presented.

## POPULARITY OF TRAINING AND DEVELOPMENT

Almost all private and public organizations have formal and informal training and development programs for their employees. According to *Training* magazine's 1999 Industry Report, the total dollars budgeted for formal training by

| | GOALS | | |
|---|---|---|---|
| **STRATEGIES** | *Self-Awareness* | *Job Skills* | *Motivation* |
| **Cognitive** | Career development<br>Management role<br>theory<br>Need for achievement<br>Double-loop learning<br>Sensitivity training<br>Self-directed<br>management<br>development<br>Transactional<br>analysis | Orientation training<br>and socialization<br>of new employees<br>Lecture<br>Audiovisual<br>Vroom-Yetton model<br>Case study<br>The incident process<br>Job aids<br>Computer-based<br>training<br>Teleconferencing<br>Corporate classrooms/<br>colleges<br>Seminars and<br>workshops | Role motivation<br>theory<br>Need for<br>achievement<br>Training<br>Survey feedback |
| **Behavioral** | Interactive skills<br>training | On-the-job training<br>Apprenticeship<br>Programmed<br>instruction<br>Equipment simulators<br>Computer-assisted<br>instruction<br>Rational manager<br>training<br>Conference<br>discussion<br>Assessment centers<br>Role playing<br>Management games<br>Grid seminars<br>Leader-member<br>exchange<br>Juniors boards<br>Understudy<br>assignments<br>Mentoring | Coaching<br>Behavior modeling |
| **Environmental** | Leader match | | Job rotation<br>Behavior<br>modification |

FIGURE 1.1   Goals and Strategies for Training and Development

U.S. organizations that employ 100 or more people was $62.5 billion. Since their survey respondents were asked to consider only formal training, which is defined as instruction that is deliberately planned and structured, this large sum of money actually underestimates the true amount spent each on training because it ignores the vast amount of informal, on-the-job training that goes on in organizations each and every day.[1]

The popularity of training and development activities is also surveyed each year by an organization known as the American Society for Training and Development (ASTD). Founded in 1944, ASTD represents more than 70,000 members in the field of workplace learning and performance. These training professionals work in every area within this growing industry and are from more than 150 countries around the world. One of the services that ASTD provides for its members is its benchmarking service, an annual process in which information is gathered from all types of organizations on the nature of their employer-provided training expenditures, practices, and outcomes. The 1999 ASTD State of the Industry Report[2] sheds a great deal of light on the current popularity and continued growth of training and development activities in the United States. It is based on data gathered from 801 U.S. organizations representing all major industry sectors (i.e., agriculture/mining/construction, information technology, nondurable and durable manufacturing, transportation/public utilities, trade, finance/insurance/real estate, services, health care, government) as well as firms of all sizes. According to the report, training expenditures have been increasing steadily each year, and the pattern is expected to continue. For instance, the typical organization in the benchmarking service spent $1.4 million on training in 1996, $2 million in 1997, and an estimated $2.1 million in 1998. In the 1999 report, ASTD introduced two key ratios that provide a quick snapshot of the state of the training industry: total training expenditures as a percentage of payroll and total training expenditures per employee. These ratios provide a much better basis for comparing organizations of vastly different sizes, as opposed to total training expenditure figures, because they correct for differences in organization size. Similar to the total training expenditures, these key ratios have steadily increased from year to year. By 1999, the benchmarking service firms reported spending $649 per employee and 1.8 percent of payroll. Another key ratio used in ASTD's annual reports to track the extent of employer-provided training is the percentage of employees an organization trains. The average benchmarking service firm provided training for just over 74 percent of its employees in 1997, up from 69 percent in 1996.

There are many dramatic changes occurring in our society that will demand the training and retraining of North American workers. First, as organizations experience more and more pressure to hire and promote women, minorities, individuals over age 40, and the handicapped, this area of personnel activity will become even more critical than it is now for the efficient management of an organization's human resources. Second, many workers are being left to fend for themselves when shifts in the economy or foreign competition have affected or eliminated their jobs. As we enter the twenty-first century, traditional manufacturing industries such as steel, autos, and rubber will continue to provide a smaller share of the nation's jobs. In these and other blue-collar industries, million of jobs have disappeared, and these are jobs that will never come back. Instead, employment opportunities are growing in the high-technology, service, and information sectors. Feeling most of the brunt and in need of retraining are the mechanics, assemblers, welders, and semiskilled and unskilled laborers who work in the factories of the northern industrial belt. Third, the evolution of new and more sophisticated computer-based office and plant equipment mandates the need for continued retraining. For example, it has been estimated that employers will have to retrain office workers five to eight times during their careers.[3] Fourth, with this new era of globalization and the increase in the number of multinational organizations such as General Motors and IBM, employees will be expected to learn about other cultures and new ways of operating, especially if they are asked by their organizations to take temporary overseas assignments.[4] Finally, through mergers and acquisitions, some American employees are finding that they are now being managed differently than they were before. Perhaps they are now expected to take on more responsibility in their work, to be supervised less closely, and to make more decisions for themselves. Changes such as these are not easy for many employees; they therefore need training to help them to adapt and accept these changes. Finally, as individuals change jobs because of promotion, layoffs, transfer, or mid-career frustration, they want and need training and development.

Unfortunately, the necessity for training and development programs has fostered many fads. The popularity of a program, as indicated by trainee satisfaction, has frequently overshadowed the importance of examining whether the training is bringing about a relatively permanent change in the employee's self-awareness, decision-making/problem-solving skills, or motivation. The fad cycle often occurs in the following sequence: A new technique appears with a group of followers who announce its success. A second group develops modifications of the technique. Empirical studies may appear supporting the technique. Then there is a backlash. Critics question the usefulness of the new technique, but rarely produce any data to support their contention. The technique survives until a new technique appears. Then the whole procedure is repeated.[5] For example, in the early 1980s, behavior modeling training was the fad (see Chapter 9). Many organizations required their managers to receive behavior modeling training in the hope of enhancing their level of motivation.

Why did faddism occur? For one thing, few organizations ascertained their training needs systematically. Instead, they purchased packaged programs because someone in another organization told them they were good. Also, organizations seldom rigorously evaluated the effects of the programs they purchased. They simply went by how much the participants liked the session, and how much they "felt" it would benefit them. Little or no attempt was made to see if the training increased employee productivity on the job. For this reason,

Chapter 5 explains ways of determining whether a training program is indeed worthwhile. This chapter precedes the discussion of training techniques for three reasons. First, the danger of faddism is always present. Only systematic evaluation of training effectiveness can prevent its return. Second, the way or ways effectiveness will be defined and measured must be decided on at the time the training program is selected or designed and before it is implemented. Third, an understanding of the criteria for evaluating training and the procedures to be followed in making the evaluation will allow you to appreciate the strengths and weaknesses of the training approaches described in Chapters 6 through 9.

In summary, we hope that the information in this book will help minimize, if not eliminate, all fads in training. People must systematically identify training needs, build content into programs based on job information, and evaluate training in terms of the objectives for which it was designed. Only then will the field of training and development cease to be an art form that is dependent on the persuasiveness of its advocates, and instead be a science that is replicable by others.

## THE RELATIONSHIP OF TRAINING AND DEVELOPMENT TO OTHER HUMAN RESOURCE FUNCTIONS

Training and development is only one of several functions usually performed by an organization's human resource department. In order to better understand the nature of training and development in organizations, it is worthwhile to examine how the training function relates to other human resource activities carried out by the personnel department. Specifically, we look at how training and development relates to task analysis, staffing, performance appraisal, and organization development.

The purpose of task analysis is to provide information about the duties involved in performing a job and the skills and knowledge required to do the job well. Task analysis information serves as the foundation for most training and development programs because it answers the important question, "What must a trainee be taught in order to perform a job effectively?" Chapter 3 describes how task analysis information provides a way of systematically determining the appropriate content of training and development programs.

Staffing also has a direct relationship to training. The better an organization's personnel selection procedures, the more likely it is that the people it hires will already possess some of the skill and knowledge needed to perform their jobs effectively. Because these people have been carefully selected, they may not need an extensive training and development program. Conversely, if a company has a weak selection program and hires people who have fewer skills and less knowledge, more training and development will be needed to give these new hires the expertise they lack.

Measures of employee proficiency (e.g., ratings, behavioral observations, units produced, dollars earned, scrappage) serve many different purposes within an organization. For instance, performance appraisal measures are used as a basis for making decisions regarding promotions, layoffs, separations, and transfers. They can also be used as a method of administering wages and bonuses so that these are contingent on the "goodness" or appropriateness of an employee's performance. Performance appraisal measures affect training and development in four basic ways: (1) as a means of determining the training needs for various organizational units; (2) as a basis for evaluating the worth of training programs; (3) as a means of identifying employee weaknesses that might be alleviated through additional formal training and development; and (4) as a means of improving proficiency of employees by providing each of them with feedback regarding their performance during periodic appraisal interviews with their supervisors.

Organizational development (OD) is concerned with increasing the competence and health of an entire organizational system or subsystem. It typically involves a systematic diagnosis of an organization by one or more change agents, who then attempt to bring about meaningful and lasting organizational change. In the course of stimulating organizational change, OD specialists may call on different intervention strategies such as team building, career planning, process consultation, and role analysis. OD differs from training and development in that the latter is concerned primarily with improving the self-awareness, skills, and motivation of individual organizational members. Although an OD effort might involve employee development, it would do so only as a part of its larger objective of improving the competence of the units comprising the total organization. Some of the intervention techniques that are used by OD specialists (e.g., grid OD, survey feedback, management by objectives) are also used by trainers for developing individual managers (see Chapters 8 and 9).

## OVERVIEW OF THE BOOK

Now that you have a general understanding of the nature of the training and development function within organizations, you are ready to begin learning more technical subject matter. Several years ago, we were asked to write the third[6] and fourth[7] chapters on training and development to appear in the *Annual Review of Psychology*. This third edition's content reflects some of the issues from these reviews that are still timely, two later annual review chapters by Tannenbaum and Yukl[8] and Weick, Salas, and Cannon-Bowers,[9] plus our knowledge gained over the past decade since the second edition from psychological journals, business magazines, management journals, and a large volume of training materials sent to us by different organizations (e.g., hospitals, banks, unions, retail, and manufacturing). We compiled and integrated these materials to describe what is currently happening in the field of training and, at the same time, present our views on how training should be done. This apparent tension between the "ideal" and the "typical" training program surfaces frequently throughout the remaining chapters.

Chapter 2 covers the functions of the training staff within an organization. Once the training staff is established, these people need to determine the training needs of the organization systematically. This process involves analyzing both the short- and long-term goals of the organization, developing training content to teach employees how to attain these goals, and identifying people in need of this training. Chapter 3 examines these issues with special attention given to task analysis, which should be used to determine the content of training programs.

Chapter 4 deals with what the training staff needs to know to maximize learning by the trainees. This chapter considers such important issues as the trainability (i.e., capacity to learn) of the trainees, how the training program should be arranged to facilitate trainee learning, and what can be done to ensure that what is learned during training will be transferred by trainees to their jobs.

Chapter 5 describes approaches to be used for evaluating training program effectiveness. The evaluation of training is mandatory so that the organization, not to mention the training staff itself, can see whether a specific program truly leads to the attainment of the objectives for which it was designed. Only in this way will the organization be able to assess rigorously whether a training program should be continued, modified, or discarded.

Chapters 6 through 9 are concerned with specific approaches to employee development. In reviewing these different methods, we have grouped them according to whether they are typically conducted on the job (Chapter 6) or off the job (Chapter 7). Of course, some of the methods are used in both circumstances.

Management development is the main topic of discussion in Chapters 8 and 9. Chapter 8 explains the ideas of several prominent leadership theorists and discusses their prescriptions for developing effective leaders in today's dynamic environment. In Chapter 9 we discuss approaches to management and executive development.

We describe each of the training and development methods covered in Chapters 6 through 9 in terms of its advantages and limitations. The research evidence bearing on its effectiveness is reviewed. Where there is little or no research data supporting a method, we point out the need for evaluative research.

Chapter 10 focuses on societal issues that can be influenced positively by appropriate training and development techniques. In the first decade of the twenty-first century, we can expect to see the increased training of people in society who, in the past, have had limited opportunities to realize their potential. Accordingly, the first part of the chapter discusses several special issues and groups such as basic skills training; training English as a second language; providing training for disabled employees; training of older workers; the training of adults, dislocated workers, and youth; and telecommuting training. The second part discusses six concerns that pertain to the training of managers and/or professionals—namely, training to improve rating accuracy, cross-cultural training, training directed at eliminating professional obsolescence, and company-sponsored employee assistance programs (e.g., substance abuse), as well as ways to manage stress and time. The final section discusses training issues that are relevant to all employees: training for the prevention of sexual and racial harassment, diversity training, corporate wellness training programs, safety training, customer service training, and team skills training.

## FINAL COMMENTS

We might have expected that advances in training and development in Euro-American countries would have progressed at approximately the same rate as industrial growth since the Industrial Revolution. That it did not, explained Downs,[10] was because of the eighteenth- and nineteenth-century views of the workforce. The prevalent view of that time was that "the lower orders are innately idle and depraved except when they are goaded by the spur." This philosophy influenced social legislation in England from the reign of Elizabeth I to the revival of liberalism in England in 1906.

Such ingrained attitudes, which discouraged formal training activities, noted Downs, might have changed faster if there had been any prolonged labor shortage. However, the Enclosure movement in England from 1760 to the Act of 1845 accelerated population movements from rural communities to cities. Consequently, labor costs were low because workers were plentiful. High employee turnover reinforced the attitude that any expenditure on training workers would be wasteful.

An additional factor that contributed to an attitude of indifference toward training, according to Downs, was the efficiency of new machinery, with which the labor force was compared, to its discredit. However, this view of workers changed rapidly with the advent of scientific management. Taylor[11] advocated the selection of the best workers for each task, followed by extensive training. Training was viewed as critical for breaking the practice of allowing employees to acquire inappropriate work habits.

Paralleling Taylor was the research of Munsterberg.[12] His work promoted a range of activity in selection and training of both military and civilian personnel during World War I. Between the wars, research was conducted in the United Kingdom by organizations such as the Industrial Health Research Board and the National Institute of Industrial Psychology. The outbreak of World War II again accelerated research on both selection and training.

The continuing need in England after the war for systematic training was recognized by the Industrial Training Act of 1964 and 1973. The government felt that both skill shortages and lack of adaptability to change would arise as a result of insufficient training.[13] Training was defined by the U.K. Department of Employment[14] as the systematic development of attitude–knowledge–skill behavior patterns required by an individual in order to perform adequately a given task or job.

Parallel developments in North America during the past 50 years have resulted in a push–pull philosophy between selection and training.[15] The selection or early identification philosophy stresses identifying individuals with strong potential and grooming them for positions to which they are likely to be promoted. In the case of a training philosophy, the organization is primarily interested in identifying and overcoming existing performance deficiencies for employees on their present jobs. In a survey of Canadian organizations, Mealia and Duffy[16] found that regardless of size of the organization, the primary emphasis today is on the latter philosophy.

In the United States, training (which is now a multibillion-dollar activity) is inextricably tied to selection through Title VII of the 1964 Civil Rights Act, the 1991 Civil Rights Act, and the 1990 Americans with Disabilities Act. Admission into training, as well as promotions, demotions, transfers, and the like, that are based on training performance, are considered employment decisions. Apprenticeship training programs are specifically covered in section 703d of the act. Thus, before training is conducted in the United States, understanding of Title VII is required (see Chapter 2).

The tying of training to Title VII reflects the fact that in recent years a large percentage of the workforce growth in the United States has come from women, African Americans, and people of Hispanic or Asian origin, including immigrants. White males, meanwhile, have accounted for most retirees; they have been leaving the workforce in record numbers.

Computer technology (see Chapters 6 and 10) and automation have taken, and will continue to take, the sweat and tedium out of many jobs, from coal mining to clerical work. The jobs of the early twenty-first century will involve wrenching adjustments for both managers and their employees. Many managers, as they delegate more decision making, will feel threatened about relinquishing their power. Among their employees, frustration will be felt as their jobs require problem solving, analytical skills, and teamwork that exceed their current abilities. Various chapters in the book focus on the steps that can be taken to deal with this fear and frustration.

# ENDNOTES

1. *Training* magazine's Industry Report 1999.
2. L. J. Bassi and M. E. Van Buren, "Sharpening the Leading Edge," *Training & Development 53* (1999): 23–28, 30, 32–33.
3. K. N. Wexley, "Personnel Training," *Annual Review of Psychology 35* (1984): 519–51.
4. K. N. Wexley and S. B. Silverman, *Working Scared: Achieving Success in Trying Times* (San Francisco: Jossey-Bass, 1993).
5. J. P. Campbell, "Personnel Training and Development," *Annual Review of Psychology 22* (1971): 565–602.

6. K. N. Wexley, "Personnel Training."

7. G. P. Latham, "Human Resource Training and Development," *Annual Review of Psychology 39* (1988): 545–82.

8. S. I. Tannenbaum and G. Yukl, "Training and Development in Work Organizations," *Annual Review of Psychology 43* (1992): 399–435.

9. Weick, Salas, and Cannon-Bowers (in press).

10. S. Downs, "Industrial Training," in A.P.O. Williams (ed.), *Using Personnel Research* (Hants, England: Gower, 1983).

11. F. W. Taylor, *The Principles of Scientific Management* (New York: Harper, 1911).

12. H. Munsterberg, *Psychology and Industrial Efficiency* (Boston: Houghton Mifflin, 1913).

13. S. Downs, "Industrial Training."

14. U.K. Department of Employment, *Glossary of Training Terms* (London: HMSO, 1971).

15. J. R. Hinrichs, "Two Approaches to Filling the Management Gap," *Personnel Journal 49* (1970): 1004–14.

16. L. W. Mealia and J. Duffy, "Contemporary Training and Development Practices in Canadian Firms." Paper presented at the annual meeting of the Atlantic Schools of Business, Halifax, Nova Scotia, 1985.

# CHAPTER

# The Organizational Role
# of the Training Specialist

We now turn our attention to the role of training specialists. In small companies, these individuals are usually in charge of all "people" issues and, therefore, find themselves involved in such diverse matters as hiring, benefits, safety, counseling, and possibly even labor relations. These individuals function primarily as training program developers, presenters, and in some instances, evaluators. Their job description includes discovering the training needs of specific groups, planning new programs and revising old programs to meet those needs, analyzing jobs and operations for teaching purposes, preparing course outlines, writing training manuals, furnishing and equipping classrooms, publicizing and selling training within the company, counseling individual employees on problems that might be solved through training, and measuring and maintaining employee productivity and job satisfaction. As the size of the organization increases, so do the number of operating problems and the number of people in need of training. To meet this need, the human resource department usually establishes a training unit consisting of a training manager, an assistant training manager, and one or more full-time trainers. As the training function expands and its activities multiply, the role of the training manager becomes less that of a program developer and implementer and more that of a line manager. Now the training manager must direct and control diverse activities. He or she must structure the training operation for maximum productivity, budget skillfully, employ cost control and cost reduction techniques, be aware of costs versus benefits of each training effort, select and train the staff, secure managerial support for the training unit, and ensure that the training programs satisfy legal requirements. In this chapter, six important aspects of the training manager's job are discussed:

1. Considerations in organizing the training department
2. A financial approach to training
3. Selecting the training staff

4. Training the trainer
5. Maintaining ongoing managerial support
6. Legal aspects of training and development

## CONSIDERATIONS IN ORGANIZING THE TRAINING DEPARTMENT

Large variations exist in the scope and organization of the training function across companies. For instance, some organizations have one-person training units; others may have as many as 150 or more professional staff people. Some training staffs report locally to the line organization; others operate out of corporate headquarters and report to the vice presidential level. Some training staffs are involved with training employees ranging from unskilled laborers to company presidents; others are restricted solely to middle management or hourly employee development. Some training staffs act primarily as purchasers of commercially available training programs; in other organizations, the emphasis is on the design of tailor-made in-house programs. Finally, in some organizations, the training staff acts primarily as instructors; in others, it performs largely a coordinating or administrative function.

As you can see, these variations make it difficult to make general statements regarding the organization of typical training units. However, we can examine variables that organizations take into consideration when organizing training staffs.

### The Organization's Corporate Strategy

Unfortunately, many organizations still exist that view training traditionally, that is, as merely a staff function whose services might or might not be used by individual line managers. In these organizations, training has no real linkage to the company's business strategy. In fact, the training manager seemingly has no influence on the formation of the corporate strategy, since training is seen by high-level executives as being peripheral to the real work of the organization. Conversely, in more progressive organizations, the training manager participates in the formation of the business's strategic planning. As such, the training manager understands the short- and long-term business objectives of the company and, therefore, is in a position to formulate a training plan that can support the company's business strategy. Sometimes, however, the training manager knows that he or she does not have sufficient training resources to do so. In this case, top management must decide to either increase the training department's budget so that it can support the strategic plan or else modify its plan to meet what the department can accomplish using current resources. In either case, when a strong linkage exists between business operations and training, the appropriate organizational structure of the training function will be clear. Its size and form will be determined by whatever it can get in the way of resources to contribute to its company's strategic plan. Here are two excellent examples of a healthy linkage between the training function and corporate strategy. At Travelers Insurance, top management set as one of its goals the changing over from an old-line insurance company to a preeminent financial services company. To accomplish this, the goals of the training department were that all Travelers' employees had to learn how to make the best use of data-processing technology in their jobs, and that Travelers' managers had to be taught how to manage a company in continual change as a result of the onset of high technology. But only when the training manager took the initiative to explain what support the training function needed to accomplish these goals did it receive the necessary resources. A state-of-the-art training center was built; 5,000 of Travelers' employees went through the company's computer literacy program; a management redevelopment program was being prepared; the training department itself was automated; individual computer work stations for managers were designed; and all of the training materials now incorporate the main themes (e.g., customer service, low cost, innovation) of the company's corporate strategy. At Ebasco Services, what appeared to be a reasonable corporate strategic plan was tentatively decided on. However, when the training manager estimated the costs of retraining Ebasco's employees in the new skills, top management decided that its strategies could not be adequately met. Rather than going ahead and implementing mediocre training programs, as some other organizations would do, Ebasco's top management chose to adopt a more affordable set of business strategies.[1]

## Organization Structure

Some organizations have a centralized group that controls all training programs; other organizations place trainers in key locations who are free to operate independently of corporate headquarters. We have found that in organizations with several large divisions it is advisable to have both a corporate and a regional training staff. The role of the corporate people should be primarily one of advising and coordinating the training activities of the various plants or regions and informing the regions of new or revised corporate objectives. Occasionally, the central training staff can be used to develop special training programs to be conducted by trainers at the divisional level. Anything more will usually be viewed by the regions as autocratic and paternalistic. Consequently, they resist corporate training policies. Typical of the many comments heard in these circumstances are "The training doesn't give the grass-roots people what they need," "The training fails to meet the current needs of our people," and "Corporate doesn't realize that we know what we need." Thus, in these situations, the role of the regional training staff people should be one of developing, implementing, and objectively evaluating their own programs. They must continually interact with the corporate staff so that successes in one region can be communicated to other regions.

In organizations in which many small locations exist, no one location may be able to support a full-time training person. In these situations, a centralized staff is typically needed to either travel from location to location or else have trainees assemble at one place. For example, a specialty food chain with numerous stores scattered throughout the country develops master programs at its corporate headquarters on topics such as cheese preparation, cash control, and product ordering. Since no one store can support its own trainer, individuals from various stores receive training at the company's training center in Dayton, Ohio.

Other organizations have one location with many employees performing essentially the same types of jobs. For example, a large insurance company has the majority of its clerical employees and underwriters located in Milwaukee, Wisconsin, where there is a central group of five training people who control all training activities.

## Technology

Some organizations are involved in rapidly changing technologies; others find themselves in a stable environment. Organizations with highly changing technologies require continual retraining of both employees and managers. These organizations have difficulty finding persons in the job market to meet their needs. They have no choice but to continually upgrade their people via specialized training programs. It is in these kinds of organizations, in particular, that a training staff is essential. For example, employees at organizations such as Dell and Microsoft that are heavily into computer-based technology have to be continuously provided with new product development information. This requires the continual retraining of its manufacturing, sales, and maintenance personnel.

The number and complexity of the products and services provided by an organization also influence the size of its training staff. Training needs will not be as great where there is one simple product or service involved as compared with several complex products or services. For instance, we would expect a greater need for in-service training in a large metropolitan medical center than in a small country hospital. Finally, products that are mass produced using highly automated processes require employees with less training than products made in small batches following customer specifications. For example, individuals on American automobile assembly lines require less training than their counterparts in Scandinavian auto factories, where jobs are less automated.

## Attitude Toward Training

Some organizations have had training programs for years and are convinced of the benefits. Others are oriented primarily toward the valid selection and placement of experienced applicants and, therefore, deemphasize the training function. The organization's emphasis on personnel selection versus employee training depends a great deal on the attitude of key persons within the company. Specifically, the attitudes of the chief executive officer and the executives in charge of the various divisions or locations are the main source of company training philosophy. Quite often, their attitudes toward training depend on their own past experiences with it. Also important are their perceptions of the labor market; that is, are there prospective employees who have the necessary skills and experiences, or must unskilled people be hired and trained? A third factor that influences their attitude is their philosophy of promoting from within versus hiring from the outside. Organizations that promote from within typically provide their people more opportunities to prepare themselves for future advancements than organizations who hire primarily experienced individuals.

## A FINANCIAL APPROACH TO TRAINING

As we mentioned in Chapter 1, the typical organization spends about $2.1 million dollars annually on training and development programs. The average firm provides training for just over 74 percent of its employees.[2] In light of these expenditures, one would think that organizations would closely monitor the benefits of their training efforts. However, many companies do not know what benefits they receive from their expenditures on training and development.

Unless training specialists can show the contribution of their efforts to profits in relation to costs, training budgets are likely to get slashed whenever there is a downturn in business. This may be especially problematic in the early 2000s, as it was in the 1990s. In order for training to be seen by management as an integral part of an organization's operating plan, it must be viewed like any other business activity. This entails sound budgeting, cost control, and cost–benefit analyses by the training director and his or her staff.

Ideally, the training budget should contain both training and financial objectives and, basically, should include the following[3]:

1. *The training programs that the staff plans to conduct during this coming year to meet specific organizational needs that have been systematically determined.* For example, the training staff may want to conduct programs for managers in successful delegation, management by objectives, planning cash flow, effective letter writing, and time management.

2. *The direct and indirect costs of each of these programs broken down into the finest detail possible.* Direct costs are those involved in operating particular programs. They include such things as wages or salaries of the participants and trainers; costs for travel, meals, and lodging; supplies and materials; and cost of the facilities. Indirect costs include the costs of operating the entire training unit (e.g., secretarial and clerical help, telephones, audiovisual equipment) and developing new training programs.

3. *The estimated savings, or increased profits, that will likely result from this training.* This should be calculated in terms of increased productivity, reduced waste, reduced expenditures for equipment breakage, increased attendance, and punctuality.

The budget needs to be supplemented with details about each program's intended length, space requirements, number of trainees per session, audiovisual equipment and materials required, and development and administrative costs.

Once the budget is accepted by management and training begins, the training unit should receive a monthly summary of its actual expenditures compared with budgeted expenditures. This summary from the accounting department should be detailed enough to allow for easy identification of problem areas. Continual cost comparisons against the financial plan are necessary to ensure cost control and, hopefully, bring about cost reduction.

Finally, a utility or cost-benefit analysis of each training program is desirable. This analysis, discussed in detail in Chapter 5, involves a comparison of the actual total costs of the program against all profit improvements. It is important to realize that certain training programs can be expected to affect the organization sooner than others. For example, a sales training course intended to cut selling expenses or a manufacturing course focused on productivity improvement should produce results within the immediate accounting period. In these cases, utility analyses can be conducted soon after training is completed. The rotation of junior executives through various organizational units in preparation for key positions several years hence, or the sending of top-level managers to residential programs offered by various colleges and universities may be expected to enhance profits or recover costs within five to ten years. In these instances, utility analyses cannot be done as quickly, nor as easily. Admittedly, cost–benefit analyses are more difficult to conduct with higher level management development programs than traditional lower level skills training programs because of the intangible nature of much of their work.

Various approaches have been suggested for determining the utility of a training or development program.[4] In Chapter 5, we describe an approach that estimates the dollar value of a training and development program to the organization. As you will see, the utility formula includes important factors affecting a program's usefulness such as the number of years the training program has affected an employee's job performance, the number of employees trained, the strength of the impact of the training on their job performance, the dollar value of the training program's impact, the company's marginal tax rate, the effects of variable costs, as well as the direct and indirect costs of designing and implementing the training.

Regardless of how the utility of a training program is determined, the training's payoff for the company will be mazimized by finding creative ways of cutting training costs. Ideas on cutting back on costs while still maintaining high-quality training include[5]:

1. Conduct a thorough needs assessment (to be discussed in Chapter 3) to focus the training directly at the specific skills, knowledge, and abilities that are really needed by the organization.
2. Look into the training services available at local community colleges.

3. Consider offering training programs in partnership with other companies, especially if your company is small.
4. Emphasize computer-based training combined with prereading.
5. Whenever feasible, use line managers as trainers.
6. Design training programs for managers around the same competencies (e.g., Strategic Planning, Empowering Employees), for which they are held accountable in their performance reviews.

## SELECTING THE TRAINING STAFF

The selection of qualified people for corporate and regional training positions is obviously a critical decision for the life of any training department. Unfortunately, this hiring process is frequently treated too lightly by many organizations. Their attitude seems to be that anyone who has adequate verbal skills and is enthusiastic about speaking in front of groups can be a trainer. Often, employees from sales, engineering, and marketing who could not perform adequately in line functions are transferred to the training department. Sometimes, certain employees decide that they want to "work with people" and manage to find their way into the role of a trainer when perhaps they are not qualified to do the job.

We see the trainer's job as requiring extensive skill. The position of corporate or regional trainer requires someone who is a learning specialist, that is, someone skilled in the ability to use learning theory and methods to meet organizational training needs. There is more to the trainer's job than just instructing. The trainer must be able to do such things as determine the organization's training needs, design and implement appropriate programs, present them in such a way as to maximize trainee learning, and rigorously evaluate these programs. To illustrate the many facets of what trainer's actually do, let's consider the job of trainer at Procter & Gamble. Here, the job of "trainer" actually breaks down into four distinct types of positions: (1) researchers, (2) designers, (3) deliverers, and (4) administrators. Researchers are the training people who interview and survey people in various P&G business units to ascertain what types of training they feel they need and what this training should look like. Based on the information gathered, these researchers outline the overall content of the training. Designers are the training personnel who are responsible for developing specific training programs (e.g., designing Web-based training sites) or else shopping around to systematically locate the most appropriate off-the-shelf educational or learning experiences for the company as a whole or particular business units. The deliverers are the people who are not necessarily good at research or designing programs, but excel in getting up in front of a classroom and delivering programs. The company looks for people who are extremely dynamic, have a great deal of energy, are great listeners, have good eye contact, possess good group facilitation skills, are able to handle difficult situations well (e.g., disruptive participants or individuals who ask off-the-wall questions), and are adept at incorporating various learning principles and training techniques. Administrators comprise the fourth type of trainer at P&G. These are the people in the training function who are responsible for handling all of the logistics surrounding the delivery of the training. They are responsible for such tasks as scheduling training sessions, registering participants, ensuring that all the training materials are available on-site when needed, and keeping records of who in the company has participated in various educational and training experiences.

Keeping in mind the complexity of this job, let's discuss some of the many knowledge and skills that a person would need to adequately fill this staff position.

1. *The individual must be adept in the skills and knowledge to be imparted.* A good instructor is expected to be skillful in the crafts and technology that he or she is passing on to others. If instructors are perceived by trainees as not knowing enough about the job being taught or the organization, trainees will quickly lose their desire to learn. When the subject involves complex technical systems, it often makes sense to let a subject-matter expert, such an experienced technician or a first-line supervisor do the training.[6] How important it is to know the subject matter in detail depends, of course, on the particular subject matter being taught. For a lot of training topics, many trainer managers believe that being good in the classroom is more than than the instructor's being expert in the skills and knowledge to be taught. There are many instructors who are quite skillful at training others without possessing the skills themselves. One trainer we know is extremely good at teaching listening skills to participants, but he himself is not a particularly good listener.

2. *The individual should have knowledge of, and ability to use, various learning principles and training methods.* Each trainee is an individual with strengths and weaknesses, and a certain potential for learning. The instructor's role requires that he or she recognize each trainee as an individual and use those specific training methods (e.g., programmed instruction, role playing, case study) and learning principles (e.g., feedback, active practice, overlearning) that maximize each person's performance.

3. *The individual must be well grounded in organization, task, and individual analyses as well as experimental design, criterion development, and statistics.* These skills are essential for systematically determining an organization's training needs and evaluating the organizational effects of training and development programs.

4. *The individual must possess certain personal qualities that facilitate learning.* The individual should be an organized person. This entails being adept at preparing ahead of time and anticipating questions and problems that trainees are likely to encounter. The person must be flexible enough to deal with each training situation so as to choose the best possible learning strategy. He or she must be flexible enough to cope with the diverse personalities among the trainees and their differences in speed of learning. The person must be amenable to change, regardless of whether an emergency arises during the conduct of a training session, a modification is indicated in the program by management, or constructive suggestions are provided by the trainees themselves.

The individual must be someone from whom the trainees want to learn. Trainers must be able to display, or "model," the very characteristics that they are teaching such as being friendly toward others, observing safety rules, using tools and equipment correctly, having a sense of humor, and keeping calm under pressure. It's also important for trainers to be enthusiastic about their training products and able to convey this enthusiasm to the trainees. It's difficult for trainees to be motivated if the trainer presents the program as an imposed chore. Finally, trainers must be capable of treating all trainees fairly (e.g., play no favorites) and be firm enough to hold them all to their performance responsibilities.

From where should these trainers be recruited? Actually, this is a controversial issue. Some organizations choose to recruit from the ranks and to encourage these individuals to remain in the training function. For example, Cosmair Inc., a New York City–based cosmetics and fragrance firm, recruits its trainers from its sales force. These salespeople have the opportunity to return to the field if they feel, after a while, that they do not like training. Otherwise, the position is permanent. Becoming a trainer is considered a promotion into management, accompanied by a significant increase in salary. Other organizations use a *pass-through* philosophy when it comes to selecting trainers. At companies such as Pitney Bowes, Inc., salespeople receive several years of sales training experience in the training department; then they are usually promoted to a management job. At Lederle Laboratories, young promotables spend two years in the training department rotating through various activities such as management, hospital oncology, and communications training. The career trainer approach is superior to the pass-through approach because it selects individuals from the ranks who are committed to a career in employee training. Moreover, their promotion and salary adjustment give them the status they need to be taken seriously by the employees whom they are expected to teach. Realizing their long-term commitment as trainers, their organizations are usually willing to give them the training that they will need to do their job effectively. For example, at General Motors' Saturn plant in Spring Hill, Tennessee, each team or work unit is composed of 5 to 15 people, including one team member who acts as "training point person." Each team member has an individualized training plan that is used to identify what skills are most needed to be developed to get the biggest benefit for their team. Every team member is expected to achieve at least 92 hours of training a year. The training point person's responsibilities include such activities as identifying their team's training needs with respect to new products, processes, and equipment; helping team members to prepare their annual training plans; enrolling team members in various classes; and presenting regularly at team meetings the training status of team members toward achieving their annual goals. Team members receive training in areas such as human skills training, safety, quality, managing conflict, problem solving, and computer training.

Saturn has a tiered arrangement of teams, and each level has its own training focus. Three to five work teams form what is called a "module," and each module has a training representative known as a "training coordinator"). The highest level involves either a business unit (e.g., one of their three plants) or a resource team (e.g., a department such as Finance, Human Resources, or Information Systems). Their training specialist is referred to as a "training leader." Training coordinators and leaders have the same basic responsibilities as the training point person, but deal with larger and larger databases.

## TRAINING THE TRAINER

If an organization is to be effective, supervisors should be held responsible for the overall training of the employees who report directly to them. Moreover, many supervisors want to train their subordinates because they are in the best position to teach new employees what is expected of them. Other supervisors may delegate the responsibility for training to their most experienced employees. These individuals are expected to provide on-the-job training to new hires and, occasionally, classroom instruction as well. Where, then, does the training department fit into all this? The training department is typically responsible for planning and conducting training sessions for supervisors and staff personnel (e.g., quality control, research and development, engineering). It either conducts the program using training materials that it has developed, or else it uses materials that have been purchased from outside vendors. Often, the training department assists supervisors in the planning and organizing of special programs for their own work units.

The need to give instruction to supervisors, employees, and training department members in the best methods of training is an important one. This is true even when these individuals possess the abilities mentioned in the previous section. These people must be made aware of the knowledge and skills necessary to make training highly effective and not just a "nice thing to do" when time and money happen to be available to the organization.

What, then, should trainers be taught in order to make the training process work? It is important to realize, first of all, that there is no universal course for all those who instruct others. A review of 37 train-the-trainer programs found that they vary from one to nine days and from general topics (e.g., communications, career transitions) to specific instructional skills and techniques.[7] Thus, it would appear that the length and specific content of a train-the-trainer course must depend on a needs assessment (see Chapter 3) of the particular participants involved. For instance, a consulting firm implemented a training-for-trainers course for about 100 first-line supervisors in a paper mill. The initial step in the project involved a needs assessment to determine exactly what the foremen needed to learn to conduct their own technical training classes for their crews. Based on the needs assessment, a four-day workshop was developed that included such topics as how adults learn, audiovisuals, questioning techniques, individualized learning problems, use of different methods of instruction, and proper instructional design.

We believe that there are common elements that should exist in all train-the-trainer programs. First, trainers must be taught to establish specific training objectives (e.g., to point out fire hazards in a chemical plant, to be familiar with the common terms used by state troopers, to design and lay out newspaper ads). Trainers must learn how these objectives can be used to influence the planning and execution of their training sessions. They need to understand the importance of communicating these objectives clearly, so that the trainees understand the program's purposes at the outset.

Second, the trainers need to be taught basic principles of how adults learn. They must understand the factors that facilitate and interfere with the learning process and what they as trainers can do about them.[8] For instance, it is important that trainers understand that their own level of expectations about a trainee affects the nature of their social interactions with the trainee, which in turn affects how well the trainee learns.[9] This phenomenon, known as the *Pygmalion effect,* was demonstrated in the Israeli army by Eden and Shani.[10] One hundred five trainees in a 15-week combat command course were matched on aptitude and randomly assigned to high, regular, and unknown trainer-expectancy conditions. Trainees from whom trainers had been induced to expect better performance (i.e., "likely to move quickly into a command position") scored significantly higher on objective achievement tests, exhibited more positive attitudes, and perceived more positive trainer leadership behavior than those trainees labeled trainees in the "regular expectations" (average movement), or "unknown" conditions.

Third, the trainers must be taught how to communicate more effectively. This should involve the actual presentation of lessons during training, and receiving feedback from other participants as to the adequacy of their oral, written, and nonverbal (e.g., facial expressions, tone of voice, eye contact) communications. Ideally, the lessons should be videotaped so that trainees can also critique their own performances. In addition, the trainers should be made aware of various visual and audio devices (e.g., overhead transparency projector, videotape recorder, tape recorder, slide and filmstrip projector, flip chart) that can facilitate effective communication. For instance, trainers need to learn that their communication style plays an important role in creating either an "adaptable" trainee, who has accepted responsibility for his or her own learning, or a "trainer-dependent" trainee, who has greater difficulty in transferring his or her learning from the specific instance in which it occurred.[11]

Fourth, the trainers must be taught how to plan each training session so that the material is presented clearly. It is also important that the trainers learn to sequence their training sessions and decide on the length and the time interval between them.

Fifth, the trainers should be taught how to choose the most effective method(s) of instruction (e.g., Web-based distance learning, behavior modeling, on-the-job training) depending on the particular type(s) of learning involved. They should be given an opportunity to develop their skills in those particular training methods they will eventually be using (e.g., role-playing exercises, lectures, or case studies). In addition, they should be shown how to pose questions so as to arouse interest and curiosity, stimulate discussion, channel the trainees' thinking, and determine how well trainees understand the material.

Sixth, trainers must be taught how to deal with individual trainees. They must learn how to get appropriate participation by drawing out the underinvolved and toning down the overinvolved. They must understand resistance to change and anxiety on the part of certain trainees, and what they as trainers can do about it. They need to be shown how to use feedback techniques, praise, and goal setting to motivate certain individuals.

Seventh, it is important for trainers to be aware of certain behaviors that are considered improper or unethical for training professionals. Table 2.1 presents the major categories of behavior considered unethical by a nationwide sample of members of the American Society for Training and Development. Incidents such as those shown in the table should be discussed during the training of trainers.

**TABLE 2.1    Major Categories of Behavior Considered Improper or Unethical for Training and Development Professionals**

| *Major Categories of Behavior Considered Unethical* | *Typical Response* |
|---|---|
| Lack of Professional Development | 1. "Not 'keeping up'—expanding their own knowledge."<br>2. "I've seen lots of 'good ol' boys' who are not educated in the training profession transferred into training."<br>3. "Application of 'technology' without understanding concepts, theory, etc." |
| Violation of Confidences | 4. "Breaking the trust of classroom participants."<br>5. "Relating information gathered in the classroom back to the organization."<br>6. "Identifying client deficiencies to others."<br>7. "Reporting information given in confidence." |
| Use of "Cure All" Programs | 8. "Consultants selling programs without any effort to even estimate the needs of the client."<br>9. "Continuing use of 'sacred cow' type programs when need for them is no longer valid."<br>10. "Continuation of programs long after they have served their purpose." |

**TABLE 2.1** *(Continued)*

| Major Categories of Behavior Considered Unethical | Typical Response |
|---|---|
| Dishonesty Regarding Program Outcomes | 11. "Concealing truth on program results." |
| | 12. "The assurance that a training program produced results when in fact it was only a good 'show.' " |
| | 13. "Falsifying training records to make results look better than they are." |
| Failure to Give Credit | 14. "Failure to give credit for work done by others (includes materials, instruments, and even whole courses)." |
| | 15. "Not giving credit when using another's research." |
| | 16. "Illegal copies of printed and taped matter from existing suppliers' programs." |
| | 17. "Copyright violations." |
| Abuse of Trainees | 18. "Treating course participants as children." |
| | 19. "Treating training participants as 'lesser' individuals of little importance." |
| | 20. "Racist and sexist remarks." |
| | 21. "Use of profanity." |
| | 22. "Unwillingness to obtain input from the trainees." |
| | 23. "Using trainees to practice training techniques and exercises to meet trainer rather than group needs." |
| | 24. "Using sexual relations with seminar participants as a portion of training." |
| Other Improper Behavior | 25. "Consultants designing programs that give people what they want rather than what they need." |
| | 26. "Acting as entertainers rather than trainers." |
| | 27. "Lack of follow-up in order to see that programs are properly implemented after the classroom training." |

*Source:* From "Unethical and Improper Behavior by Training and Development Professionals" by Ronald W. Clement, Patrick R. Pinto, and James W. Walker. Reproduced by special permission from the December 1978 *Training and Development Journal.* Copyright 1978 by the American Society for Training and Development, Inc. All rights reserved.

How do organizations go about training their trainers? We surveyed several different companies to find out the answer to this very question. We were surprised to find that most organizations train their trainers in a similar manner. Basically, they seem to follow a four-step procedure. The first step involves requiring that all future trainers go through the actual training program itself. It is felt that it is more beneficial for future trainers to actually participate in the training process itself as trainees rather than to merely sit in the back of the room and take notes on what the trainer is doing. Step two is typically referred to either as "Certification" or "Trainer Training." There are certain training programs, either home-grown or purchased off-shelf, wherein it is critical that trainers are highly skilled at administering a specific tool (e.g., a diagnostic psychological instrument) or highly knowledgeable about a particular subject matter (e.g., a situational leadership model). These programs require that trainers be certified; this is especially needed when the training can be expected to impact trainees' self-image or how they will think about themselves. Trainer Training typically involves an experienced trainer working through a Trainer's Guidebook with one or more future trainers. These guidebooks usually spell out, step by step, how to facilitate the training sessions. The third step entails hands-on practice for future trainers with other future trainers. Each individual is given an opportunity to either teach one or more of the modules, or else conduct the entire program. Individuals receive constructive feedback from the master trainer as well as from one another. The final step involves giving each individual an opportunity to co-train with a master trainer who has proven himself or herself to be outstanding with live participants. After the session is completed, the master trainer provides them with videotaped feedback on what they did effectively and ways that they can improve.

## MAINTAINING ONGOING MANAGERIAL SUPPORT

It is important for training managers and their staff not only to develop effective training and development programs but also to ensure that these programs are adopted where they are needed in the organization. Unless the training unit is able to maintain training and development programs, even effective programs may quickly fade away. What, then, can a training staff do to make certain that its training and development programs have staying power?

As pointed out by Latham and Wexley,[12] there must be significant senior management support for the training program, as opposed to passive tolerance. Such support is essential as an umbrella under which new norms and expectations can flourish without constant pressures to revert back to the more comfortable and known ways of operating. Active senior management support is necessary for ensuring a high level of commitment by middle managers to the program.

A critical mass must be reached in order for a program to be sustained. In other words, the training must be diffused throughout a significant portion of the organization so as to become a way of life for employees. For these reasons, a new program must be installed on key fronts within an organization simultaneously, rather than implemented in only one area. Change has to spread throughout a substantial segment of the organization and be backed by the managers and employees if it is to remain. This reaching of a critical mass is particularly important when the objective of the training effort is directed at changing the culture of an entire organization.

The initial strategy should be to "go with the winners." That is, one must be careful to ensure that the system is implemented in several parts of the organization where there is a good chance of achieving positive results, so that success can be demonstrated early. Once the concepts become widely accepted, it will be easier to tackle the more complex and resistant segments of the organization.

The implementation of the training system should be reviewed quarterly with the vice presidents of operations and human resources. A major topic of each meeting should be the cooperation and active efforts exerted by the managers reporting to these vice presidents in making the training a way of life with the people whom these managers supervise. These managers should know that they run the risk of transfer, demotion, or even termination if they receive poor evaluations from the vice presidents in meeting this objective.

It is important to start thinking of training and development as part of the business. To gain managerial support, the training department must identify its customers and consumers and begin doing first those programs that satisfy these two constituencies. The customers for the training department include all critical members of the client base *within* the organization. Ultimately, the training department's client is the highest member of management who is impacted by the training activities. For example, the sales trainers within a large operating unit should consider the regional sales vice president as their primary customer. To satisfy this customer, the sales trainers must talk with this individual to understand the unit's business objectives as well as its specific short- and long-term needs. It is imperative that they can see the direct and immediate relevance of the training on their sales behaviors and on sales results. By satisfying consumers, the training department will get the support it needs to be effective. Top management (i.e., customers) will start hearing throughout the organization that the training is useful and realistic.[13] An excellent example of this support is Pacific Bell's Capability 97 program. Capability 97 was designed to help all Pacific Bell employees make the transition from analog to digital transmission. It has the full support of top management and business-unit leaders because it was developed in the first place in response to a business problem articulated by the executive vice president—the need to build employee capability that would be appropriate to the company's business goals and that would give it competitive advantage.[14]

Many problems in organizations (e.g., low morale, poor employee motivation, employee dissatisfaction) cannot be solved through training and development efforts. In these cases, training managers have to say no to requests by managers for training. Instead, they need to recommend to management alternative solutions to their problems (e.g., motivational interventions). To secure top management support, it is better to say "sorry, no" than to implement an expensive and time-consuming training program that ultimately fails.

Finally, to maintain ongoing managerial support, it is advisable to get away from a program orientation. Rather than always trying to solve every new problem with another training program, it is better to think more of ongoing learning. For example, Buick-Oldsmobile-Cadillac (BOC) recently trained all of its managers and supervisors in ways of improving their ongoing communication and coaching skills with their employees. Providing ongoing communication and coaching to employees is the key to "continuous improvement and development," one of BOC's most cherished philosophical concepts.

## LEGAL ASPECTS OF TRAINING AND DEVELOPMENT

We now turn to a very important topic: the impact of federal fair employment regulations and issues of workers' rights on training practices. It might be helpful for us to begin by briefly reviewing the history of these regulations.

Although the federal requirement of equal treatment under the law dates back to the Bill of Rights and the Thirteenth and Fourteenth Amendments of the Constitution, it was the 1964 Civil Rights Act that specifically brought employment practices under the jurisdiction of the courts. Title VII of this act specifically states that "it shall be an unlawful employment practice for an employer to . . . discriminate against any individual with respect to compensation, terms, conditions, or privileges of employment, because of the individual's race, color, religion, sex, or national origin" (Sec. 703). Furthermore, Title VII established the Equal Employment Opportunity Commission (EEOC) as an enforcement agency of fair employment practices. In 1978, the EEOC and three other federal agencies (i.e., the Civil Service Commission, Department of Justice, and Department of Labor) issued the Uniform Guidelines. The guidelines' primary concern is an organization's selection procedure, but they have important implications for training as well.

Often, certain kinds of training are required before an employee can be considered for entry into a particular job. For example, a clerk in a retail store might be required by the personnel department to have a college degree in order to be admitted into a training program for buyers. Or a person may be expected to pass a pole-climbing course prior to becoming a telephone installer or repair technician. In such cases, the potential for discrimination exists. It can be especially problematic in situations in which women or nonwhites are less likely to pass a training course than white males, and the company has no proof that the training requirements are relevant to later job proficiency.

Any company that intends to use the successful completion of training as a job prerequisite should attempt to show that their training program has no negative (i.e., adverse) impact on women and minorities. In other words, women and minority group members must have as much chance of successfully completing the training as white males. If the training does have a negative impact, however, the organization must stand ready to demonstrate the validity (i.e., job related-ness) of its training requirements in the event of a lawsuit or a government compliance review. That is, the company must be able to show that persons with this training perform the job better than persons without the training. To carry out such a study, it is necessary for the company to permit persons without this prerequisite training to be placed on jobs in order to measure their later performance. The performance of the trained and untrained groups should not only show statistically significant differences, but the differences must be great enough to be of practical significance as well.

If for some reason the strategy just described is not technically feasible, another strategy known as *content validation* may be used. Content validation of training requirements would first necessitate an analysis of the skills and knowledge needed on the job (see Chapter 3), and then a systematic documentation that the training content covers these things. For example, we might find through a careful job analysis that building maintenance mechanics must understand advanced heating systems and refrigeration absorption systems. Therefore, a content-valid training program would deal with the electrical and mechanical maintenance, operation, and wiring of common heating plant components. In addition, it would cover common absorption principles and specific differences between the major manufacturers' systems. The course also would allow trainees to gain hands-on experience with various maintenance routines and troubleshooting procedures. The objective, then, is to document that the training content is representative of the skills and knowledge that will be required in doing the job.

Admission into a training program is another situation in which potential discrimination exists. Selection of trainees is almost always based on some informal or formal selection procedure such as testing, interviewing, reference checking, or supervisory recommendation. Where negative impact exists against females and nonwhites, the selection procedure may be discriminatory and should not be used unless it can be demonstrated to possess *criterion-related validity.* That is, it must be shown statistically that an applicant's level of performance on the selection procedure will, on the average, be indicative of his or her level of performance on the job. The advisability of validating selection procedures by correlating them with measures of success taken during training (e.g., scores on achievement tests and trainer's ratings) is open to question. In our opinion, a relationship should always be established between measures of trainees' success and actual job performance before training measures are used in criterion-related validity studies.

Several years ago, we established a skilled-trades training program to provide an opportunity for disadvantaged employees to receive on-the-job work experience and off-the-job training to qualify eventually for skilled maintenance job openings. The program involved a three-year training period during which selected applicants were given direct learning opportunities in a designated maintenance skill area. Each trainee was under the immediate supervision of the maintenance supervisor in the department (e.g., electrical, mechanical, instrumentation) in which he or she was being trained. The supervisor assigned the responsibility of instructing the trainee to one or more qualified tradespeople. Each trainee was assigned to certain departments (e.g., curing, calendaring, extruding, final finish) for three months, during which time he or she became familiar with and knowledgeable about the maintenance assignments in the respective departments. Each trainee was exposed to the most troublesome and frequent maintenance-related breakdowns within the trainee's skill designation while in each department. The training also consisted of correspondence school-work during the first two years of the program.

Based on the skilled-trades training program, a battery of tests were assembled to choose objectively those employees who had the necessary learning capabilities for this training program. The test battery measured such things as mental alertness, mechanical reasoning ability, tool knowledge, ability to visualize and mentally manipulate objects in space, skill in using ordinary mechanics' tools, and fine eye–hand coordination. It was found that the tests had no negative impact on the selection of minority employees. Moreover, each test was shown to have criterion-related validity, in that there was a relationship between scores on the selection tests and appraisals of job performance subsequent to the completion of training.

Sometimes women, members of minority groups, or trainees over 40 may allege that the training process itself has shown disparate treatment toward them. According to the Uniform Guidelines,[15] "disparate treatment occurs where (members of a minority) have been denied the same employment opportunities as have been available to other employees or applicants" (p. 38300). For example, female plaintiffs might testify that the training equipment was designed primarily for males, thereby making it difficult for some females to use because of their shorter legs and arm reach than most males. Hispanic plaintiffs might maintain that the vocabulary level in their company's training manuals requires reading ability in English far above that which is required for performing the job adequately. If an organization provides training that involves outdoor activity or strenuous physical exertion, it might incur liability if older trainees feel that they must participate in it so as to receive a promotion.

Proof of disparate treatment by plaintiffs in such court cases normally follows a three-step procedure:

1. The plaintiffs must establish a prima facie case of discrimination by demonstrating that they belong to a minority group, are qualified for the employment opportunity, and were denied the employment opportunity while others in nonprotected classes were not.

2. The employer must either specify that the actions were taken for legitimate, nondiscriminatory reasons, or the actions were required by business necessity.

3. The plaintiff must then either prove that the employer's reasons cannot be substantiated by the facts of the case or prove that the employer was more likely to have been motivated by discriminatory reasons.

What should training managers do to prevent court cases in which disparate treatment is alleged by plaintiffs? If the training process consistently results in inferior performance by women or minorities, a redesign of the training program may be required unless such differential performance is reflected in similar on-the-job performance by nonminorities. Although our example goes back several years, it still does a good job of illustrating our point. A demand for smaller pole-climbing gear began to develop in the Bell System as a result of the entry of women into outside craft positions. In response, AT&T formally requested the Western Electric Company to develop smaller equipment for use by employees of slight stature. Size and strength data on the male and female adult population of the United States was obtained by Western Electric in its design effort. It also prepared a questionnaire to obtain data from women who used climbers as part of their assignments and from short men who had difficulty using full-size climbers. By 1976, Western Electric had completed its small climber design. Some of the design changes included:

1. The stirrup width was made about one-half inch narrower than the standard climber to accommodate the narrower work boot of the smaller individual.
2. The stirrup depth was decreased to produce a snug fit in front of the work boot heel for the smaller size boot.
3. The stirrup end was modified to permit the foot strap to firmly hold the smaller size work boot.

Based on the results of a questionnaire study, AT&T found that the new design met the needs of 98.6 percent of the female employees.[16]

Another example of the need for redesign of training content that takes into account the unintentional effect of adverse impact comes from a chemical company that examined the reading difficulty of its training materials compared to that required on the job by chemical operators. The company used a readability index that took into account both the number of syllables per 100 words as well as average sentence length. It learned that the training manuals were excessively difficult to comprehend, which partially explained why some Spanish-surnamed trainees were dropping out of the program. Based on this information, the training department revised the training manuals by shortening words and sentences.

Training managers also need to ensure that everyone is treated the same by trainers during training sessions regardless of their race, sex, or ethic background. Managers of training need to make it clear to their trainers what their company stands for and what behaviors won't be tolerated. For example, one training manager told us about a trainer who had a tendency to talk down to older, gray-haired trainees. The trainer spoke down to them and acted as though they were too old to learn new things. This trainer was warned that his behavior was illegal and objectionable. Subsequently, he was fired after he told a training class that "it's impossible to teach old dogs new tricks." Derogatory comments made by training program participants may also be alleged to be discriminatory. For example, in a U.S. District Court case, a group of female and black employees alleged that the food store chain they worked for discriminated against women and minorities by not promoting them into management positions. They further alleged that comments made about women and minorities during training sessions for managers confirmed that the company's management had discriminatory attitudes. When discussing the promotion of females and minorities into managerial positions, several participants were heard to make comments that characterized women as being the weaker sex, not wanting to work the late shift, merely producing a second income for their families, possessing no incentive to be managers, that the store's customers might object to seeing female and minority managers, and that store employees would not produce for such managers.[17]

A potential source of discrimination related to training occurs when measures collected during training are used in certain career decisions about trainees. These measures might be used for making decisions about a trainee's retention in the program. Or they may be used to give those who performed better in training the preferred job assignments after training is completed. In these two situations as well as others, if there is a differential performance for minority groups, then the training performance measures must be validated. For example, a large banking firm used paper-and-pencil quizzes, work sample tests, and trainer's ratings to evaluate trainee performance during an 18-day training class for bank tellers. Trainees were assessed on how effectively they could issue new bonds, open new accounts, and record deposits and withdrawals on computer terminals. A validation study was conducted, which showed that performance on each of these measures correlated substantially with the trainees' performance six months later as tellers. Performance ratings were obtained from each teller's bank manager, who had no knowledge at all of the individual's performance during training. The bank showed that there was no differential performance for minority group trainees on any of the measures used during training.

Another aspect of legislation that training specialists must be sensitive to is the Equal Pay Act, passed by Congress in 1963. This act prohibits pay discrimination between males and females whose jobs require equal skill, effort, and responsibility and who work under similar conditions. The courts will not tolerate pay differentials between males and females due to "flaws" in the training provided. The courts' standards were laid down in *First Victoria Bank* when the Fifth Circuit Court ruled that the bank's training program was fatally flawed because[18]:

1. Employees were not hired with the understanding that they were to be in a training program.
2. The training program was not in writing.
3. Employees were not rotated to predetermined jobs and, moreover, assignments were apparently based on the employer's needs.
4. No formal instruction was given to the "trainees."
5. The training program had historically excluded women.
6. Advancement from the training program to fully qualified employment was sporadic.

Since the bank violated all six of the court's training standards, it was ordered to grant equal pay to its female employees. To prevent future litigation of this kind, training managers should obviously take steps to ensure that these types of training flaws do not exist.

Recently, there have been lawsuits concerning two additional training issues. First, the popularity of so-called New Age training programs is creating legal challenges by employees who claim that these programs violate their religious or philosophical beliefs. These New Age programs vary widely, but may include such controversial things as Eastern mysticism, emotional confessions, positive thinking, and hypnosis. The groups that promote these programs all have a common aim—to alter people and their corporation by unleashing in them energies that purportedly remain unused in most people. They seek to liberate the mind by allegedly breaking the chains of habit and passivity.

In an article in *Fortune* magazine that is highly critical of this training,[19] Carl Raschke, an expert in religion and society at the University of Denver, was cited as describing these techniques as an attempt by its advocates to transplant culturism and mysticism from the counterculture of the 1960s and 1970s to the corporate world. Robert Tucker, head of the Council of Mind Abuse in Toronto, an organization that helps people break from cults, was quoted as stating, "It's one thing if an individual walks in off the street and signs up for a course, but quite another if your boss sends you. Then there is a level of coercion. Does my boss have the right to put me through training that conflicts with my religion and any worldview?"

The *Fortune* article argues that corporations are building an enormous potential liability. That the number of known lawsuits is currently small in number reflects the fact that many cases are shrouded in medical and legal confidentiality. Moreover, many employees are understandably reluctant to publicly criticize training that is strongly endorsed by their bosses.

The most well-documented case of employees in revolt, stated *Fortune,* is that of Pacific Bell. *Fortune*'s description of the event is quoted here:

> After the breakup of AT&T, Pacific Bell, a subsidiary of Pacific Telesis, decided that it needed to overhaul its corporate culture, which had been standard Bell. To help, it hired two associates of Charles Krone, a trainer who for years has served the likes of Scott Paper and Du Pont. Krone, who often veils his ideas in impenetrable language, claims to make people rethink the way they think and hence arrive at new ways of solving problems. The Krone consultants worked with Pacific Bell for two years and obviously made an impression on corporate culture: This year's corporate statement of principles was worked in a manner even Krone might find indecipherable. It defined interaction, for example, as the "continuous ability to engage with the correctedness and relatedness that exists and potentially exists, which is essential for the creations necessary to maintain and enhance viability of ourselves and the organization of which we are a part."
>
> When the mounting resentment inside Pac Bell was revealed by the San Francisco *Chronicle* in March, the California Public Utilities Commission investi-

gated and asked a consulting firm, the Meridian Group, to survey the utility's employees. Guaranteed anonymity, employees by the hundred complained furiously. They hated the jargon and obscure language, the perceived threats that those who didn't adopt the new-think would have no future at Pac Bell, the "facilitators" who sat in as "thought police" at meetings to make sure the Krone procedures about agendas and note-taking were followed, and the implication that anyone who didn't get the new routine was stupid. There were, admittedly, also some pluses. Company meetings became more purposeful, and managers got to know each other better.

The commission found, too, that the Kroning of Pac Bell was enormously expensive. It is recommended that $25 million of the $40 million cost of the program in 1987 be charged to the stockholders, not the rate payers. Pac Bell suspended further training and ordered its own study. The company's president, Theodore Saenger, took early retirement, and his heir apparent, Executive Vice President Lee Cox, the chief supporter of the Krone program, was demoted to the presidency of a subsidiary, PacTel Corp.[20]

The need to guard the rights of the individual is discussed in Chapter 10. Suffice it to say here that Title VII of the Civil Rights Act of 1964 requires an employer to "reasonably accommodate" a worker's religious beliefs unless it creates undue hardship. To prevent these kinds of lawsuits, we recommend that employees be informed of the training techniques beforehand and be allowed to truly choose whether to attend.

Second, the issue of stress on the job has gathered more and more attention by the media and the courts. Recent court decisions clearly suggest that employers will sometimes be held financially liable for stress created on the job. In response, experts have counseled that managers learn to identify the potential stress trouble spots in their organizations (i.e., training programs), try to relieve these where possible, and document their efforts.[21]

As you can see so far, the training specialist's role in the twenty-first century requires a clear understanding of a host of legal issues related to the training and development efforts in their organizations. Let's take a look at a few additional legal issues and requirements that training specialists should know about:

- *Workplace safety and emergency training.* The Occupational Safety and Health Act, which has been in effect since 1971, together with related regulations require businesses in certain industries to train their employees on various safety and emergency procedures. For example, chemical companies would be required to train their workers in handling hazardous materials and cleanup, as well as using emergency medical procedures for treating workplace burns.
- *Sexual harassment prevention.* The U.S. Supreme Court has ruled that if an organization has developed a sexual harassment policy and has taken reasonable steps to educate its employees about this policy so that the policy is followed when a complaint is made, the company may avoid liability in hostile environment cases.
- *Drug-free workplace procedures.* Companies doing business with the federal government must comply with the Drug Free Workplace Act along with numerous

state and local government regulations. Companies must train their managers and supervisors about conforming to detailed posting, notice, and testing procedures so as to ensure their protection against losing their federal contracts. The training may also protect them against wrongful discharge suits filed by employees who are fired when caught using drugs during work.

- *Trade-secret handling procedures.* Many organizations are concerned with protecting trade secrets such as technology that has not yet been patented, recipes, or confidential customer lists. The quality of training given to employees about their company's trade-secret protection procedures (e.g., clearing and locking one's desk and file cabinet each night) is a key legal factor in determining whether the state should permit the organization to robe those secrets with protection.

- *Preventative training measures.* Training specialists have come to realize that there are certain training processes that, if ignored by them, could bring about federal and state compliance agency investigations or else litigation. Using training as a preventative measure, these organizations make available online information to managers and supervisors about such things as proper hiring procedures, affirmative action compliance, termination procedures, correct handling of family and medical leave requests, proper conducting of annual performance reviews, and ways of reducing the risks of employee injuries.[22]

We turn now to a discussion of a sweeping piece of legislation that is very important for training specialists to know about because it affects millions of employees—the Americans with Disabilities Act (ADA).

# AMERICANS WITH DISABILITIES ACT

Although the ADA was passed by Congress in 1990, it didn't go into effect until 1992 for employers with 25 or more employees, and 1994 for employers with 15 to 24 employees. Its main purpose is to prohibit discrimination against qualified individuals with physical or mental disabilities, and to require employers to make reasonable accomodations for such individuals unless that would cause undue hardship for the employer. *Undue hardship* means that the accomodations are either excessively costly, substantial, or disruptive, or would fundamentally alter the nature or operation of the business.

This act affects many different areas of employment (e.g., hiring, promotion, retention), including training and development. According to the ADA, employees with disabilities must be provided equal opportunities to participate in training to improve job performance and provide opportunities for advancement. Training opportunities cannot be denied merely because of the need to make a reasonable accomodation, unless that accomodation would be an undue hardship. Examples of reasonable training accomodations include:

- Accessible locations and facilities for employees with mobility disabilities.
- Interpreters and note-takers for employees who are deaf.

- Materials in accessible formats or readers for people who are visually impaired, for people with learning disabilities, and for people with mental retardation.
- If audiovisual materials are used, captions for people who are deaf, and voice-overs for people who are visually impared.
- Good lighting on an interpreter, and good illumination for people with visual impairments and other disabilities.
- Clarification of concepts presented in training for people who have reading or other disabilities.
- Individualized instruction for people with mental retardation and certain other disabilities.

In addition, if an employer contracts for training with a training group, or contracts for training facilities such as hotels or conference centers, the employer is responsible for ensuring accessibility and other needed accomodations. According to the ADA, it is advisable that "any contract with a company or facility used for training include a provision requiring the other party to provide needed accomodations."

## FINAL COMMENTS

The underlying theme of this and the subsequent two chapters is that training cannot be viewed as an isolated process. It is affected by a wide variety of organizational factors that can enhance or reduce its value. These include the organization's corporate strategy, structure, technology, and attitude toward selecting the most effective employees versus training to develop their capability.

The company's financial health obviously affects the company's training department. A financial downturn usually is the direct cause of a reduction in training staff and budget. Tying the training budget to the company's financial health, however, may sometimes be a mistake, especially if the company is experiencing the results of an economic recession.

Haveman and Saks[23] wrote an essay on transatlantic lessons for training policy. The Swedish government has argued that training should be emphasized rather than deemphasized during an economic recession so that skilled workers will be available during a recovery to relieve inflationary pressures and rapidly expand the industries. Thus, training is expanded to include some 5 percent of the labor force during peaks of recessions by paying companies to expand in-house training.

To ensure ongoing managerial support for training departments, the training staff must be selected on the basis of their knowledge, skill, and ability as trainers. They must receive ongoing training of trainers to ensure that they maintain their knowledge, skills, and ability. In addition, the training staff needs to take it upon themselves to stay abreast of the organization's short- and long-term goals so that they can show upper management how the various training processes are playing a key role in the effective implementation of the corporate strategy. Organization analysis is the subject of the next chapter. The steps to maximizing trainee learning are the subject of Chapter 4. The ways of determining whether the training accomplished the objectives for which it was designed are discussed in Chapter 5.

Another step that training staffs can take to ensure senior management support is to keep abreast of legal issues that affect the way organizations develop the capability of their people. More than one leader has reached a plateau or, even worse, ended his or her career because of ignorance of Title VII implications that led to a class-action lawsuit against the company in question. Ensuring that managerial decisions and training processes are in compliance with the law is a vital service that training staffs can perform for the organization. We discuss this subject further in Chapter 10.

## ENDNOTES

1. J. M. Rosow and R. Zager, *Training—The Competitive Edge* (San Francisco: Jossey-Bass, 1988).

2. L. J. Bassi and M. E. Van Buren, "Sharpening the Leading Edge," *Training & Development 53* (1999): 23–28, 30, 32–33.

3. J. S. Jenness, "Budgeting and Controlling Training Costs," in R. L. Craig (ed.), *Training and Development Handbook: A Guide to Human Resource Development* (New York: McGraw-Hill, 1976): 4-1–4-2.

4. W. F. Cascio, "Using Utility Analysis to Assess Training Outcomes," in I. L. Goldstein and Associates (eds.), *Training and Development in Organizations* (San Francisco: Jossey-Bass, 1989): 63–88; S. B. Parry, "Measuring Training's ROI," *Training & Development 50* (1996): 72–77; and J. J. Phillips, "ROI: The Search for Best Practices," *Training & Development 50* (1996): 42–47.

5. M. R. Callahan, "Training on a Shoestring," *Training & Development,* December 1995, 18–23.

6. C. J. Reiss, "Turning Technicians into Trainers," *Training,* July 1991, 47–50.

7. A. J. DiPaolo and A. C. Patterson, "Selecting a Training Program for New Trainers," *Training & Development Journal 37* (1983): 96–101.

8. S. Downs and P. Perry, "Can Trainers Learn to Take a Back Seat?" *Personnel Management 18* (1986): 42–45.

9. D. Eden, "Self-Fulfilling Prophecy as a Management Tool: Harnessing Pygmalion," *Academy of Management Review 9* (1984): 64–73.

10. D. Eden and A. B. Shani, "Pygmalion Goes to Boot Camp: Expectancy, Leadership, and Trainee Performance," *Journal of Applied Psychology 67* (1982): 194–99.

11. S. Downs, J. Petford, and J. McHale, "Learning Techniques for Driver Training," *International Review of Applied Psychology 31* (1982): 511–22.

12. G. P. Latham and K. N. Wexley, *Increasing Productivity Through Performance Appraisal* (Addison-Wesley: Reading, MA, 1994).

13. W. N. Yeomans, "How to Get Top Management Support," *Training & Development Journal 36* (1982): 38–40.

14. P. A. Galagan, "Business Units Take the Lead in Capability 97," *Training & Development,* February 1995, 29–31; and C. J. Tunis, "Linking Capability 97 to Our Business," *Training & Development,* February 1995, 26–28.

15. *Uniform Guidelines on Employee Selection Procedures.* Federal Register, 43, No. 166, August 25, 1978.

16. E. I. Smith, *Small Climber Development* (Basking Ridge, NJ: AT&T Co., November 1978).

17. Society for Human Resource Management, 1999.

18. J. S. Russell, "A Review of Fair Employment Cases in the Field of Training," *Personnel Psychology 17* (1984): 261–74.

19. J. Main, "Trying to Bend Managers' Minds," *Fortune,* November 23, 1987, 95–108.

20. Ibid.

21. J. M. Ivancevich, M. T. Matteson, and E. P. Richards III, "Who's Liable for Stress on the Job?" *Harvard Business Review 63* (1985): 60–65.

22. Society for Human Resource Management, 1999.

23. R. H. Haveman and D. H. Saks, "Transatlantic Lessons for Employment and Training Policy," *Industrial Relations 24* (1985): 20–36.

# CHAPTER

## Identifying Training Needs

Too often, training and development programs get their start in organizations simply because the program was well advertised and marketed, or because "other organizations are using it." It makes little sense for any organization to adopt an expensive and time-consuming training effort simply to "keep up with the Joneses." However, because organizations often imitate one another, training techniques (as pointed out in Chapter 1) can be faddish. This faddish nature of training can be minimized by systematically determining training needs. In this way, organizations will use training and development interventions only for the people and the situations where needed. Unfortunately, only about 27 percent of companies report having procedures for systematically determining the training and development needs of their managers.[1]

In this chapter, we discuss the most comprehensive and sophisticated system of determining an organization's training needs. This approach consists of three kinds of analyses: organization, task, and person.[2] These analyses provide answers to the following three questions: Where is training needed in the organization? What must a trainee learn in order to perform the job effectively? Who needs training and of what kind?

Before proceeding, it is important to keep several things in mind about this approach to training needs. First, these analyses require time and human resources to be conducted properly. It is clearly not something that a few individuals in an organization can complete overnight. Second, it is a process that needs repeating when the organization's products, services, or technology changes. Third, the three analyses are usually performed simultaneously since they interrelate so highly with one another. Even if an organization cannot afford financially to carry out each step mentioned in this chapter, it should attempt to do whatever it can to approach this ideal.

## ORGANIZATION ANALYSIS

Organization analysis looks at the organization as a whole. This involves examining its interface with the external environment in which it operates, the attainment of its stated objectives, its human resources, and its culture. The primary purpose of an organization analysis is to determine where in the organization training activities should be conducted (i.e., "Are they needed?") and could be conducted (i.e., "Will they be successful?"). It is unusual for all units within an organization to have the same training and development needs. To implement an organizationwide training program without assessing where the training is needed makes little sense from a cost–benefit standpoint. Nevertheless, some organizations adopt expensive "organizationwide" programs with little or no regard to where the training was actually required.

The environment in which an organization operates can be a critical factor in determining whether training and development should be conducted. For one thing, if a training function is to survive, it must be supported financially by the organization. The amount of support the organization gives can be affected by its overall profitability or vitality in the competitive market, as well as by the resources available (i.e., labor, raw materials, capital, technology, markets) for its continued success. Further, the larger environment in which an organization operates can affect the organization itself, which in turn can affect training needs. For one thing, the environment can affect the way the organization's managers design jobs, supervise their employees, and make decisions.[3] The environment may also influence the structural nature of the organization itself. Organizations operating in dynamic, uncertain environments where there are frequent scientific discoveries, technical inventions, and changes in market conditions (e.g., electronics firms) need structural features (e.g., flexible roles, open communications that cut across hierarchical levels, coordination by committees) that will allow them to adapt rapidly to changing environmental conditions. On the other hand, organizations functioning within relatively stable commercial and technological environments (e.g., banks, insurance companies) can function well using a more bureaucratic or mechanistic structure.[4] Designing a bureaucratic structure may involve clearly defining roles and responsibilities, instituting a one-way chain of command from the top to the bottom of the authority hierarchy, and delegating sufficient authority to each manager to carry out his or her responsibilities.

Unless it is known what the organization and its subunits are trying to accomplish, there is little basis for determining where training is needed. Knowing, for example, that an organization's 90 retail stores had a net profit of $150 million last year tells us little unless we can evaluate this outcome in relation to store objectives. Once we know the objectives, we can examine how closely these goals are being achieved.

An organization's overall objectives should first be stated in broad terms and then stated more specifically for the organization's various divisions, departments, and sections. In this way, training programs can be directed toward the improvement of those organizational units that are currently the weakest.

Furthermore, both short- and long-term goals must be established. Programs should not focus solely on solving immediate problems to the extent that long-term, preventive training is completely forgotten. For example, Table 3.1 presents

**TABLE 3.1    Short- and Long-Term Objectives of the Medical Records and Housekeeping Departments of a Small Hospital**

| *Medical Records Department* | *Housekeeping Department* |
|---|---|
| • Develop five-year capital and manpower plan in accordance with long-range plan for hospital | • Compliance with hospital requirements for audit activities |
| • No more than one complaint per month as to the organization, operation, or attitude of personnel in department from members of medical staff |   (a) No deficiences on audit cited by survey |
| |   (b) Be in compliance within current standards |
| • No more than three formal grievances per year from members of the deparment | • Maintain all necessary records for |
| • Written and current policies and procedures for the operations of the medical records department will be maintained, "current" being defined as semi-annual |   (a) Infection control |
| |   (b) State license |
| • No medical record shall ever be lost |   (c) Legal documents |
| • Medical records shall be completed within time frames set up in Medical Staff Bylaws | • Annual operating budget will be prepared according to timetable presented by the director of finance. Year-end variance will not exceed ± 5% |
|   (a) All charts will be assembled and deficiency slips made out and put in physician's box within 48 hours of discharge | • Monthly status report will be turned in to administrative head by the 10th of each month |
|   (b) If chart is still incomplete 1 week later, physician will be notified that he or she has 8 days to complete the chart | • Develop five-year capital and manpower plan in accordance with long-range plan for hospital |
| • All registered and professional employees will maintain continuing education requirements | • No more than four complaints per month as to the organization, operation, or attitude of personnel in department from members of medical staff |
| • All other employees to receive some form of continuing education at a minimum of one hour per month. | • No more than five formal grievances per year from members of the department |
| | • All employees to receive some form of continuing education at a minimum of one hour per month |
| | • Educational activities to include at least 12 hours of management education per year for the housekeeping supervisor |
| | • Written and current policies and procedures for the operations of the housekeeping department will be updated during the next five years in accordance with the hospital's projected expansion |

a few of the short- and long-term objectives established by the medical records department and housekeeping department of a small midwestern hospital. Suppose that the medical charts of some patients had been misplaced in the past and that some members of the medical staff had voiced their complaints regarding the operation of the medical records department. Suppose also that the housekeeping department had been meeting or exceeding its stated objectives. All of this may suggest that members of the medical records department, but not the housekeeping department, need training of some kind. As you can see, one of the main purposes of performing an organization analysis is to identify "gaps," which are simply a difference between what an organization expects to happen and what actually happens.[5]

It is important to remember, however, that not all performance gaps can be dealt with by means of training. It could be that such nontraining factors as boredom with the work itself, low wages, inefficient work procedures, and poor physical working conditions are causing the problems. Furthermore, if employees know how to engage in certain behaviors but do not want to engage in those behaviors, the problem may be one of motivation rather than training. The important point here is that the training specialists performing the organization analysis must ultimately decide why a particular organizational unit is not meeting its stated objectives (i.e., training versus nontraining causes). These professionals must refrain from jumping to the conclusion that training is the answer the problem. Instead, they need to leave the question open of whether there should be training at all.[6] This is a real challenge for training specialists! In the "real world," too many training specialists do just what they are asked to do by their organizations—deliver training. They do not do what they are *not* asked to do—to improve human performance in the workplace. So, their organizations do not ask them to deliver what is really needed (i.e., performance improvement), but instead to deliver merely what their organizations believe they can provide.[7] It is crucial that training managers consider eliminating or reducing performance gaps through alternate means such as hiring the right people, communicating performance expectations, removing obstacles, creating a supportive work environment, and providing positive consequences for achieving excellence at work.

Another aspect of organization analysis is the estimation of how many people need to be trained immediately and in the future. This can be determined by conducting two processes, one known as *employment planning* or human resource analysis, the other called *concept testing*.

Every organization performs employment planning, on either an intuitive or a formal basis. Formal planning is especially necessary for large organizations with high growth rates, high employee turnover, and rapid changes in technology and product lines. The techniques used in forecasting vary from guesses by experts to sophisticated mathematical approaches.

Table 3.2 presents hypothetical information to illustrate how human resource analyses can be used to shed light on a department's training needs. Items 1 and 2 indicate that there is an immediate need to train one new

**TABLE 3.2    A Human Resource Analysis of One Hypothetical Department**

1. Number of employees in the job classification:    37
2. Number of employees needed:                        38
3. Age levels:          29      33      45      47      50      51      53      55      69
   No. per age group:    2       8       7      10       3       2       2       1       2

| Factors | Satisfactory | Questionable | Unsatisfactory |
|---------|-------------|-------------|----------------|
| 4. Skill | 32 | 2 | 3 |
| 5. Knowledge | 33 | 3 | 1 |

6. Skill and knowledge for other jobs within the company:

| Classification | Number | Jobs |
|----------------|--------|------|
| No other jobs | 35 | none |
| One other job | 1 | Job Z, Dept. Y |
| Two or more other jobs | 1 | Job Z, Dept. Y; Job A, Dept. B |

7. Potential replacements and training time:

| Outside Company | Within Company | Training Time |
|-----------------|----------------|---------------|
| 0 | 1 | Less than 1 week |
| 0 | 1 | 3 weeks to 6 weeks |
| 10 | 0 | 12 weeks to 16 weeks |

8. Training time on job for novice:    12 to 16 weeks
9. Turnover (two-year period):    Five employees; 13.5%

employee. Item 3 shows that two employees will be retiring within the next year. Their replacements will require training and development. Items 4 and 5 indicate that as many as nine present employees are either "questionable" or "unsatisfactory" in skill and knowledge about their jobs. This suggests that they may need retraining to improve their current performance levels.

It is evident from item 6 that the problem with these employees cannot be solved simply by transferring them to other jobs, since so few of the employees in this department have the skill and knowledge levels for other company jobs. Items 7 and 8 show that most replacements will have to come from outside the company and that their training time will take 12 to 16 weeks. Finally, item 9 indicates that, assuming the current rate of turnover, five new employees will have to be trained within a two-year period.

Concept testing is another approach for determining where within an organization training might be needed. Procter & Gamble, for example, has randomly selected 500 people throughout its 110,000-person organization to function as a permanent, core concept testing panel. This core panel is supplemented each year by 1,000 additional employees who are randomly chosen to represent all the various business units within the organziation. Whenever a new training program is being considered for possible purchase or home-grown design, the 1,500 panel members are contacted, provided a detailed description of the objectives and content of the program, and then asked to complete an eight-item "global learning concept testing model." Following are a few examples of what the panel members are asked about the proposed training description:

- The purpose of this training is to _____. To what extent is this an outage/barrier for you? (Place a check by only one)
  Definitely an outage or barrier                           _____
  Probably an outage or barrier                             _____
  Might or might not be an outage or barrier                _____
  Probably is not an outage or barrier                      _____
  Definitely is not an outage or barrier                    _____
- Which statement best describes how well you think you would VALUE or NOT VALUE this training to improve your capability versus other interventions of which you are aware? (Place a check by only one)
  Value extremely well                                      _____
  Value very well                                           _____
  Value quite well                                          _____
  Value somewhat                                            _____
  Not value at all                                          _____
- How likely would you be to participate in this training? (Place a check by only one)
  Definitely would participate                              _____
  Probably would participate                                _____
  Might or might not participate                            _____
  Probably would not participate                            _____
  Definitely would not participate                          _____

After gathering information from their 1,500-member concept testing panel, the organization analyzes the data broken down by various business units and organization level. By analyzing these data, the company's learning center is able to decide whether there is a need big enough to warrant offering this training and, if so, where in the organization it is needed.

A final aspect of organization analysis sometimes involves an organizational culture survey. A culture survey is used to determine the way employees perceive specific aspects of their work (e.g., compensations, opportunities for advancement, supervision received) and their membership in the organization (e.g., policies, goals, procedures, benefits, concern for human resources). If a group of employees perceive the company and their jobs as congruent with their own personal needs, goals, and aspirations, then the environment within their organizational unit will be one of trust and willingness to cooperate. However, if employees see the company and their jobs as being antagonistic to their personal needs, goals, and aspirations, then the environment in their unit will be characterized by mistrust and resistance to change.

Why would we want to assess an organization's culture? First, the environment may affect whether training can produce changes in behavior that will contribute to organizational effectiveness. Often, if the environment is very poor, employees will resist any kind of training given by the company. We have witnessed excellent training and development programs doomed to failure because the social–psychological environment basically made employees say to themselves, "I refuse to change." Second, a careful examination of an organization's culture using a technically sound attitude survey can help pinpoint problem areas within the organization.

An organizational culture survey is typically conducted by using a questionnaire that is completed by all employees. One such organizational diagnosis questionnaire is known as *Perspectives,* a computer-scored 57-item core questionnaire that provides information about 13 core dimensions of organizational culture, including:

Overall job satisfaction
Satisfaction with the work itself
Satisfaction with pay and benefits
Opportunities for advancement
Satisfaction with leadership and supervision
Motivation
Total quality management

In addition, based on the diagnosis, most users choose to add customized survey items that deal with unique issues facing their organization. Examples include:

Customer focus
Teamwork
Reaction toward merger
Continuous learning environment
Reaction toward downsizing

Table 3.3 shows some of the items found in this questionnaire. As you can see, all of the questions employ a multiple-choice answer format. Table 3.4 presents some of the data obtained after computer scoring of the questionnaire. The table gives summary data for all 879 respondents from one organization as to their satisfaction with pay, benefits, and opportunities for promotions. The table also compares the attitudes of the office clerical employees with those of all 879 respondents.

In summary, an organization analysis prevents training from being viewed as an isolated activity or series of activities by training specialists. As we go further into the twenty-first century, two themes should be kept in mind in order for training departments to be considered effective by senior-level management. First, training needs must be linked strongly to corporate strategy. Second, organizations have an ethical responsibility for developing training programs that minimize the technical obsolescence of their employees.

**TABLE 3.3 Sample Content of an Organization Culture Questionnaire**

The following questions are to be answered using the number associated with the choice that comes closest to your own feelings:

1 = not at all, or none
2 = very little
3 = somewhat
4 = quite a bit
5 = a great deal, or to a great extent

1. Does your job make the best of your own particular
   skills and abilities?                                1  2  3  4  5

2. Are the people in your work group encouraged to work
   together as a team?                                  1  2  3  4  5

In this section several aspects of your job are listed. Please indicate the importance of each of these for your overall job satisfaction by selecting one of the five choices below:

1 = very unimportant
2 = unimportant
3 = neither important nor unimportant
4 = important
5 = very important

1. Promotions                                           1  2  3  4  5

2. Benefits                                             1  2  3  4  5

The following questions are to be answered using the number associated with the choice that comes closest to your own feelings.

1 = almost never
2 = seldom
3 = sometimes
4 = often
5 = almost always

1. How often do you leave work with a good feeling of accomplishment
   about the work you did that day?                     1  2  3  4  5

2. Do you get conflicting orders or instructions and, as a result,
   don't know what you are supposed to do?              1  2  3  4  5

---

With regard to the first theme, Brown and Read[8] concluded that the productivity gap between U.K. and Japanese companies can be closed by taking a strategic view of training policies. This should be done by ensuring that the training plan is constructed in the same context and by the same process as the business plan, and more importantly, that it is viewed in direct relationship to it. Thus, achievement of training goals should be regularly monitored and subjected to a thorough annual review alongside the business plan.

**TABLE 3.4   Sample Data from an Organizational Culture Questionnaire**

### Summary Data for All 879 Respondents
### from Consolidated Corporation

| Attitude Dimension | Percentage Responding | | | | |
|---|---|---|---|---|---|
| | *LO* | | | | *HI* |
| | *1* | *2* | *3* | *4* | *5* |
| SATISFACTION WITH | | | | | |
| Pay | 9 | 11 | 34 | 32 | 14 |
| Benefits | 3 | 3 | 11 | 34 | 49 |
| Promotions | 13 | 28 | 28 | 24 | 8 |

### Comparative Summary
### of 136 Office Clerical (C)
### 879 Overall Company (O)

| Attitude Dimension | | Percentage Responding | | | | |
|---|---|---|---|---|---|---|
| | | *LO* | | | | *HI* |
| | | *1* | *2* | *3* | *4* | *5* |
| SATISFACTION WITH | | | | | | |
| Pay | C | 14 | 33 | 25 | 25 | 3 |
| | O | 9 | 11 | 34 | 32 | 14 |
| Benefits | C | 3 | 0 | 3 | 39 | 56 |
| | O | 3 | 3 | 11 | 34 | 49 |
| Promotions | C | 16 | 38 | 25 | 18 | 3 |
| | O | 13 | 28 | 28 | 24 | 8 |

It has been argued that training objectives, especially for management development, should be reviewed by top management whenever a major switch in strategic emphasis is planned.[9] However, in a survey of U.K. companies, it was found that only one-third of the respondents saw the necessity for doing so. Most managers felt that training objectives should be tailored to the individual rather than to corporate needs. Hussey also argued for a shift in thinking regarding the purpose of training. Training should not be solely for the improvement of the individual with the hope that it will benefit the organization; training should be for the benefit of the firm, knowing that this, in turn, will benefit the individual. Such training should ensure that strategy is communicated and implemented effectively throughout the organization.

As stated earlier, organization analysis focuses on the organization as a whole, including the external environment in which it operates. It attempts to answer the question, "*Where* is training and development needed and where is it likely to be successful within an organization?" It consists of an analysis of the following:

1. How the organization relates to its external environment, in order to assess how these external variables influence the need for training and development
2. How well the organization and its various subunits are achieving their stated objectives
3. The short- and long-range training and development needs of its employees
4. A need or market in the organization for this type of training
5. What factors in the internal and external environment are likely to present problems and to what extent can they be dealt with through the training and development of the organization's human resources

Once questions of *where* and *why* training is needed have been answered, the design or content of the program itself can be considered. This is done through a systematic task analysis.

## TASK ANALYSIS

As shown in Figure 3.1, there are five steps in conducting a task analysis:

1. Obtain a copy of the company's job description and any other information available about the job.
2. Identify the tasks involved in performing the job for which the training program is being designed.
3. Identify the knowledge (K), skills (S), and abilities (A) needed for performing these tasks.
4. Develop course objectives.
5. Design the training program.

Suppose we wanted to develop a training program for newly hired tire store managers. Figure 3.2 shows the types of information that would be generated at each step of the task analysis.

### Job Description

The first step in determining the content of a training and development program is to develop a description of the target job. A job description is essentially a narrative statement about what a person does on the job, including the conditions

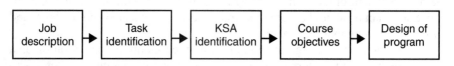

**FIGURE 3.1** Steps in Course Development Using Task Analysis

**Job Description**
Supervises and coordinates activities of the workers engaged in servicing and repairing automobiles and truck tires and tubes. Examines damaged, defective, or flat tires to determine feasibility of repair and assigns workers to tasks.

**Task Identification**
Attends meetings with district manager.
Communicates Occupational Safety and Health Administration (OSHA) regulations to employers.
Selects employees to train a new worker.
Schedules overtime as needed.

**KSA Identification**
Oral communication skills.
Tolerance of stress.
Numerical ability.
Persuasiveness.

**Course Objectives**
To be knowledgeable about company overtime policies and procedures.
To be knowledgeable about store return policies.
To handle customer complaints on the phone and in person.
To maintain the security of the tire store building.
To know and be able to communicate OSHA regulations to employees.

**Design of Program**
Methods: lecture, behavioral modeling, computer-assisted instruction, and on-the-job training (OJT)
Length: 15 days
Place: Corporate Training Center
Trainers: HRD, Inc. + 3 in-house trainers
Trainees: 75 new hires per year

**FIGURE 3.2**    An Example of the Information Collected at Each Step of the Task Analysis

(e.g., cold weather, excessive time pressures, dealing with irate customers) under which the job is performed.

Some organizations already have written job descriptions that are filed in the personnel department. Often, however, these descriptions are not comprehensive enough for course preparation purposes. Thus, the training staff must frequently rewrite them. This entails observing current employees performing their jobs and questioning them about what they are doing. In some instances, the training analyst may perform some of the job duties him- or herself in order to obtain firsthand knowledge of exactly what is involved in doing the work. More often than not, this cannot be done because the work is either too complex or dangerous for a novice to perform.

There may be other sources of information available about the job that training specialists often use in addition to a job description, such as:

• *Job inventory questionnaire:* Completed by employees asking them to evaluate the tasks they perform in terms of importance and relative amount of time spent.

- *Performance standards:* A listing of the expectations of the job expressed in terms of both effective behaviors and desired bottom-line outcomes or results.
- *Analyses of operating problems:* Training specialists can review various reports showing such things as downtime, waste, repairs, late deliveries, and the frequency and nature of customer complaints.
- *Observing, questioning, and performing the job:* Training specialists can observe employees performing the job; ask incumbents, supervisors, and managers about the work; and, if feasible, perform parts of the job themselves.[10]

Two examples of job descriptions are presented in Figures 3.3 and 3.4. The first one, a description of an investment specialist, comes from the securities department of a large life insurance company. The second one describes the job of a medical librarian in a small hospital. In writing these two descriptions, the training specialists tried to include those things that are critical to performing these jobs satisfactorily, no matter how infrequently or briefly they occur. Moreover, the training specialists took care to describe these jobs as they exist now, not as the training specialists or the supervisors would like them to be in the future.

## Task Identification

As discussed in the last section, a job description portrays the job in some detail, but it does not give us enough specific information to put together a training and development course. This is where task identification comes in.

Task identification focuses on the behaviors that are involved in performing a job. A task listing of a home telephone installer might include the following behavioral statements:

1. Reads and interprets service orders
2. Climbs pole to hook up the drop wire
3. Runs drop wire from pole to house
4. Checks protector to make sure it is functioning correctly
5. Uses ladder on side of house to hook up drop wire

Several different approaches can be used for identifying tasks. Although the procedures differ somewhat from one another, they all break down human work into task units that can then be used for determining the content of a training and development program. In this section, the following six procedures are described:

1. Stimulus–response–feedback
2. Time sampling
3. Linear sequencing
4. Critical incident technique
5. Job inventories
6. Future-oriented job analysis

The incumbent reports to a manager of investments and an investment officer. The manager, along with three other managers, an assistant manager, the investment research officer, the investment officer (markets), and the assistant treasurer-assistant secretary, reports to the vice president–securities and treasurer.

The incumbent frequently accompanies the manager or investment officer on trips made to the site of borrowing corporations, and may occasionally make such trips alone. She or he actively participates in negotiation conferences both in the home office and in the field between JMW and potential borrowers and/or their investment banking representatives. After mutually satisfactory terms have been reached and the investment has been finally approved, the incumbent works closely with the law department to review the loan agreement and assure that it conforms to the conditions and stipulations approved by the finance committee.

The incumbent spends much of his or her time performing various necessary service and analytical functions for JMW's offshore oil and gas project. She or he is required to maintain liaison with joint venture partners for the purpose of acquiring and updating information. He or she is further responsible for authorizing the disbursement of funds, updating the project budget periodically, and projecting future expenditures. Finally, the incumbent performs various research activities for the project such as computing the probable rate of return on JMW's investment.

The incumbent also has major responsibility for evaluating consent requests for changes in existing investment loan agreements. She or he pursues the financial and legal aspects of the requested changes to assess their investment consequences. The incumbent then presents oral and/or written recommendations concerning the requested changes to a manager of investments and/or an investment officer for approval.

The incumbent occasionally prepares special projects related to portfolio analysis, securities department procedures and activities, and so on. He or she is generally expected to be knowledgeable about the portfolio, and to monitor its status periodically in order to identify and anticipate problem areas.

The incumbent assists a manager of investments and an investment officer in the analysis of new investment opportunities. This involves an appraisal of the credit worthiness of potential borrowers, including the general state of the borrower's industry, a thorough understanding of the terms of the loan agreement, and analysis of the yield required to make the deal attractive to JMW. The incumbent is expected to research and analyze these investment offerings with minimum supervision, developing and incorporating meaningful data on her or his own initiative. Based on this research, the incumbent's recommendation on a proposed investment is presented orally and in a detailed written memorandum to the manager and investment officer for approval. They direct any necessary revisions, and accompanied by the incumbent, present the proposal to the vice president–securities. Investment proposals approved by the vice president are subsequently presented to the finance committee by the manager and/or investment officer.

**FIGURE 3.3** An Example of a Job Description for the Job of Investment Specialist

According to the stimulus–response–feedback method, each task activity consists of the following components.[11] An indicator may be any object that provides the cue for making a response. It may be an aircraft instrument, a pressure gauge, a millivolt meter, a circuit tester, or even a written message. The indicator cue that triggers the response may appear all at once, or it may have to be pieced

**GENERAL RESPONSIBILITIES**

Under general, but limited, supervision the librarian assumes responsibility for the administration, operation, organization, and expansion of a professional hospital library providing document delivery, bibliographic and reference services, and containing current books, serials, other appropriate print material, audiovisual material and bibliographic tools necessary for the use of the medical staff, medical and nursing students, and employees serving the hospital.

**SPECIFIC RESPONSIBILITIES**

1. Works with and makes recommendations to the library committee in the selection of appropriate books, serials, and audiovisual material for acquisition through purchase, gift, and/or exchange and in the establishment of library policies and procedures.
2. Classifies, catalogs, and indexes books, serials, and audiovisual material.
3. Issues materials to qualified library users and keeps pertinent records of lending in order to locate material when necessary or prevent material from remaining outside of the library for undue periods of time.
4. Performs reference services for library users including requests for factual information and for subject or bibliographic searches to be done manually and/or with MEDLINE terminal.
5. Provides document reproduction/delivery services as requested consistent with the Copyright Law of the United States (Title 17, U.S. Code).
6. Contacts other medical libraries and/or intertype library networks with shared services arrangements for material requested but not available in the hospital library.
7. Performs routine library clerical procedures including taking care of the library mail and correspondence, recording acquisitions, and checking in journals.
8. Coordinates through all medical center departments the purchase and/or subscription of reference materials or journals.
9. Develops annual departmental budget recommendations.
10. Develops annual plan of short-term and long-range departmental objectives.
11. Develops and establishes coordinated program of library service with the director of staff development and the hospital education council for in-house and community education.
12. Keeps all staff aware of library services and materials and orients the new medical staff, students, and employees to use of the library, its services, and materials to assure that effective use is made of the library.
13. When possible, participates in the professional organization, medical library consortia, and intertype library networks for the purpose of continuing education in librarianship and to be aware of and/or influence legislation, activities, and programs that may affect the hospital library.

**FIGURE 3.4**   An Example of a Job Description for the Job of Medical Librarian

together by the worker from recall through periods of time. In its broadest sense, it is an out-of-tolerance signal that there is a difference between present conditions and how conditions ought to be. Examples here might include the excessive vibrations of a piece of machinery, exhaust sounds from an automobile, or a clock that runs too slowly. The control object refers to any means the employee uses to correct the out-of-tolerance situation. It may require the use of a tool, a piece of machinery, or even another worker. The activation or manipulation deals with the employee's actual use of the control object. Here, it is important to describe the actual use of the tool or machinery or even the message conveyed by one employee to another regarding the situation. The indication of response adequacy is the feedback that the employees receive regarding the adequacy of their behaviors. The indication of response adequacy may be proximal (as by the feel of a switch when a machine is being adjusted), or distal (as when one hears the machine starting up again). In short, this approach basically calls for the analysis of each task in terms of a stimulus–response–feedback framework. This paradox is illustrated here for two different tasks.

This approach to task identification is of value when describing simple structural tasks that are amenable to a stimulus–response–feedback dissection. However, the method is limited with complex tasks (e.g., executive management) because of the difficulties in specifying cues, responses, and feedback involved. Nevertheless, the approach can be particularly useful in training where equipment simulators need to be developed. Imagine how much easier it would be to design a truck simulator or a punch press simulator after identifying the exact stimuli and responses involved in each aspect of the truck driver's or press operator's job.

A second task identification approach is called time sampling. Here, direct observations of work activities are made by trained observers. Time sampling enables trainers to determine through direct observation exactly what employees do on the job and how frequently they do it. By making randomized observations of employee behavior, trainers can learn in a relatively short time how employees perform their jobs. For example, in an analysis of entry-level clerical jobs, 37 clerical workers representing 10 clerical positions were selected for observation.[12] At 25-minute intervals, an observer made "rounds" of observations that took him or her past the work stations of each of the 37 persons being observed. As the observer passed each work station, he or she simply noted the job duty (e.g., filing, checking, typing, receiving information, giving information) the worker was performing. Each observer's "rounds" were begun at random times throughout the workday. Over 1,900 individual observations were made in all. This information enabled the organization to identify the tasks performed in each of these clerical positions.

In another organization, four observers were trained to monitor customer contacts of telephone company service representatives for a three-day period.[13] Well over 100 service representatives in two district offices were monitored while handling almost 1,000 telephone calls. The monitoring procedure required the observer to follow a "new" call through to completion (a new call was signaled by a light on a switchboard in an observation room). When the contact was completed, the observer switched off that representative, recorded the behavior(s) engaged in by the service representative, and waited for the next call. Randomization of service representative positions was ensured because the positions were connected to the central switchboard on a rotary number basis; that is, the next call was automatically connected to the next service representative available. Several interobserver agreement checks were conducted to assess the consistency of their task identification procedure. Correspondence between pairs of observers listening to the same 30 telephone calls was found to be quite high, ranging from 90 percent to 100 percent agreement. A major deficiency of the time sampling method is its inability to determine what an employee is thinking. Therefore, if a job is extremely cerebral in nature (e.g., a Designer at Mack Trucks who works at a CAD [Computer Assisted Design] updating and creating new truck parts), this method may not be very effective.

The third task identification procedure, called linear sequencing, was designed expressly for specifying training content.[14] The method is applicable for trainers who want to analyze the basic steps of any job so that they can successfully teach these steps to someone else. To do this, the task description must be sufficiently detailed so that trainees who know nothing about the procedure to be performed can read the analysis and perform the job correctly without guidance. This approach can be illustrated by using another telephone example and asking you to imagine for a moment a person who has never seen or used one. The trainer would use the following procedure:

1. Write each step on a card, with each card containing a stimulus and a response.

   **Stimulus:**   The phone rings.

   **Response:**   Pick up the receiver (the part that is attached to the base by a wire).

   **Stimulus:**   You hear nothing.

   **Response:**   Say "hello."

2. Make certain that the response portion of the card begins with an imperative verb telling the reader to do something. For example, when taking an outgoing call, some of the response cards could read: Press the buttons corresponding to the seven-digit telephone number of the person you are calling. Next, listen for a series of long tones interspersed with long pauses.

3. Technical terms commonly used by subject-matter experts should be included in the write-up and defined.

   **Example:**   If you do not hear a DIAL TONE (steady buzzing signal), HANG UP (replace the receiver on the phone as you found it).

4. If it seems desirable to record the rationale for a step (i.e., the reason why the step is performed) for future reference, the rationale should be recorded on the back of the card.

5. The trainer places the cards in the proper sequence. A series of steps that follow one another without any alternatives is called a linear sequence. If the steps are not always followed in exactly the same manner, and the trainees are required to make procedural decisions, the procedure is known as branching. The following are examples of these two types of sequences:

   **Linear:**   (5) Next, insert the letter in the envelope. (6) Next, close the envelope. (7) Next, moisten the stamp. (8) Next, affix the stamp to the envelope.

**Branching:** (5) Next, insert the letter in the envelope. (6) Next, close the envelope. (7) Next, determine if there is a postage meter in the office. (8) If there is a postage meter, . . . (instructions telling how to use it). (8a) If there is no postage meter, moisten a stamp.

As you can imagine, branching sequences occur more frequently as jobs become more complicated. This is an excellent method for determining training content with any job involving certain prescribed procedures (e.g., orthopedic surgery, dentistry, pipe fitting) because it specifies the exact things to be taught.

A fourth approach to task identification is known as the *critical incident technique* or CIT.[15] The CIT requires observers who are aware of the aims and objectives of a given job and who frequently (e.g., daily) see people perform the job, to describe to a task analyst incidents of effective and ineffective job behavior that they have observed over the past 6 to 12 months. This means that supervisors, peers, subordinates, and clients may be interviewed about the critical requirements of a specific job. The specific steps in conducting a task identification based on the CIT are listed here[16]:

1. (Introduction): "I am conducting a job analysis to determine what makes the difference between an effective and an ineffective _____ (e.g., foreman, pipe fitter, administrative assistant). By effective performance, I mean behavior you have seen in the past that you wished all employees would do under similar circumstances. By ineffective performance, I mean behavior that, if it occurred repeatedly or even once under certain circumstances, would make you doubt the competency of the individual.

   "I am asking you to do this because you are aware of the aims and objectives of the job, you frequently observe people in this job, and you are able to discern competent from incompetent performance. Please do not tell me the names of any individual to whom you are referring."

   Job incumbents are not interviewed concerning their own behavior. This is because incumbents are usually objective in describing their effective behavior, but there is sometimes a tendency for them to attribute their ineffective behavior to factors that were beyond their control.

2. (Interview): "I would like you to think of specific incidents that you personally have seen occur over the past 6 to 12 months." The emphasis on the past 12 months is to ensure that the information is currently applicable. For example, behaviors that were critical for a salesperson in the 1950s may no longer be critical in the 2000s. Moreover, memory loss may distort the facts if the analysis is not restricted to recent incidents. The requirement that the interviewer report only firsthand information maximizes the objectivity or factual nature of the information to be reported.

For each incident that is recalled, the same three questions are asked, namely:

1. "What were the circumstances surrounding this incident?" In other words, what was the background? What was the situation? This question is important because it establishes when a given behavior is appropriate.

2. "What exactly did the individual do that was either effective or ineffective?" The purpose of this second question is to elicit information concerning observable behavior.

3. "How is the incident an example of effective or ineffective behavior?" In other words, how did this affect the task(s) the individual was performing?

Generally, an interviewee is asked to report five effective and five ineffective incidents. Attention is given to both types of incidents because an effective incident is not necessarily the opposite of an ineffective incident. For example, setting a specific goal has been found to be effective for increasing productivity in many jobs, but not setting goals does not necessarily decrease productivity.[17]

A total of 10 incidents are collected because they can usually be collected within one hour. This is the maximum time period that many employees can be away from the job without disrupting their workday. No more than 10 incidents are collected from any one individual so that the data are not biased by talkative people. In order to obtain a comprehensive sample of incidents, it is recommended that at least 30 people be interviewed for a total of roughly 300 incidents.[18]

The interviewer must be skilled in collecting information describing observable behaviors. If the interviewee responds to question b with the answer, "The employee really showed initiative in solving the problem," the interviewer must ask, "What exactly did the individual do that indicated initiative?"

This procedure has particular utility when training specialists want to develop programs that concentrate on critical tasks. For example, a restaurant's waiters and waitresses may know how to set up tables and clean them after customers have left. The same waiters and waitresses may have difficulty, however, taking customer orders and relaying these orders accurately to the kitchen. Therefore, the training program should be concerned with these critical tasks.

The fifth approach to task identification involves the development of a job inventory (sometimes referred to as a task inventory). A job inventory is a structured questionnaire that consists of a listing of tasks comprising a particular job. Once the questionnaire is constructed, it is administered to employees who currently perform the job since they are considered to be among the most knowledgeable about it. In many cases, supervisors are asked to describe the job as well.

One or more small groups of persons (8 to 12 in a group) are initially selected to generate an exhaustive list of job tasks necessary to perform a particular job adequately. The individuals in these groups are not randomly selected, but are chosen on the basis of their exhaustive knowledge of the job. A technique known as *group brainstorming* is used by the training specialist during the meetings to encourage the group members to list as many tasks as possible. Employees and supervisors usually participate in separate meetings, as the presence of a supervisor may inhibit the employees from speaking openly. Tasks that were generated during group sessions we held with tire store managers included:

- Takes a physical inventory monthly
- Reviews salespersons' expense reports
- Arranges for outside collection of bills through independent agencies
- Holds safety meetings with store personnel
- Informs employees of all company benefits
- Assigns sales quotas to sales and service personnel
- Makes certain that customers are informed of all warranties and guarantees

Following the group meetings, a job inventory is constructed by the training specialist and mailed to a random sample of employees. These employees are asked to rate each task in terms of both importance and amount of time spent. An example of a typical job inventory is presented in Figure 3.5. Both low and high performers can be used to complete job inventories, since both groups of employees provide similar ratings of importance and time spent on tasks.[19]

After the questionnaire is completed by a number of employees, the training specialist calculates the average rating for each task for both importance and time spent. These ratings help to identify true training needs rather than just training wants.[20] The end product of this analysis is a comprehensive picture of the job's tasks as seen by not just one person or a few people, but by many knowledgeable employees currently working on the job.

A sixth and final approach to task analysis anticipates the dynamic environment in which organizations will be operating throughout the twenty-first century. It is called *future-oriented task analysis.* This concept at the present time is admittedly a fuzzy one. It is based on research which has indicated that the jobs of the future will require less memorizing of facts and procedures, fewer physical skills, and far more conceptual ability than is true at the present time.

Consistent with these findings, it can be argued that an organizational analysis must focus on future objectives of the organization rather than only present ones. Only in this way can the development and training of senior executives be effective (see Chapters 8 and 9).

The purpose of future-oriented task analysis is to link the management succession process, individual executive learning, with the business strategy. In this way, future executive requirements are defined in terms of the future strategic organizational objectives. To do this, the organization's executives speculate on the future mission and future goals of the organization.

In updating, the critical incident technique described earlier can be used to develop behavioral observation scales (also discussed in this chapter) that specify what a person must do to engage in updating behaviors (e.g., keep abreast of technical journals, periodicals, and in-house publications; allocate working time for developmental purposes; volunteer for special assignments and tasks that represent a change in present job assignments).

### Summary

We have described six different task analysis procedures. Any of these methods can be recommended for determining job tasks. The stimulus–response–

|  | Importance | Amount of Time Spent |
|---|---|---|
| **INSTRUCTIONS:** For each task activity, *circle* the number corresponding to its importance for *your* job and the amount of time you spend on it. | 1 = *Not at all* important<br>2 = *Slightly* important<br>3 = *Moderately* important<br>4 = *Very* important<br>5 = *Extremely* important | 0 = *Never* do this task<br>1 = *Very little time* compared to other tasks<br>2 = *Somewhat less time* compared to other tasks<br>3 = *Same amount of time* as other tasks<br>4 = *More time* compared to other tasks<br>5 = *A great deal more time* compared to other tasks |

| Task | Importance | | | | | Amount of Time Spent | | | | | |
|---|---|---|---|---|---|---|---|---|---|---|---|
| 1. Assign and define duties to *all* new store employees. | 1 | 2 | 3 | 4 | 5 | 0 | 1 | 2 | 3 | 4 | 5 |
| 2. Take a physical inventory monthly. | 1 | 2 | 3 | 4 | 5 | 0 | 1 | 2 | 3 | 4 | 5 |
| 3. Assign accounts to salespeople for collection. | 1 | 2 | 3 | 4 | 5 | 0 | 1 | 2 | 3 | 4 | 5 |
| 4. Monitor overtime payments to employees. | 1 | 2 | 3 | 4 | 5 | 0 | 1 | 2 | 3 | 4 | 5 |
| 5. Make sure the inside and outside of building is maintained in a presentable condition. | 1 | 2 | 3 | 4 | 5 | 0 | 1 | 2 | 3 | 4 | 5 |
| 6. Schedule and place advertisements in newspapers and on radio. | 1 | 2 | 3 | 4 | 5 | 0 | 1 | 2 | 3 | 4 | 5 |
| 7. Make certain customers are greeted when coming into store and properly handled upon leaving. | 1 | 2 | 3 | 4 | 5 | 0 | 1 | 2 | 3 | 4 | 5 |
| 8. Establish a probationary period for new hires and review their performance periodically. | 1 | 2 | 3 | 4 | 5 | 0 | 1 | 2 | 3 | 4 | 5 |
| 9. Advise staff accountant of store claims. | 1 | 2 | 3 | 4 | 5 | 0 | 1 | 2 | 3 | 4 | 5 |
| 10. Arrange promissory notes payable at customer's bank if deemed necessary. | 1 | 2 | 3 | 4 | 5 | 0 | 1 | 2 | 3 | 4 | 5 |
| 11. Ensure that trucks are routed profitably. | 1 | 2 | 3 | 4 | 5 | 0 | 1 | 2 | 3 | 4 | 5 |
| 12. Hold safety meetings with store personnel. | 1 | 2 | 3 | 4 | 5 | 0 | 1 | 2 | 3 | 4 | 5 |
| 13. Make telephone solicitations to customers. | 1 | 2 | 3 | 4 | 5 | 0 | 1 | 2 | 3 | 4 | 5 |
| 14. Ensure that advertised products are available to customers. | 1 | 2 | 3 | 4 | 5 | 0 | 1 | 2 | 3 | 4 | 5 |
| 15. Discuss career goals with employees. | 1 | 2 | 3 | 4 | 5 | 0 | 1 | 2 | 3 | 4 | 5 |

**FIGURE 3.5** An Example of a Job Inventory Used with Tire Store Managers

feedback and linear sequencing methods are extremely time consuming and microanalytic. With these methods, the training specialist essentially observes employees at work and records stimulus–response links. Of the two methods, stimulus–response–feedback is more microanalytic, since tasks are broken down even further than in linear sequencing. Time sampling is a sound method of ascertaining what employees do and how frequently they do it simply by making direct observations of their behavior. The soundness of this approach, however, depends on the randomness of the "rounds" and the comprehensiveness of the checklist on which job duties are noted. The CIT involves interviewing individuals who have themselves made direct observations. This method is particularly useful when we are interested in identifying critical aspects of the job. The use of job inventories is quite appealing because employees participate in the construction of the inventory. The inventory is mailed to a large sample of employees who report their opinions about the importance and the relative amount of time they spend on each task. The end result is their averaged view of the job. Finally, the use of future-oriented task analysis captures the dynamic environment in which organizations find themselves in the twenty-first century.

## KSA Identification

Once the tasks involved in performing the job have been identified, the training specialist must identify the knowledge, skill, and ability needed to perform these tasks. A *K* (knowledge) refers to factual material that an employee needs to learn (e.g., marketing strategies, company overtime policies and procedures, store return policies). An *S* (skills) pertains to the hands-on, overt doing of things (e.g., delegating responsibility to subordinates, handling irate customers, operating the cash register, operating car lifts). An *A* refers to basic abilities that new hires are typically expected to possess, but that can be developed through training (e.g., multilimb coordination, deductive reasoning, selective attention).

The identification of K's, S's, and A's can be accomplished using a panel of about 10 people who are very familiar with the particular job. Typically, a combination of one's best job incumbents and supervisors of the job constitute an appropriate panel. Once the panel members understand the meaning of KSAs, they should be asked to brainstorm the K's, S's, and A's for each and every job task.

## Course Objectives

The information obtained from KSA identification is used to construct the course objectives, which consist of statements that specify the desired behavior of the trainee at the end of training. That is, these statements explicate what the training specialist expects the trainee to know and to do after participating in the training program. Following are examples of the many course objectives that participants are expected to achieve upon completion of a four-week tire store manager training and development program:

1. Set down conditions of employment for new hires (i.e., spell out exactly what their jobs are).
2. Maximize one's employees through efficient scheduling and use of part-time people.
3. Critique the appearance of different stores, and offer cost-effective solutions to any problems discovered.
4. Fill out a customer invoice.
5. Be familiar with the proper use of safety cages for safely dismounting and mounting split-run truck tires.
6. Handle customer complaints effectively.
7. Make a complete diagnosis of any car malfunctions in order to deal with customer service questions.
8. Handle radio advertisements, newspaper ads, and direct mailings.
9. Be familiar with some of the more critical Occupational Safety and Health Administration (OSHA) guidelines affecting store operations (e.g., proper stocking of aisles, storage of flammable materials, use of safety equipment in service area).
10. Be familiar with all types of store inventory (i.e., truck tires, passenger tires, brake and mechanical parts) and paperwork.

Although course objectives are based on the KSA identification, they differ in two important ways. First, KSA identification describes all of the personal characteristics involved in performing a job. Course objectives do not include those things that trainees are expected to know or be able to do before entering a course. For example, if prospective store managers already know how to complete a monthly inventory, there would be no need to include this task as a course objective.

Course objectives also do not include those KSAs called for in performing a job that are impractical to teach during a training course and are better left to learn on the job. For example, the handling of certain store operations may not be taught during a four-week store manager program since the training specialist may feel that it can be learned better on the job. Second, the KSAs describe the job as it is performed by an experienced employee. Course objectives need only describe the KSAs we can reasonably expect at the end of a training program. For example, an experienced store manager may be totally knowledgeable about all safety regulations affecting his or her store operations. It would be unrealistic to expect a trainee to know all of this upon course completion. It is far more realistic to expect the graduate to know the more critical regulations and learn the remainder through managerial experience.[21]

It is important to remember that course objectives are tailored to people who will take the training course. Their level of motivation and their abilities (see Chapter 4) will influence the quality of terminal performance that can reasonably be expected at the conclusion of the course. Finally, although the course objectives are expressed in terms of the KSAs, the actual material taught during the training pertains to the job's tasks. Only in this way can we expect to maintain the trainee's level of motivation and positive transfer (see Chapter 4).

## Design of Program

The final step in task analysis involves making decisions about the actual design of the training program. Of course, these decisions must be based on the particular set of course objectives. The first decision that needs to be made is whether to "make" or "buy." The answer, of course, depends on whether there exists a ready-made program that meets one's objectives as well as the program's quality and costs. If the training staff decides that it is advisable to make their own program, decisions must be made about its length, the techniques and methods to be used, where and when it will be conducted, who the trainers should be, the type of training the trainers will be given, who will train the trainers, and, finally, who the trainees will be. If the decision is to buy, then the trainers must take steps to ensure that the program teaches the critical KSAs identified in the task analysis. This is done by examining the content validity of the training.

## Content Validity

A training program can be judged as possessing *content validity* if (1) it trains individuals on the KSAs that have been identified previously through the task analysis as being important for performing the particular job, and (2) it does *not* train individuals on KSAs that are irrelevant for the particular job. If we should find, after designing a certain training program, that it lacks content validity, then we must revise it.

For example, the content validity of an existing police officer training program was conducted using the following procedure.[22] First, several panels of experts (i.e., training staff members, instructors, members of the most recently graduated recruit class) were asked to generate a list of KSAs that were currently taught in the training program. These panels defined the content domain of the training program as consisting of 383 KSAs. Second, the training content domain was evaluated for job relatedness by 114 experts—64 experienced patrol officers who trained recruits on the job, 31 patrol sergeants from the target city, and 20 police personnel from similar-sized communities outside the target city. These experts independently rated the importance of each KSA to job performance. They used a seven-point rating scale ranging from "no importance" to "extreme importance." A decision rule was used in which KSAs with rating above average importance or high (i.e., 5, 6, or 7) were considered important; KSAs with ratings of average importance or below (i.e., 4, 3, 2, 1) were considered to be unimportant. Third, the degree of consensus was determined by calculating a content validity ratio (CVR) for each KSA. The CVR was determined by taking the number of experts who stated that a KSA was important *(Ni)*, minus the number of experts who stated that a KSA was unimportant *(Nu)*, divided by the total number of experts (i.e., 114) involved *(Nt)*. Finally, the job relatedness of the total police officer training program was determined by calculating the average value of all the CVRs—the content validity index (CVI). The CVR and CVI values supported the conclusion that the content of this training program had a substantial degree of job relatedness. Specifically, it was found that of the 383 KSAs defining the training content domain, 62 percent had statistically significant CVR values. In addition, the CVIs for both the target city sample of officers and sergeants and the outside city sample were statistically significant, as was the CVI for the total combined sample of 114 experts.[23]

Even though these findings confirmed the content validity of the training program, Ford and Wroten proceeded to improve the program's content validity by trying to eliminate two types of misses: deficiencies and excesses. Training deficiences are KSAs that are important for job success but are not matched by a high degree of emphasis in the training program. The most extreme example of a deficiency would be a K, S, or A that is omitted from the training. On the other hand, training excesses are KSAs receiving an excessive amount of emphasis in the training relative to their importance on the job. The most extreme example of an excess would be a K, S, or A that is being covered in training but is not needed at all on the job.

The fact that a training program possesses content validity does *not* necessarily guarantee that the trainees learned the material taught, *nor* does it mean that the trainees were able to transfer what they were taught back to their jobs. Checking to see that a training program possesses content validity is important simply to ensure that it is, in fact, teaching what it should be teaching. Content validity by itself, however, is not sufficient. One must also use the various criteria (i.e., reaction, learning, behavior, and results), experimental designs, and quasi-experimental designs discussed in Chapter 5 to make certain that the trainees both learned the material and were able to apply this knowledge to their jobs.

## INDIVIDUAL ANALYSIS

Individual analysis focuses on the individual employee. It deals with the question, "Who needs training and of what kind?" For example, one company found that its salespeople spent, on the average, only three hours a day with genuine sales prospects. The rest of their time was spent on various nonsales activities such as joking with one another and making personal telephone calls. The vice president of marketing decided that the entire sales force needed a course teaching them how to make more productive use of their work time. Although the one-day workshop on time management was effective for most people, it was obvious to the trainer that not every salesperson needed this type of training.

What is involved in conducting individual analysis? Step 1 is concerned with how well a specific employee is performing his or her job. The term *performance appraisal* is used to refer to the techniques employed by training specialists to measure an employee's job proficiency. The results of the performance appraisal determine whether or not step 2 (referred to here as diagnosis) is needed. If the appraisal indicates that an employee's work performance is acceptable, there is no need for step 2. If, on the other hand, the employee's performance is found to be below standard, this is a signal that diagnosis is needed. The diagnosis involves carefully determining what specific skills and knowledge must be developed if the employee is to improve his or her job performance.

## Step 1

Since step 1 involves employee performance appraisal, let us turn to an overview of some of the methods that are available for evaluating whether an employee is performing a job adequately. These methods can be conveniently categorized into three general areas: (1) behavioral measures, (2) economic measures, and (3) proficiency tests.

### Behavioral Measures

Behavioral measures involve ratings based on observations of an employee's on-the-job behaviors by superiors, peers, subordinates, or outside evaluators. A major characteristic of behavioral measures is that they are dependent on human observation, and accuracy in reporting observations is often affected by factors irrelevant to job performance. For example, an individual's physical attractiveness, race, seniority in the organization, personality, and level of education may contaminate the performance appraisal. Simply warning or lecturing raters about judgmental errors does not reduce them to any appreciable degree.[24]

Fortunately, managers and supervisors can be taught to eliminate certain errors when observing and evaluating their employees (see Chapter 10). For example, in one program, corporate managers were trained to eliminate the following judgmental errors: halo error (the tendency to rate an employee either high, average, or low on many factors simply because the rater believes the employee is high, average, or low on one single factor); similarity effect (the tendency on the part of a rater to judge more favorably individuals perceived as similar to him- or herself); first impressions (the tendency to evaluate another person on the basis of a judgment made primarily after an initial meeting); and contrast effect (the tendency to evaluate subordinates in comparison to one another rather than against preestablished job requirements).

During the one-day workshop, trainees saw videotapes of hypothetical employees being appraised by a manager. The trainees estimated how the manager in the videotape evaluated the employee, and how they themselves would rate the individual. The program provides an opportunity for trainees to actively participate in discovering the degree to which they themselves are prone to making judgmental errors, to receive immediate feedback as to the accuracy of their own ratings, and to practice job-related tasks so as to minimize any errors being committed.[25]

The training specialist has a number of behavioral procedures available for appraising employee proficiency. Two of the better ones are known as behavioral expectation scales (BES)[26] and behavioral observation scales (BOS).[27] Figures 3.6 and 3.7 provide examples of BES and BOS rating scales. The two procedures

**Directions:** First read the name of the behavioral dimension and its definition. Then notice the examples that illustrate various points on the rating scale. These examples are included to give you clear anchor points to help you make more accurate evaluations. Don't worry about whether or not your employee has actually exhibited the behavior described in the example. By knowing your employee, you should be able to judge whether he or she "could be expected" to display the type of behavior described in the example. After reading all the examples on a dimension, decide where on the rating scale the individual belongs by making a checkmark in the appropriate box. The box you check can range anywhere from the bottom of the scale, which represents low or poor performance, to the top of the scale, which represents high or good performance. Finally, on the next page, describe actual behaviors you have observed that support your rating. This same procedure should be followed for each dimension.

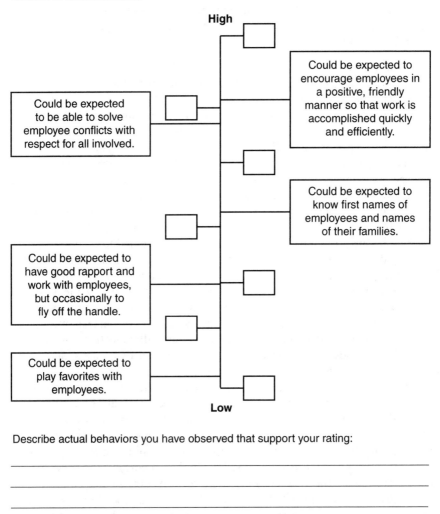

Describe actual behaviors you have observed that support your rating:

_____

_____

_____

_____

**FIGURE 3.6**   Example of a Behavioral Expectation Scale (BES)

**Directions:** This checklist contains performance-related job behaviors that foremen, their supervisors, and their subordinates have reported as critical to the foreman's job success. Please consider the above-named individual's behavior on the job for the past three months. Do not consider other foremen or this individual's behavior at other times in the past in making your ratings.

Read each statement carefully. On the basis of your actual observations or on dependable knowledge (e.g., hard evidence or reliable reports from others), circle the number that indicates the extent to which this particular foreman actually demonstrated each of the following behaviors. For each behavior, a 4 represents "Almost Always" or 95 through 100% of the time. A 3 represents "Frequently" or 85 through 94% of the time. A 2 represents "Sometimes" or 75 through 84% of the time. A 1 represents "Seldom" or 65 through 74% of the time. And a 0 represents "Almost Never" or 0 through 64% of the time.

---

### Dimension I. Interactions with Subordinates

1. Asks an employee to do a job rather than tells him or her.
   Almost Never    0   1   2   3   4    Almost Always
2. Tells workers that if they ever have questions or problems with their jobs to feel free to ask him or her.
   Almost Never    0   1   2   3   4    Almost Always
3. Gives employees suggestions on how to do the job more easily.
   Almost Never    0   1   2   3   4    Almost Always
4. After assigning a difficult job, checks back to see if the worker is having any problem.
   Almost Never    0   1   2   3   4    Almost Always
5. When there is conflict (e.g., between two employees, between foremen and worker), takes the time to sit down and discuss the causes and potential solutions.
   Almost Never    0   1   2   3   4    Almost Always

Total = _____

| Below Adequate | Adequate | Full | Excellent | Superior |
|:---:|:---:|:---:|:---:|:---:|
| 0–4 | 5–8 | 9–12 | 13–16 | 17–20 |

In the space below, record observations to support your rating.

_____

_____

_____

_____

**FIGURE 3.7**   Example of Behavioral Observation Scale (BOS)

are similar in that both are variations of the critical incident technique, both are based on observable job behaviors that are viewed by others as critical to job success, and both take into account the multifaceted nature of job performance. The BES and BOS methods differ, however, in at least one important way. Behavioral expectation scales require that each dimension be arranged on a continuous vertical rating scale with a behavioral anchor listed near each of the seven points ranging from ineffective to effective behavior. Raters simply examine the respective dimension and place a check mark beside the one behavioral anchor that they believe best describes the behavior that the employee could be expected to demonstrate. This expectation is based on what the rater has seen the employee do over a period of time. Thus, the manager is required to extrapolate from actual behaviors observed to those that could be "expected" as defined by the scale anchors. The BOS is different in this respect, in that it requires no such extrapolation. With BOS, each critical behavior is listed in a questionnaire format and the rater indicates the frequency with which he or she has observed each behavior. An employee's total score on each dimension or criterion of job performance is then determined by totaling his or her scores on the five-point BOS scales. Although the example in Figure 3.7 contains only effective behaviors, in practice ineffective ones are listed as well. As can be seen from the two formats, BOS allows a more comprehensive analysis than does the BES.

The frequently heard complaints of managers and supervisors that the items on performance appraisal instruments are either sufficiently vague to defy understanding or completely inappropriate can be minimized with BES and BOS. The behavioral statements used are expressed in the rater's own terminology. In addition, by actively participating in the construction of the scales, the raters are more inclined to complete the ratings carefully and candidly.

### Economic Measures

Here, someone in the organization simply records the number of units produced in a given amount of time, sales volume, number of injuries, scrappage weight, and so on. In general, economic measures can be broken down into two subcategories: those dealing with production (e.g., units produced, number of rejects, dollars earned) and those dealing with personnel information (e.g., attendance, tardiness, grievances, training time needed to reach an acceptable standard of performance).

These variables may serve as excellent indicators of an organization's effectiveness, but they often present problems as measures of an individual's job performance. First, they cannot be meaningfully applied to many organizational positions. They are usually appropriate for such jobs as assembly-line worker or press operator, in which an employee's performance can be evaluated by recording the number of units produced in a given time period, the number of rejectable items produced, or the scrappage weight. However, on such nonproduction jobs as manager or chemist, neither quantitative measures of output nor job-related personal information are typically available.[28] For such jobs, behavioral measures should be used.

### Proficiency Tests

An entirely different approach to measuring employee proficiency is to use proficiency tests. One variant of this approach is to take a work sample whereby, in either the actual work setting or a simulation of it, the employee is asked to perform the duties required in a job. Examples of this approach would include simulated telephone calls to operators, typing tests for administrative personnel, and flight simulators for pilots. The assessment center (discussed in Chapter 9) illustrates the use of simulation devices for evaluating the proficiency of managerial personnel. For example, 36 managers at a Wisconsin plant that manufactures wooden doors were put through an assessment center, six managers at a time, by two industrial/organizational psychologists. Each of the managers was observed for two days while participating in the assessment center exercises, and then evaluated in terms of 14 management dimensions needed for managerial success at this particular plant (e.g., delegation, decision making, innovativeness, written communications). Each manager also received a written and oral report detailing his or her strengths and areas for improvement.

Another variant of this approach involves the use of written job-knowledge tests to assess employees. For example, pipe fitters might be given a battery of tests measuring such things as knowledge of fittings, accessories, and tools.

The major advantage of using proficiency tests is that they permit the employee's skills and knowledge to be compared to known standards under controlled and uniform conditions. Their main drawback is that the employee's performance during testing may not accurately reflect daily performance on the job.

We have now reviewed different performance appraisal methods that can be used in carrying out step 1 of individual analysis. This step involves determining whether each employee in the organization is adequately performing his or her job. By using a combination of behavioral, economic, and proficiency measures, the training specialist can make an astute assessment of who is not fulfilling job requirements. If an individual is performing satisfactorily, there is no need for training. However, if an individual is not performing satisfactorily, then the next step in person analysis is warranted.

## Step 2

Step 2 in individual analysis involves determining the specific skills and knowledge that an employee needs to acquire in order to perform the job acceptably. This step requires a systematic diagnosis of each employee's strengths and weaknesses using the performance appraisal information collected during step 1.

Let us consider two examples of how diagnosis can help pinpoint the kind of training and development that an employee may need. Betty is employed as a copy editor for a medium-sized southwestern newspaper. Her job involves writing headlines, editing copy, selecting stories and other news material, laying out pages, and managing production flow. Betty's performance has been below standard ever since she was hired six months ago from another newspaper. Her performance has been evaluated using BOS by both her city editor and the paper's managing editor. Their evaluations indicate that Betty's weaknesses are primarily in the area of writing headlines. Specifically, she often writes inaccurate headlines, misses the point of a story with her headlines, occasionally misses deadlines, and uses poor grammar in headlines. As a result of this diagnosis, Betty is currently being coached by one of her department's most capable copy editors on headline writing. She is also taking a grammar course several nights per week at a community college.

The second example involves Bill who went through a one-day assessment center conducted for developmental purposes at the door plant mentioned previously. Bill went through the center with five other people and was rated on 15 KSAs by a panel of three assessors. Besides getting feedback on his strengths and areas for improvement, Bill was told such things as, he should: (1) attend a training course on using different types of motivational techniques with his employees, as well as when and how to use them; (2) attend a training seminar on time management to improve his organizing and planning skills; (3) attend a training workshop to enable him to give constructive individual feedback to his people and to deal with difficult employees; and (4) seek out his manager's help in increasing his knowledge about the company's quality assurance system in conformance with ISO 9000 standards. A written copy of Bill's feedback report was sent to his manager and the plant's training manager so they could each help Bill to follow through on his developmental plan.

An alternative way of performing step 2 is to simply ask employees to assess their own individual training needs. Many organizations use self-reports as an important source of training needs information. For example, one organization asks all its supervisors and managers to complete a need-for-training questionnaire. Each respondent is asked to review a list of 100 skills (e.g., "confronting unsafe behaviors," "resolving conflicts among employees") that are normally used by supervisors and managers in their daily jobs. Respondents are asked the extent to which they feel that they personally need training in each of the skill areas.

The use of self-ratings with respect to individual analysis has its strengths and limitations. On the one hand, this approach prevents the problem of forcing employees to attend training programs that they believe do not address their needs. In these cases, individuals become dissatisfied with the training and do not have the motivation to learn or to transfer skills back to their jobs. On the other hand, what employees report they "need" in the way of training may be more an expression of preference or demand and not an observable discrepancy in performance produced by a lack of skill. Further, what they feel they need is also influenced by their attitudes toward training utility. Specifically, it has been shown that managers who have negative attitudes toward training will report less need for training than managers with favorable attitudes.[29] Finally, more research is clearly needed on the interobserver reliability and construct validity of self-ratings with regard to person analysis. For instance, several studies have found that employee and supervisor needs assessments do not correlate highly with one another.[30]

Procter & Gamble (P&G) illustrates yet another way of determining the specific competencies that a particular employee needs to acquire or increase to perform his or her job effectively. P&G, like many other organizations today, encourages their employees to take more responsibility for their own careers and their own development rather than having the organization take a traditional paternalistic approach. Therefore, the company expects employees to meet yearly with their manager to discuss the employee's business results and future plans for the upcoming year. Based on how the employee performed historically and his or her upcoming projects and responsibilities, the two of them discuss the relative importance of what the company calls its seven "Success Actions for Winning" (SAWs) (i.e., Leadership, Capacity, Risk-Taking, Innovation, Solutions, Collaboration, Mastery). These SAWs and the behaviors that comprise them are considered to be the "what counts factors" that make for success at P&G throughout the organization. Typically, the manager and employee use an assessment tool that is based on these seven SAWs. The way the assessment tools works is that an individual scores him- or herself, the manager scores the employee, and additional feedback is obtained from others with whom the employee has worked. This assessment instrument is intended to be simply a discussion tool and, therefore, does not impact salary or promotion decisions. So, for example, an employee could find out from his or her manager that he or she is going to be in charge of three large projects next year. This individual headed up two projects last year and did well in all the SAWs, except for innovation. Although the employee got the projects completed, others felt that he or she did not exhibit enough out-of-the-box thinking. So, in this case, the employee and the manager would focus on discussing those particular behaviors that were rated within the Innovation SAW. This, in turn, would help shed light on the employee's specific strengths and deficiencies in this SAW area. Based on the SAW ratings from all three sources (i.e., self, manager, others) as well as the employee's previous job performance, the employee and the manager would work together to generate a training plan for the individual.

There are numerous small companies, ranging from 15 employees to a few hundred employees, that cannot possibly afford to conduct individual analyses in the same manner as does a Procter & Gamble. These companies typically consist of one human resource generalist who performs a wide range of human resource functions such as recruiting, interviewing, compensation and benefit administration, and training. In these small companies, the training person would determine an employee's training needs by using one or more of the following sources of information:

- Examine employee performance problems such as low productivity, customer grievances, equipment downtime, excessive absenteeism or tardiness, waste, and equipment utilization.
- Conduct discussions with the employee as well as the employee's supervisor, manager, peers, and customers to ascertain what they believe the individual needs to learn.
- Observe the employee's behaviors (e.g., during customer sales calls) and, when appropriate, evaluate the bottom-line results or outcomes of these behaviors (e.g., sales in dollars). For instance, in a small printing and imagining company, the training person determined that one of the employees needed to attend a training session on how to become a better team player after observing that this individual put personal goals far ahead of team goals, failed to utilize the resources of other team members, and tended to form strong opinions before listening to others' viewpoints.

# THE FINAL PRODUCT: A TRAINING PLAN

The end result of this systematic process of identifying an organization's training needs is a training plan. This plan is constructed by the training department and is used to strategically plan what kinds of training will be conducted in the near future.

For each training program to be implemented in the future (e.g., five years), certain key information should be included in the training plan. Consider this information for the tire store manager program as an example.

| | |
|---|---|
| Course Title: | Tire Store Manager Training I |
| Classification: | Management Development |
| Needs Analyses: | Organization (employment planning, store diagnoses) |
| | Task ( job inventory) |
| | Individual (self-report) |
| Course Objectives: | Effectively handle customer complaints |
| | Handle radio advertisements, newspaper ads, and direct mailings |
| Length: | 15 days (3 days/week for 5 weeks) |
| Trainees: | 75 new hires per year |
| | 15 trainees per class |
| Trainers: | ABC, Inc. + three in-house trainers |
| Place: | Corporate Training Center (Annapolis, Maryland) |
| When: | Classes will start the first week of February, April, June, August, October |
| Training Methods: | Lecture, Behavioral Modeling, Computer-Assisted Instruction, On-the-Job Training |
| Measures of Achievement During Training: | Weekly paper-and-pencil achievement tests |
| | Weekly proficiency testing |
| Evaluation Reaction: | End of training and 6 months later |
| Learning: | End of training + 6 and 12 months later |
| Behavior: | 6 and 12 months later |
| Store Results: | 6 and 12 months later |
| Utility Analysis: | 18 months later |
| Transfer: | Immediate supervisor |
| Job Follow-up: | Relapse prevention |
| | Weekly meetings with trainer |
| Estimated Cost to Develop: | $130,500 |
| Estimated Cost to Implement: | $187,500 per year |

# FINAL COMMENTS

We have presented several approaches that organizations can use for determining training and development needs systematically. Obviously, not all organizations will be able to afford the time and money to do every phase of organization, task, and individual analyses as presented here. Yet we offer these approaches as an ideal to strive for. Even a reduced application of these approaches is better than what many organizations are doing today to determine training and development needs.

Let us look for a moment at a few current organizational practices. Some organizations break down each of their jobs into a list of detailed parts or steps arranged in a logical sequence. A copy of this list is given to employees whose opinions are valued. The employees check off items for which they would like to have more skill. Lists of all kinds are assembled. The one for salespeople might include prospecting for new business, conducting a fact-finding interview, sales closing, and sales follow-through. The list for retail store managers might include credit management, inventory control, building maintenance and security, sales management, customer relations, expense control, and community relations. One for industrial truck mechanics might include assembling distributors, changing generator brushes, replacing contacts and coils, reading blueprints, and so on.

Other organizations have a committee established for each special area of training such as orientation, sales, clerical, technical, supervisory, and executive. Each committee advises the training staff as to what particular training and development programs they think are needed. Sometimes the advisory committees also get involved in constructing the content of the courses and even evaluating course results.

Still other organizations purchase canned training and development programs from vendors who call on them periodically. The salesperson may be promoting programs on effective reading, improved human relations skills, or increased assertiveness. A vice president of manufacturing, marketing, or personnel may decide that this type of program is needed and purchase it on the spot or after giving it a short trial run.

Although these methods of determining training needs have their merit, it should be obvious that they are not as rigorous as the approaches presented in this chapter. Their biggest drawback, in our opinion, is that they are based solely on the assumption that someone can simply look at a list of training needs and accurately indicate what they themselves need or someone else needs in the way of personal development. Further, these methods tell us nothing about where within the organization a particular type of training is needed or who needs it. The end result is the indiscriminate use of a training and development program across company locations and people. It is no wonder that employees are often heard making statements such as, "I have no idea why I've been told to go to that training course," "I know just about everything they taught me in this program," and "Why doesn't the company just leave me alone and let me get on with my work!"

# ENDNOTES

1. L. Saari, T. R. Johnson, S. D. McLaughlin, and D. M. Fimmerle, "A Survey of Management Training and Education Practices in U.S. Companies," *Personnel Psychology 41* (1988): 731–44.
2. W. McGehee and P. W. Thayer, *Training in Business and Industry* (New York: Wiley, 1961).
3. S. W. J. Kozlowski and E. Salas, "A Multilevel Organizational Systems Approach for the Implementation and Transfer of Training," in J. K. Ford and Associates (eds.), *Improving Training Effectiveness in Work Organizations* (Hillsdale, NJ: LEA, 1996).
4. T. Burns and G. M. Stalker, *The Management of Innovation* (London: Tavistock, 1961).
5. J. A. Miller and D. M. Oseñski, "Training Needs Assessment." SHRM White Paper.
6. C. Carr, "Total Quality Training," *Training,* November 1990, 59–65.
7. G. A. Regalbuto, "Targeting the Bottom Line," *Training & Development,* April 1992, 29–38.
8. G. F. Brown and A. K. Read, "Personnel and Training Policies—Some Lessons for Western Companies," *Long Range Planning 17* (1984): 48–57.
9. D. E. Hussey, "Implementing Corporate Strategy: Using Management Education and Training," *Long Range Planning 18* (1985): 28–37.
10. Miller and Oseñski, "Training Needs Assessment."
11. R. B. Miller, "Task Description and Analysis," in R. M. Gagné (ed.), *Psychological Principles in System Development* (New York: Holt, 1962).
12. M. R. Blood, *Job Analysis of Entry-Level Clerical Jobs in the South Central Bell Company* (American Telephone and Telegraph Company, 1975).
13. K. N. Wexley, *A Job Analysis Study of the Position of Residential Service Representative* (American Telephone and Telegraph Company, 1975).
14. E. C. Dean and R. A. Jud, "How to Write a Task Analysis," *Training Directors' Journal 19* (1965): 9–22.
15. J. C. Flanagan, "The Critical Incident Technique," *Psychological Bulletin 51* (1954): 327–58.
16. G. P. Latham and K. N. Wexley, *Increasing Productivity Through Performance Appraisal* (Reading, MA: Addison-Wesley, 1994).
17. Ibid.
18. Ibid.
19. K. N. Wexley and S. B. Silverman, "An Examination of Differences Between Managerial Effectiveness and Response Patterns on a Structured Job Analysis Questionnaire," *Journal of Applied Psychology 63,* no. 5 (1978): 646–49.
20. K. M. Nowack, "A True Training Needs Analysis," *Training & Development Journal,* April 1991, 69–73.
21. R. F. Mager and K. M. Beach Jr., *Developing Vocational Instruction* (Belmont, CA: Fearon, 1967).
22. J. K. Ford and S. P. Wroten, "Introducing New Methods for Conducting Training Evaluation and for Linking Training Evaluation to Program Design," *Personnel Psychology 37* (1984): 651–65.
23. Ibid.
24. K. N. Wexley, R. E. Sanders, and G. A. Yukl, "Training Interviewers to Eliminate Contrast Effects in Employment Interviews," *Journal of Applied Psychology 57* (1973): 233–36.
25. G. P. Latham, K. N. Wexley, and E. D. Pursell, "Training Managers to Minimize Rating Errors in the Observation of Behavior," *Journal of Applied Psychology 60* (1975): 550–55.
26. P. C. Smith and L. M. Kendall, "Retranslation of Expectations: An Approach to the Construction of Unambiguous Anchors for Rating Scales," *Journal of Applied Psychology 47* (1963): 149–55.
27. G. P. Latham and K. N. Wexley, "Behavioral Observation Scales for Performance Appraisal Purposes," *Personnel Psychology 30* (1977): 255–68; and G. P. Latham and K. N. Wexley, *Increasing Productivity Through Performance Appraisal* (Reading, MA: Addison-Wesley, 1994).
28. G. P. Latham and K. N. Wexley, *Increasing Productivity Through Performance Appraisal* (Reading, MA: Addison-Wesley, 1994).

29. J. K. Ford and R. A. Noe, "Self-Assessed Training Needs: The Effects of Attitudes Toward Training, Managerial Level, and Function," *Personnel Psychology 40* (1987): 39–53.

30. J. McEnery and J. M. McEnery, "Self-Rating in Management Training Needs Assessment: A Neglected Opportunity," *Journal of Occupational Psychology 60* (1987): 49–60; and C. C. Staley and P. Shockley-Zalabak, "Communication Proficiency and Future Training Needs of the Female Professional: Self-Assessment Versus Supervisors' Evaluations," *Human Relations 39* (1986): 891–902.

# C H A P T E R

# *Maximizing the Trainee's Learning*

This chapter focuses on what the trainer needs to do to maximize learning on the part of trainees. Here, three main questions are of interest:

1. Is the individual trainable?
2. How should the training program be arranged to facilitate learning?
3. What can be done to ensure that what was learned during training will be retained and transferred to the job?

Since there are no well-developed and tested theories of learning to answer these questions, trainers must rely on two main sources for guidance. First, there are principles of learning that have been derived over the years by psychologists in their study of human and animal behavior. These principles are useful in maximizing learning if they are regarded as guiding principles and not as immutable laws. Second, there are theories of motivation that are very helpful in inculcating in the trainee the desire to learn and apply the skills and concepts being taught during training.

This chapter is divided into three main sections: (1) trainability, (2) arrangement of the training environment, and (3) retention and transfer of learning. Let's first examine the issue of trainability.

## TRAINABILITY

The largest component of training costs is the labor cost of the trainee. When large numbers of trainees are involved, course development and administrative costs become only a fraction of trainee labor costs.[1] This clearly suggests that substantial cost savings in training are possible through a reduction in training time. Such a reduction is best accomplished by selecting and retaining in training only those individuals who are clearly trainable.

Trainability is a function of the individual's ability and motivation. Ability refers to the extent to which the individual possesses the aptitude or skills to perform the tasks at hand. For example, does the individual possess the muscular coordination to perform the motor tasks required of him? Does she have the visual acuity needed for learning watchmaking, radar monitoring, or surgery? Does he possess personality characteristics such as self-confidence, persuasiveness, sociability, decisiveness, and assertiveness needed to perform the job effectively? Does she have the mental ability to learn complex concepts and rules for computer programming, financial planning, or electronics? The many abilities that have been found to be associated with trainees' capacity to learn include:

- Reading level, educational level, educational preparation, aptitude[2]
- General intelligence[3]
- Cognitive ability[4]
- Ability to visualize how a piece of paper could be folded to form a three-dimensional object, ability to infer a rule from patterns of letters, knowledge about mechanical facts and principles, ability to perceive changes in direction and position[5]
- Conscientious, dependable, conforming, well socialized[6]
- Analytical learning strategy and learning anxiety[7]

Motivation is concerned with those variables which influence the trainee's effort, persistence, and choices. Such variables as the individual's need for achievement or competence are included here. Included here, too, are an individual's feeling of job involvement as well as their level of career interest. Trainees' involvement in their jobs and careers are important antecedents of learning during training and behavior change after training. Research shows that if trainees personally agree with the assessment of their skill weaknesses on which their training assignments were based, they are then more likely to be satisfied with the training program's content as compared to trainees who disagree with the assessment of their weaknesses.[8] Also important is the individual's expectancy that participation in training will lead to desired outcomes such as feelings of accomplishment, greater responsibility, opportunity for advancement, higher pay, job security, status, stimulating colleagues, or a good geographic location. Another crucial motivational variable worth noting here is anxiety. Anxiety has been shown to facilitate performance in relatively simple types of learning (e.g., assembly-line operations), but to interfere with learning complex tasks. It is reasonable to expect that anxiety will interfere with most classroom-type learning, which generally consists of teaching concepts of a fairly complex nature. One possible way of reducing anxiety and thereby increasing motivation to learn the material is to give trainees a choice of whether to attend training. In making this choice, they should be provided detailed and accurate information about the program. In one study, it was found that managers who were given complete freedom to participate in a two-day workshop on performance appraisal–related issues had higher self-assessed mastery of the workshop content and achievement test performance than managers who were given little freedom of choice.

The same positive effects were found when managers were given detailed and accurate information about the workshop as opposed to a traditional (brief, overly positive) announcement.[9] Trainees' anxiety can also be lowered by changing their conception of their own ability. In a field experiment involving microcomputer training, Martocchio[10] demonstrated that anxiety could be decreased by inducing in trainees the conception of ability as an acquirable skill rather than as a fixed entity. Apparently, when trainees construe ability as a fixed entity, they focus primarily on evaluative concerns about their personal competence. Any mistakes they make are threatening to them, causing them to dwell on their personal deficiencies rather than on learning. In contrast, when trainees view ability as an acquirable skill, they believe that their trainability can be continually increased by gaining knowledge and increasing their competencies through practice. Martocchio[11] also showed that computer anxiety can be reduced and learning increased by labeling the context as an opportunity as opposed to using neutral labeling. For instance, "opportunity labeling" involves introductory statements such as:

> You can expect to *gain* quite a lot in the workplace by using a microcomputer. Many experienced microcomputer users . . . have said many encouraging things about microcomputers such as using microcomputers provides greater job opportunities and using microcomputers enhances their reputation in the eyes of their supervisors.
>
> Many new microcomputer users have also said that using a microcomputer has been a very positive experience for them. For example, many have said that time flies by when using a microcomputer, working on a microcomputer is like playing a game.[12]

"Neutral labeling" is what, unfortunately, is typically used without any "opportunity labeling" with trainees. The following is an example of neutral labeling:

> There are four specific objectives of this class:
>
> To teach you the basics of microcomputer hardware. We'll do this through discussion and "show and tell."
>
> To teach you the basics of software and how to perform some common functions on the microcomputer. We'll do this through lecture and hands-on experience.
>
> To teach you the basics of word processing. We'll do this primarily through hands-on experience.
>
> To teach you the basics of spreadsheets. We'll also do this primarily through hands-on experience.[13]

The relationship between ability and motivation is expressed by the following formula:

$$\text{Performance} = \text{Ability} \times \text{Motivation}$$

According to this formula, a trainee's performance will have a value of zero if either ability or motivation is absent, and it increases as each factor rises in value. The objective, then, is to train individuals who possess both the ability and motivation to perform what is taught in training.

Ability and motivation can be assessed by various measurement instruments in order to predict performance of prospective trainees. For example, the Navy School for Divers has used a motivational instrument to predict success in their 10-week training program in SCUBA and Deep Sea Air (DSA) procedures.[14] Briefly, SCUBA training consists of instruction in diving medicine and physics, as well as the use of the neoprene wet suit and SCUBA breathing equipment. It concludes with ocean dives to a depth of 60 feet. DSA training involves learning to dive in a canvas suit and metal helmet. The training includes underwater communication and the use of underwater tools. DSA concludes with ocean dives to a depth of 180 feet. Research has shown that a trainee confidence measure is significantly related to eventual graduation from the program. Each of the following questions are answered on a six-point scale ranging from disagree strongly (score of 1) to agree strongly (score of 6):

- I have a better chance of passing this training than most others.
- I volunteered for this training program as soon as I could.
- The knowledge and experience that I gain in this training may advance my career.
- Even if I fail, this training will be a valuable experience.
- I will get more from this training than most people.
- If I have trouble during training, I will try harder.
- I am more physically fit for the training than most people.

Another example of the value of predicting trainability involved a welding program that was used to train unemployed and underemployed individuals from East Tennessee for entry-level work in various vocational fields.[15] The plate welding section of the training program consisted of 14 separate welding tasks ordered in terms of increasing complexity. The last three welding positions were used as test positions to decide whether a trainee should receive certification. It was found that the time required by a trainee to complete the first four welding tasks was an excellent predictor of the time the trainee required to complete the entire training course. Although this research was conducted years ago, it nonetheless clearly demonstrates that a sampling of a trainee's ability level can be used as a valid predictor of subsequent success in training. This research also supports the widely accepted truism in psychology that an excellent predictor of future behavior is past behavior.

Another approach for assessing trainability is known as the "miniature job training and evaluation approach."[16] For example, suppose we wanted to use this approach for selecting applicants for a machinist training program for the navy. First, we would isolate a sample of tasks typically performed by naval machinists using task analytic procedures (Chapter 3). Second, we would build short training sessions (15 to 30 minutes) around each of these identified tasks. Once the training was completed, the evaluation phase would begin. The evaluation, of course, would involve administering performance tests which would measure the amount learned by each applicant during training. For example, a machinist task might be "ability to start up and shut down a motor and pump apparatus." The miniature training session might teach applicants how to follow a 33-step procedure, including safety precautions. After training, each applicant would be rated by knowledgeable judges on how well he or she started and shut down the apparatus. This approach has been used for selecting telephone company switching technicians.[17] Applicants were given a minicourse that was designed to be a self-paced content valid sample of a lengthy and complex Electronic Switching Systems (ESS) training program. They found that a combination of time to complete the minicourse and performance on several objective tests was predictive of the time it took trainees to complete the self-paced ESS training. In another study, the added value of using training performance in predicting trainees' success in an air intercept and controller's task was demonstrated.[18] Specifically, how trainees did during a short training program added significantly to how well ability tests, by themselves, could predict success. In fact, this research demonstrated the value of using a two-stage sequential selection procedure—Stage 1, ability testing; Stage 2, training performance.

Excellent research on trainability testing has also been conducted in the United Kingdom.[19] Trainability tests have been used to improve the selection process of untrained applicants for training programs. Most of these trainability tests have taken the following form:

1. Using a standardized form of instruction and demonstration, the instructor teaches the applicant a task.
2. The applicant is asked to perform the task unaided.
3. The instructor records the applicant's performance by noting errors on a standardized error checklist (prepared and different for each trade) and by making a rating of the applicant's likely performance in training, usually on a 5-point scale.

For example, trainability tests have been developed for welding and carpentry. The carpentry test involved making a half-lap T joint; the welding test involved making several straight runs along chalk lines on mild steel. Both tests took 30 to 45 minutes to administer and score. Robertson and Downs[20] completed a meta-analysis of trainability tests in which they concluded that these tests produce a worthwhile level of validity. More specifically, they found that these tests are quite useful for predicting an untrained applicant's subsequent success in training and job performance. They also concluded that in order to attain a high level of trainability test validity, it is essential that the instructional procedures used during the tests simulate those involved subsequently during actual training and later learning on the job itself. For instance, to predict success in a sewing machine operator training program, we might decide to teach and test the following tasks to be encountered by operators: joining pieces of cloth, joining two pieces to make an open bag, and operating a lockstitch machine. The researchers also found that the greater the length of the training program, the smaller the size of the validity coefficient. In fact, attempts to predict success in training over a one-year period resulted in considerably smaller validities. Apparently, more complex jobs and longer training periods may expose trainees to a wider variety of instructional processes and call for a greater range of learning abilities from trainees, some of which may not have been captured in the initial learning period during the trainability test.

Trainability is frequently best measured by using a combination of ability and personality assessment measures. For instance, trainee success in a two-month naval basic electricity and electronics training course was predicted *best* when scores on the Armed Services Vocational Aptitude Battery (ASVAB) were supplemented with various personality scores. Although the ability tests were reliably associated with learning ability and academic performance, the personality assessment measures predicted the motivational factors that also affected training success.[21]

## ARRANGEMENT OF THE TRAINING ENVIRONMENT

In the previous section we discussed the importance of measuring ability and motivation levels that exist in the individual before training occurs. These are the *internal* conditions necessary for learning to occur by an individual.

A second major category of learning conditions is *external* to the learner. These are the environmental arrangements that the trainer can control so as to facilitate learning. Before examining these external conditions and how they can be arranged to enhance learning, it is important to agree on a definition of what is meant by learning.

*Learning* is defined as a relatively permanent change in behavior that occurs as a result of practice. *Behavior* includes the knowledge and skills acquired by people. When we say that an individual has learned something, we are not referring to temporary changes in behavior. Instead, we are referring to enduring behavioral changes.

In order to arrange the training program to facilitate learning, the following variables need to be taken into account:

1. Conditions of practice
   a. Active practice
   b. Overlearning
   c. Massed versus distributed practice sessions
   d. Size of the unit to be learned
   e. Sequencing the training sessions

2. Feedback
3. Meaningfulness of the material
4. Individual differences
5. Behavior modeling
6. Maintaining motivation

## Conditions of Practice

### Active Practice

Whether a trainee is learning a new skill or acquiring knowledge of a given subject, the individual should be given the opportunity to practice what is being taught. During the early stages of learning skills, the trainer should be available to guide the trainee's practice. This minimizes the risk of the individual developing inappropriate behaviors. The trainer might tell the novice cab driver to "return your cab to the home base location on 'weekends only'" or "turn your wheels in the direction in which you are skidding." It is not enough during skills learning for the trainees to merely verbalize what they are expected to do, nor to listen to the trainer or to other trainees repeat the directions again and again. Rather, the trainee must actively practice the skill. Only by actually repeating the essential movements can the trainee be provided with the internal or proprioceptive cues that regulate motor performance. As practice continues, internal cues leading to errors are progressively discarded, and internal cues associated with smooth and precise performance are retained.

Traditional approaches to training have aimed at trying to reduce or eliminate trainees' mistakes for the purpose of shortening the learning period and avoiding the negative motivational effects of making errors.[22] However, recent studies indicate that training programs which encourage trainees to make errors and allow them freedom to explore and try out alternate solutions to problems is superior to training that guards against making mistakes.[23] Today, it is acknowledged that practice works best with small doses of errors because these errors have both an informational and motivational role in learning.[24]

Active practice also works best when: (1) trainees are given advice before beginning practice about the process or strategy that should be used to achieve optimal performance,[25] (2) trainess have mastery goals that focus their attention on the process itself as opposed to outcome goals that focus their attention on only end results,[26] (3) expectations are clarified and roles are established among team members before team practice sessions,[27] and (4) trainees practice skills on either the job itself or in an environment that simulates the functional and cognitive aspects of the actual one.[28]

### Overlearning

Closely related to the principle of active practice is that of overlearning: providing trainees with continued practice far beyond the point when the task has been performed correctly several times. It is relevant to those activities that must be practiced under simulated conditions (e.g., missile firing) because the real situation is either too expensive or too dangerous. It is even more crucial in tasks that are designed so that individuals cannot rely on lifelong habit patterns, as, for example, in certain emergency procedures. It pertains less to those types of work (e.g., press operators, pipe fitting, carpentry) in which individuals practice their skills on a daily basis.

An actual example of overlearning can be found in the U.S. Air Force training school:

> Boldface Emergency Procedures are procedures that must be accomplished immediately and in the proper sequence after an indication of a specific system malfunction. Failure to initiate these procedures promptly or in sequence could result in loss of aircraft and/or pilot injury or death. Therefore, all procedures that are printed in bold type in the aircraft flight manual must be committed to memory. The pilot must also be familiar with all other emergency procedures discussed in the emergency procedures section of the flight manual. During Undergraduate Pilot Training (UPT), student pilots must write or orally recite the Boldface Emergency Procedures for the aircraft he or she is flying. Unsatisfactory performance on the daily quiz usually results in counseling, remedial instruction, and grounding from flying that day. Pilots in operational squadrons must indicate their knowledge of Boldface Emergency Procedures weekly and before training flights. (Personal communication with Captain Frank Tetreault, United States Air Force)

Overlearning is important for several reasons. First, it increases the length of time that training material will be retained. By continually pairing a response with a particular stimulus, the bonds between the two will be strengthened, thereby making the response less likely to be forgotten. Second, it makes the learning more reflexive, that is, the trainee will have to concentrate less strongly on the task as it becomes "automatic" with practice. Third, trainees will be more likely to maintain the quality of their performance on their jobs during periods of emergency and added stress. For example, those professional athletes who have thoroughly mastered their sport are more likely to perform effectively despite such factors as unfavorable weather conditions and large crowds of spectators. Finally, overlearning helps trainees transfer what they have learned during training to their job settings.

The claims made for overlearning in the training community was finally confirmed a few years ago by a statisitical process known as meta-analysis. The effects of overlearning were examined across 15 studies involving 3,771 subjects.[29] The analytical results confirmed the benficial effects of overlearning on retention for both physical and cognitive tasks, although the effects were found to be somewhat stronger with cognitive tasks. The results also showed that 50 percent additional practice beyond initial mastery should be considered as a minimum practical operationalization of overlearning, and that small improvements in performance can be expected from this amount of overlearning. The findings also revealed that 100 percent additional practice results in moderate effects on retention, while 150 percent more practice can be expected to yield large effects.

### Massed Versus Distributed Practice Sessions

Another consideration in designing a training program is the problem of whether to divide the practice period into segments or plan one continuous session. For example, if you decided to give trainees eight hours of practice, which of the following schedules would be best to follow?

One eight-hour nonstop session
Four hours a day for two days
Two hours a day for four days

The answer depends on the nature of the task being trained. For years, psychologists have known that distributed practice sessions interspersed with reasonable periods of rest permit more efficient learning of skills than continuous practice. Therefore, in the case of training someone to operate a sewing machine or a printing press, it would be advisable to schedule practice sessions for two hours a day for four days.

Unfortunately, this principle of spreading the effort of the trainee over a period of time is often ignored in organizations. Management is frequently anxious to get the individual trained to standard as quickly as possible. The result is often inadequately trained employees.

Some organizations have used ingenious ways to obtain the advantages of distributed practice and, at the same time, make efficient use of the trainee's time. For example, a supermarket chain trains its checkout clerks on using computerized cash registers by having each of them work two hours on the new equipment and the remainder of the day on their former equipment. A large furniture retail chain trains its salespeople by alternating their time on the floor with performing other beneficial activities such as reading decorator catalogs, studying fabrics, telephoning customers, and rearranging store merchandise.

Why, we might ask, is distributed practice better for learning motor skills than massed practice? The answer seems to be that the rest periods between practice sessions allow for dissipation of the fatigue that builds up when we continually perform the same set of responses over and over.

The effectiveness of massed versus distributed practice becomes less clear-cut when it comes to learning factual information. Should the learning be massed, as in cramming for an exam, or distributed over time? The less meaningful the material to be learned and the greater its length or difficulty, the better distributed practice becomes relative to massed practice. Moreover, the less trainability the trainee possesses, the more that person will benefit from distributed practice.

The benefits to be realized from using distributed practice will become more apparent in the years ahead as more organizations move from using "closed" to "open" learning settings.[30] In open learning settings, individuals work on their own to learn material that is presented to them through an interactive video system, by a computer, via audio or videotapes, or in writing. Open learners have more freedom to decide what is studied, as well as when, where, and at what pace they will progress.[31] The learning may take place either at work or at home. Since open learning is often interpresed among other activities, it can be expected to be more distributed over time. According to Warr and Bunce, this type of learning is likely to be become more common in the future as organizations seek to train employees flexibly, to capitalize on technological advances, and to encourage employees to take more reponsibility for their own development.

### Size of the Unit to Be Learned

When designing any training program, the following questions naturally arise: What is the optimum size of the unit to be learned? Should you attempt to teach the entire task at each practice session, or is it more efficient in the long run to teach individual subtasks initially and as the trainee starts mastering each subtask begin the process of combining them?

Many different approaches can be used in scheduling a training program, but all seem to be derivations of three basic strategies. Suppose you have a task that can be divided into three distinct parts or subtasks: A, B, and C. The three basic strategies would proceed as shown in the diagram.

| | Phase I | Phase II | Phase III | Phase IV |
|---|---|---|---|---|
| Whole Training | A + B + C | A + B + C | A + B + C | A + B + C |
| Pure-Part Training | A | B | C | A + B + C |
| Progressive-Part Training | A | A + B | A + B + C | A + B + C |

As you can see, whole training consists of practicing all subtasks during all phases of training. In pure-part training, successive subtasks are practiced separately in successive phases of training. Progressive-part training involves practicing the first subtask in the first phase of training: the first and second subtasks in the second phase; the first, second, and third subtasks in the third phase, and so on.

Which strategy is superior? There are some writers who mean well, but incorrectly advocate one best way of training. For example, Strauch[32] advocates using a so-called holistic approach to employee training which always makes the object of attention the whole activity and never an isolated piece. More accurately, which strategy to use depends on two components of the task itself: *task complexity* and *task organization*. Task complexity refers to the difficulty of each of the subtasks comprising the total task. Task organization refers to the degree of interrelationship among the set of subtasks. For highly organized tasks, the whole method seems to be more efficient than the part methods. Both part methods, however, are superior to the whole method when task organization is low. These two statements are especially true as task complexity increases.[33]

For example, when learning to operate a bulldozer (a task of high organization), a person must learn skills like starting the engine, steering, braking, backing up, and shifting. It makes little sense to learn each of these subtasks individually because all of them are so highly interrelated. In contrast, secretarial work often consists of a number of subtasks that are largely independent of one another (i.e., low task organization). Secretaries typically type letters, answer telephone calls, take dictation, photocopy reports, greet visitors, and so on. Each of these subtasks can be learned and practiced separately. Indeed, it would be impractical to teach all of these subtasks at every training session.

The examples just described offer situations which are relatively clear-cut. In many situations, however, a combination of whole and part training is used to optimize the benefits of both approaches. For example, suppose you wanted to train someone to be a pipe fitter. Certain training sessions would be devoted to specific topics such as valves, gaskets, traps, and strainers. Other sessions would concern themselves with larger chunks of the job such as cutting, bending, and threading pipe. Suppose for a moment that a politician is memorizing a speech to be given at a fund-raising dinner. Where the different parts of the material are logically related, the whole method should be employed. Where the material is very complex and long, it should be broken down into parts and learned progressively, one section at a time.

### Sequencing the Training Sessions

The sequencing of the training sessions is another important consideration when one is trying to maximize trainee learning. According to Anderson's theory of skill acquisition, learning occurs in a series of three stages: (1) declarative learning, (2) knowledge compilation, and (3) proceduralized knowledge. Declarative learning involves obtaining factual knowledge about a task. The trainee needs to be involved in memorizing, comprehending, and remembering essential facts, rules, policies, and procedures. For instance, if we were training operators in a pharmceutical packaging plant to operate a new packaging machine, the trainees would first be taught through lectures, technical manuals, and/or online instruction such things as the safety and packaging procedures that need to be followed. During the next stage, knowledge compilation, the training sessions would be aimed at teaching the trainees to turn their declarative knowledge into a cognitive understanding of how they are to perform these safety and packaging procedures using the new equipment. During the final stage of training, training sessions would focus on instilling proceduralized knowledge, which involves learning to carry through the actual hands-on application. During the final training sessions, the pharmaceutical operators would actually operate the new packaging equipment in the plant or else learn to do it using equipment simulators (see Chapter 7). It is not only important to sequence these training sessions properly but also, according to instructional theory, incorporate enough practice (i.e., overlearning) at each stage to ensure that the trainees' responses are *automated* and thus require very little of their attentional capacity.

When sequencing the training sessions, it is also important to keep in mind that the particular abilities (e.g., trunk strength, coordination, speed of limb movement, verbal reasoning, inductive reasoning) needed to learn to perform a particular task change at different stages of learning. In a series of studies, Fleishman and associates showed that a trainee's ability differs at subsequent stages of learning. Specifically, they have found that general cognitive abilities (e.g., problem sensitivity, deductive reasoning, inductive reasoning, information ordering) on motor-type tasks decline in importance with practice, and that motor skill abilities (e.g., strength, coordination, finger dexterity) increase in importance.[34] In other words, during Anderson's declarative learning and knowledge compilation stages, trainers will need to encourage trainees to use their cognitive abilities. During the proceduralized knowledge stage, these same individuals will need to rely more on their motor skill abilities.

## Feedback: Knowledge of Results

### Practice Without Evaluative Feedback Retards Learning

Feedback or knowledge of results is critical for both learning and motivation.[35] Trainees should be informed when and how they have done something correctly. Feedback, whether in the form of verbal praise, test scores, productivity reports, or performance measurement, serves three functions in promoting learning and motivation[36]:

1. It tells trainees whether their responses were correct, thereby allowing them to make the necessary adjustments in their subsequent behavior.
2. It makes the learning process more interesting for the trainees, thereby maximizing their willingness to learn.
3. It leads to the setting of specific goals for maintaining or improving performance.

Imagine for a moment how difficult and frustrating it would be for people to learn a job such as assembling television sets or building radial tires if they received little or no feedback. Without the trainer's specific comments about what they are doing right and wrong, supplemented with reasons and explanations, it would not be long before trainees would discontinue learning.

To be effective, feedback should be provided as soon as possible after the trainee's behavior. It is not necessary that feedback be instantaneous, only that the relationship between behavior and feedback be clearly evident to the learner. For example, it has been shown that college students learn better when their instructors give them verbal feedback on the correctness of their test answers. The beneficial effect of this verbal feedback occurred even when a delay of 30 minutes ensued between the students' test taking and the feedback session.[37]

The specificity or amount of feedback provided must be appropriate to the particular capabilities and stage of development of the learner. Too much feedback at one time, or too early in the learning process, can be confusing and lead to a decline in trainee performance. Likewise, too little information at critical stages can lead to similar consequences. It appears that, for each trainee and each stage of learning, there is an optimum level of feedback which should be given.

It is important that trainers be cognizant of this inverted-U relationship when designing training programs (see Figure 4.1).

Praise can be a powerful source of positive feedback. For example, a trainer may look at certain indices of trainee performance (e.g., sales records, attendance, production figures) and compliment the positive aspects of the individual's performance as it relates to established goals or to the trainee's previous level of performance. Making praise the consequence of behavior will usually strengthen that behavior.[38]

Feedback is basically a form of persuasion that can be conveyed to trainees in oral or written form, and it is expected to increase a trainee's belief that he or she can master the task. Recent research by Martocchio and Dulebohn[39] has shown that trainees who receive feedback that attributes past performance to factors *within* their control have heightened feelings of self-efficacy (a concept that will be discussed at greater length in the motivation section in this chapter), goal commitment, positive mood, and learning, compared to feedback that attributes past performance to factors outside the trainees' control. Apparently, it is important that the feedback that trainees receive provide them with the feeling that they are in control over their own performance.

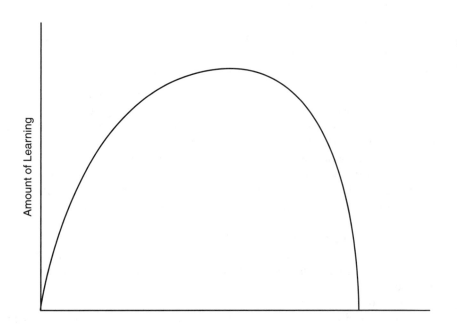

Specificity of Feedback

**FIGURE 4.1** Hypothesized Relationship Between Specificity of Feedback and Amount of Learning

*Source:* Adapted from Blum and Naylor, 1968.

Should trainers provide negative feedback? Positive feedback is perceived and recalled more accurately and accepted more readily than negative feedback. It has also been found to bring about more learning than does negative feedback.[40] Negative feedback is often denied, especially by trainees with low self-esteem, due to their unwillingness to accept critical comments about themselves. However, most trainees will accept and respond to negative feedback from trainers whom they view as trustworthy, knowledgeable about the subject matter being taught, and powerful enough to influence the trainee's receipt of certain valued outcomes such as pay increases, promotions, and retention in training. Similarly, it has been found that negative feedback is more effective when the supervisor who gives it has a relatively close and friendly relationship with the employee than when the relationship is distant and unfriendly.[41] Perhaps counter to common sense is their finding that punishment is more effective when it is given on a continuous rather than on an intermittent schedule. Finally, the effect of punishment is enhanced if the employee is made aware of alternative acceptable behaviors. Thus, trainers should provide both positive feedback (e.g., "Now you're igniting that acetylene torch correctly," "Your sales presentation this morning was perfect," "Your auditing report was submitted on time") and negative feedback (e.g., "You've got too much amperage on that torch," "You spoke down to the prospective customers during your sales presentation," "Your report was two days late"), so long as the negative feedback does not become punitive for the trainee. Of course, what will be experienced as punitive will depend on the particular interpersonal relationship (i.e., trust, respect, liking) between the trainer and trainee.

It is interesting to note that in the behavioristic tradition,[42] error feedback was conceptualized as being a form of punishment, and punishment was to be avoided. Erroneous performance was thought of as being disruptive to learning. Programmed instruction (Chapter 7), which strives to prevent trainees from making errors, grew out of this Skinnerian tradition. As was mentioned earlier, error training can have positive effects because one has to learn to deal efficiently with errors on both a strategic and an emotional level. Clearly, training programs need to be designed so that trainees have an opportunity to make errors, receive immediate feedback on these, and be encouraged by the trainer to solve these problems by themselves, thereby enhancing their error management skills.

Another important issue for training specialists concerns the effects of *intrinsic feedback* on learning. Obviously, a trainee can derive knowledge of results from the trainer (extrinsic) as well as from the task itself (intrinsic). An example of feedback emanating from the task itself would include a tailor looking at a finished suit that he or she has made and realizing the workmanship is perfect. In certain situations, individuals may be able to judge their own performances and thereby generate their own intrinsic feedback. How much these individuals rely on this self-generated intrinsic feedback depends on their experience in the job being taught and their particular level of self-esteem.

An effective learning strategy should include both intrinsic and extrinsic feedback. For example, in a large midwestern telephone company, employees performing service-type jobs (i.e., building equipment mechanic, motor mechanic, building servicer, cleaner, stocker) received intrinsic and extrinsic feedback. Each Friday, the employees rated themselves in terms of the number of days absent, accidents, amount of money spent compared to the amount budgeted, and their subjective evaluation of their service quality (intrinsic feedback). Every Monday, the supervisors met with the people they supervised to establish goals for the coming week and to tell how many employees had met the previously determined weekly goals (extrinsic feedback). The results of this project showed that the combination of intrinsic and extrinsic feedback (in conjunction with goal setting) was successful in reducing actual dollar expenditures and number of accidents.[43]

The relationship between feedback and goals is an interesting one. Trainees are more likely to seek feedback about their performance when they are working toward achieving assigned goals than when no goals exist.[44] Feedback is effective only when it affects a person's goals.[45] Finally, feedback works best when it involves simultaneously both behavioral feedback (e.g., "Joe, as a salesperson, you need to smile when greeting our customers") and end-results (e.g., "Joe, your level of sales volume has fallen 10 percent during the past month") feedback.

## Meaningfulness of the Material

Factual material is more easily learned and remembered better when it is meaningful to the trainees. Meaningfulness refers to material that is rich in associations for the trainees and is thus easily understood by them. Material can be structured to maximize its meaningfulness in the following ways:

1. At the outset of training, trainees should be provided with an overview of the material to be presented. Seeing the overall picture allows the trainees to understand how each unit of the program fits together as well as the objective of the program. An excellent illustration of this would be the instructor who provides a detailed course outline during the first day of a new semester or quarter.

2. The material should be presented using examples, terms, and concepts familiar to the trainees in order to clarify key learning points. For instance, a supervisory development program for head nurses in a medical center should employ examples concerning patient care. Visual aids can be used to augment abstract concepts. For example, one vocational training program teaches its educable mentally retarded students the concepts of city, county, state, and country by having them play darts using a board similar to the one shown in Figure 4.2.

3. Meaningfulness is also facilitated when the material is sequenced in a logical order. For instance, it has been shown that trainees learn best when they are told the function of a piece of machinery (i.e., what is it used for and when will they need to use it) before they learn its operations or its structure.

4. Complex intellectual skills are invariably composed of simpler skills, and the attainment of these subordinated skills is necessary before the complex skills can be assimilated. For instance, a mechanical trainee must first learn to discriminate

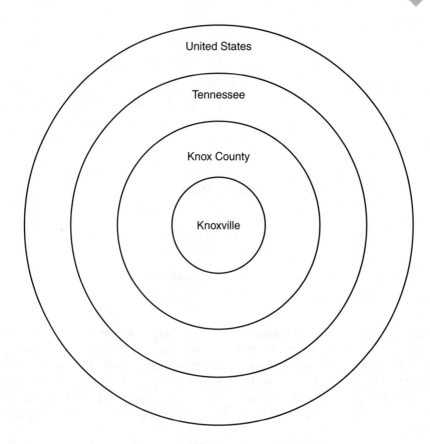

**FIGURE 4.2**   An Example of a Visual Aid for Teaching the Handicapped

successfully among various machine components before being able to understand such concepts as gears, sprockets, bushings, and couplings. Once these discriminations and concepts are absorbed, the trainee is ready to learn sample rules (e.g., how a reduction gear operates) and higher-order rules (e.g., how to put together a complex set of reduction gears to solve a specific mechanical application problem). Figure 4.3 suggests the most meaningful sequence for learning intellectual skills. Each level of learning requires as a prerequisite that one learn all levels underneath it.

## Individual Differences

In the years to come, there is likely to be an increase in interest in providing alternative modes of instruction for the needs and aptitudes of the individual trainee. This concern can be attributed to governmental pressure to hire and train members of minority groups, including women and older employees. It can also be attributed to the capacity of sophisticated computer-based instructional techniques (see Chapters 6 and 7) to adapt to the unique characteristics of individual

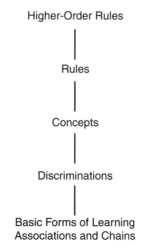

Higher-Order Rules

|

Rules

|

Concepts

|

Discriminations

|

Basic Forms of Learning
Associations and Chains

**FIGURE 4.3** Prerequisites in the Learning of Intellectual Skills

*Source:* Adapted from Gagné, 1977.

trainees. For example, regarding age, a survey was conducted that focused on perceptions of workers aged 40 and older in order to determine their training needs in the technological and management areas within the U.S. Geological Agency of the Department of the Interior. The younger age group, 40 to 49, preferred management training; the upper age group, 50 to 59, preferred training in technological areas; the age 60-and-above group showed little interest in any kind of training.[46]

In another study, management hierarchy was used to determine the audience to which training courses should be directed. Through the use of a correlational technique called factor analysis, 28 training courses were reduced to six factors. First-line supervisors had as their highest need technical factors (e.g., record keeping, written communications), mid-level managers rated human resource courses as most important for meeting their needs (e.g., leadership skills, performance appraisal), and upper management rated conceptual courses (e.g., goal setting, planning skills) as most important for their development.[47]

Gordon et al. found that trainees with greater seniority tended to require more time than standard to complete training than people with less seniority. Interjob similarity, not surprisingly, was a strong predictor of training time.[48]

Berryman-Fink focused on male and female managers' views of the communication needs and training needs of women in management.[49] Both male and female managers identified four communication skills for which women managers need training: assertiveness, confidence building, public speaking, and dealing with males. Male managers need training in listening, verbal skills, non-verbal communication, empathy, and sensitivity. However, in her survey of government workers, Tucker (1985) found no significant difference between women's and men's expressions of training needs. Nevertheless, her study demonstrated the need for human resource planning with regard to organizational analysis. Such planning, she showed, reveals the necessity for discouraging the early retirement of older workers from the U.S. Department of Interior because fewer people are entering the workforce.

Streker-Seeborg et al. investigated whether training economically disadvantaged women for male-dominated occupations increases the probability of their achieving employment. The results showed that despite training, they were much less likely than their male counterparts to become employed in male-dominated occupations.[50]

Because of projections of a lack of qualified personnel in male-dominated technical jobs, the West German Ministry of Science instigated a large-scale study of the apprenticeship of women in mechanical-technical occupations. Schuler found that the training could develop job-relevant aptitudes for women, but could not diminish the initial differences that existed between males and females prior to training.[51]

The studies just cited are demographic in nature. In contrast, learning curves are used to depict an *individual's* rate of learning as a function of continued practice. Figure 4.4 illustrates the unique patterns of learning of four trainees. It can be seen from the slope of the curves that some trainees learn faster (e.g., trainee A learns fastest), some begin learning at higher initial levels of expertise (trainee B), others are capable of higher terminal levels of performance (trainee C), and still others improve very little despite their continued practice (trainee D). These variations in learning patterns are the result of individual differences in levels of motivation and ability among trainees. The effective trainer is flexible enough to modify his or her training strategies to accommodate these differences in learning patterns among trainees.

Most graphs of learning progress usually follow the S-shaped pattern depicted in Figure 4.5. Rapid improvement comes during the early practice trials, but then the curve levels off, or plateaus, and may remain level for quite a while. There are several reasons for the plateau: The trainee may have reached the level of his or her capability, the trainee's interest may have waned temporarily, the person may be in the process of integrating levels of different skills, or the individual may need a different method of instruction. Regardless of the cause, the trainer should recognize that this leveling process is normal for most trainees, and that it is essential to provide encouragement to the learner at this time. Unless this encouragement is present, the learning process may be stopped prematurely.

Could it be that the same training approach may not work as well for all trainees? Since the late 1970s, the answer to this question has been examined by a research approach that has come to be known as *Aptitude-Treatment Interaction* (ATI). ATI is focused on providing each trainee with the most appropriate model of instruction based on the individual trainee's aptitude level. An aptitude refers to any characteristic of the trainee that may affect his or her capa-

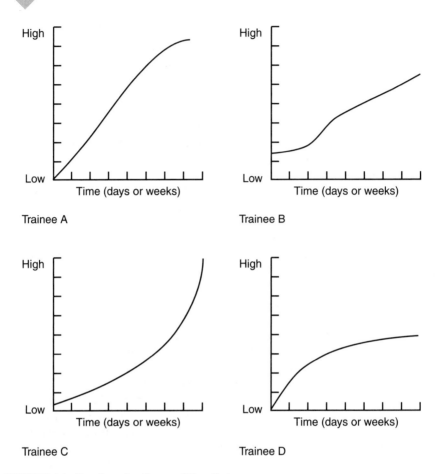

**FIGURE 4.4** Four Learning Curves of Four Trainees

bility to learn. Figures 4.6 and 4.7 illustrate two types of ATI relationships. In both figures, performance has been plotted for each training group with payoff on one axis and aptitude on the other. Figure 4.6 depicts the case where the treatment lines do not cross. This indicates that one method (treatment A) is best for all trainees regardless of their aptitude level. A *disordinal aptitude-treatment interaction* (see Figure 4.7) occurs when the treatment lines cross, and can be interpreted as evidence for a meaningful aptitude-treatment interaction; that is, trainees should be assigned differentially to alternative training methods in order to maximize instruction payoff. Specifically, trainees with high aptitude levels (those to the right of the cutoff line) will learn best with treatment A; persons with lower aptitude levels (those to the left of the cutoff line) will learn best with treatment B. For example, entry-level auditors conduct financial analyses of an organization's plants, stores, and/or distribution centers. One company found that trainees with high aptitude as measured by an accounting test, a numerical

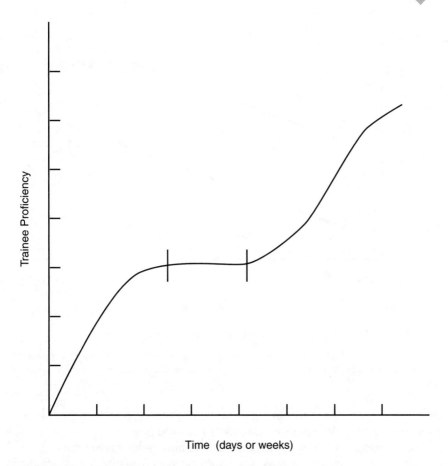

**FIGURE 4.5**   An S-Shaped Learning Curve with a Plateau

reasoning test, and a bookkeeping test learned most effectively by means of on-the-job coaching conducted by senior auditors. Those trainees with less aptitude learned best when their on-the-job coaching was supplemented with special lectures and programmed levels.

What else is known about the effect of individual differences on learning? First, differences among trainees in abilities, motivation level, interests, and prior history will affect performance and attribution in training programs. By measuring applicants' individual differences by means of various aptitude and personality tests, we can select applicants for training programs who possess trainability. Second, individual differences in trainee abilities (e.g., memorization, deductive reasoning, multilimb coordination, static strength) have been found to relate to a number of different learning phenomena such as performance during massed versus distributed practice sessions, whole versus part training, as well as retention and transfer. These individual differences have

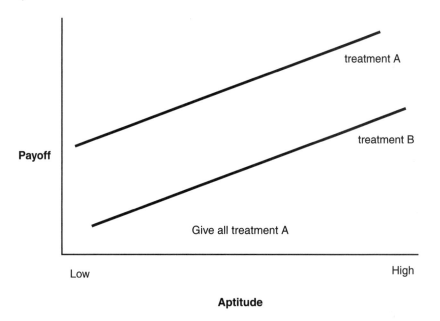

**FIGURE 4.6**    Illustration of No Aptitude-Treatment Interaction

*Source:*From L. J. Cronbach, "The Two Disciplines of Scientific Psychology," *American Psychologist 12* (1957): 671–84. Copyright 1957 by the American Psychological Association. Reproduced by permission.

enormous implications for training design. For instance, a shorter training program may be possible if trainees are experienced and possess high levels of task-related abilities. On the other hand, longer training programs are advisable for relatively inexperienced trainees, since they need to focus on fact acquisition, knowledge-structure development, and certain basic abilities. Third, we know that trainees differ in the kinds of "mental models" that they formulate, and that these mental models affect how well they learn what is being taught. Mental models are similar to schemata in that they are descriptions of a trainee's conceptualizations of physical devices or systems, and they are used by the trainee to explain and predict the system's behaviors. Frese et al.[52] were interested in comparing alternative training approaches for teaching the word-processing program Wordstar. They found that the training approach which encouraged trainee exploration and the active development of an integrated mental model led to better performance as compared to the approach that did not help trainees to actively develop a mental model. With the better approach, the trainees did not get any written material on the computer, since they were supposed to develop their own coherent mental model. Before beginning to work on the computer, they received a hard copy of the flawed text and were asked to develop hypotheses about the commands to be used to correct these mistakes. They were encouraged to try out all solutions that came to mind. After a while, the correct com-

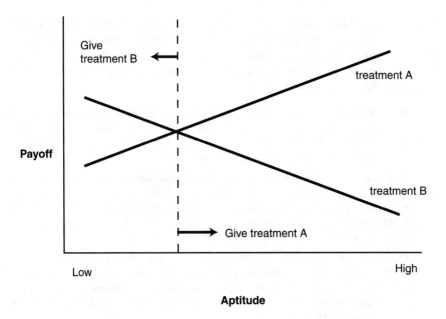

**FIGURE 4.7**   Illustration of a Disordinal Aptitude-Treatment Interaction

*Source:* From L. J. Cronbach, "The Two Disciplines of Scientific Psychology," *American Psychologist* *12* (1957): 671–84. Copyright 1957 by the American Psychological Association. Reproduced by permission.

mand was mentioned by the trainer, and the trainees were asked to write down what they learned. With the poorer approach, the trainees received written material which told them step by step every keystroke that needed to be used to correct each flaw. They were given no explanation as to *why* a particular command had to be used, and no mnemonic aids were provided. As long as the trainees followed the step-by-step directions, they could not make any errors. Finally, on the average, older trainees require longer to reach proficiency levels than younger trainees, and they may have developed alternative ways of organizing information which could conflict with the requirements of the training program.[53] Perhaps the older trainees need slower presentation rates, longer periods for study, greater self-confidence by sequencing their learning from simple to complex tasks, greater help in their organizational and memory processes, and the greater use of training techniques that provide active (rather than passive) participation in the learning process.[54]

Working in the United States, David Kolb was one of the first to develop a theory to explain the nature of experiential learning. Kolb identified four stages in the learning cycle: (1) having a here-and-now experience, (2) thinking about that experience by bring in more data and recollections about previous experiences in the past, (3) continuing to think about the experience by fitting the results into one's personal view of reality, and (4) testing one's conclusions by using a modified approach the next time a similar set of circumstances occurs.[55] Kolb's theory has been further developed by recognizing that each trainee has four channels in which they learn, and that each trainee prefers to use certain channels over others. These channels are referred to as "learning styles." They are clearly described below by Inglis[56]:

> **Activists:** Enjoy the here and now, dominated by immediate experiences, tend to revel in short-term crises, firefighting. Tend to thrive on the challenge of new experiences, but are relatively bored with implementation and long-term consolidation. They are the life and soul of the managerial party.

> **Reflectors:** Like to stand back and ponder on experiences and observe them from different perspectives. They collect data and analyze it before coming to any conclusions. They like to consider all possible angles and implications before making a move so they tend to be cautious. They actually enjoy observing other people in action and often take a back seat at meetings.

> **Theorists:** Are keen on basic assumptions, principles, theories, models, and systems thinking. They prize rationalty and logic. They tend to be detached, analytical, and are unhappy with subjective or ambiguous experiences. They like to assemble disparate facts into coherent theories. They like to make things tidy and fit them into rational schemes.

> **Pragmatists:** Positively search out new ideas and take the first opportunity to experiment with applications. The sort of people who return from management course brimming with new ideas that they want to try out in practice. They respond to problems and opportunities as a "challenge" (the activists would probably not recognize them as problems and opportunities).

An effectively designed training program should allow for the use of all four learning styles. Trainers should make it their responsibility to develop an understanding of each trainee's learning style through observation and assessment. They should communicate this to each trainee so that each individual can take greater charge of their own learning. If this is achieved, activists will come to the fore when fact-finding visits need to be made to other locations, crises need to be tackled, and volunteers are needed for challenging assignments. Reflectors will feel comfortable shifting through data; organizing these data into flowcharts, graphs, and models; and listening to others during training sessions before drawing meaningful conclusions. Trainees who are theorists will feel most comfortable organizing all the lose ends as well as playing "the devil's advocate" by asking difficult questions of the trainer and other trainees. The pragmatists will desire to ensure that whatever developmental activities are decided upon are, in fact, implemented efficiently and effectively.

It is important in the years to come that we increase our understanding of how individual differences between trainees affect learning and also training design. It is imperative that we continue to deal more and more with trainees on an individual basis through such training methods as Web-based and Internet training (Chapter 6). Training practitioners must be on the lookout for differences among trainees as well as disordinal interactions. This will require measuring various trainee characteristics prior to training and using more than one training method, if deemed necessary. For example, Snow's[57] work has shown that less able learners do better when instruction is tightly structured and lessons are broken down into a sequence of simplified units. Because they are structured, one would expect various computer-based training methods to result in better learning in highly anxious trainees. In two studies conducted in 1989, Gist[58] found that different methods of teaching computer software worked best with trainees who possessed high versus low feelings of self-efficacy. Specifically, she was able to show that those with low self-efficacy scores learned best from going through a one-on-one tutorial, whereas trainees with self-efficacy scores in the higher ranges benefited most from behavioral modeling, discussed in the next section.

## Behavior Modeling

Learning would be exceedingly laborious and hazardous if everything we learned resulted from our actually performing the behaviors involved. Fortunately, a large majority of our behavioral repertoire can be acquired through observing others. That is, we can learn by imitating those actions of others that we see as leading to desirable outcomes. If the consequences of their actions are positive, the models' actions come to function as a cue to what constitutes appropriate behavior.[59] For example, the head nurse in a hospital's cardiac care unit had a reputation for being a demanding, hard-working manager. She received a great deal of admiration and loyalty from her floor nurses and took a lot of pride in developing them for supervisory positions in other departments. When her nurses eventually got promoted to supervisory positions, they tended to exhibit the same hard-hitting managerial style as their mentor.

Despite the fact that each day people observe hundreds of behaviors by other people, they only choose to imitate some of them. What are some of the factors that cause people to model others?

Modeling occurs when the person who is imitated is seen as being competent, powerful, friendly, and of high status within an organization. This identification occurs because the model's behavior is seen as desirable and appropriate by the observer. Modeling is increased when the person to be imitated is seen as being rewarded for how he or she acts, and when the rewards received by the model (e.g., status, influence, friendship) are things that the observers would like for themselves. However, in a training context, observer identification with the model is maximized when the model is similar to the observer. If the observer sees little similarity between him- or herself and the model, it is very unlikely that the model's behaviors will be imitated.[60]

Greater modeling also occurs when the modeling "display" (either a live physical demonstration or a pictorial representation) portrays the behaviors in a clear and detailed manner. The effectiveness of behavior modeling is maximized when a combination of positive and negative model displays are used.[61] Clarity is enhanced by presenting trainees with a list of specific key behaviors (commonly referred to as *learning points*) that the trainer wants the trainees to attend to when observing the model. Following are examples of four learning points which were used in training supervisors to improve their interpersonal skills while orienting new employees.[62]

1. Welcome the employee to her or his area in a warm and friendly manner.
2. Put the employee at ease by getting the person to talk about him- or herself.
3. Tell the employee you are confident that she or he is going to do well on the job.
4. Tell the employee you're going to do everything you can to help him or her succeed.

Mann and Decker[63] found that when creating a behavior-modeling display, attaching learning points closely to the key behavior performed (especially for key behaviors that are not naturally distinctive) enhances both the acquisition and the recall of these behaviors. Trainees were unable to identify key behaviors from simply observing the model. As was found in Latham and Saari,[64] giving trainees the learning points in the absence of the model did not affect trainee behavior.

That the absence of learning points can have unintended and undesirable effects on trainees was discovered serendipitously by Manz and Sims.[65] The exposure to a reprimanding model inadvertently led to a decrease in both goal setting and positively reinforcing behaviors.

Hogan et al.[66] showed that trainees should not be restricted to the use of learning points written by trainers, even if trainer-generated points are assessed by subject-matter experts to be of higher quality than trainee-generated learning points. Their study revealed that when trainees developed their own mnemonics in organizing the material presented via modeling and displays, better performance occurred on a generalization test one week later than was the case when trainees were restricted to learning trainer-generated rules.

The effectiveness of the modeling process can also be aided by sequencing the behaviors to be modeled from least to most difficult. For example, if we were training supervisors how to coach their employees, the first modeled performance should be with an employee who has a minor performance problem, the second modeled performance with an employee whose problem is more severe, and so on. It is also important to show the modeled behaviors with enough repetition to make overlearning possible as well as to have the behaviors portrayed by several models rather than just one.[67] An interesting question is whether it is advisable to expose trainees to a variety of model of varying competence. There is some research suggesting that the inclusion of a negative model (i.e., showing a trainee the incorrect way of doing something) together with a positive model appears to facilitate transfer of learning to other situations.[68] However, there is also contradictory evidence in the research literature as to the advisability of using negative models along with positive ones.[69] A definitive answer to this particular question will have to await additional research on this question.

Behavior modeling is clearly a highly effective way of maximizing trainees' learning. This was evident in a study where behavior modeling was found to be superior to both traditional classroom instruction and a self-study course with regard to teaching computer skills to 160 novice users from a U.S. Naval Construction Battalion. Various measures of training effectiveness were gathered immediately after training, as well as one month after the training was completed. Measures of cognitive learning and skill demonstration were found to be the highest for behavior modeling during each of the two measurements. In addition, satisfaction with the computer system, one month after training, was found to be highest for those who had been trained using behavior modeling.[70] You can learn more about behavior modeling in Chapter 8 when we discuss the theoretical underpinning of this important component of learning—Albert Bandura's social learning theory.

## Maintaining Motivation

No one doubts the importance of trainee motivation for facilitating the effectiveness of any training program. If you think back over your own experiences, you will remember how much more readily you learned ideas and skills that you believed were relevant for you. Conversely, when you were disinterested in what was being taught, often little progress was made, despite your ability to learn what was being taught. What ways are there to motivate trainees? To answer the question, we need first to examine three theories of motivation which are particularly relevant to trainee motivation: goal setting, reinforcement theory, and expectancy theory. After discussing these three theories, we will offer several additional ways that trainee motivation can be enhanced.

Goal setting as formulated by Locke and Latham[71] states that an individual's conscious goals or intentions regulate one's behavior. A goal is anything an individual is consciously trying to achieve. Given that the goal is accepted, hard goals result in higher levels of performance than do easy goals, and specific hard goals result in higher performance levels than do no goals or even a generalized goal such as "do your best." Numerous laboratory experiments and field studies conducted in a wide variety of organizational settings have demonstrated the practical feasibility of goal-setting programs as means of increasing employee performance.[72]

The research findings on goal setting have three important implications for motivating trainees. First, the learning objectives of the training program should be conveyed clearly to the participants at the outset of training and at various strategic points throughout the training process. Second, training goals should be difficult enough so that trainees are adequately challenged and thus are able to derive satisfaction from the achievement of objectives. However, the goals should not be perceived as being of such difficulty that trainees feel they are unable to reach them. Third, the distal goal of "finishing the program" should be supplemented with periodic subgoals during training such as trainer evaluations, work sample tests, and periodic quizzes. In this way, the trainee can derive a feeling of goal accomplishment and, consequently, look forward to tackling the next hurdle. For example, department heads from large urban hospitals participated in an effective management development program designed to improve their human relations skills in dealing with their employees.[73] The department heads actively took part in a series of role-playing exercises. The trainer assigned specific and moderately difficult performance goals to the trainees prior to each exercise. The trainer also met with each trainee on his or her job to review performance and to assign specific performance goals for their subsequent meeting. The results were an improvement in the interpersonal skills of the department heads and a reduction in the absenteeism of their employees.

Trainers need to be aware that high levels of anxiety may debilitate one's feelings of self-efficacy. *Self-efficacy* refers to the person's conviction that he or she can master a given task.[74] Self-efficacy has been found to predict performance in computer software training,[75] interpersonal skills training,[76] newcomer training,[77] and military training programs.[78]

In a training program, goal setting can be a two-edged sword. For example, goal setting is important for increasing self-efficacy because without specific goals people have little basis for judging how they are doing, or for gauging their capabilities. Self-motivation is sustained by adopting specific attainable subgoals that lead to large future ones.[79] Subgoal attainment provides clear markers of progress which, in turn, verifies a person's sense of self-efficacy. Thus, it is important that a trainer coach trainees to set specific goals that are difficult, but attainable, for the trainee.

Trainers must realize that the trainee's perception of their adequacy of performance is measured against their personal standards. Depressive reactions often arise from stringent standards of self-evaluation. Trainees who are prone to giving up are often people who impose high performance demands and then devalue their accomplishments because they fall short of their exacting goals. Thus, it cannot be overemphasized that trainers must help trainees to set specific goals that are difficult, but attainable.

Finally, trainers must distinguish between process (i.e., behavioral) and outcomes goals. The latter can be detrimental to the learning process. For example, learning theorists describe skill acquisition as a three-phase process: (1) declarative knowledge, (2) knowledge compilation, and (3) procedural knowledge. It has been found that the effectiveness of goals set with regard to performance outcomes are moderated by the attentional demands of each specific learning stage. The higher the attentional demands of the learning stage, the less effective the goal-setting intervention.[80]

In the first phase of learning, declarative knowledge, the trainee acquires a basic understanding of what is required to perform the task. During this phase, the training content often includes a lecture on the general principles of the task, observation of task performance, and strategies on how to perform the task. The declarative knowledge phase involves high attentional demands, which makes it difficult for trainees to concentrate on additional information-processing demands.

During the second phase of learning, knowledge compilation, trainees integrate the sequence of cognitive and motive processes required to perform the task. Performance improvement results from task practice and trying out various methods of simplifying or reducing each task component. As performance stabilizes during this phase, attentional demands are reduced and attention may be diverted to other areas without substantial decrements in performance.

In the third phase of skill acquisition, procedural knowledge occurs when the learner has essentially automatized the skill. After sufficient practice, performance becomes rapid and accurate; thus, it can usually be performed with minimum attention devoted to the learned task.

Based on the attentional demands of each acquisition phase, Kanfer and Ackerman[81] derived and tested hypotheses on the effectiveness of performance outcome goals. Since the self-regulation required in attaining a specific performance outcome requires attentional demands, the researchers hypothesized that attentional resources would be diverted from the learning task.

Kanfer and Ackerman tested this hypothesis using U.S. Air Force trainees who were learning an air traffic control computer simulation task. The task involved accepting and landing planes on appropriate runways based on specific rules (e.g., weather conditions, amount of fuel) over ten trials. In a series of experiments, subjects received either no goal ("do your best") or an outcome goal on early trials ("achieve score of 2200 during trials 5, 6, and 7"). The results showed that only outcome goals assigned late in the skill acquisition process exerted a significant positive effect on task performance.

With regard to goal commitment, there is evidence to suggest that trainees should make their goals known to peers. For example, in one study, students set goals on a number of questions they would answer correctly on reading passages of the Graduate Record Examination. Students in the "public condition" handed their goals to the experimenter, who then read them aloud. Students in the "private condition" deposited their goals into an anonymous box. Although the goal difficulty levels of the public and private conditions were not significantly different, the public goal group did perform better than the private goal group.

In a second study by the same researchers, students read a series of modules on improving their study skills. They set goals on both the number of modules that they would read, and on their posttest performance. Students in the public condition read their goals aloud to the group; those in the private condition placed their goals anonymously in the box. Similar to the results of the first study, students in the public condition significantly outperformed students in the private condition. Again, this result occurred in spite of the fact that the two groups did not differ greatly in the difficulty level of the goals they set.[82]

In another study investigating the effects of public commitment, subjects set goals for the grade point average (GPA) they would obtain the following term. Subjects were randomly assigned to either a public goal or a private goal condition. In the public goal condition, students' GPA goals were distributed to other individuals within that condition, and a copy of their respective goals was sent to a self-determined significant other person. The results of this study revealed that subjects in the public goal condition had higher goal commitment than those in the private goal condition. Further, there was a significant effect for commitment on performance that was independent of goal level.[83]

Reinforcement theory, otherwise known as behavior modification or operant conditioning, is another approach for stimulating a trainee's desire to learn. One of its major principles is that "the frequency of behavior is influenced by its consequences." If the consequence is positive for the individual, the likelihood that the behavior will be repeated is increased. Rapid behavior change results when the consequence follows immediately or shortly after a behavior being taught in training is demonstrated by the trainee.

The consequences of behavior can be categorized into two major types: positive reinforcers (rewards) and punishers. The use of positive reinforcement is generally more effective for modifying behavior than punishment.[84] Punishment often has unfortunate side effects such as anxiety, hostility, and withdrawal. More important than the magnitude of a reinforcer is the schedule with which reinforcers occur. A continuous schedule involves administering a reinforcer after every correct response; a partial or intermittent schedule entails administering reinforcers only after a certain number of correct responses have been emitted or to the first correct response after a specified period of time has elapsed.

In applying reinforcement theory, it is crucial that the trainer define precisely the target behaviors that the trainee is expected to learn. Answers such as "improving attitudes," "providing job knowledge," and "increasing performance" are much too general. The key question for the trainer to ask is, "What should the trainee be able to do at the end of training that will enable that person to become an effective employee?" This is why task analysis, particularly the critical incident technique discussed in Chapter 3, is so important. Examples of appropriate course objectives would include: "Punch in at 7:30 A.M. every workday"; "Produce an error-free typed letter"; and "Be familiar with terms commonly used by operating room technicians." Unless the desired behaviors are specified in advance, it is difficult for the trainer to know what to reward during the training program.

Just as the target behaviors[85] and ideas must be identified, so must the positive reinforcers be used. It is important for the trainer to make certain that the most powerful positive consequences are used for each trainee. Again, individual differences must be taken into account because the same reinforcers are not effective with all trainees.

Once the effective reinforcers for an individual have been identified, it is important that they are administered as soon as possible after the desired behavior. Delay of reinforcement can strengthen irrelevant behavior in lieu of the appropriate behavior. For example, a trainee learning to make an electrical assembly will perform considerably better if the trainer rewards correct behaviors immediately after they occur rather than informing the individual about them weeks after. If the trainer waits too long, there is an increased possibility that the trainee will develop bad habits.

It is best to provide continuous reinforcement when the trainee begins the learning of new behaviors. As the behaviors become better established, the schedule of reinforcement should be stretched. In other words, a partial schedule should be used, since it not only makes the new behaviors more stable or resistant to extinction, but it can also lead to an increase in the rate of desired behavior.[86] An example of a partial schedule would be the trainer who occasionally drops by a trainee's work station without prior notice to formally recognize appropriate behavior.

Rather than frustrating trainees by forcing them to perform behaviors that they are presently incapable or unwilling to exhibit, the trainer can use a process called *shaping:* the procedure of reinforcing any behavior that approximates the terminal behavior desired by the trainer while refraining from rewarding all other behaviors. As time proceeds, closer and closer approximations to the terminal behavior are required of the trainee before any reinforcement is given. For example, suppose a particular trainee is attending a three-week training program. At the outset of the program, the trainer notices that the trainee shows up 15 minutes late several days in a row. The trainer decides that she wants to teach him to be punctual. At first, the trainer praises any attempt by the individual to show up more punctually, even if this may mean rewarding him for being only 14 minutes late. After a while, the trainer demands more and more by praising only closer approximations to the desired response of being on time. Finally, the trainee is praised only when he is truly punctual.

*Expectancy theory* also has important implications for motivating trainees. Although a number of versions of expectancy (also called *instrumentality*) theory have been proposed,[87] they all share certain common features. Each version proposes that an individual will be motivated to choose a behavior alternative that is most likely to have favorable consequences. When deciding whether to expend effort on a given activity, the individual asks, "What am I going to get out of that?" A decision to put forth effort is made if it is perceived that there is a good chance it will result in obtaining something of value. The key concepts in the theory are (1) outcome, (2) valence, (3) *E* (effort) *P* (performance) expectancy, and (4) *P* (performance) *O* (outcome) expectancy. Outcomes in a work context include such things as salary increase, promotion, dismissal, illness, injury, peer acceptance, recognition, and achievement. Valence refers to the desirability or attractiveness of an outcome to the individual. For instance, one worker may value pay more than recognition; another may feel just the opposite. The *EP expectancy* concerns itself with the employee's perceived probability that a given amount of effort will result in improved performance (i.e., quantity and/or quality of work). The perceived probability that improved performance will lead in turn to the attainment of valued outcomes (e.g., bonus, pay increase, promotion) is called the *PO expectancy*. The theory assumes that, before deciding how much effort to exert, employees ask themselves whether or not (1) the action has a high probability of leading to better performance *(EP)*; (2) improved performance will yield certain need-related outcomes *(PO)*; and (3) those need-related outcomes or organizational rewards are of value (valence). The two expectancies are affected by different conditions. The *EP* expectancy depends in part on relatively stable characteristics of the worker such as intelligence, motor abilities, and personality traits. In addition, the individual's perception of what makes for a successful employee will influence whether effort can be transformed into effective performance. The *PO* expectancy depends on a person's perceptions of the reward contingencies presently found in the organization.

Expectancy theory has several important implications for motivating trainees. First, for any program to be successful, the trainee must believe that "there's something in it for me." The individual must perceive that his or her participation in training will lead to more desirable rewards than not being in training. Unless trainees can expect the program to lead to valued outcomes (e.g., higher wages, opportunities for advancement, skill acquisition, less fatiguing, and safer work), it will be viewed as merely a waste of time. Trainees will either expend minimal effort or simply drop out. This is precisely the problem that has been encountered in training underprivileged individuals. These individuals often do not expect these behavior-reward contingencies and, consequently, see their training as just another futile exercise leading them nowhere.

Second, trainers should not assume that their trainees have accurate perceptions of reward contingencies. Trainers should explain the contingencies in a manner that will ensure accurate *PO* expectancies. Trainees must be told exactly what outstanding performance during training will mean to their careers.

Third, the organization should ensure that each trainee has a high *EP* expectancy by providing effective instructors, eliminating obstacles to effective performance, providing accurate role perceptions, and selecting trainees with requisite ability and motivation. Finally, the valence attached by an individual to potential need-related outcomes should be investigated by the organization, since this will differ among trainees and even within the same trainee over time. Only high-valence outcomes should be used as incentives for superior trainee performance.

The practical implications of goal theory, reinforcement theory, and expectancy theory are compatible with one another. These theories can all be applied for motivating learning by making certain that trainees see the value *for them* of participating in the training, understanding the goals or target behaviors of the program, and clearly perceiving the link between their actions during training and their receipt of valued rewards.

Additional things that training specialists can consider doing to maximize trainee motivation include:

- Give trainees a choice of the training modules or training programs that they would like to attend, and make certain that they can actually attend the training that they choose. This is preferably to either forcing trainees to attend training sessions or not delivering on the choices they have made.[88]
- Make participating in training programs voluntary rather than mandatory.[89]
- Interview trainees prior to training to get them to talk about previous negative events that they have experienced related to the purpose of training.[90] For instance, if one were implementing an assertiveness, one would contact future participants to discuss those times in the past when negative consequences occurred as a result of their not being assertive enough.
- Work on maintaining a favorable reputation of the training function throughout the organization so that trainees perceive more intrinsic reasons to attend training and have a more favorable view of the training department's efforts.[91]
- Frame the purpose of attending the training to superior performance (i.e., advanced training) rather than to poor performance (i.e., remedial training). Assignment to training is a form of positive or negative feedback depending on the reason given for the assignment.[92]

Most training programs are based on the assumption that what is taught in training will be used by trainees when they complete the training program. For example, astronauts are taught complex procedures using simulated space capsules on the assumption that these procedures will carry over to their actual flights into space. Medical students are taught surgical procedures on cadavers in the hope that this instruction will transfer someday to their live patients. Supervisors are shown films about handling employee complaints and grievances with the expectation that this new knowledge will be applied by them to their jobs. In the section that follows, we attempt to answer the question "What can be done to ensure that what is learned in training will be retained and transferred to the job?"

## RETENTION AND TRANSFER OF LEARNING

Transfer refers to the extent to which what was learned during training is used on the job. Three transfer possibilities exist:

*Positive transfer:* Learning in the training situation results in better performance on the job.

*Negative transfer:* Learning in the training situation results in poorer performance on the job.

*Zero transfer:* Learning in the training situation has no effect on job performance.

Training that results in negative or zero transfer is either detrimental or of no value to an organization from a cost–benefit viewpoint. Nevertheless, instances of negative and zero transfer occur frequently in organizations. For example, one organization followed the practice of fostering competition among its trainees in the hope of increasing their motivation to learn. Trainers provided special monetary awards for those trainees who showed the highest rates of production at the end of each two-week period. The organization found that the quantity of production of their fiberglass auto bumpers did, in fact, increase during the two-month training period. Unfortunately, the organization also found that, after the training was completed, the individuals involved had considerably more scrappage and waste than comparable employees who had not been exposed to this training strategy. Management soon realized that they were teaching their fiberglass production employees the wrong thing, that is, to maximize quantity of production at the expense of quality.

In a large-sized insurance company, newly appointed department managers were exposed to a week-long lecture series designed to help them plan and organize by maximum output, manage their own time more effectively, set realistic departmental objectives, and develop their employees to their fullest potential. A rigorous evaluative study of the program revealed that the training had no effect whatsoever on the managers' behaviors back in their home departments.

Is positive transfer and retention of training a problem? Let us look at the facts. First, it is estimated that merely 10 percent of the training dollars spent result in actual and lasting behavioral change back on trainees' jobs.[93] Second, according to training professionals, only about 40 percent of the content of training programs is actually transferred to the work environment immediately after training, about 25 percent is still being applied six months later, and a mere 15 percent is still being used at the end of a year.[94]

How can we optimize the possibility of getting positive transfer? In discussing various strategies for maximizing retention and transfer, we separate our recommendations into three time periods—before, during, and after training.

## Before

- **Conduct a needs analysis that includes multiple constituencies.** A training needs analysis procedure that includes representatives from the training department, the customer (i.e., the people who initially requested some sort of training), as well as the potential participants and their managers, is appropriate if the training is really going to be taken and applied seriously.[95]
- **Seek out supervisory support for training.** Supervisory support for training is considered to be a key work variable affecting the transfer process.[96] Clearly, when employees perceive that the training is important to their supervisor they will be more motivated to attend, learn, as well as retain and transfer what was learned to their jobs.[97] In light of this, an advance letter to the trainee's supervisor stressing the expected benefits of the training for his or her unit and asking for the manager's help in supporting the behavior changes is a good idea.[98] Better yet, this could be accomplished face to face at a briefing session conducted by the training department for the supervisors.
- **Inform the trainees regarding the nature of the training.** Trainees should be informed ahead of time regarding such things as the training program's purpose, specific behavioral objectives, methods, length, location, trainers, successful grad-

uates, and examples of potential skill applications back on their jobs. According to expectancy theory, it is important that trainees believe that they are capable of performing well in training and that completion of the training will lead to valued rewards.[99]

- **Assign tasks prior to the training sessions.** To stimulate interest, trainers will sometimes assign advanced readings, provide a realistic case study that is to be analyzed, or else ask trainees to fill out various self-analysis materials in advance.[100]

- **Maximize organizational commitment and eliminate cynicism.** It has been shown that trainees are more likely to apply what they have learned during training back on their jobs when they have higher organizational commitment and lower feelings of cynicism about their organization.[101] It makes sense to deal with these issues before expending the effort, time, and money to design and implement training programs.

## During

- **Maximize the similarity between the training situation and the job situation.** Positive transfer will be maximized to the degree that there are identical stimulus and response elements in the learning and job situations.[102] Suppose, for example, that an individual is to be trained as a typist. The job involves typing auto and homeowner insurance policies in a noisy, fast-paced work environment using an electric typewriter. In this case, the training should involve typing alphanumeric symbols accurately and quickly in a noisy setting using a typewriter identical to that found on the job.

- **Provide as much experience as possible with the task being taught.** Positive transfer increases, and negative transfer decreases, with more and more practice on the original task.[103] This is true regardless of whether a trainee is learning a physical or a cognitive task. For example, operator packers in a soap plant spent most of their shift time packing four-bar bundles of soap into shipping cartons. The more practice and feedback that these employees were given during their initial training, the better they were able to adjust to occasional defects—caused by the wrapping machines, fluctuations in the speed of the bundling machines, changes in the size of the cartons, and variations in the sizes of the soap bars. Supervisory trainees in a paper mill need to learn certain safety rules so that they know and understand them without referring to a safety manual. The trainees, during the safety training program, assess each others' understanding and memory of the rules by posing hypothetical situations at one another until each trainee remembers and applies them perfectly.

- **Have the trainees practice their newly learned skills in actual situations that they will encounter back on their jobs.** To help transfer newly learned skills to the trainees' own work environment, each trainee should choose an actual work situation from his or her own unique job environment. It is advisable to videotape the trainee practicing the skill during a role play with one or more other trainees. Immediately after taping, the trainee should critique his or her performance with the help of the trainer and other trainees.[104]

- **Provide for a variety of examples when teaching concepts or skills.** Provide several examples of instances that do and do not represent the concept being taught. For instance, investment counselors are taught about different tax shelters for their clients. During training, they are given examples of shelters and nonshelters depending on a customer's particular income tax bracket. In skill training, the individual should be given adequate opportunity to practice the skill under a wide range of conditions. A powerhouse trainee, for example, might be taught to fire a boiler under varying temperature and pressure conditions.

- **Label or identify important features of a task.** Labeling helps the trainee to distinguish important features of the task being taught. In training someone to operate a piece of machinery, for example, give a label to each step involved in its operation. In addition, place a label on the various parts of the machine. For instance, in one organization, building maintenance mechanics were shown several types of boilers, each painted various colors to signify their parts (i.e., firebox, compressor, gas cock, water pump). This teaching aid enabled the trainees to detect unique as well as common features across the various types of boilers.

- **Make sure that general principles are understood before expecting much transfer.** Transfer is facilitated when the trainee truly understands the general rules and principles that are needed in solving new problems. For example, the newly trained polymer chemist can only apply her knowledge to tire development if she understands the basic principles of her field and has not merely memorized facts.

- **Provide trainees with the knowledge, skills, and feelings of self-efficacy to self-regulate their own behaviors back on their jobs.** Research has shown that, without the benefit of training, employees do little in the way of self-regulating their own job performance.[105] Self-regulating entails goal setting, self-monitoring, as well as self-reward and self-punishment depending on the discrepancy between one's behavior and one's goal.[106] Recent research has shown that employees can be successfully trained to set goals, formulate written behavioral contracts, self-monitor their own behavior, and self-administer rewards and punishments. For instance, Latham and Frayne[107] found that unionized state government employees trained in self-management skills increased the work attendance and their feelings of self-efficacy significantly more than employees in a control group. Most importantly, this increase in job attendance continued over 12 months. In another study, self-management instruction was found to maximize positive transfer as part of a negotiation skills training program.[108] The self-management instruction involved presenting examples of previous self-management programs, discussing goal setting as a self-management technique, identifying obstacles to success, planning how to overcome these obstacles, self-monitoring progress in the implementation of plans, and using self-reinforcement methods to motivate interim accomplishments.

- **Design the training content so that the trainees can see its applicability.** It has been shown that individuals who feel that the training course they attended helped them learn skills and ideas directly related to their job situations are more likely to transfer their learning on return to their companies. Positive transfer is also facilitated when trainees feel that the trainers understand their unique job problems. Conversely, training programs felt to be too difficult and poorly organized have been found to generate less positive transfer.

- **Use adjunct questions to guide the trainee's attention.** Research in factual learning has found that questions inserted in instructional materials can influence trainees' retention.[109] Questions in a text that precede the material containing the answers often facilitate the trainee's learning and retention of the information which the questions asked about, but reduce the learning and retention of other information presented. These results suggest that, if adjunct prequestions are to be used, they should be broad enough in scope to cover the entire content domain being taught (see, for example, the three broad questions posed at the beginning of this chapter).

## After

After completing a training program, trainees should be assigned specific behavioral goals. In addition, the trainees and/or their supervisors should complete behavioral progress reports to monitor the extent of the goal achievement back on the job. Wexley and Baldwin[110] investigated the effectiveness of three post-training strategies for facilitating transfer of transfer: (1) assigned goal setting, (2) participative goal setting, and (3) a behavioral self-management approach. Their results showed that both the assigned and participative goal-setting conditions were superior to behavioral self-management and control conditions in inducing maintenance of behavioral change over a two-month period. In another study, Wexley and Nemeroff[111] incorporated assigned goal setting and behavioral checklists as an element of their management development program for hospital supervisors. Trainees completed a two-day workshop intended to improve their leadership and interpersonal skills. After finishing training, but before returning to their jobs, trainees received a set of behavioral checklists and instructions in monitoring and recording their own on-the-job use of their new skills. The trainees expected to fill out the behavioral checklists three times per week in order to record their progress in achieving the program's behavioral goals. The specific items on the checklists were derived directly from the learning points of the training program. Their results indicated that the treatment group using this assigned goal-setting and behavioral feedback approach was significantly better at applying learned skills than was a control group. In another study, trainees were assigned behavioral goals based on 10 learning points presented during a behavior modeling workshop aimed at increasing assertiveness.[112] The subjects received activity checklists that they were to use twice a week for four weeks. The trainees were asked to consider, when filling out the checklist, to think back about the most challenging situation calling for assertiveness that they had faced and to check how many learning points (i.e., goals) they had achieved. After the four weeks, the trainees submitted all their completed checklists to the trainers. This post-training intervention impacted both learning and behavior measures.

- **Give trainees an opportunity to practice the trained tasks on the job.** The opportunity to perform trained tasks consists of three dimensions: (1) *breadth*—trainees usually learn during training a variety of tasks; breadth refers to how many of these tasks they actually get to perform once they are on their jobs; (2) *activity level*—refers to the number of times the trainees get to perform the trained tasks on their jobs; and (3) *type of tasks*—some trainees may perform on their jobs only the simplest of the tasks they have learned while others perform the difficult tasks; this dimension relates to how critical, complex, or difficult the tasks are that trainees have the opportunity to perform on the job. Research has shown that positive transfer is increased when trainees have an opportunity to experience these three indices of opportunity.[113]

- **Have the trainer collaborate with each of the trainees in using the application plan principle.** The application plan principle consists of several basic steps designed to assist the trainee in choosing relevant material (i.e., learning points) from the training program and applying them through a set of measurable behaviors or activities. First, each trainee is asked to force rank the learning points in terms of importance in their own particular work setting. Next, each trainee is asked to address the highest ranked learning point and to reduce that learning point to a basic goal that will fit the context of the trainee's job. Third, the trainee is asked to generate specific activities that will help to apply the goal as well as who will be affected by these new activities. The application plan form includes all of the information previously described as well as several self-rating dates. The form also includes a performance improvement section to be used after each one of the first two rating sequences. This section assists trainees in identifying *why* they have not been very successful in achieving behaviors that are rated as 3 or lower, with 3 being "performed this behavior, but can use much improvement." Other important learning points may be addressed in successive or concurrent application plans.

- **Make certain that the trained behaviors and ideas are rewarded in the job situation.** A trainee will transfer what he or she has learned during training only if it is supported by the reward structure on the job. The most crucial person in this reward structure is the trainee's immediate supervisor. It is therefore imperative that this individual understand and endorse the objectives of training. For instance, in one organization, it was realized that it would be virtually impossible to change the behaviors and thinking of supervisors without first changing the managerial climate that descended on them from above. The company decided to begin supervisory training at the top and then work down in this way, so each trained level could support the training of the level immediately below it. What other ways are there for training specialists to elicit managerial and supervisory support? Consider the following suggestions: (1) make sure managers and supervisors know the training requirements, (2) solicit their input on the training content, (3) show them how to reinforce desired behaviors on the job, (4) explain to them the expected benefits and expected outcomes of the training, and (5) enlist their help in collecting evaluation data.[114]

- **Use the relapse prevention strategy, which relies heavily on behavioral self-management.** Marx[115] proposed the use of a strategy called *relapse prevention,* which was originally designed and successfully implemented in the treatment of various addictive behaviors such as smoking, eating, and drinking.[116] Marx argued that this approach seems particularly applicable as a post-training strategy for management development. The strategy consists of both cognitive and behavioral components designed to facilitate long-term maintenance of learned behaviors by teaching trainees how to understand and cope with the problem of relapse. In a work context, *relapse* refers to reversion to pretraining behavior in certain on-the-job situations.

How does one implement the relapse prevention strategy? First, the trainees must be made aware of the relapse process itself. Second, each trainee is asked to pinpoint situations that would likely sabotage their attempts to maintain their new learning back on their jobs. This should be done for each of the training program's learning points. Next, each trainee is asked to develop lists of potential coping responses for these situations. They are also told that temporary difficulties or slips are normal and that they should not feel guilty when these temporary slips occur. Each trainee leaves the training session with a self-generated list of coping responses corresponding to each of the learning points. However, a relapse prevention strategy must be supplemented by goal setting, monitoring, and feedback from supervisors and/or trainers if it is to result in transfer of training.[117]

## ORGANIZATIONAL FACTORS AFFECTING TRANSFER OF TRAINING

Latham and Crandall[118] have described organizationwide factors that can affect the transfer of training to the job. Under this rubric fall such factors as pay and promotion policies and environmental constraints. These variables affect transfer of training to the job because they affect trainee outcome expectancies.

### Pay and Promotion

Outcome expectancies, a concept similar to instrumentality that we discussed earlier in this chapter, are trainee beliefs about whether particular behaviors will lead to desired outcomes.[119] Trainees may believe that they are capable of performing a specific behavior, but may choose not to do so because they believe it will have little or no effect on their status in the organization. Thus, high outcome expectancies are critical to the transfer of training to the job setting.

Researchers in the behaviorist tradition have long known that the environment shapes behavior. Although this finding should be a platitude by now, there is evidence to suggest that our knowledge of environmental reinforcers such as pay and promotion practices is not being applied in the training context.[120] For example, research suggests that pay for performance systems are effective methods for bringing about and sustaining performance.[121] Thus, newly acquired skills should be incorporated into merit pay plans in order to increase the probability that these skills will be used on the job. Robinson and Robinson[122] cited an example of the importance of incorporating newly learned skills into a merit pay plan. Customer service representatives (CSRs) in an organization received training in customer relations. They were taught to handle customer complaints by obtaining sufficient knowledge over the phone and then empathizing with the customer regarding the problem. The CSRs were provided incentives based on the dollar value of orders received each day. When handling a customer complaint, however, the CSRs would spend twice as long on the phone compared with the time it took to take an order. Fortunately, management anticipated the reinforcement problem inherent in this situation and modified the incentive system so the newly learned customer relations skills would be utilized.

Caplow[123] described a study of clerical workers who subsequent to training were allowed to work without close supervision. The result was lower productivity and morale than those in the control group. Interviews with the clerks who had received the training disclosed that after they were given autonomy they thought themselves entitled to higher pay than the other clerks. They become so disgruntled at not receiving it that their output eventually declined to a much lower level than that of the control group.

As people progress up the organizational hierarchy, the opportunities for promotion, remuneration, and honors are greater than for the organization's rank and file employees. Paradoxically, the opportunities for disappointment not only increase, but they are often more severe than they are lower in the organization. To have completed successfully an executive development program (e.g., Harvard's or MIT's—see Chapter 9) and then just miss becoming an executive vice president is probably a greater disappointment than to have just missed a promotion to an assistant supervisory position. Moreover, the likelihood that others will want to model this person's behavior of taking time away from the job to attend similar executive programs is decreased. The likelihood that the disaffected employee will leave the organization for another is increased.

## Environmental Constraints

Environmental constraints can obviously have a deleterious effect on a trainee's outcome expectancies. In the context of training, there are at least 11 constraints that can hinder the transfer of training to the job setting, namely, the lack of job-related information, tools and equipment, materials and supplies, budgetary support, required services and help from others, task preparation, time availability, work environment (i.e., physical aspects), scheduling of activities, transportation, and job-relevant authority.[124]

Several empirical investigations have demonstrated the effect of environmental constraints on an individual's behavior. For example, Peters et al.[125] found that three types of situational constraints (completeness of task information, ease of use of materials and supplies, similarity of work environment to training environment) affected performance on a goal-setting task. When these situational constraints were low, goal level correlated significantly with performance ($r = .63$); when these situational constraints were high, the correlation was reduced to nonsignificance. To minimize the probability of low outcome expectancies, Robinson and Robinson[126] suggested conducting an organizational assessment to identify any barriers to transfer before training begins. This assessment should be made in addition to the traditional organizational and person training needs assessment (see Chapter 3). For example, a survey can be distributed to supervisors and potential trainees for the purpose of identifying perceived situational constraints. Barriers to performance should be corrected prior to training in order to facilitate high outcome expectancies and maximum transfer of training to the work setting.

Other environmental variables are social in nature, and stem from interactions with peers and supervisors. The social variables can have a positive or a deleterious effect on a cognitive variable that is crucial to training success, namely, self-efficacy. Self-efficacy, as described earlier in this chapter, is the extent to which one believes one can perform a specific task. The ways peers and supervisors can increase self-efficacy are described next.

## Social Variables Affecting Transfer of Training

### Peer Group

A potent force in the socialization process within an organization is the interactive dynamics between the individual and his or her peers. Such interaction can provide support and reinforcement for not only learning what is being taught in the training program but also in applying what was learned to the job. Conversely, failure to secure such support can result in alienation during training or on the job. For example, it has been found that avoidable terminations were significantly lower when a trainee was assigned to a department with two or more trainees than when the person was assigned to a department either alone or with only one trainee. This finding suggests that a trainee who has the substantive support of other trainees will have higher self-efficacy in dealing with the stresses and ambiguities created by a new job than would be the case without such social facilitation.[127]

The beneficial effects of interactive learning was pointed out years ago by the Swiss developmentalist Jean Piaget.[128] Piaget noted that collaborative learning plays a crucial role in constructive cognitive development. This type of learning, he believed, was in sharp contrast with adult–child or teacher–student interactions, whereby the former is in control and the latter merely follows what the former professes, thereby not following their own natural learning process. Reg Revans,[129] the originator of "action learning" (to be discussed at further length in Chapter 9), observed years ago how scientists working at the Cavendish Laboratory at Cambridge University shared their problems, as well as sought and received help from others in the group. According to Revans, there is nothing really new about action learning since people have always been learning from one another. Action learning is a process that brings people together (known as a *set*) to find solutions to real problems confronting their organization and, in so doing, develops both the participants as well as the organization.[130] The set typically consists of a group of about five to eight people who interact with one another, with their "set advisor" (a knowledgeable person about the action learning process who facilitates the sets learning process), with their "client" (the person who owns the problem being confronted by the set), and with their "tutor" (an expert who periodically delivers needed knowledge to the set and encourages the members to ask insightful questions). It is interesting to note that the educational psychology literature contains made articles about a new instructional method known variously as *collaborative learning* and *cooperative learning*.[131] The method essentially involves students at various performance levels working together in small groups in pursuit of a common goal. These students are responsible for one another's learning in addition to their own.

No studies, to our knowledge, have been conducted on the optimal peer group size for training effectiveness. However, since it is known that enactive mastery is critical to bringing about high self-efficacy (see Chapter 8), it would appear safe to conclude that the training class must be small enough to allow ample practice with the subject matter being taught.

Similarly, no studies to our knowledge have been conducted on the optimal composition of the training group in terms of learning effectiveness. However, there is indirect evidence suggesting that the trainees should be comparable in attitude and skill prior to entering the training class. For example, the mere presence of a highly confident person can sometimes undermine the effective use of routine skills. Moreover, when people are assigned inferior labels that imply limited competence, they perform activities at which they were skilled less well than when they were not so labeled.

## Supervisory Support

To increase the probability of transfer of training to work in the workplace, supervisors need to reinforce the application of what was learned in training to the job. To do this effectively, the supervisors must be fully aware of the training objectives as well as the content of the training for attaining those objectives. Although we know of no research on the subject, it has been our experience that this can be done effectively when a supervisor or manager serves as either the trainer or co-trainer. This not only increases supervisory understanding of and appreciation for the training, but it increases trainee outcome expectancies that demonstrating the learned skills will be valued by the organization.

When the trainee returns to the job, supervisors should adopt the same strategies as those used by trainers in the classroom. That is, early assignments should be given that allow the employee to experience success in applying their newly acquired skills. The supervisor should continually model these skills. The verbal and nonverbal cues exhibited by the supervisor should connote a positive expectation that the employee will constantly apply the newly acquired knowledge and skills. Moreover, the supervisor should coach the employee to set specific difficult but attainable goals. These goals, as noted earlier, should be made public.

One way to publicize commitment to training objectives is to have the supervisor and the trainee sign a contract which explicitly lists the long-term goals of the training program and the conditions under which the learned behavior will occur on the job.[132] By setting goals in advance, trainees can focus their attention on the important components of the training program content. In addition, having supervisors publicly commit to the objectives of the training program helps increase their investment in the outcome of training. The contractual goals should be specific and measurable so that progress toward the goals can be evaluated through the use of behavior-based performance appraisals such as behavioral observation scales.[133]

## Transfer Climate, Continuous-Learning Culture, and the Learning Organization

Transfer climate has been defined by Rouiller and Goldstein[134] as "those situations and consequences which either inhibit or facilitate the transfer of what has been learned in training to the job situation." They proposed that a positive transfer climate consists of various cues (i.e., goal cues, social cues, task and structural cues, self-control cues) and consequences (i.e., positive and negative feedback, punishment, no feedback) that serve to remind trainees to use their newly acquired knowledge and skills once they return to their jobs. They conducted research that involved new assistant restaurant managers who completed a week-long training program focusing on such topics as employee relations, shift management, customer service, and food preparation and handling. Each new assistant manager was then randomly assigned to one of 102 restaurant units. In those units that had a more positive transfer climate, trainees exhibited more of the trained behaviors even after Rouiller and Goldstein statistically corrected for amount of learning during training and for unit performance. This research underscores the need for training practitioners to assess the transfer climate during their organizational analysis (see Chapter 3) and, if needed, to work on changing the work environment to support subsequent transfer.[135]

Several authors have suggested that a continuous-learning work environment is an important construct for understanding the positive transfer of learned behaviors.[136] A continuous-learning work environment is one where knowledge and skill acquisition is a major responsibility to each employee, learning is supported through social interaction and work relationships, there are formal systems that reinforce achievement and provide opportunities for personal growth, and innovation and competition exists both within and outside the organization. Tracey, Tannenbaum, and Kavanagh[137] conducted a field study involving 200 experienced supermarket department managers who attended a supervisory skills training program. Their findings are important for three reasons. First, they showed that not just transfer climate, but continuous-learning culture as well, were both directly related to the application of newly trained behaviors. Second, they extended Rouiller and Goldstein's[138] findings by showing that the concept of transfer climate generalizes to the training of experienced employees. Third, they confirmed that the social support system (i.e., the encouragement a trainee receives from managers and coworkers) plays a central in facilitating positive transfer.

Closely related to transfer climate and continuous-learning culture is Peter Senge's vision of what he calls "The Learning Organization."[139] According to Senge, "learning organziations" are companies that can overcome inherent obstacles to learning, develop dynamic ways to pinpoint the threats that face them, and can recognize new opportunities. His integrated corporate framework is structured around five basic disciplines:

### Systems Thinking
Rather than focus on snapshots of isolated parts of the organizational system, and wonder why our deepest problems never get solved, systems thinking is a conceptual framework that makes the fuller patterns clearer. It helps us to see how to change them effectively.

### Personal Mastery
People enter businesses as bright, well-educated, high-energy people, full of the desire to make a difference. By the time they're 30, a few are on the "fast track" and the rest "put in their time." In a learning organization, everyone has a high level of personal mastery, which involves continuing clarifying and deepening their personal vision, focusing their energies, developing patience, and seeing reality objectively.

### Mental Models
Mental models are deeply ingrained assumptions, generalizations, or even pictures or images that influence how we understand the world and how we take action. Many insights into new markets or outmoded organizational practices fail to get put into practice because they conflict with powerful people's mental models. The discipline of working with mental models starts with turning the mirror inward as well as learning to unearth our internal pictures of the world. It also includes carrrying on conversations in which people expose their own thinking effectively and make their thinking open to the influence of others.

### Building Shared Vision
In the learning organization, management has a genuine vision (as opposed to the all-to-familiar "vision statement") that are translated into a shared vision that galvanizes everyone in the organization. This shared vision causes people to excel, not because they are told to do so, but because they want to.

### Team Learning
Team learning is vital because teams, not individuals, are the fundamental learning unit in modern organizations, according to Senge. When teams are truly learning, they not only produce extraordinary results, but the individual members are growing more rapidly than could have happened otherwise. The discipline of team learning dialogue, the capacity for team members to suspend assumptions and enter into a genuine "thinking together." This dialogue also involves learning how to recognize the patterns of interactions in teams that undermine learning.

When you think about these disciplines that comprise Senge's learning organization, it should be apparent why such an organization would ensure the transfer of learning.

## FINAL COMMENTS

The underlying theme of this chapter and the preceding chapter is that if training is to be effective, it cannot be viewed as an isolated set of activities within an organization. It must affect and be affected by the organization's culture, strategy, systems, and structure.

Culture refers to the values, often unwritten, that senior-level management wishes to infuse throughout the organization. Included in this culture are written statements regarding the organization's vision and mission. For training to be viewed as effective by senior management, training programs must be tied directly to the vision and mission statements.

Values are not always easily articulated. Vision and mission statements are often expressed very abstractly. Training departments, through an organizational analysis, can be invaluable in developing strategies for clearly communicating and instilling these values throughout a diverse workforce. In short, training objectives must be tied to "business purpose."

Imbedded in strategy are the training processes for attaining the training objectives. The processes must incorporate ways of maximizing trainee learning that take into account demographic and individual differences as well as the transfer of what is learned to the job. The extent to which the latter is accomplished is affected directly by other organizational systems such as staffing, performance appraisal, and compensation.

Staffing can have an adverse effect on training if the people hired and placed in an organization lack the aptitude to learn what is required of them. Training affects staffing in two ways. First, it often serves as the criterion for ascertaining whether the right person or persons were hired in terms of trainability. Second, it develops and facilitates the growth of the aptitudes that the person brings to the organization. Thus, staffing and training are interconnected in that both are designed to increase the probability that employees will be able to execute the corporate strategies that enable the attainment of the organization's goals.

The late Mason Haire, an industrial/organizational psychologist who served on the faculties at Berkeley and MIT, is credited with the maxim, "That which gets measured gets done." Of importance to trainers is this: That which gets appraised and rewarded gets performed on the job. Thus, appraisal and compensation systems can facilitate or hinder transfer of training. Training, in turn, can affect the effectiveness of these two systems by teaching managers how to give constructive feedback to, set specific goals with, and reward people properly. In addition, trainees can help develop appraisal instruments that reflect the organization's values and the behaviors that must be engaged in to implement the corporate strategy for achieving the business's objectives. It is a sad commentary that many organizations often spend too much time developing vision statements and strategy, but spend too little time on the systems that need to be put into place to ensure that people can and will implement the mission.

It was Chandler[140] who originally pointed out that structure usually follows strategy or, more precisely, that a strategy of diversity fosters a decentralized structure. A decentralized structure characterizes many of today's organizations. The result could be fragmented training programs and an inflation of training budgets to meet the needs of relatively autonomous businesses within the organization. Training departments can bring unity to such situations by retaining a focus on the overall cultural values and vision of the organization. This can be done by getting the key managers from each business to reach consensus on the communalities, ensuring that the appraisal and reward systems reinforce the organizational demonstration of this knowledge and skill, and removing barriers in the environment to this demonstration. In Chapter 5, we discuss the criteria and measurement designs for determining training success.

---

## ENDNOTES

1. P. C. Ross, "A Relationship Between Training Efficiency and Employee Selection," *Improving Human Performance 3* (1974): 108–17.

2. M. D. Mumford, J. L. Weeks, F. D. Harding, and E. A. Fleishman, "Relations Between Student Characteristics, Course Content, and Training Outcomes: An Integrative Modeling Effort," *Journal of Applied Psychology 73* (1988): 443–56.

3. M. J. Ree and J. A. Earles, "Predicting Training Success: Not Much More than g," *Personnel Psychology 44* (1991): 321–32.

4. J. A. Cannon-Bowers, E. Salas, S. I. Tannenbaum, and J. E. Mathieu, "Toward Theoretically Based Principles of Training Effectiveness: A Model and Initial Experimental Investigation," *Military Psychology 7* (1995): 141–64.

5. K. A. Hanisch and C. L. Hulin, "Two-Stage Sequential Selection Procedures Using Ability Performance: Incremental Validity of Behavioral Consistency Measures," *Personnel Psychology 47* (1994): 767–85.

6. J. E. Driskell, J. Hogan, E. Salas, and B. Hoskin, "Cognitive and Personality Predictors of Training Performance," *Military Psychology 6* (1994): 31–46.

7. P. Warr and D. Bunce, "Trainee Characteristics and the Outcomes of Open Learning," *Personnel Psychology 48* (1995): 347–75.

8. R. A. Noe and N. Schmitt, "The Influence of Trainer Attitudes on Training Effectiveness: Test of a Model," *Personnel Psychology 39* (1986): 497–523.

9. W. D. Hicks and R. J. Klimoski, "The Process of Entering Training Programs and Its Effects on Training Outcomes." Paper presented at the 44th annual meeting of the Academy of Management, Boston, 1984.

10. J. J. Martocchio, "Effects of Conceptions of Ability on Anxiety, Self-Efficacy, and Learning in Training," *Journal of Applied Psychology 79* (1994): 819–25.

11. J. J. Martocchio, "Microcomputer Usage as an Opportunity: The Influence of Context in Employee Training," *Personnel Psychology 45* (1992): 529–51.

12. Ibid., p. 540.

13. Ibid.

14. D. H. Ryman and R. J. Biersner, "Attitudes Predictive of Diving Training Success," *Personnel Psychology 28* (1975): 181–88.

15. M. E. Gordon and S. L. Cohen, "Training Behavior as a Predictor of Trainability," *Personnel Psychology 26* (1973): 261–72.

16. A. I. Siegel, "The Miniature Job Training and Evaluation Approach: Additional Finding," *Personnel Psychology 36* (1983): 41–56.

17. R. R. Reilly and W. R. Manese, "The Validation of a Minicourse for Telephone Company Switching Technicians," *Personnel Psychology 32* (1979): 83–90.

18. Hanisch and Hulin, "Two-Stage Sequential Selection Procedures Using Ability Performance."

19. I. T. Robertson and S. Downs, "Work-Sample Tests of Trainability: A Meta-Analysis," *Journal of Applied Psychology 74* (1989): 402–07.

20. Ibid.

21. Driskell, Hogan, Salas, and Hoskin, "Cognitive and Personality Predictors of Training Performance."

22. K. Ivancic and B. Hesketh, "Making the Best of Errors During Training," *Training Research Journal 1* (1995/1996): 103–25.

23. T. Dormann and M. Frese, "Error Training: Replication and the Function of Exploratory Behavior," *International Journal of Human–Computer Interaction 6* (1994): 365–72; M. Frese, F. Brodbeck, T. Heinbokel, C. Mooser, E. Schleiffenbaum, and P. Theimann, "Errors in Training Computer Skills: On the Positive Function of Errors," *Human Computer Interaction 6* (1991): 77–93; and S. B. Sitkin, "Learning Through Failure: The Strategy of Small Doses," in B. M. Staw and L. L. Cummings (ed.), *Research in Organizational Behavior* (Greenwich, CT: JAI Press, 1992): 484–91.

24. S. L. Feinzig, "Individual Differences in Feedback Preferences: Development of a Questionnaire." Paper presented at the 8th annual meeting of the Society for Industrial and Organizational Psychology, San Francisco, CA, 1993; R. Fuller, "Learning to Make Errors: Evidence from a Driving Task Simulation," *Ergonomics 33* (1990): 1241–50; and R. M. Hogarth, B. J. Gibbs, C. R. M. McKenzie, and M. A. Marquis, "Learning from Feedback: Exactingness and Incentives," *Journal of Experimental Psychology: Learning, Memory, and Cognition 17* (1991): 734–52.

25. G. Phye, "Schemata Training and Transfer of an Intellectual Skill," *Journal of Educational Psychology 81* (1989): 347–52; and G. Phye and C. Sanders, "Advice and Feedback: Elements of Practice for Problem Solving," *Contemporary Educational Psychology 19* (1994): 286–301.

26. S. W. J. Kozlowski, S. M. Gully, E. A. Smith, K. G. Brown, M. Mullins, and A. E. Williams, "Sequenced Mastery Goals and Advanced Organizers: Enhancing the Effects of Practice," in K. A. Smith-Jentsch (chair), When, how, and why does practice make perfect? Symposium conducted at the 11th Annual Conference of the Society for Industrial and Organizational Psychology, San Diego, CA, 1996.

27. K. A. Smith-Jentsch and S. I. Tannenbaum, "Training Research on Guided Self-Correction for Shipboard Teams." Presentation made to the TADMUS Tactical Advisory Board Naval Command, Control, and Ocean Surveillance Center, 1995.

28. J. Jacobs, C. Prince, R. Hays, and E. Salas, "Flight Simulator Training Effectiveness: A Meta-Analysis," *Military Psychology 4* (1992): 63–74.

29. J. E. Driskell, R. P. Willis, and C. Copper, "Effect of Overlearning on Retention," *Journal of Applied Psychology 77* (1992): 615–22.

30. Warr and Bunce, "Trainee Characteristics and the Outcomes of Open Learning."

31. J. Stewart and R. Winter, "Open and Distance Learning," in S. Truelove (ed.), *Handbook of Training and Development* (Oxford: Blackwell, 1992).

32. R. Strauch, "Training the Whole Person," *Training & Development Journal 38* (1984): 82–86.

33. J. C. Naylor and G. D. Briggs, "The Effect of Task Complexity and Task Organization on the Relative Efficiency of Part and Whole Training Methods," *Journal of Experimental Psychology 65* (1963): 217–24.

34. E. A. Fleishman, "On the Relationship Between Abilities, Learning, and Human Performance," *American Psychologist 27* (1972): 1017–32.

35. R. B. Ammons, *Knowledge of Performance, Survey of Literature, Some Possible Applications and Suggested Experimentation* (WADC Technical Report 54–14, Wright Air Development Center, 1954); and J. Arnett, "The Role of Knowledge of Results in Learning: A Survey," *U.S. NAVTRADEVCEN Technical Document Report* 342–43 (May 1961).

36. E. A. Locke and G. P. Latham, "Work Motivation and Satisfaction: Light at the End of the Tunnel," *Psychological Science 1* (1990): 240–46.

37. K. N. Wexley and C. L. Thornton, "Effect of Verbal Feedback of Test Results upon Learning," *Journal of Educational Research 66,* no. 3 (1972): 119–21.

38. G. P. Latham and K. N. Wexley, *Increasing Productivity Through Performance Appraisal* (Reading, MA: Addison-Wesley, 1994).

39. J. J. Martocchio and J. Dulebohn, "Performance Feedback Effects in Training: The Role of Perceived Controllability," *Personnel Psychology 47* (1994): 357–73.

40. J. J. Martocchio and J. Webster, "Effects of Feedback and Cognitive Playfulness on Performance in Microcomputer Software Training," *Personnel Psychology 45* (1992): 553–78.

41. R. D. Arvey and J. M. Ivancevich, "Punishment in Organizations: A Review, Propositions and Research Suggestions," *Academy of Management Review 5* (1980): 123–32.

42. B. F. Skinner, *Science and Human Behavior* (New York: Free Press, 1953).

43. J. S. Kim and W. C. Hamner, "Effect of Performance Feedback and Goal Setting on Productivity and Satisfaction in an Organizational Setting," *Journal of Applied Psychology 61* (1976): 48–57.

44. E. W. Morrison and E. Weldon, "The Impact of an Assigned Performance Goal on Feedback Seeking Behavior," *Human Performance 3* (1990): 37–50.

45. Latham and Wexley, *Increasing Productivity Through Performance Appraisal.*

46. F. D. Tucker, "A Study of the Training Needs of Older Workers: Implications for Human Resources Development Planning," *Public Personnel Management 14* (1985): 85–95.

47. E. L. Bernick, R. Kindley, and K. K. Pettit, "The Structure of Training Courses and the Effects of Hierarchy," *Public Personnel Management 13* (1984): 109–19.

48. J. Gordon, "Games Managers Play," *Training 22* (1985): 30–47.

49. C. Berryman-Fink, "Male and Female Managers' Views of the Communication Skills and Training Needs of Women in Management," *Public Personnel Management 14* (1985): 307–13.

50. I. Streker-Seeborg, M. C. Seeborg, and A. Zegeye, "The Impact of Nontraditional Training on the Occupational Attainment of Women," *Journal of Human Resources 19* (1984): 452–71.

51. H. Schuler, "Females in Technical Apprenticeship: Development of Aptitudes, Performance and Self-Concept," in S. E. Newstead, S. H. Irvine, and P. L. Dann (eds.), *Human Assessment: Cognition and Motivation* (The Hague: Nijhoff, 1986).

52. M. Frese, K. Albrecht, and A. Altmann, "The Effects of an Active Development of the Mental Model in the Training Process: Experimental Results in a Word Processing System," *Behavior and Information Technology 7* (1988): 295–304.

53. H. L. Sterns and D. Doverspike, "Aging and the Training and Learning Process," in I. L. Goldstein and Associates (eds.), *Training and Development in Organizations* (San Francisco: Jossey-Bass, 1989): 229–332.

54. E. Belbin and R. M. Belbin, *Problems in Adult Retraining* (London, England: Heineman, 1972); C. Mullen and L. Gorman, "Facilitating Adaptation to Change: A Case Study in Retraining Middle-Aged and Older Workers at Aer Lingus," *Industrial Psychology 15* (1972): 23–29; and F. A Schmidt, M. D. Murphy, and R. Sanders, "Training Older Adults' Free-Recall Rehearsal Strategies, *Journal of Gerontology 36* (1981): 329–37.

55. S. Inglis, *Making the Most Out of Action Learning* (Brookfield, VT: Gower Publishing Limited, 1994).

56. Ibid.

57. R. E. Snow, "Individual Differences and the Design of Educational Programs," *American Psychologist 41* (1986): 1029–39.

58. M. E. Gist, "The Influence of Training Method on Self-Efficacy and Idea Generation Among

Managers," *Personnel Psychology 42* (1989): 787–805; and M. E. Gist, C. Schwoerer, and B. Rosen, "Effects of Alternative Training Methods on Self-Efficacy and Performance in Computer Software Training," *Journal of Applied Psychology 74* (1989): 884–91.

59. A. Bandura, *Social Foundations of Thought and Action* (Upper Saddle River, NJ: Prentice Hall, 1986).

60. A. P. Goldstein and M. Sorcher, *Changing Supervisor Behavior* (New York: Pergamon Press, 1974).

61. T. T. Baldwin, "Effects of Alternative Modeling Strategies on Outcomes of Interpersonal-Skills Training," *Journal of Applied Psychology 77* (1992): 147–54.

62. G. P. Latham and L. M. Saari, "Application of Social-Learning Theory to Training Supervisors Through Behavioral Modeling," *Journal of Applied Psychology 64* (1979): 239–46.

63. R. B. Mann and P. J. Decker, "The Effect of Key Behavior Distinctiveness on Generalization and Recall in Behavior Modeling Training," *Academy of Management Journal 27* (1984): 900–10.

64. Latham and Saari, "Application of Social-Learning Theory to Training Supervisors Through Behavioral Modeling."

65. C. C. Manz and H. P. Sims, "Beyond Imitation: Complex Behavioral and Affective Linkages Resulting from Exposure to Leadership Training Models," *Journal of Applied Psychology 71* (1986): 571–78.

66. P. M. Hogan, M. D. Hakel, and P. J. Decker, "Effects of Trainee-Generated Versus Trainer-Provided Rule Codes on Generalization in Behavior-Modeling Training," *Journal of Applied Psychology 71* (1986): 469–73.

67. P. J. Decker and B. R. Nathan, *Behavior Modeling Training: Principles and Applications* (New York: Praeger, 1985); and Goldstein and Sorcher, *Changing Supervisor Behavior.*

68. T. T. Baldwin, "Effects of Stimulus Variability on Trainee Outcomes," PhD dissertation, Michigan State University, East Lansing, MI (1987).

69. S. I. Tannenbaum and G. Yukl, "Training and Development in Work Organizations," *Annual Review of Psychology 43* (1992): 399–435.

70. S. J. Simon and J. M. Werner, "Computer Training Through Behavior Modeling, Self-Paced, and Instructional Approaches: A Field Experiment," *Journal of Applied Psychology 81* (1996): 648–59.

71. Locke and Latham, "Work Motivation Satisfaction"; and E. A. Locke and G. P. Latham, *A Theory of Goal Setting and Task Performance* (Upper Saddle River, NJ: Prentice Hall, 1984).

72. G. P. Latham and T. W. Lee, "Goal Setting," in E. A. Locke (ed.), *Generalizing from Laboratory to Field Settings: Research Findings for Industrial–Organizational Psychology, Organizational Behavior, and Human Resource Management* (Lexington, MA: Health Lexington, 1986).

73. K. N. Wexley and W. F. Nemeroff, "Effectiveness of Positive Reinforcement and Goal Setting as Methods of Management Development," *Journal of Applied Psychology 60* (1975): 446–50.

74. Bandura, *Social Foundations of Thought and Action.*

75. Gist, Schwoerer, and Rosen, "Effects of Alternative Training Methods on Self-Efficacy and Performance in Computer Software Training."

76. M. E. Gist, C. K. Stevens, and A. G. Bavetta, "Effects of Self-Efficacy and PostTraining Intervention on the Acquisition and Maintenance of Complex Interpersonal Skills," *Personnel Psychology 44* (1991): 837–61.

77. A. M. Saks, "Longitudinal Field Investigation of the Moderating and Medicating Effects of Self-Efficacy on the Relationship Between Training and Newcomer Adjustment," *Journal of Applied Psychology 80* (1995): 211–25.

78. D. Eden and G. Ravid, "Pygmalion v. Self-Expectancy Effects of Instructor and Self-Expectancy on Trainee Performance," *Organizational Behavior and Human Performance 30* (1982): 351–64; and S. I. Tannenbaum, J. E. Mathieu, E. Salas, and J. A. Cannon-Bowers, "Meeting Trainees' Expectations: The Influence of Training Fulfillment on the Development of Commitment, Self-Efficacy, and Motivation," *Journal of Applied Psychology 76* (1991): 759–69.

79. Locke and Latham, "Work Motivation Satisfaction."

80. R. Kanfer and P. Ackerman, "Motivation and Cognitive Abilities: An Integrative Aptitude-Treatment Interaction Approach to Skill Acquisition," *Journal of Applied Psychology Monograph 74* (1989): 657–90.

81. Ibid.

82. S. C. Hayes, I. Rosenfarb, E. Wulfert, E. D. Munt, Z. Korn, and R. D. Zettle, "Self-Reinforcement Effects: An Artifact of Social Standard Setting?" *Journal of Behavior Analysis 18* (1985): 201–14.

83. J. R. Hollenbeck, C. R. William, and H. J. Klein, "An Empirical Examination of the Antecedents to Commitment to Difficult Goals," *Journal of Applied Psychology 74* (1989): 18–28.

84. B. F. Skinner, *Contingencies of Reinforcement* (New York: Appleton-Century-Crofts, 1969).

85. G. P. Latham, "Behavioral Approaches to the Training Process," in I. L. Goldstein and Associates (eds.), *Training and Development in Organizations* (San Francisco: Jossey-Bass, 1989): 256–95.

86. G. P. Latham and D. L. Dossett, "Designing Incentive Plans for Unionized Employees: A Comparison of Continuous and Variable Ratio Reinforcement Schedules," *Personnel Psychology 31* (1978): 47–61; and G. Yukl, K. N. Wexley, and J. D. Seymore, "Effectiveness of Pay Incentives Under Variable Ratio and Continuous Reinforcement Schedules," *Journal of Applied Psychology 56* (1972): 19–23.

87. D. R. Ilgen and H. G. Klein, "Organizational Behavior," *Annual Review of Psychology 40* (1989): 327–51.

88. T. T. Baldwin, R. J. Magjuka, and B. T. Loher, "The Perils of Participation: Effects of Choice of Training on Trainee Motivation and Learning," *Personnel Psychology 44* (1991): 51–65.

89. Noe and Ford, "Emerging Issues and New Directions for Training Research."

90. K. A. Smith-Jentsch, F. G. Jentsch, S. C. Payne, and E. Salas, "Can Pretraining Experiences Explain Individual Differences in Learning?" *Journal of Applied Psychology 81* (1996): 110–16.

91. J. D. Facteau, G. H. Dobbins, J. E. A. Russell, R. T. Ladd, and J. D. Kudisch, "The Influence of General Perceptions of the Training Environment on Pretraining Motivation and Perceived Training Transfer," *Journal of Management 21* (1995): 1–25.

92. M. Quiñones, "Pretraining Context Effects: Training Assignment as Feedback," *Journal of Applied Psychology 80* (1995): 226–38.

93. M. L. Broad and J. W. Newstrom, *Transfer of Training: Action-Packed Strategies to Ensure Payoff from Training Investments* (Reading, MA: Addison-Wesley, 1992).

94. Ibid.

95. A. Trost, "They May Love It but Will They Use It?" *Training & Development Journal 39* (1985): 78–81.

96. T. T. Baldwin and J. K. Ford, "Transfer of Training: A Review and Directions for Future Research," *Personnel Psychology 41* (1988): 63–105.

97. A. A. Huczynski and J. W. Lewis, "An Empirical Study into the Learning-Transfer Process in Management Training," *Journal of Management Studies 17* (1980): 227–40.

98. M. S. Leifer and J. W. Newstrom, "Solving the Transfer of Training Problems," *Training & Development Journal,* August 1980, 34–46.

99. C. N. Jackson, "Training's Role in the Process of Planned Change," *Training & Development Journal 39* (1985): 70–74.

100. Leifer and Newstrom, "Solving the Transfer of Training Problems."

101. P. E. Tesluk, J. L. Farr, J. E. Mathieu, and R. J. Vance, "Generalization of Employee Involvement Training to the Job Setting: Individual and Industrial Effects," *Personnel Psychology 48* (1995): 607–32.

102. K. N. Wexley and D. G. McCellin, "The Effects of Varying Training Task Difficulty on Training Transfer." Paper presented at the 95th Annual Convention of the American Psychological Association, New York, 1987.

103. J. K. Ford, M. A. Quiñones, D. J. Sego, and J. S. Sorra, "Factors Affecting the Opportunity to Perform Trained Tasks on the Job," *Personnel Psychology 45* (1992): 511–27; and E. M. Smith, J. K. Ford, D. A. Weissbein, S. M. Gully, and E. Salas, "The Effects of Goal Orientation, Metacognition, and Practice Strategies on Learning Outcomes and Training Transfer." Paper presented at the annual convention of the Society for Industrial and Organizational Psychology, Orlando, FL, 1992.

104. T. B. Green, J. T. Knippen, and J. P. Vincelette, "The Practice of Management: Knowledge Versus Skills," *Training & Development Journal 39* (1985): 56–58.

105. A. P. Brief and J. R. Hollenbeck, "An Exploratory Study of Self-Regulating Activities and Their Effect on Job Performance," *Journal of Occupational Behavior 6* (1985): 197–208.

106. G. P. Latham, "Human Resource Training and Development," *Annual Review of Psychology 39* (1988): 545–82.

107. G. P. Latham and C. A. Frayne, "Increasing Job Attendance Through Training in Self-Management: A Review of Two Studies," *Journal of Applied Psychology 74* (1989): 411–16.

108. M. E. Gist, A. G. Bavetta, and C. K. Stevens, "Transfer Training Method: Its Influence on Skill Generalization, Skill Repetition, and Performance Level," *Personnel Psychology 43* (1990): 501–23.

109. M. C. Wittrock and A. A. Lumsdaine, "Instructional Psychology," *Annual Review of Psychology 28* (1977): 417–59.

110. K. N. Wexley and T. T. Baldwin, "Posttraining Strategies for Facilitating Positive Transfer: An Empirical Investigation," *Academy of Management Journal 29* (1986): 503–20.

111. Wexley and Nemeroff, "Effectiveness of Positive Reinforcement and Goal Setting as Methods of Management Development."

112. J. M. Werner, A. M. O'Leary-Kelly, T. T. Baldwin, and K. N. Wexley, "Augmenting Behavior-Modeling Training: Testing the Effects of Pre- and Post-Training Interventions," *Human Resource Development Quarterly 5* (1994): 169–83.

113. Ford, Quiñones, Sego, and Sorra, "Factors Affecting the Opportunity to Perform Trained Tasks on the Job."

114. P. L. Garavaglia, "How to Ensure Transfer of Training," *Training & Development,* October 1993, 63–68.

115. R. D. Marx, "Relapse Prevention for Managerial Training: A Model for Maintenance of Behavior Change," *Academy of Management Review 7* (1982): 433–41.

116. K. D. Brownell, G. A. Marlatt, E. Lichtenstein, and G. T. Wilson, "Understanding and Preventing Relapse," *American Psychologist 41* (1986): 765–82.

117. C. Stark, "Ensuring Skills Transfer: A Sensitive Approach," *Training & Development Journal 40* (1986): 50–51; and Wexley and Baldwin, "Posttraining Strategies for Facilitating Positive Transfer."

118. G. P. Latham and S. R. Crandall, "Organizational and Social Influences Affecting Training Effectiveness," in J. E. Morrison (ed.), *Training for Performance* (Chichester, England: Wiley, 1991).

119. Bandura, *Social Foundations of Thought and Action.*

120. Leifer and Newstrom, "Solving the Transfer of Training Problems"; and D. G. Robinson and J. C. Robinson, "Breaking Barriers to Skill Transfer," *Training & Development Journal 39* (1985): 82–83.

121. R. L. Henemen, "Merit Pay Research," in G. R. Ferris and K. M. Rowland (eds.), *Research in Personnel and Human Resource Management,* 8th ed. (Greenwich, CT: JAI Press, 1990): 203–63; and G. P. Latham and V. L. Huber, "Problems Encountered in Pay Research," *Journal of Organization Behavior Management* (in press).

122. Robinson and Robinson, "Breaking Barriers to Skill Transfer."

123. T. Caplow, *Managing an Organization* (New York: Holt, 1983). *Careers in Management: A Video-Based Self-Directed Management Development System.* Sterling Institute, Washington, DC.

124. L. H. Peters, E. J. O'Connor, and J. R. Eulberg, "Situational Constraints: Sources, Consequences, and Future Considerations," in J. Ferris and K. Rowland (eds.), *Research in Personnel and Human Resources Management 3* (1985): 79–114.

125. L. H. Peters, M. B. Chassie, H. R. Lindholm, E. J. O'Connor, and C. R. Kline, "The Joint Influence of Situational Constraints and Goal Settings of Performance and Affective Outcomes," *Journal of Management 8* (1982): 7–20.

126. Robinson and Robinson, "Breaking Barriers to Skill Transfer."

127. W. M. Evan, "Peer-Group Interaction and Organizational Socialization: A Study of Employee Turnover," *American Sociological Review 28* (1963): 436–40.

128. J. Piaget, *Judgment and Reasoning in the Child* (London: Routledge and Kegan Paul, 1928).

129. R. W. Revans, *Action Learning* (London: Blond & Briggs, 1980).

130. Inglis, *Making the Most Out of Action Learning.*

131. A. A. Gokhale, "Collaborative Learning Enhances Critical Thinking," *Journal of Technology Education 7* (1995): 1–8; and D. W. Johnson, R. T. Johnson, and E. J. Holubec, *Cooperation in the Classroom,* 6th ed. (Edina, MN: Interaction Book Company, 1993).

132. Leifer and Newstrom, "Solving the Transfer of Training Problems."

133. Latham and Wexley, *Increasing Productivity Through Performance Appraisal.*

134. J. Z. Rouiller and I. L. Goldstein, "The Relationship Between Organizational Transfer Climate and Positive Transfer of Training," *Human Resource Development Quarterly 4* (1993): 377–90.

135. Tannenbaum and Yukl, "Training and Development in Work Organizations."

136. S. S. Dubin, "Maintaining Competence Through Updating," in S. L. Willis and S. S. Dubin (eds.), *Maintaining Professional Competence* (San Francisco: Jossey-Bass, 1990): 9–43; J. M. Juran and F. M. Gyrna, *Quality Planning and Analysis* (New York: McGraw-Hill, 1993); R. A. Noe and J. K. Ford, "Emerging Issues and New Directions for Training Research," in G. R. Ferris and K. M. Rowland (eds.), *Research in Personnel and Human Resource Management* (Greenwich, CT: JAI Press, 1992); J. M. Rosow and R. Zager, *Training—The Competitive Edge* (San Francisco: Jossey-Bass, 1988); and P. M. Senge, *The Fifth Discipline: The Art and Practice of the Learning Organization* (New York: Currency Doubleday, 1990).

137. J. B. Tracey, S. I. Tannenbaum, and M. J. Kavanagh, "Applying Trained Skills on the Job: The Importance of the Work Environment," *Journal of Applied Psychology 80* (1995): 239–52.

138. Rouiller and Goldstein, "The Relationship Between Organizational Transfer Climate and Positive Transfer of Training."

139. Senge, *The Fifth Discipline.*

140. A. D. Chandler, *Strategy and Structure: Chapters and the History of the American Industrial Enterprise* (Cambridge, MA: MIT Press, 1962).

# CHAPTER

# Evaluating Training Programs

5

Once the organizational analysis has been completed and steps have been taken to maximize trainees' learning, the training specialist's attention should shift to the way or ways the actual effectiveness of the training will be discerned. Typically, the training and development is reviewed with one or two vice presidents at the corporate office, various managers in the field, and perhaps a group of prospective trainees. If the program looks good, the organization uses it. In fact, the program may be used again and again until it becomes all but institutionalized. It continues to be used until someone in a position of authority decides that the program has outlived its usefulness. All of this is done on the basis of opinion and judgment. In the end, no one really knows whether the training attained the objective(s) for which it was designed. The result can be an ineffective training program that is perpetuated or an effective program that is terminated or modified inappropriately.

The objective of this chapter is to answer the question, "How can training programs be evaluated?" First, we discuss the various criteria or measures that can be used in evaluating training programs. Then, we review the various ways of designing the evaluation procedures. Finally, we describe the measurement process itself.

## MEASURES OF TRAINING EFFECTIVENESS

The effectiveness of a training program can be evaluated using Kirkpatrick's[1] taxonomy of measures (i.e., reaction, learning, behavioral, and results), as well as utility analysis. Before discussing each of these measures, let's talk about how often they are used by looking at the *2000 ASTD State of the Industry Report*. This report provides the most comprehensive review available of employer-provided training in the United States. The report is based on the findings of the ASTD (American Society for Training and Development) Benchmarking Service, an annual process that collects information from all types of organizations on the nature of their training expenditures and practices. The 2000 report shares findings from 501 U.S. organizations (out of a total of more than 1,200 worldwide) that participated in the Benchmarking Service in 1999 by providing data on training activities for the previous year. As part of their survey, the Benchmarking Service asked participants to report on their evaluation methods using Kirkpatrick's four levels of evaluation. The results showed that about three-fourth of the organizations (77 percent) used reaction measures in 1998. In addition, more than a third (36 percent) used learning evaluations, and a small minority of organizations (15 percent and 8 percent, respectively) used the other two levels of evaluation—behavior and results. It is interesting to note that these measures were up slightly from the previous year's figures.

## Reactions

Reaction criteria measure how well the participants liked the program, including its content, the trainer, the methods used, and the surroundings in which the training took place. The ASTD conducted a survey to determine the evaluation practices of several large organizations. They found that almost all of the companies reported that they collected trainee reactions, while only 10 percent reported evaluating trainees' behavioral improvements back on their jobs.[2]

When reaction criteria are used, the specific trainee reactions the organization is interested in examining should be decided on at the time the training program is being developed. Unless reaction objectives are established, irrelevant data are likely to be gathered from the trainees. One might, for instance, gather information about how much trainees enjoyed the training, when enjoyment per se was not a primary objective of the program.

Once specific reaction objectives are formulated, a comment sheet similar to the one presented in Figure 5.1 can be designed. It should elicit reactions to training objectives, permit anonymous answers, and allow the trainees to write additional comments not covered by the questions. In addition, two or three items that have no relationship to the training program might be included on the reaction questionnaire to determine whether the trainees are responding thoughtfully or blindly (e.g., everything was great or the converse). For example, suppose a training program was designed to teach finance and accounting to nonfinancial managers. We would not expect the responses to items dealing with basic accounting, budgeting, and inventory valuation (assuming that the training program was a good one) to be the same as responses to irrelevant items dealing with data processing techniques or the cost effectiveness of various computer storage systems. If there are no significant differences between the responses to the two sets of items (e.g., relevant versus irrelevant ones), we know that the reaction measures are somehow contaminated.

The form shown in Figure 5.1 has been used by the training staff of an electric company for gathering trainee reactions to a supervisory training program. As you can see, the training staff was interested in reactions to the utility

**Evaluation Questionnaire**
(Please return this form unsigned to the Training and Development Group)

1. Considering everything, how would you rate this program? (Check one)
   Unsatisfactory _____ Satisfactory _____ Good _____ Outstanding _____

   Please explain briefly the reasons for the rating you have given:

2. Were your expectations (Check one) exceeded _____ matched _____ fallen below _____?

3. Are you going to recommend this training program to other members of your department?
   Yes _____ No _____. If you checked "yes," please describe the job titles held by the people to whom you would recommend this program.

   _____

   _____

4. Please rate the relative value (1 = very valuable; 2 = worthwhile; 3 = negligible) of the following components of the training program to you:

   | | | | |
   |---|---|---|---|
   | Videocassettes | _____ | Role-playing exercises | _____ |
   | Workbooks | _____ | Small group discussions | _____ |
   | Small group discussions | _____ | Lectures | _____ |
   | Cases | _____ | Readings: Articles | _____ |

5. Please rate the main lecturer's presentation (1 = not effective; 2 = somewhat effective; 3 = effective) in terms of:

   | | |
   |---|---|
   | Ability to communicate | _____ |
   | Emphasis on key points | _____ |
   | Visual aids | _____ |
   | Handout materials | _____ |

6. Please rate the following cases, readings, and videocassettes by placing a check mark in the appropriate column:

   | | Excellent | Good | Fair | Poor |
   |---|---|---|---|---|
   | Overcoming Resistance to Change | | | | |
   | Reviewing Performance Goals | | | | |
   | Setting Performance Goals | | | | |
   | Handling Employee Complaints | | | | |
   | Improving Employee Performance | | | | |
   | Slade Co. | | | | |
   | Superior Slate Quarry | | | | |
   | McGregor's Theory X and Y | | | | |
   | Henry Manufacturing | | | | |
   | First Federal Savings | | | | |
   | Claremont Industries | | | | |

**FIGURE 5.1** An Example of a Trainee Reaction Questionnaire

7. Was the ratio of lectures to cases (Check one): High _____ OK _____ Low _____?

8. Were the videocassettes pertinent to your work? (Check one)

   To most of my work? _____
   To some of my work? _____
   To none of my work? _____

9. To help the training director and the staff provide further improvements in future programs, please give us your frank opinion of each case discussion leader's contribution to your learning. (Place your check marks in the appropriate boxes.)

| | Excellent | Above Average | Average | Below Average | Poor |
|---|---|---|---|---|---|
| DAVIS | | | | | |
| GLEASON | | | | | |
| LAIRD | | | | | |
| MARTIN | | | | | |
| PONTELLO | | | | | |
| SHALL | | | | | |
| SOMMERS | | | | | |
| WILSON | | | | | |
| ZIMMER | | | | | |

10. How would you evaluate your participation in the program? (Check)

    Overall workload:      Too heavy _____   Just right _____   Too light _____
    Case preparation:      Too much _____   Just right _____   Too little _____
    Homework assignments:  Too heavy _____   Just right _____   Too little _____

11. What suggestions do you have for improving the program?

    _____

    _____

    _____

12. Please add any additional comments, criticisms, or suggestions that you think might be helpful for the training group to know before scheduling future programs.

    _____

    _____

    _____

**FIGURE 5.1** *(Continued)*

of the training, the relative value of different components of the program, and the effectiveness of the head lecturer and the case leaders. A few items irrelevant to the program were included within questions 6 and 9.

A somewhat different approach for collecting trainee reactions is used by the Life Office Management Association (LOMA), a nonprofit organization supported by insurance companies. By using the type of form shown in Figure 5.2, LOMA gives its trainees an opportunity to select at the beginning of the program the course objectives that specially apply to them, a means of expressing the relative importance of each objective selected, and a way of expressing how well each objective has been fulfilled.[3]

Favorable reactions to a training program do not guarantee that behavior of the trainees will change as a result of the program.[4] Nevertheless, reaction measures are important to collect for several reasons.

First, certain types of reaction measures have been found to correlate moderately with immediate learning. Utility-type reaction measures (e.g., "To what degree will this training influence your ability later to perform your job?", "Was this training job relevant?", "Was the training of practical value?") that tap the perceived usefulness of the training program correlate stronger with immediate learning than do affective-type measures ("To what extent did you find this training to be enjoyable?") that tap trainees' liking of the training.[5]

Second, positive reactions help ensure organizational support for a program. Many programs have been canceled prematurely by top management because a few participants told them, "This program was a waste of time."

Third, these measures can be used by the training staff to assess the success of their efforts, and to provide them with information that may help them plan future programs. In addition, a comment sheet should be obtained on each trainer as well as on each subject taught. In this way, program weaknesses as perceived by trainees can be pinpointed. Figure 5.3 shows a form that has been used for obtaining trainee reactions to various instructors.

Fourth, favorable reactions can enhance a trainee's motivation to learn.[6] That is, trainees are likely to be motivated to learn material when they believe the program is useful to them and they perceive the learning experience to be a positive one.

Fifth, it is sometimes useful to take the reactions of particular groups of trainees and analyze them separately. For example, it may be informative to compare the assessments of trainees from the maintenance department with those given by trainees from production. The trainers may also want to compare the responses of older versus younger, line versus staff, or unionized versus nonunionized employees to particular facets of the program or to the program as a whole.

Sixth, it is important to collect reaction measures again several months after the training program has taken place. This allows the trainee to assess realistically the effectiveness of the training for his or her job. It also permits the training staff to see if the ratings collected immediately after training were

Systems Design
Workshop

Your Name _____

| OBJECTIVES | ✔ | DEGREE OF IMPORTANCE × | DEGREE OF FULFILLMENT = | INDEX OF OBJECTIVE FULFILLMENT |
|---|---|---|---|---|
| Check those that are important to you. (Ignore those that are not.) | | *Weight each checked objective for its importance to you, allocating exactly 100 points *among* all of those checked. A total of 100 points *must* be assigned. | **Rate each objective you checked (from 0–10) to indicate how well it was fulfilled. | |
| Be able to | | | | |
| 1. Identify and describe the various elements in the systems development process and understand their significance. | | | | |
| 2. Understand the use and value of systems feasibility studies. | | | | |
| 3. Identify essential considerations (critical factors) in a systems design problem. | | | | |
| 4. Design a management report. | | | | |
| 5. Design an input form. | | | | |
| 6. Develop an overall systems flow. | | | | |

**FIGURE 5.2**    A Reaction Form Used by the Life Office Management Association (LOMA)

| | | | |
|---|---|---|---|
| 7. Understand the objectives and techniques of designing input/output controls. | | | |
| 8. Select among and be able to use basic database structures. | | | |
| 9. Prepare an oral presentation of design recommendations for management. | | | |
| 10. Exchange ideas with other participants. | | | |
| | 100 | TOTAL = | |

**FIGURE 5.2** *(Continued)*

\* If you checked only one objective, assign all 100 points to it; if you checked two objectives, spread the 100 points between them, etc.

\*\* 0 is unsatisfactory; 1–2 poor; 3–4 below average; 5 average; 6 above average; 7 good; 8 very good; 9–10 excellent.

*Source:* D. Fast, "A New Approach to Quantifying Training Program Effectiveness," *Training & Development Journal* 28:9 (1974): 8–14. Reproduced by special permission from the September 1974 *Training & Development Journal.* Copyright 1974 by the American Society for Training and Development, Inc. All rights reserved.

inflated due to enthusiasm for the trainers, or the enjoyment derived from sharing experiences with new and old acquaintances. Nevertheless, collecting reaction measures immediately after training is important for two reasons: (1) Memory distortion can affect measures taken at a later point, and (2) there is often a low return rate for questionnaires mailed to people long after they have completed the training.

A different type of reaction measure is the *self-report.* Here, trainees are asked to evaluate themselves on variables related to the purpose of the training such as skill in conference leadership, budgeting, or time management. Research suggests that valid self-report measures for evaluating training programs can be collected as follows: At the end of the training program, ask each participant to complete a self-report questionnaire, answering each item as viewed at this time (i.e., "Post" rating) and as viewed at the start of training (i.e., "Then" rating).[7]

**Rating Scale for Instruction**

TRAINING COURSE: _____

DATE STARTED: _____

LOCATION: _____

TRAINER: _____

NOTE TO TRAINERS: To keep conditions as nearly uniform as possible, it is important that *no instructions* be given to the trainees. The rating scale should be passed out without comment.

NOTE TO TRAINEES: Following is a list of qualities that tend to determine if the trainer (instructor) is effective or ineffective. Of course, nobody approaches the ideal in all of these qualities, but some do so more than others. You can provide information that will be used in improving subsequent training programs by rating your trainer on the qualities shown below. Please circle one of the ten numbers along the line at the point which most nearly describes him or her with reference to the quality you are considering.

This rating is entirely confidential. Do not sign your name or make any other mark on the paper that could serve to identify yourself.

| | | | | | | | | | | | |
|---|---|---|---|---|---|---|---|---|---|---|---|
| Interest in Subject . . . . . . . . . . . . . | 10 | 9 | 8 | 7 | 6 | 5 | 4 | 3 | 2 | 1 | |
| | Always appears full of his subject. | | | Seems mildly interested. | | | | Subject seems irksome to him. | | | |
| Considerate Attitude Toward Trainees . . . . . . | 10 | 9 | 8 | 7 | 6 | 5 | 4 | 3 | 2 | 1 | |
| | Always courteous and considerate. | | | Tries to be considerate, but finds this difficult at times. | | | | Entirely unsympathetic and inconsiderate. | | | |
| Stimulating Intellectual Curiosity . . . . . . . . . . | 10 | 9 | 8 | 7 | 6 | 5 | 4 | 3 | 2 | 1 | |
| | Inspires students to independent effort; creates desire for investigation. | | | Occasionally inspiring; creates mild interest. | | | | Destroys interest in subject; makes work repulsive. | | | |
| Presentation of Subject Matter . . . . . . . . . . . . . | 10 | 9 | 8 | 7 | 6 | 5 | 4 | 3 | 2 | 1 | |
| | Clear, definite, and forceful. | | | Sometimes mechanical and monotonous. | | | | Indefinite, uninvolved, and monotonous. | | | |
| Relevance . . . . . . . . . . | 10 | 9 | 8 | 7 | 6 | 5 | 4 | 3 | 2 | 1 | |
| | Ties ideas and facts back to the job. | | | Occasionally goes off onto irrelevant tangents. | | | | Is too academic and school-like. | | | |
| Depth of Knowledge . . . | 10 | 9 | 8 | 7 | 6 | 5 | 4 | 3 | 2 | 1 | |
| | Knows the area thoroughly. | | | Sometimes has to look things up to answer questions. | | | | Kows little more than trainees. | | | |

**FIGURE 5.3** An Example of a Form for Evaluating Trainers

For example, in evaluating a training program to improve interviewing skills, each workshop participant was asked to rate twice (i.e., "Post" and "Then") the degree to which he or she possessed the following six interviewing skills: questioning techniques, interviewing structure, interviewer supportiveness, techniques of rapport building, active listening, and attention to relevant material.[8] The difference between the two sets of self-report measures serves as a way of assessing the trainees' reactions to the usefulness of the program. Later in this chapter we discuss problems that might be encountered when using self-report measures of change.

## Learning

Learning criteria assess the knowledge gained by the trainees. The results of research indicate that trainees' learning correlates moderately with immediate job behavior.[9] Knowledge is typically measured by paper-and-pencil tests. The following multiple-choice items are examples of those that might be used in a test of electrical knowledge at the conclusion of a skilled trades training program:

1. On a DC motor starter, what is the function of a field accelerating delay?
   (a) to prevent excessive current from damaging the armature
   (b) to protect the field coils
   (c) to prevent the motor from starting if the field current is open
   (d) to stabilize motor RPM
2. To phase two three-phase feeders together, you would use a(n)
   (a) tachometer
   (b) pyrometer
   (c) oscilloscope
   (d) voltmeter

Quite often, true/false questions are used because they are relatively easy to compose. Multiple-choice and true/false questions assess the trainee's capacity to recognize information or misinformation put before them rather than using their memory to recall the answers. For this reason, we prefer the completion of fill-in type items like those shown in Figure 5.4.

Performance tests are used to determine if trainees have mastered a particular skill. Figure 5.5 presents the instructions for two different performance tests. One performance test is used to determine whether a mechanical trainee has acquired the skills necessary to assemble a reduction gear properly. The other test is used to assess whether a painter apprentice can use a boatsman chair and a spray gun. Similarly, at the managerial level, trainees might be asked to participate in various role-playing exercises or business games to measure their human relations skill after attending a management development program. A very intriguing way of measuring how well trainees have mastered particular skills is the use of written case studies. For example, three staffing and place-

*Instructions:* Notice that there are seven circles on the print. Notice that there is a list of answers numbered 1 through 12 on the right-hand side of the print. Seven answers are correct; five answers are wrong and do not apply. Write one of these seven correct answers in each of these seven white circles. Use the numbers. Use each number only once.

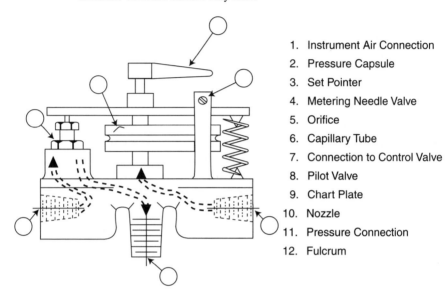

1.  Instrument Air Connection
2.  Pressure Capsule
3.  Set Pointer
4.  Metering Needle Valve
5.  Orifice
6.  Capillary Tube
7.  Connection to Control Valve
8.  Pilot Valve
9.  Chart Plate
10. Nozzle
11. Pressure Connection
12. Fulcrum

**FIGURE 5.4** An Example of a Completion or Fill-In Item

ment classes taught by Navy Civilian Personnel Command (NCPC) instructors had to be rigorously evaluated. To accomplish this, the course goals were distilled into competencies (e.g., trainees understand and can apply the Department of Defense priority placement program when filling vacancies) so that a series of case studies could be written that addressed these competencies. Trainees were asked, three to six months after the training, to describe how they would handle

*MECHANICS:* "You have in front of you a gear reducer, a line shaft, bearings, and coupling. I want you to assemble and adjust the proper alignment so that the finished assembly is a right-hand (or left-hand) driven assembly. Set the coupling gap ⅛″ apart. You do not have to put the grid member in place or fasten the coupling covers. After you are finished, I will ask you where and how the grid member should go in. You will have 45 minutes to complete this job."

*PAINTERS:* "I want you to boost yourself up about 10 feet off the floor using this boatsman chair, and then tie yourself off so that you don't fall. After that, I would like you to hook this spray gun to the air supply, set the regulator to the correct pressure, and then spray this wall."

**FIGURE 5.5** Instructions to Performance Tests for Mechanics and Painters

the case studies if they arose as part of the job. They were scored on their use of the learned competencies in solving the work-related problems.[10]

Regardless of the type of learning test used, it is essential that it be tied directly to the program's learning objectives. As discussed in Chapter 3, these learning objectives should be based on the knowledge that has been determined through the task analysis to be truly necessary prerequisites for performing satisfactorily on the job. For example, there is nothing wrong with an electrician's learning about Ohm's law, but this knowledge may not be essential for functioning effectively as a skilled craftsman. If it is not strictly necessary, then learning Ohm's law should be neither a learning objective nor a test item.

Based on our experience in the training field, measures of learning are important to incorporate in one's evaluation strategy for two reasons. First, by using multiple measures of learning that tap both knowledge and skill mastery, training specialists are better able to pinpoint exactly what content needs to be modified if their training programs don't bring about intended behavioral outcomes.[11] Second, learning exams often have a beneficial impact on both trainees' and trainers' motivation levels. For instance, it was found at General Dynamics during a computer-based manufacturing resource planning program that competency testing not only increased trainees' motivation level, but also kept the trainers on their toes during the actual training process.[12] Apparently, learning measures have the added value of ensuring feelings of accountability on the part of both trainees and trainers.

## Behavior on the Job

The importance of collecting behavioral measures of training effectiveness is illustrated by the following story:

> During the week I was particularly impressed by a foreman named Herman from a Milwaukee company. Whenever a conference leader asked a question requiring a good understanding of human relations principles and techniques, Herman was the first one who raised his hand. He had all the answers in terms of good human relations approaches. I was very impressed and I said to myself, "If I were in industry, I would like to work for a man like Herman." It so happened that I had a first cousin who was working for that company. And oddly enough Herman was his boss. At my first opportunity, I talked with my cousin, Jim, and asked him about Herman. Jim told me that Herman might know all the principles and techniques of human relations, but he certainly did not practice them on the job. He performed like the typical "bull-of-the-woods" who had little consideration for the feelings and ideas of his subordinates. At this time I began to realize there may be a big difference between knowing principles and techniques and using them on the job.[13]

This example illustrates how training programs can effectively disseminate knowledge without providing the skill to do the job effectively. It shows clearly the need for assessing changes in a trainee's overt behavior in addition to the knowledge that was acquired. There may be a large gap between knowing facts or principles and demonstrating them on the job. Likewise, it is possible for trainees to do well on performance tests administered during training, yet not be able or willing to exhibit these same skills on their jobs (i.e., zero transfer of learning). It is therefore important that measures be gathered on how a trainee behaves in the actual job environment.

The following examples illustrate how behavioral measures have been used to evaluate training. First, a program designed to train managers to conduct better appraisal feedback interviews with employees was implemented in an engineering section of the General Electric Company. Two years after the adoption of the program, a questionnaire was used to obtain the employees' views about changes in their managers. The questions shown in Figure 5.6 asked the respondents to compare present conditions with what they were two years ago.

A more behaviorally oriented questionnaire was used to evaluate the effectiveness of a two-month training program for tire store managers. Figure 5.7 presents a portion of this BOS (Behavioral Observation Scales) questionnaire, which was completed by each store manager's district supervisor one year after the program.

An interesting method of rating trainee behavior involves developing job-related scenarios such as the one shown below. This scenario was one of 29 situational items used for evaluating the effectiveness of a two-day training program designed to improve the interpersonal and administrative skills of educators.

**Compared to two years ago:**

|  | (CHECK ONE) | | |
|---|---|---|---|
|  | YES | NO | ? |
| 1. Does your manager have a better understanding of how you perform your job? | | | |
| 2. Does he or she have a better understanding of you as an individual? | | | |
| 3. Does he or she better indicate recognition of your good work? | | | |
| 4. Does he or she better utilize your particular skills? | | | |
| 5. Do you have a better picture of what he or she expects from you in terms of job performance? | | | |
| 6. Do you have a better picture of how you stand with him or her overall? | | | |
| 7. Does he or she discuss your job performance with you more frequently? | | | |
| 8. Do you have a greater opportunity to present your side of a story during those discussions? | | | |
| 9. Does he or she take a greater personal interest in you and your future? | | | |
| 10. Does he or she make a greater effort to help you develop yourself? | | | |

**FIGURE 5.6** An Example of a Behavioral Questionnaire Completed by Subordinates

*Source:* Adapted from C. G. Moon and T. Hariton, "Evaluating an Appraisal and Feedback Training Program," *Personnel,* November–December (1958). New York: American Management Association, Inc., 40.

Store Manager _____

District Supervisor _____

Date _____

INSTRUCTIONS: Please consider the above-named individual's behavior on the job for the past 12 months. Read each statement carefully, and on the basis of your actual observation or on dependable knowledge, circle the number that best indicates the extent to which this particular store manager actually demonstrated each of the following behaviors. For each behavior, a "5" represents "Almost Always" or 95 to 100% of the time. A "4" represents "Frequently" or 85 to 94% of the time. A "3" represents "Sometimes" or 75 to 84% of the time. A "2" represents "Seldom" or 65 to 74% of the time. A "1" represents "Almost Never" or 0 to 64% of the time.

An example of an item is shown below. If the store manager comes to work 95 to 100% of the time you should circle "5."

Example: Comes to work
Almost Never     1          2          3          4          (5)     Almost Always

1. Holds weekly credit collection meetings with his/her sales personnel and credit manager.
   Almost Never     1          2          3          4          5     Almost Always

2. Keeps his or her salespeople informed of competitive conditions in the local market.
   Almost Never     1          2          3          4          5     Almost Always

3. Personally reviews all invoices for correct billing and merchandise received.
   Almost Never     1          2          3          4          5     Almost Always

4. Takes inventory monthly, checks discrepancies, and promptly corrects any items requiring correction.
   Almost Never     1          2          3          4          5     Almost Always

5. When there is a conflict among employees, takes the time to sit down and discuss the causes and resolution.
   Almost Never     1          2          3          4          5     Almost Always

**FIGURE 5.7** An Example of a Behavioral Observation Questionnaire Completed by Supervisors

The administrator receives a letter from a parent objecting to the content of the science section. The section topic is reproduction. The parent objects to his daughter having exposure to such material and demands that something be done. The administrator would (check one):

_____ Ask the teacher to provide handouts, materials, and curriculum content for review

_____ Check the science curriculum for the board-approved approach to reproduction and compare board guidelines to course content

_____ Ask the head of the science department for his/her own opinion about the teacher's lesson plan

_____ Check to see if the parent made similar complaints in the past

The 29 situational items were written to tap the six skill areas (e.g., problem analysis, decisiveness, leadership) taught during the training program. Each of the situational items consisted of a short paragraph describing a typical situation faced by educators and four to six possible responses to the situation. Each of the possible responses were statistically weighted based on the degree to which they differentiated between effective and ineffective educators. For instance, for the scenario above, if a supervisor chose to rate an educator using response 1, the educator received a score of 0; if response 2 was selected, the educator got a score of 2; if response 3 was chosen, a score of −8 was given; and if response 4 was selected, a score of 3 was given.[14]

The appraisal of on-the-job behavior can be collected from various sources such as supervisors, coworkers, or subordinates.[15] This trend of using of multiple sources, known as *360° feedback,*[16] has been extremely popular in recent years for both evaluating training programs and for performance improvement (see Chapter 9 for more information about the use of 360° feedback). The appraisal can take place soon after training, but it should also be done several months later, so that the trainee is given adequate opportunity to put into practice what has been learned during training. Quite often, there is a *sleeper effect;* that is, it takes time for trainees to exhibit on the job what they have acquired during training.

Many training specialists ardently believe that it is infeasible to get a pure ROI (return-on-investment) index of a training program's impact because it is impossible to factor out other things that may have affected the training's impact. For example, at Procter & Gamble, behavioral measures are designed and used to find out from internal customers the degree to which training courses delivered against stated objectives. Another example is Anderson Consulting Education. They use stakeholder expectations to both design and evaluate their training courses. They do this based on the idea that managers know what skills and behaviors their employees need to perform their jobs effectively, and that training them successfully in these areas will bring about bottom-line results.[17] So, they develop behavioral measures to assess these particular skills and behaviors, and then determine whether individuals who have received training are now using them on their jobs.

Years ago, reaction, learning, and behavioral measures were collected from trainees using written questionnaires. Today, more and more organizations are gathering this information through e-mail. Individuals who have been through training simply click 3, 4, or 5 keys on their computers to answer a series of questions that will assess their reactions, learning, and behaviors.

## Results Criteria and Utility Analysis

The objectives of many training programs can be stated in terms of cost-related results or behavioral outcomes rather than the behaviors themselves, for example, a reduction in turnover, an increase in attendance, an increase in quantity and quality of units produced, an increase in sales, and a reduction in accidents. At General Electric, a training program for supervisors was instituted in a manufacturing plant. The cost-related measure used to evaluate the program was an index that reflected the effective utilization of employee and equipment resources by a foreman, calculated by the following formula:

$$\text{Performance} = \frac{\text{Actual Productivity}}{\text{Standard Productivity}}$$

Actual productivity was the production level achieved by a foreman's work group within a production cycle or period. Standard productivity referred to the production level that management had estimated through time and motion study that employees were expected to achieve during a given production period.[18]

To determine the actual dollar value of the training, a utility analysis can be conducted. The concept of utility is synonymous with evaluating a training program in terms of its costs versus its benefits in financial terms.[19] A utility analysis is important because it is possible for a training program to bring about favorable reactions, increase trainee learning, change employee behavior on the job, and improve cost-related results. However, it is also possible that this same training program is *not* worth implementing in an organization because it is not cost effective; its monetary costs outweigh its monetary benefits to the organization.

In order to estimate the utility of any training program, the following formula has been recommended[20]:

$$U = (T')\ (N')\ (d_t)\ (SD_y)\ (1 + V)\ (1 - TAX) - NC\ (1 - TAX)$$

where     $U$ = the dollar value of some training program.

$T'$ = T (the number of years' duration of the training effect on performance) reduced by the Discount Factor (see Table 5.1).

$N'$ = number of people trained who are still employed by the organization in the particular job.

$d_t$ = the true difference in job performance between the average trained and untrained employee expressed in standard deviation (SD) units. Preferably, this should be calculated empirically by using one of the recommended evaluation designs employing a control group discussed later in this chapter. Alternately, it can be estimated from published research literature evaluating the particular training method (see, for example, Burke and Day, 1986).

**TABLE 5.1** Values of the Discount Factor (DF) Adjustment Computed Using Illustrative Combinations of Values for the Discount Rate (i) and the Duration of the Program's Effects (T)

| | | | T | | |
|---|---|---|---|---|---|
| i | 1 | 2 | 5 | 7 | 10 |
| .00 | 1.00 | 2.00 | 5.00 | 7.00 | 10.00 |
| .05 | .95 | 1.86 | 4.33 | 5.79 | 7.72 |
| .10 | .91 | 1.74 | 3.79 | 4.87 | 6.14 |
| .15 | .87 | 1.62 | 3.35 | 4.16 | 5.02 |

*Note:* Table values are computed using the formula

$$DF = \sum_{t=1}^{T} [1/(1+i)^t].$$

*Source:* Reprinted by permission of the publisher, from "Economic Considerations in Estimating the Utility of Human Resource Productivity Improvement Programs," by J. W. Boudreau, *Personnel Psychology 36,* 1983, © Personnel Psychology, Inc., 567. All rights reserved.

$SD_y$ = the standard deviation of job performance in dollars of the untrained (i.e., control) group. It can be estimated by asking a group of people knowledgeable about the particular job to estimate the dollar value of job performance of an employee who falls at the 15th, 50th, and 85th percentile. The dollar difference between the 85th and 50th percentiles or between the 50th and 15th percentiles reveals a measure of the variability (standard deviation) of job performance in dollars of an untrained group of people. An alternative approach is to simply calculate 40 percent of the average salary level on the particular job.

$(1 + V)$ = the effects of variable costs (V) on $SD_y$ (see Table 5.2).

$(1 - TAX)$ = the effects of the organization's marginal tax rate on $SD_y$ and on NC (see Table 5.1).

$N$ = the number of people initially trained, regardless of whether they stayed or left the job.

$C$ = the costs of training for each trainee, including all direct and indirect expenses.

Now, let us apply this formula to estimate the utility of a five-day program used to improve the selling skills of route salespeople who drive around in trucks to promote the company's products to supermarkets and grocery stores.

**TABLE 5.2** **Illustrative Adjustments to Correct Utility Estimates for the Combined Effects of Variable Costs (V) and Taxes (TAX)**

| V | TAX | | | | | |
|---|---|---|---|---|---|---|
| | **0** | **.05** | **.10** | **.30** | **.45** | **.55** |
| .33 | 1.33 | 1.26 | 1.20 | .93 | .73 | .60 |
| .10 | 1.10 | 1.04 | .99 | .77 | .60 | .50 |
| .05 | 1.05 | 1.00 | .94 | .74 | .58 | .47 |
| .00 | 1.00 | .95 | .90 | .70 | .55 | .45 |
| −.05 | .95 | .90 | .86 | .68 | .52 | .43 |
| −.10 | .90 | .86 | .81 | .63 | .50 | .40 |
| −.20 | .80 | .76 | .72 | .56 | .44 | .36 |
| −.30 | .70 | .67 | .63 | .49 | .39 | .32 |
| −.40 | .60 | .57 | .54 | .42 | .33 | .27 |
| −.50 | .50 | .48 | .45 | .35 | .28 | .22 |

*Note:* Table values equal $(1 + V)(1 - TAX)$. These values would be multiplied by the sales value of increased productivity to adjust for variable costs and taxes.

*Source:* Reprinted by permission of the publisher, from "Economic Considerations in Estimating the Utility of Human Resource Productivity Improvement Programs," by J. W. Boudreau, *Personnel Psychology 36*, 1983, © Personnel Psychology, Inc., 562. All rights reserved.

$T = 3$ Suppose it is estimated by management that the effects of this training program last about three years on a typical route salesperson job performance.

$T' = 2.2$ By entering Table 5.1, where $T = 3$ and i (interest rate) = .15, T is discounted to a T′ of 2.2. Remember, all of the money that the company has invested in designing and implementing this training program could have been otherwise invested in other ways such as stocks and bonds. Assuming that this company could have gotten an annual yield of 15 percent on these monetary investments, i = .15.

$N' = 954$ This is the total number of route salespeople who have gone through the training program and are still employed by the company.

$d_t = +1.00$ Suppose we use a Pretest–Posttest Control Group Design (see Figure 5.8) and find that the true difference in job performance between the average trained and untrained route salesperson in standard deviation units is +1.00.

$SD_y = \$14{,}500$ Suppose that the average annual salary of route salespeople in the company is $36,250. Forty percent of this figure is $14,500.

| Group A (Trained) | Measures taken before training | Training | Measures taken after training |
|---|---|---|---|
| Group B (Not Trained) | Measures taken before training | — | Measures taken after training |

**FIGURE 5.8** The Pretest–Posttest Control Group Design

$(1 + V) = 1 + (-.05) = +.95$  In this case, the effects of the training improved the job performance of the route salespeople. This increase in sales performance, in turn, increased variable costs (V) by 5 percent. Thus, the company will derive only +.95, or 95 percent, of the dollar value of this improvement in job performance. Why? Because the route salespeople will receive higher pay in the form of sales commissions.

Conversely, in other training situations, an increase in job performance might reduce variable costs (V) by some percentage. For example, well-trained programmers may produce better programs and also help the company train other programmers who are new and less experienced. In this case, variable costs might be lowered by 5 percent. Now, $(1 + V)$ equals +1.05. Thus, the company will derive 105 percent of the dollar value of the improvement in job performance.

$(1 - TAX) = 43$ percent  Suppose the company's marginal tax rate is 57 percent. So, $1 - TAX$ equals .43. A company's marginal tax rate is a function of its level of profitability in the past.

$N = 1,200$  Suppose this many route salespeople have been trained in the past. As you can see from $N'$, 246 route salespeople have either left the company or else been transferred to other jobs.

$C = \$1,083$  Suppose that a panel of training specialists and company accountants estimated that the total cost of the training program is $1,083 per trainee.

Substituting all of these values into the formula just described tells us that this training program is worth $11,955,530 to the company over a period of 2.2 years with 954 route salespeople trained. This also means that the training program is worth $5,429,331.80 per year and $5,691.12 per trainee.

What kind of a return is the company getting on their training investment? This can easily be calculated by figuring out the benefits/costs per trainee. Thus,

$5,691.12/$1,083 = 525 percent. Simply stated, this training program is yielding in benefits over five times its costs.

There is often a temptation for training specialists to sell the benefits of a proposed training program solely on the basis of anticipated increases in cost-related measures. Although we realize that if human resources hopes to take a place in the strategic management of organizations, it needs to justify things like training and development in cost-effectiveness terms. However, this is not enough. Doing this would be a mistake for at least three reasons.[21] First, although these measures usually serve as excellent indicators of an organization's effectiveness because they are almost always deficient. That is, they often omit important factors for which a person should be held accountable (e.g., team playing as defined by a manager in one district loaning equipment to a manager in another district of the same company). This deficiency is a major criticism of management by objectives (MBO), in which the performance standards or goals are usually set in terms of cost-related targets. Emphasis is placed primarily on tangible results that are perceived to be easily measurable. Consequently, many employees feel that there is an overemphasis on quantitative goals because they are not measured on nor do they receive credit for important aspects of their jobs that cannot be spelled out in quantitative terms. For example, a marketing manager might specify that a major objective of the forthcoming year is to increase the number of accounts by 10 percent in the Vancouver area. A human resources manager, however, would have difficulty expressing the desired end results of a new career development program in percentage figures.

Second, cost-related measures are affected positively as well as adversely by factors beyond the trainee's control. A senior-level manager who returns from an executive development program (see Chapter 9) may find that his or her performance is either lavishly praised or criticized severely even though the obtained results were due more to the relation of the dollar to the yen rather than to his or her own behaviors (e.g., sales based on log exports to Japan).

Third, there are certain training and development programs that are not designed to bring about the tangible bottom-line results in the traditional sense of the word. Outdoor management training (OMT) serves as a good example of where the clarion call for results-oriented evaluation may be misguided.[22] OMT typically consists of a series of high-risk activities, most involving teamwork and problem solving among a group of managers or executives. Interspersed with the activities are debriefing sessions where participants analyze and discuss their feelings, and talk about their learning with one another (see Chapter 9 for further discussion). The objectives of OMT include such things as increasing participant self-awareness and insight, developing supportive communications with others, and building and maintaining effective work teams.

Even utility analysis, despite its current level of sophistication, needs to be viewed with caution. Researchers such as Boudreau[23] and Cascio[24] are among those who advocate utility analysis as a way of developing credible bottom line estimates of the value of training programs that may soften the criticisms of those executives who view training as little more than the source of burdensome overhead expenses. A critical flaw in utility analysis models, however, is that the standard deviation of job performance in terms of dollars (i.e., $SD_y$) is estimated simply by asking the opinion of supervisory employees. According to Dreher and Sackett,[25] (1) there is no evidence that a rational estimate approach to assessing the standard deviation of job performance approximates the true value, (2) agreement among job experts (i.e., supervisors) is not a guarantee that the estimates are valid, and (3) the procedure lacks credibility in that the basis of each supervisor's judgment is unknown. Tenopyr reported that utility may eventually be discarded along with its predecessors of the 1950s and 1960s, namely, the dollar criterion and human resource accounting.[26]

The appropriate question to ask is, "What do executives take into account when determining whether training programs should continue?" As noted in Chapter 3, a major impediment to upper-management support for training may be the failure of managers to see how training has had a positive impact on employee behavior with regard to the attainment of organizational objectives. Seeing a positive behavior change on the part of employees may result in upper management treating training more seriously than if presented with dollar estimates that justify time spent on training. Research is needed on managerial decisions regarding the continuation of training programs as a result of seeing observable job-related behavior change versus utility estimates.

In the interim, it would appear wise for training specialists to use utility analysis as well as all four criteria (reactions, learning, behavioral, results). These four criteria are a way of showing the training program's construct validity. The construct of interest is on-the-job effectiveness. Each measure supplements the others by providing information on why the training worked or failed to work in improving trainees' performance on their jobs. Each measure provides the trainers with information on the steps that can be taken to strengthen and improve training effectiveness. The advisability of using multiple measures is particularly evident when measuring the effects of training on team performance. Here, you would want to gather both process (e.g., information exchange, flexibility, assertiveness) and outcome (e.g., error reduction, increased safety, quality of decision making) measures, and do it at *both* the individual and the team level.[27]

## Summary

Measures of training success fall into four categories:

1. Reaction—how do the trainees feel about the program they attend?

2. Learning—to what extent have the trainees absorbed the knowledge and skills that have been taught?

3. Behavior—to what extent can the trainees apply what they have learned during training to their job settings?

4. Results—to what extent have cost-related behavioral outcomes been affected by the training? Do these cost-related benefits outweigh the costs of developing and implementing the training?

A statistical technique known as *meta-analysis* was used to investigate the relationship among reaction, learning, behavior, and results measures across a total of 34 different studies that involved 115 correlations.[28] The researchers expanded Kirkpatrick's taxonomy of reactions, learning, behavior, and results by examining two types of reactions (affective reactions and utility reactions) and three types of learning (i.e., immediate knowledge, knowledge retention, and behavior/skill demonstration). Affective reactions—how much the trainees liked and felt good about the training—were discussed earlier in this chapter. Utility reaction focuses on something different. It asks trainees such questions as "To what degree will this training influence your ability later to perform your job?", "Was this training job relevant?", and "Was the training of practical value?"

Immediate knowledge is the type of learning we discussed earlier. Knowledge retention involves measuring knowledge at a later time (e.g., 6 months) rather than (or in addition to) immediately after training. Behavior/skill demonstration deals with any indicators of behavioral proficiency when these are measured *within* the training, rather than the job environment.

This meta-analytical research yielded several findings, the most interesting of which are as follows:

- There are modest correlations among the various types of training criteria. This suggests to us that since each criterion measure is tapping something unique, multiple measures of training success are recommended.
- Utility reactions correlated more highly with subsequent trainee job performance than did affective reactions. In other words, utility reactions are better to use because, when asked about training's value, trainees are probably taking into considerations the environmental constraints (discussed in Chapter 4) that they will face when they return to their jobs.
- Both immediate knowledge and knowledge retention measures correlated positively with behavior/skill demonstration. Although these linkages were only moderate, they suggest that it is advisable to assess trainee learning immediately after training and again at a later time.
- Regardless of their relationship with other training measures, from a practical viewpoint, trainee reactions are important. Although they do not ensure organizational support for the training program, negative reactions can have a negative impact on the training department's reputation. However, no type of reaction measure should ever be used as a surrogate for other measures.

# HOW SHOULD A TRAINING EVALUATION STUDY BE DESIGNED?

Once the measures or criteria of training effectiveness are selected, attention must be given to choosing the proper design, or experimental procedure, in which to do the measurement. Unfortunately, the two designs most frequently used in the training literature are also the most absurd for evaluation purposes. These two designs, commonly referred to as *case study* and *pretest–posttest* are as follows:

*Case Study*

Training  →  Measures Taken After Training

*Pretest–Posttest Design*

Measures Taken
Before Training  →  Training  →  Measures Taken
After Training

In the case study, employees are trained and measures of trainee effectiveness are then taken (e.g., reaction, learning, behavior, and/or results). In one instance, a company evaluated a two-day assertiveness training course by asking each manager who had participated to fill out a short assertiveness quiz. The primary problem with this design is that there are no measures taken prior to training. Consequently, there is no way to know whether the assertiveness training brought about any change. The person might have known the answers to the questions prior to receiving the training. In other instances, companies in Australia, Canada, South Africa, and the United States use a process known as *Training Impact Assessment* (TIA) to evaluate both technical and nontechnical training programs. With TIA, a group consisting of the trainees' managers meet to look collectively at what happened to their employees as a result of the training. These managers gather data on the impact of training in their units and then meet, initially in subgroups and then all together, to discuss the achieved and unachieved results. Senior executives may sometimes attend the sessions to witness the excitement and findings. Although TIA has certain merits such as the systematical collection of data by the various subgroups, one must not lose sight of the fact that is merely a "case study" approach to evaluation.[29]

The pretest–posttest design assesses such changes because measures are taken before and after training. Nevertheless, this design also is of little value, because a multitude of unknown factors could be the real cause of a change in performance. For example, if a post-training measure of performance showed that safety improved (i.e., fewer accidents) after a safety training program had been conducted, there would be no way of knowing whether the training program in any way contributed to this result. If the trainees consisted of newly hired applicants, it could be that the trainees had simply become more experienced by the time the post-training measure of performance was taken. If new equipment and better lighting had been installed, if management suddenly emphasized safety over production, if the workday were shortened, or if any other of a host of factors occurred at the time the training program took place, it would be impossible to identify what variable or variables were responsible for the change and what variable or variables were a waste of time, money, and energy on the part of the organization.

Research suggests that value of the pretest–posttest design can be increased when an evaluator is using learning criteria. Haccoon and Namtiaux[30] suggested using what they call *Internal Referencing Strategy* (IRS). It is a simple procedure for inferring that trainees really did learn what they were taught. With IRS, the evaluator purposely incorporates in the pre- and post-training measures items that are relevant to the training (i.e., that ought to change because the course content covered them) and items that are not expected to change because the course content did not deal with them. The pre–post differences are then determined for the relevant and for the irrelevant items. Training effectiveness is inferred when changes on the relevant items are significantly greater than changes on the irrelevant ones. Haccoun and Hamtiaux used IRS to evaluate a 45-hour training course on the management of human resources for intermediate-level managers at a large university. The pre- and posttest performances were measured using multiple-choice questions. Some of the multiple-choice items focused, as the course did, on applications (e.g., "Providing job performance feedback to employees implies . . .") or on the knowledge of content (e.g., "McGregor's theory suggests that underlying managerial behaviors are assumptions about . . ."). Other multiple-choice questions tapped applications and knowledge that were germane to the management of human resources, but were not treated in the course. Their research suggests that evaluators working in situations in which better designs are not feasible might decide to use the IRS approach.

Two designs that do permit a stringent evaluation of training programs are (1) the pretest–posttest design with a control group (see Figure 5.8), and (2) the after-only design with a control group.

In the pretest–posttest control group design, individuals are randomly assigned to either a group that receives training or a group that does not receive training until after the program has been evaluated. Random assignment ensures that a positive change in performance in Group A relative to Group B cannot be attributed to the fact that the Group A people were more intelligent, experienced, or motivated prior to training than the Group B people. The advantages of a pretest are at least twofold. First, they tell us whether the groups are truly equal prior to training. Second, they allow us to use statistical techniques to correct for imbalance between groups. In short, they minimize the probability we will conclude erroneously that the training was effective or ineffective.

The key factor in this design is the control group (Group B). Any change in equipment, lighting, management policy, hours worked, and the like, are exactly the same for both groups. The only difference between the two groups is that one received training. Therefore, any improvement in learning, behavior, or result measures can only be attributed to the training. If the training was of value, the trained group should perform significantly better in learning, behavior, or results than the control (i.e., untrained) group. The use of a control group allows us to say with more assurance that the changes in the trained group were due to the instructional treatment per se, and were not brought about by extraneous factors such as the passage of time, maturational changes in the trainees themselves, or certain events happening within the organization. Thus, a fairly strong case can be made when using this design for continuing, modifying, or even discarding the training program.

Consider the use of this design as used for an evaluation of a training program on self-management conducted with state government unionized workers in Washington State. In this study, people were randomly assigned to an experimental (i.e., training) or a control group, and several measures of training effectiveness were taken.[31]

Assessing employee reactions to the training was important because many trainees had argued that sick leave is a personal privilege. Moreover, in the initial session, the trainees in the original trained group expressed hostile reactions to the training in the form of self-depreciating and aggressive comments (e.g., "I guess we are the delinquent bunch"; "The trainer is a spy for management"). A fistfight occurred in the first class as a result of name calling between two trainees. Thus, it was important to determine what, if anything, the trainees perceived was especially effective or ineffective about the program.

Data were collected 3, 6, 9, and 12 months after the training program was completed. Favorable reactions were maintained over time because the trainees reported that the training they had received enabled them to identify obstacles preventing them from coming to work, helped them overcome these obstacles, led them to set specific goals for increasing their job attendance, and increased their self-confidence in their ability to control their own behavior.

An important issue was to understand in what other ways the training was effective. A second criterion was *learning.* Did the trainees learn ways of responding to attendance-related issues? Did they acquire problem-solving principles that enabled them to deal effectively with coming to work? To answer these questions, a learning test was developed on the basis of interviews with the supervisors of the employees. The learning test consisted of 12 situational items with a scoring guide. Here is a sample item: "The reason I can't come to work is that I do not get along with a particular person with whom I work. Whenever she is on shift, I call in sick. I noted that when I do have contact with her on the job, we get into arguments. I decided to set a goal of getting along with her, but it does not seem to be working. What should I do?" The data analysis revealed that the trained group learned significantly more problem-solving skills than the individuals assigned to the control group.

To determine whether people retained the information presented during the training program, the learning test was administered and scored 6 months and again 9 months later. The trainees had not been informed of their scores. Again, the performance of the trained group was significantly higher than that of the control group. Thus, any decrease in job attendance could not be blamed on lack or loss of knowledge.

Of crucial importance to the evaluation of training effectiveness is whether the training truly changed the trainees' behavior. The behavioral measures of job attendance of those people who received training in self-management was significantly superior to that of the control group. Later, when the control group people were trained, it was found that their reaction measures were as positive, their learning test scores were as high, and their job attendance was as good as that of the people who were in the original trained group.

In the after-only control group design (see Figure 5.9), individuals available for training are randomly assigned to either a training group or a control group. The control group consists of individuals who will not receive training until after the program has been evaluated. No pretest measures are necessary prior to training because random assignment ensures that the two groups have been equalized prior to training (especially when a large number of individuals are involved). This is particularly true when a process known as *matching* is used. With matching, pairs of workers are found who are alike on relevant variables such as age, sex, experience, and ability. One member of each pair is randomly assigned to the training group while the other is assigned to the control group.

This design is particularly useful where the time required to collect pretest measures is not available, or it is believed that the pretesting of trainees may in some way facilitate their learning and thus contaminate (inflate) the measures of training effectiveness. If this were the case, we would not know whether the same positive effects would have been obtained without giving the pretest. Further, it has been shown that the after-only control group design will often be more advantageous than the pretest–posttest control group design when one has a fixed budget and strict cost constraints. In this situation, the after-only control group design has greater power to detect any significant differences between the trained and untrained groups.[32]

An example of the use of this design is found in the evaluation of a behavioral modeling program, known as *Supervisory Relationships Training* (SRT), designed by AT&T to help line supervisors interact more effectively with their subordinates. Two months after the experimental group completed SRT, each

| Group A (Trained) | Training | Measure performance after training |
|---|---|---|
| Group B (Not Trained) | — | Measure performance after training |

**FIGURE 5.9** The After-Only Control Group Design

supervisor from the trained and the untrained groups was given a series of three simulated problem-solving discussions by a staff of assessors. Only the posttest measures of the trained and untrained supervisors were compared.[33]

A minor disadvantage of using either of these two designs is that it is highly desirable to have a minimum of 20 employees for an adequate statistical evaluation of a training program; that is, 10 individuals would need to be randomly assigned to training; the remaining 10 individuals would form the control group. If the number of employees involved in these designs are too small, then the statistical power of detecting any difference between the training and control groups is so low that trainers attempting to evaluate their programs will seldom find any positive results. This is a minor problem, because most employers are interested in training a large number of employees. However, where the number of employees is inadequate for either one of these designs, at least two alternatives may be considered.

The first alternative is called a *time-series design* (see Figure 5.10), in which a series of measures are taken prior and subsequent to training. The logic of this design is that if performance was consistently hovering at a given level before training was introduced, and performance suddenly increased and remained high following training, we can conclude that the training program brought about the change in performance. The important feature of this design is that there must be a sufficient number of pretest data points covering a sufficiently extended period of time so that all possible patterns of variation can be ascertained.[34] Shown in Figure 5.11 is a hypothetical example of a successful training program. In this example, the purpose of training was to increase employee attendance. Attendance was expressed in terms of the percentage of scheduled work-hours actually worked. As you can see, attendance data were collected for 15 weeks prior to training and 12 weeks after training.

A major drawback of this design is the chance that some fortuitous event will occur at the same time that training is initiated, and that the event (and not the training) is the cause of the increase in performance. The result is even worse if, instead of an increase, a decrease occurs. Training may indeed have improved performance, but this improvement will not show up, because some extraneous negative variable occurred when the posttest measures were taken. The effects of weather and season can be particularly bothersome. For example, five monthly measures of production were taken on several logging operations. The loggers were then given training in goal setting, and five more monthly measures were taken. The results are shown in Figure 5.12.

$M_1\ M_2\ M_3\ M_4\ M_5\ M_6\ M_7\ M_8\ M_9\ M_{10}$  TRAINING  $M_1\ M_2\ M_3\ M_4\ M_5\ M_6\ M_7\ M_8\ M_9\ M_{10}$

M = daily or weekly measures

FIGURE 5.10  The Time-Series Design

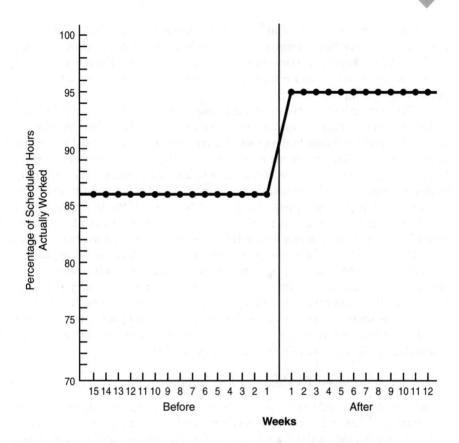

**FIGURE 5.11** Mean Attendance Data for the 15 Weeks Before and 12 Weeks After a Hypothetical Training Program to Increase Attendance

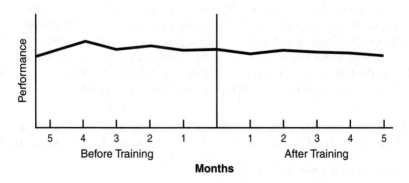

**FIGURE 5.12** Time-Series Line for Loggers Who Received Goal-Setting Training

It might be concluded that training neither helped nor hurt production. However, there was heavy rainfall in the months after training occurred. It may be that, without training, performance would have decreased. The point is, we do not know the answer because there is no control group against which performance can be compared.

The time-series design can be vastly improved by adding a control group. Unlike the pretest–posttest control group and the after-only designs, employees are not randomly assigned to the group that receives training or to the group that does not. This design, commonly known as the *multiple time-series design* (portrayed in Figure 15.13), is used frequently in applied settings where naturally occurring groups must be used (e.g., department A and department B; individuals from the East Lansing plant and the Seattle plant). If the design had been used in evaluating the effects of training loggers to set goals, the effects of heavy rainfall following training might have led to the drawing shown in Figure 5.14.

In this hypothetical situation, the control group's performance dropped significantly while the training group maintained production despite the rain. The employees' performance across the two groups was approximately the same prior to training. Moreover, both groups were exposed to the same factors prior to and during training, except that the control group did not receive training. The only logical conclusion we can draw is that training maintained production by counteracting the negative effects of the heavy rainfall.

## More Sophisticated Evaluation Designs

Because of its increased complexity, the Solomon Four-Group design is ideal for ascertaining whether a training intervention had a desired effect on trainees' behavior. Unlike the designs discussed so far, this design involves the use of more than one control group.

Solomon[35] argued that the very act of taking pretest measures prior to training may reduce the possibility of observing the training effect as it would have occurred naturally (i.e., in the absence of training). That is, there is possibility that merely taking pretest measures changes the trainees' attitudes and behaviors toward the training procedures. Or it may conceivably alter the set or attentional factors important to the effectiveness of training. For instance, if a group of supervisory trainees were given a pretest on leadership ability and the test contained a lot of items on participative decision making, it is quite conceivable that the trainees would pay attention to certain relevant portions of the training program in a manner different than if they had not received the pretest at all.

$M_1 M_2 M_3 M_4 M_5 M_6 M_7 M_8 M_9 M_{10}$  TRAINING  $M_1 M_2 M_3 M_4 M_5 M_6 M_7 M_8 M_9 M_{10}$
$M_1 M_2 M_3 M_4 M_5 M_6 M_7 M_8 M_9 M_{10}$ $\qquad\qquad\quad$ $M_1 M_2 M_3 M_4 M_5 M_6 M_7 M_8 M_9 M_{10}$

$M$ = daily or weekly measures

FIGURE 5.13   The Multiple Time-Series Design

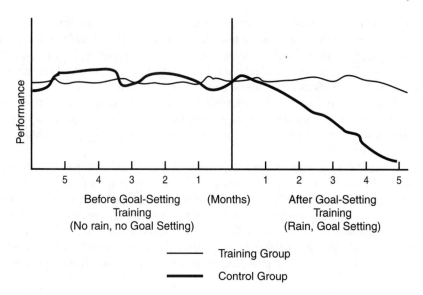

**FIGURE 5.14**   Multiple Time-Series Lines for Loggers Who Received and Did Not Receive Goal-Setting Training

This source of contamination is called *pretest sensitization,* and it cannot be adequately measured or controlled using the traditional two-group designs. Solomon, therefore, suggested extending the two-group model to include two additional control groups.

The Solomon Four-Group design is illustrated in Figure 5.15. Note that the first two groups are treated in the same way as in the pretest–posttest control

| | | | |
|---|---|---|---|
| **Group 1**<br>**(Trained)** | **A**<br>Measure performance<br>before training | Training | **B**<br>Measure performance<br>after training |
| **Group 2**<br>**(Untrained)** | **C**<br>Measure performance<br>before training | — | **D**<br>Measure performance<br>after training |
| **Group 3**<br>**(Trained)** | — | Training | **E**<br>Measure performance<br>after training |
| **Group 4**<br>**(Untrained)** | — | — | **F**<br>Measure performance<br>after training |

**FIGURE 5.15**   Solomon Four-Group Design

group design. However, two additional non-pretested control groups have been added. Notice that the effects of training can be assessed in four different ways in this design: Measure B should be larger (>) Measure A, Measure B > Measure D, Measure E > Measure F, and Measure E > Measure C. Also, if there is no pretest sensitization, then Measure E should be the same as Measure B.

Although the Solomon Four-Group is an excellent design, it continues to be rarely used in organizations. One reason for this is that it requires a sizable number of employees (e.g., 80 or more) and their random assignment into four, instead of two, groups.

Despite its infrequent use, let's look at a good illustration of how the Solomon Four-Group design has been used to evaluate the effectiveness of a training program for telephone installer-repair technicians. This training program involved a combination of text reading, audiovisual presentations, and hands-on exposure to the basic AC/DC characteristics of electronic and telephone systems. As part of the evaluation study, 131 employees were randomly selected from the employee pool and assigned to one of the following conditions.

1. Pretested, Trained, Posttested
2. Pretested, Untrained, Posttested
3. Non-Pretested, Trained, Posttested
4. Non-Pretested, Untrained, Posttested

The pretest and posttests used were equivalent forms of a 50-item multiple-choice examination developed by an electronics expert. Of special significance is the fact that the added costs associated with incorporating the two non-pretested control groups into the design were quite small compared to the expenses associated with the training program itself and the traditional two-group evaluation model. In fact, total expenditures for the evaluation (i.e., employee costs, lost work time, data analysis, etc.) were estimated to be about 10 percent of the amount invested in training program development and implementation. As for the total evaluation costs, 25 percent could be attributed to the extension of the design.[36]

Technical Educational Resources (TER) at Kodak was responsible for delivering a three-day training program on manufacturing resource planning (MRP) to over 10,000 Kodak employees over a two-year period. MRP is a method for effectively planning, coordinating, and integrating the use of all resources within one's manufacturing facility. TER was interested in determining whether a new method of presenting MRP would be effective. This new approach, referred to as IL (integrative learning), involved generating a classroom atmosphere that minimized various learning barriers (e.g., negative reinforcement, fear of failure, boredom, anxiety) and created a positive affect among trainees. From the outset, it was clear to the researchers[37] that Kodak was unwilling to assign any of its employees randomly to untrained groups (i.e., Solomon

Groups 2 and 4). In other words, everyone had to receive MRP training of some type. In light of this, the researchers decided that the most appropriate control group would involve training lecture-training rather than no treatment. So, in this case, the Solomon four groups consisted of: (1) a group that received pretests, IL-based training, and posttests; (2) a group that received pretests, traditional training, and posttests; (3) a group that received IL-based training and posttests only; and (4) a group that received traditional training and posttests only. Membership in this Solomon Four-Group design was determined by random assignment. Moreover, even though Kodak was unwilling to assign employees randomly to a no-treatment group, the researchers did their best to include the best no-treatment group they could considering the constraints placed on them by the organization. Their "quasi" no-treatment group included volunteers (all from TER) and was significantly smaller than the four treatment groups. What is most important thing for you to learn about this research at Kodak? The Solomon Four-Group cannot always be conducted in a perfect textbook manner in field settings. But we would rather see it modified, as Bretz and Thompsett did, than ignored completely.

Within-group designs have been embraced by some training specialists because of the difficulty often encountered in obtaining control groups in organizational settings. A within-group design useful for evaluating training programs is the multiple-baseline design.[38] This design does not require having more than one group. Rather, comparisons are made between individuals or groups. That is, each person or group serves as his or her own control. Therefore, there is no need to have any separate control groups to infer cause-effect relationships between training and its outcomes. It is often difficult to arrange a suitable group that is similar to the experiment group in every way except for exposure to training. With the multiple-baseline design, the trainer can evaluate the effectiveness of training without using a control group.

This design includes two basic components: (1) concurrent baselines—baseline data taken repeatedly over a period of time across either multiple behaviors or groups of people, and (2) staggered interventions—the treatment is first introduced with one behavior or group of people. When the desired change occurs (or after some predetermined number of training sessions), the treatment is then introduced with a second behavior or group of people. Again following an observed change, the training is introduced with the next behavior or group of people. Again following an observed change, the training is introduced with the next behavior or group, and so on, until the training has been introduced with all behaviors or groups.

To evaluate the effects of the training, comparisons are made between baseline and intervention phases to determine whether the effects of training are replicated at different times. If performance improves after, but not before, the training phase and this happens each time the training is introduced (in its staggered fashion), then it can be concluded with a great deal of confidence that the training itself was responsible for the favorable results.

Let us look at a few examples. A multiple-baseline design across behaviors was used to evaluate whether a training program was effective with clerks in a small grocery store.[39] The objective of the training was to improve performance on three desired behaviors: (1) remaining in the store, (2) assisting customers, and (3) stocking merchandise. The training was introduced initially with the first behavior. The training involved clarifying the desired behavior and its rationale during an initial half-hour session. Trainees were also given time off with pay whenever they attained at least 90 percent or more of the desired behaviors. In addition, they were given feedback on their progress in the form of a graph posted regularly on a bulletin board by the trainer. The clerks also learned to give themselves feedback by recording on a specially designed checklist whether or not they had engaged in any of the desired behaviors.

When improvements were noted in the percentage of time spent in the store (after 24 observational sessions), the training approach was reintroduced with the second behavior. When the clerks had begun to assist customers regularly and had continued to remain in the store (after 30 observational sessions), they were given training for the third behavior. Figure 5.16 shows the percentage of time the three target behaviors were performed across the 12 weeks of the study. The mean performance level of the three behaviors improved from 53, 35, and 57 percent to 86, 87, and 86 percent, respectively. Based on these data, it was concluded that the improvements in behavior were due to the training, since performance increased only after, and never prior to, the introduction of each training intervention.

Sometimes, instead of examining the effects of training across behaviors, we are interested in evaluating its effectiveness across groups of people. The groups may consist of different units within a single organization (e.g., sales, quality control, product development), different shifts within a department (e.g., nurses on the 8 to 4, 4 to 12, 12 to 8 shifts), or different branches within a statewide organization (e.g., Flint, Lansing, and Saginaw). For instance, an industrial safety program was instituted in a wholesale bakery that makes, wraps, and transports pastry to retail outlets throughout the United States. The groups, selected because of their high number of accidents during the previous year, consisted of personnel in the second-shift wrapping and makeup departments. Employees in the makeup department measure and mix ingredients, prepare dough, and manually depan and package pastries as they come out of the ovens. Employees in the wrapping department bag, seal, and label the packages and then stack them on skids to be shipped. After collecting baseline data on the percentage of incidents performed safety in both departments, a training intervention was introduced in the wrapping department. During this training, employees were presented with safety information and rewarded for desired behaviors. Following continued improvement by personnel in the wrapping department, the intervention was implemented in the makeup department.[40]

The multiple-baseline design across groups is a particularly powerful approach for evaluating training programs. Unlike the designs we have discussed

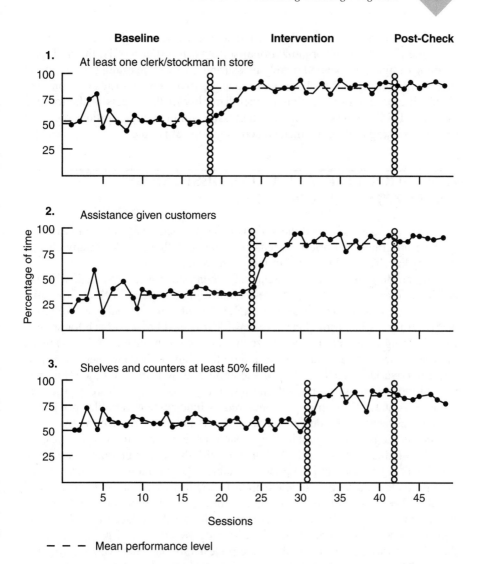

**FIGURE 5.16** Example of Multiple-Baseline Design Across Behaviors; Percentage of Time the Three Target Behaviors Were Performed by the Grocery Personnel During a 12-Week Period

The first intervention took place after 18 sessions (3 weeks), the second after 24 sessions (4 weeks), and the third after 30 sessions (3 weeks).

*Source:* From J. Komaki, W. M. Waddell, and M. G. Pearce, "The Applied Behavior Analysis Approach and Individual Employees: Improving Performance in Two Small Businesses," *Organizational Behavior and Human Performance 19,* 1977, 342.

thus far, it allows us to determine to what degree the beneficial effects of training can generalize to other organizational settings. In other words, the multiple-baseline design goes beyond merely measuring how well learning transfers from the training setting to the job setting for one group of people. Instead, it concerns itself with the interorganizational generalizability of the effects of the training program. This, of course, is an important issue within an organization where the training is going to be implemented across groups of people.

## HOW SHOULD EVALUATION DESIGNS BE ANALYZED STATISTICALLY?

Now that we have examined the various measures and designs used to evaluate training programs, we briefly discuss the statistics that can detect any change that may have resulted from the training intervention.

According to various researchers,[41] when one considers statistical power and lower costs, the preferred choice for analyzing a training intervention statistically is to use analysis of variance (ANOVA) with an after-only control group design. If for some reason this is not feasible, the next best approach for analyzing a training intervention is to utilize analysis of covariance (ANCOVA) using the pretest score as a covariate. An alternative, but equivalent, method of performing covariance analysis can be accomplished by using multiple regression procedures whereby the pretest and a dummy-coded variable (e.g., training group = 1; control group = 2) are entered as independent variables predicting posttest scores (i.e., the dependent variable). Another alternative to covariance analysis is the use of hierarchical regression. Here, we construct two regression models, a reduced model and a full model. With the reduced model, the posttest variable is regression onto the pretest variable. The full model involves regressing the posttest variable on *both* the pretest variable as well as the dummy-coded variable. Then, we examine the $R^2$ values for each of these models. If the $R^2$ for the full model is significantly larger than the $R^2$ for the reduced model, we can conclude that group membership (i.e., training versus control groups) predicts the posttest variable, over and above the pretest variable. However, according to Arvey and associates, all that has been presented here is based on the assumption that the training and control groups are equivalent at pretest. Usually, this situation is arranged via random assignment of employees to the two groups. The existence of nonequivalent groups at pretest can produce biased, misleading results.

In many evaluations of training studies, there is relatively little difficulty in measuring change because the variables of interest are straightforward and reliable (e.g., amount of scrap produced, incidents of customer complaints, amount of productivity). Recent research suggests that, particularly with regard to self-report data (e.g., questionnaires, interviews, personality tests), the measurement of change is far more difficult than just discussed.[42] Self-respect measures greatly complicate the measurement of change due to training, not so much because of the statistical procedures we have described but because of the problems involved in the definition of change itself.[43] Specifically, there are three types of change that can occur with self-report data: alpha, beta, and gamma.

*Alpha change* occurs when the observed difference between the pretest and posttest measures represents a true change due to the training intervention.

*Beta change* occurs when the alpha change is confounded by a recalibration of the scale(s) used to measure the variable of interest. Arvey and Cole[44] provide an excellent example of beta change. During pretest, a supervisor rates herself as being of "average" supervisory competence. After the training is completed, two things happen: She is now a more competent supervisor than she previously realized. Consequently, after training, she rates herself again as being "average," thereby giving the erroneous impression that the training had no impact.

*Gamma change* refers to a trainee's reconceptualization of the variable being measured. For instance, the individual's personal understanding of, say, job satisfaction might change from the pretest to the posttest period.

The best way of measuring these three measures has been suggested by Terborg, Howard, and Maxwell.[45] They recommended using a *then* (otherwise known as a *retrospective pretest*) measure after a training intervention, in addition to the usual pre- and postmeasures. Respondents are asked how they perceive themselves to have been just before the training was conducted. To assess beta change, the average of each respondent's self-reported answers to the items on the pretest measure is compared to his or her own average on the then measure. If no beta change exists, then these averages should be approximately the same for each of the respondents. Terborg et al. recommend using a t-test to assess the degree of beta change for each individual. In a similar manner, alpha change can be assessed by comparing posttest scores to then scores. Finally, to measure each person's degree to gamma change, we compute the correlation as well as the change in variance between pretest and then pretest items.[46] Of course, our hope is that the self-reported improvement from the training intervention is caused by alpha change, not by beta or gamma changes.

## FINAL COMMENTS

It is difficult to understand why the rigorous evaluation of training programs is the exception rather than the rule in North American business and industry. Grove and Ostroff[47] described four barriers that discourage training evaluation:

1. *Top management does not usually require evaluation.* Frequently, top management seems ready to take on faith that certain training programs are valuable. Moreover, some top managers reward their training staff for merely staying current with the latest training fads. When sales and profits are good, top management appears to have no problem embracing the value of most training efforts. Further, when a needs analysis implies that training in certain areas is "good to do," it appears to be

especially easy for top management to rest assured that things are being done properly by the training department.

2. *Most senior-level training managers do not know how to go about evaluating training programs.* Evaluation of training is a complex procedure. Most people simply do not know how to evaluate training programs properly.

3. *Senior-level training managers do not know what to evaluate.* Many people are not clear on what questions should be answered by an evaluation. Should they focus on the number of key people who want to attend the program? The costs per trainee? The degree of enjoyment expressed by trainees? Changes back on the job? Grove and Ostroff[48] argued that the major contributor to this problem is a lack of clear training objectives. A review of a sample corporate training catalogs substantiates their point. They described one manager of a corporate learning center who cut out of his own company's training catalog all of the different stated course objectives. Then, he tried to match these objectives to the various course descriptions. He was not able to do this because the objectives were so vague! This problem can be corrected by tying the training to the organizational analysis (see Chapter 2) where the corporate objectives and strategies for attaining them are identified.

4. *Evaluation is perceived as costly and risky.* There are at least two forces acting on training specialists that work against evaluation: cost and risk taking. Many training specialists would rather spend their limited funds on developing new and highly visible training offerings that hopefully will be seen favorably by top management rather than spending scarce dollars on evaluation. The risk with evaluation is that the results may show that a training program which top management and others like is not attaining the objectives for which it was designed.

To counteract these four barriers, we recommend the following actions:

1. Top-level management needs to be educated on the importance of rigorous evaluation and the dangers of taking on faith that a certain training and development strategy is worthwhile.

2. Training managers and their staffs need to be taught the "how to's" of training evaluation. They need to be given hands-on training where they are shown how to design questionnaires, use the correct experimental design, statistically analyze data, and calculate utility.

3. Training mangers and top-level management need to discuss what exactly needs to be evaluated. Training needs to be incorporated into the business strategy (see Chapter 3). It is important that the organization's overall strategy and the human resource management's strategy are aligned.

4. If top management really wants to reinforce rigorous evaluation, it needs to make it clear to the training director that a certain proportion of the training budget should be targeted to evaluation.

5. The risk-taking component of evaluation needs to be minimized by rethinking the purpose of evaluation. Rather than thinking of evaluation as a live or die decision for a training program, evaluation needs to be thought of as a way of finding out if there's anything wrong with the program and, if there is, correcting it.

6. It is important to remember that training effectiveness is not just dependent on the training program per se. Training program effectiveness hinges on a multitude of

factors associated with the trainees themselves (e.g., trainee motivation), with the context in which the training occurs (e.g., opportunities to practice newly acquired skills) and the environment (e.g., amount of supervisory support) to which the trainer must transfer.[49]

7. No matter how rigorous the training evaluation effort, keep in mind that it is impossible to get ironclad proof that the training program brought about the beneficial outcomes to one's organization. Fortunately, top management is not going to ask, "Can you prove it?" What they want is awfully good evidence that the training contributed what has happened, and evidence fortunately is not all that hard to come by.[50]

8. Benchmarking is an excellent method of supporting one's evaluation findings in one's company. In the past 15 years, businesses have begun to use benchmarking as a way of comparing their products, services, and practices with those of other companies within their industry.[51] Training specialists who are members the American Society for Training and Development can join the ASTD Benchmarking Forum for a modest fee. Established in 1991, the forum provides the opportunity for training professionals to compare their training and development practices with other organizations, and to identify successful training practices. By joining the forum and supplying completing their survey of one's company practices, one gets in return information about others' evaluation findings.

As stated in Chapter 1, systematic measurement is the key to the prevention or minimization of training fads. It enhances training effectiveness by showing the trainer where and why the training was effective or ineffective. Unfortunately, we have seen too many programs evaluated inappropriately. Here are two actual incidents which illustrate our experiences:

A medium-sized banking firm develops its managers by presenting a monthly series of lectures by prestigious outside speakers on such topics as participative management, mutual goal setting, and employee motivation. The effectiveness of these training sessions are evaluated ritualistically by the loudness of the audience's clapping and cheerfulness at the end of the session. Used also is a short two-item comment sheet that can be voluntarily filled out by any of the participants and mailed to the training department. The questionnaires received by the training department are largely favorable, thereby demonstrating that the fees paid to the speaker were worth it, and that the training staff is succeeding in its mission.

An office equipment manufacturer and distributor was considering whether to purchase a sales training program from a consulting firm specializing in the development of such programs. The vice president of marketing of the office equipment company wanted to evaluate the sales program before purchasing it. He therefore asked the consultants to demonstrate the two-day program on a trial basis for himself and his staff. They immediately liked the program and adopted it for training over 300 of the company's salespeople.

Although not all evaluations are this bad, there is often a sizable gap between the practice of training and the science of training evaluation as we have presented it in this chapter. Frequently, students ask us how we cope with this discrepancy in our dural roles as both teacher (i.e., telling how it should be done) and practitioner (i.e., experiencing how it is actually done). As practitioners we persuade management to implement the most sophisticated training evaluation possible. For example, a printing company wanted to have its secretarial training program evaluated in terms of reaction, learning, behavior, and results measures. We decided that the Solomon Four-Group design would be the best approach to follow and, therefore, presented it to the company's management. Their position immediately was that the current company situation could not tolerate the training of only one-half of the current secretarial force. They agreed, however, that it would be reasonable to choose half of the secretaries randomly for training now and use the remaining secretaries as a control group. This arrangement was agreed to on the stipulation that, if the training proved to be successful, the control group of secretaries would later be trained. Management also opposed the use of any pretest measures since they would take too long to collect. Management admitted that they were impatient to get the training started. The final result was the use of an after-only control group design.

As you can see from this example, organizational constraints often preclude the use of the most sophisticated designs. However, the training specialists should not throw up their hands in despair. It means essentially that, at times, something less than the ideal must be used. This is acceptable within limits. We feel strongly that the case study and the pretest–posttest without control designs are not acceptable for training program evaluation. In other words, flexibility is good, but there must be limits to anyone's level of flexibility.

With an understanding of the four criteria for evaluating training effectiveness, and the different approaches that can be used in conjunction with them, we now examine the training strategies and procedures that can bring about a relatively permanent change in a person's self-awareness, job skill, and motivation.

## ENDNOTES

1. D. L. Kirkpatrick, "Evaluation of Training," in R. L. Craig (ed.), *Training and Development Handbook: A Guide to Human Resource Development* (New York: McGraw-Hill, 1976).
2. S. I. Tannenbaum and G. Yukl, "Training and Development in Work Organizations," *Annual Review of Psychology 43* (1992): 399–435.
3. D. Fast, "A New Approach to Quantifying Training Program Effectiveness," *Training & Development Journal 28,* no. 9 (1974): 8–14.
4. G. M. Alliger and E. A. Janak, "Kirkpatrick's Levels of Training Criteria: Thirty Years Later," *Personnel Psychology 42* (1989): 331–42.
5. G. M. Alliger, S. I. Tannenbaum, W. Bennett Jr., H. Traver, and A. Shotland, "A Meta-Analysis of the Relations Among Training Criteria," *Personnel Psychology 50* (1997): 341–58.
6. J. E. Mathieu, S. I. Tannenbaum, and E. Salas, "An Influence of Individual and Situational Characteristics on Training Effectiveness Measures," *Academy of Management Journal* (1990): 25–32.
7. G. S. Howard, K. M. Ralph, N. Gulanik, S. E. Maxwell, D. W. Nonce, and S. R. Gerber, "Internal Invalidity in Pretest–Posttest Self-Report Evaluations and Reevaluation of Retrospective Pretests," *Applied Psychological Measurement 3* (1979): 1–23.

8. G. S. Howard and P. R. Dailey, "Response-Shift Bias: A Source of Contamination of Self-Report Measures," *Journal of Applied Psychology 64,* no. 2 (1979): 144–50.

9. Alliger et al., "A Meta-Analysis of the Relations Among Training Criteria."

10. P. R. Erickson, "Evaluating Training Results," *Training & Development Journal 44* (1990): 57–59.

11. K. E. Ricci, E. Blickensderfer, J. A. Cannon-Bowers, and L. Miller, "Assessing Cognitive Skill: Multiple Measures of Learning Outcomes." Paper presented at the annual convention of the Human Factors and Ergonomics Society, Orlando, FL, 1995.

12. J. E. Smith and S. Merchant, "Using Competency Exams for Evaluating Training," *Training & Development Journal 44* (1990): 65–70.

13. Kirkpatrick, "Evaluation of Training."

14. C. Ostroff, "Training Effectiveness Measures and Scoring Schemes: A Comparison," *Personnel Psychology 44* (1991): 353–74.

15. G. P. Latham and K. N. Wexley, *Increasing Productivity Through Performance Appraisal* (Reading, MA: Addison-Wesley, 1994).

16. M. R. Edwards and A. J. Ewen, *360° Feedback: The Powerful New Model for Employee Assessment and Performance Improvement* (New York: AMACOM, 1996).

17. D. J. Abernathy, "Thinking Outside the Evaluation Box," *Training & Development,* February 1999, 19–23.

18. A. P. Goldstein and M. Sorcher, *Changing Supervisor Behavior* (New York: Pergamon Press, 1974).

19. W. F. Cascio, "Using Utility Analysis to Assess Training Outcomes," in I. L. Goldstein and Associates (eds.), *Training and Development in Organizations* (San Francisco: Jossey-Bass, 1989): 63–88; S. B. Parry, "Measuring Training's ROI," *Training & Development Journal 50* (1996): 72–77; and J. J. Phillips, "How Much Is the Training Worth?" *Training & Development Journal 50* (1996): 20–24.

20. J. W. Boudreau, "Economic Considerations in Estimating the Utility of Human Resource Popularity Programs," *Personnel Psychology 36* (1983): 551–76; J. W. Boudreau, "Effects of Employee Flows on Utility Analysis of Human Resource Productivity Improvement Programs," *Journal of Applied Psychology 68* (1983): 396–406; J. W. Boudreau, "Utility Analysis for Decisions in Human Resource Management," Cornell University, School of Industrial Relations, Working Paper 88–21 (1988); and F. L. Schmidt, J. E. Hunter, and K. Pearlman, "Assessing the Economic Impact of Personnel Programs on Workforce Productivity," *Personnel Psychology 35* (1982): 333–47.

21. G. P. Latham and K. N. Wexley, *Increasing Productivity Through Performance Appraisal* (Reading, MA: Addison-Wesley, 1994).

22. G. M. McEvoy and P. F. Buller, "Five Uneasy Pieces in the Training Evaluation Puzzle," *Training & Development Journal 44* (1990): 39–42.

23. Boudreau, "Utility Analysis for Decisions in Human Resource Management."

24. W. F. Cascio, *The Financial Importance of Behavior in Organization,* 2nd ed. (Boston: Kent, 1987).

25. G. F. Dreher and P. R. Sackett, *Perspectives on Employee Staffing and Selection* (Homewood, IL: Irwin, 1983).

26. H. E. Brogden and E. K. Taylor, "The Dollar Criterion—Applying the Cost Accounting Concept to Criterion Construction," *Personnel Psychology 3* (1950): 133–54; R. L. Brummet, E. Flamholtz, and W. C. Pyle, "Human Resource Accounting in Industry," *Personnel Administration,* July –August 1969, 34–46; and M. L. Tenopyr, "Policies and Strategies Underlying a Personnel Research Operation." Paper presented at the annual meeting of the Society of Industrial-Organizational Psychology, Atlanta, 1987.

27. J. A. Cannon-Bowers, S. I. Tannenbaum, E. Salas, and C. E. Volpe, "Defining Team Competencies and Establishing Team Training Requirements," in R. Guzzo and E. Salas (eds.), *Team Effectiveness and Decision Making in Organizations* (San Francisco: Jossey-Bass, 1995): 333–80.

28. Alliger et al., "A Meta-Analysis of the Relations Among Training Criteria."

29. L. Coffman, "Involving Managers in Training Evaluation," *Training & Development Journal 44* (1990): 77–80.

30. R. R. Haccoun and T. Namtiaux, "Optimizing Knowledge Tests for Inferring Learning Acquisition Levels in Single Group Training Evaluation Designs: The Internal Referencing Strategy," *Personnel Psychology* (1994): 593–604.

31. G. P. Latham and C. A. Frayne, "Increasing Job Attendance Through Training in Self-Management: A Review of Two Studies," *Journal of Applied Psychology 74* (1989): 411–16.

32. R. D. Arvey, S. E. Maxwell, and E. Salas, "The Relative Power of Training Evaluation Designs Under Different Cost Configurations," *Journal of Applied Psychology 77* (1992): 155–60.

33. J. L. Moses and R. J. Ritchie, "Supervisory Relationships Training: A Behavioral Evaluation of a Behavior Modeling Program," *Personnel Psychology 29* (1976): 337–43.

34. T. D. Cook and D. T. Campbell, *Quan-experimentation: Design and Analysis Issues for Field Settings* (Chicago: Rand McNally, 1979).

35. R. L. Solomon, "An Extension of Control Group Design," *Psychological Bulletin 46* (1949): 137–50.

36. K. A. Bunker and S. L. Cohen, "The Rigors of Training Evaluation: A Discussion and Field Demonstration," *Personnel Psychology 30* (1977): 525–41.

37. R. D. Bretz and R. E. Thompsett, "Comparing Traditional and Integrative Learning Methods in Organizational Training Programs," *Journal of Applied Psychology 77* (1992): 941–51.

38. Cook and Campbell, *Quan-experimentation.*

39. J. Komacki, W. M. Waddell, and M. G. Pearce, "The Applied Behavior Analysis Approach and Individual Employees: Improving Performance in Two Small Businesses," *Organizational Behavior and Human Performance 19* (1977): 337–52.

40. J. Komaki, K. D. Barwick, and L. R. Scott, "A Behavioral Approach to Occupational Safety: Pinpointing and Reinforcing Safe Performance in a Food Manufacturing Plant," *Journal of Applied Psychology 63,* no. 4 (1978): 434–45.

41. R. D. Arvey and D. A. Cole, "Evaluating Change Due to Training," in I. L. Goldstein and Associates (eds.), *Training and Development in Organizations* (San Francisco: Jossey-Bass, 1989); Arvey, Maxwell, and Salas, "The Relative Power of Training Evaluation Designs Under Different Cost Configurations"; and S. E. Maxwell, D. A. Cole, R. D. Arvey, and E. Salas, "A Comparison of Methods for Increasing Power in Randomized Between-Subjects Designs," *Psychological Bulletin 110* (1991): 328–37.

42. K. N. Wexley, "Personnel Training," *Annual Review of Psychology 35* (1984): 519–51.

43. Arvey and Cole, "Evaluating Change Due to Training."

44. Ibid.

45. J. R. Terborg, G. S. Howard, and S. E. Maxwell, "Evaluating Planned Organizational Change: A Method for Assessing Alpha, Beta, and Gamma Change," *Academy of Management Review 5* (1980): 109–21.

46. Arvey and Cole, "Evaluating Change Due to Training."

47. D. A. Grove and C. Ostroff, "Training Program Evaluation," in K. N. Wexley and J. R. Hinrichs (eds.), *Developing Human Resources* (ASPA/BNA Series, Washington, DC: Bureau of National Affairs, 1990).

48. Ibid.

49. E. Salas, K. A. Burgess, and J. A. Cannon-Bowers, "Training Effectiveness Techniques," in J. Weiner (ed.), *Research Techniques in Human Engineering* (Upper Saddle River, NJ: Prentice Hall, 1995): 439–71.

50. J. Gordon, "Measuring the 'Goodness' of Training," *Training,* August 1991, 19–25.

51. O. L. E. Day, "Bench Marking Training," *Training & Development 49* (1995): 27–30.

# CHAPTER

# On-Site Training Methods

6

To this point, we have discussed four main areas of training and development: how the training staff fits in with the rest of the organization, how to determine an organization's training needs, how to maximize a trainee's learning, and how to evaluate training and development programs. After the training staff describes the job in general terms (job description), lists each of the specific tasks comprising the job (task identification), and prepares a blueprint of trainee performance desired at the completion of training (course objectives), they must decide which techniques to use to optimize trainee learning.

There are numerous techniques available for presenting information and transmitting skills, in fact, more than can be discussed here. We have chosen to review the major training techniques currently used by both small and large organizations. For convenience of presentation, these techniques are grouped into four main categories: On-Site Training Methods (Chapter 6), Off-Site Training Methods (Chapter 7), Developing and Training Leaders: Theoretical Approaches (Chapter 8), and Management and Executive Development (Chapter 9). As you will see, Chapters 6 and 7 cover those on- and off-site approaches that are used primarily for developing nonexempt (i.e., hourly) employees. Chapters 8 and 9 review those approaches employed primarily for developing managers.

In this chapter, the following on-site approaches are reviewed: orientation training and the socialization of new employees, on-the-job training (OJT), apprenticeship training, job aids, coaching, mentoring, technology-based training (TBT), job rotation, and career development. Before proceeding further, let us briefly discuss the advantages and disadvantages of using on-site methods. The main advantages are that the problems of transfer of learning (see Chapter 4) and training costs are minimized because the trainees learn the skills and knowledge in the same physical and social environment in which they will work once training is completed. Moreover, with certain of these techniques (e.g., apprenticeship training, OJT, job rotation), the trainees contribute to the organization while they are learning, thus defraying training costs. A limitation of on-site training is that sometimes coworkers or supervisors acting as trainers do not have the

| STRATEGIES / GOALS | *Self-Awareness* | *Job Skills* | *Motivation* |
|---|---|---|---|
| **Cognitive** | Career development | Orientation<br>Training and socialization of new employees<br>Job aids | |
| **Behavioral** | | On-the-job training<br>Apprenticeship training<br>Monitoring computer-based training | Coaching |
| **Environmental** | | | Job rotation |

**FIGURE 6.1** On-Site Methods Classified According to Goals and Strategies

motivation or the capability to provide trainees with worthwhile learning experiences. This can occasionally be a problem for some employees who are asked to train females and members of minority groups. They may believe that their job security is threatened by having women and minorities in their department, especially if these individuals possess more seniority than they do.

In discussing on-site techniques, we use the nine-cell framework presented in Figure 1.1, which shows that any training technique can be conceptualized in terms of its goals (i.e., purposes) and its strategies (i.e., how these goals are to be achieved). A training effort can have one or more of the following goals: (1) to improve an individual's level of self-awareness, (2) to increase an individual's skill in one or more areas of expertise, and (3) to increase an individual's motivation to perform the job well. These broad goals can be attained by directing training efforts at the trainees' cognitions (i.e., thoughts and ideas), behaviors, or the environment in which the trainees work. Figure 6.1 presents six on-site methods cross-tabulated for both goals and strategies. We begin where a new employee would—in orientation.

## ORIENTATION TRAINING AND THE SOCIALIZATION OF NEW EMPLOYEES

There's an old saying, "Well begun is half done." This is an important concept for any organization to follow after an employee is hired. Getting new employees started in the right way is important, in order to reduce their feelings of anxiety and to increase their subsequent job satisfaction and commitment. Poor orientation programs can be financially damaging to the organization because they reduce effectiveness for the first few weeks on the job and may contribute to dissatisfaction and turnover. According to the 2000 ASTD (American Society for

Training and Development) *State of the Industry Report,* organizations are spending about 7 percent of their annual training dollars on new employee orientation.[1]

Orientation training should be the joint responsibility of the training staff and the line supervisor. There must be a clear understanding of the specific obligations of each, so that nothing is left to chance. Too often, we witness situations in which both the training staff and the supervisor believe that the other is or should be responsible for orientation. The result is an inadequately trained employee. Generally, the training staff should provide information on matters that are organizationwide in nature and relevant to all new employees. The line supervisor should concentrate on those items unique to the employee's workplace. Although the content of the training will vary from organization to organization and from department to department, the items shown in Table 6.1 are typically included in any orientation. As you can see, the orientation process has as its goal the development of new employee skills. It attempts to accomplish this objective by transmitting factual (i.e., cognitive) information about the company and the employee's new job. Regardless of what is handled by the training staff versus supervision, every orientation program should accomplish at least the following 10 objectives[2]:

1. Introduction to the company
2. Review of important policy and practice
3. Review of benefits and services
4. Benefit plan enrollment
5. Completion of employment documents
6. Review of employer expectations
7. Setting of employee expectations
8. Introduction to fellow workers
9. Introduction to the facilities
10. Introduction to the job

New employees often go through a process known as *organizational socialization.* This involves learning the attitudes, standards, and patterns of behavior that are expected by the organization and its various subunits. Although the process of learning the ropes is a continuous one, it is highly intensified whenever we change organizations and/or jobs. It is important that orientation programs facilitate this socialization process by conveying to new employees the expected standards of behavior within the organization.

For example, in one Wisconsin hospital, newly appointed registered nurses and licensed practical nurses are given a one-week basic orientation program. At the end of this program, the nurses (1) recognize their own position within the structure of the nursing department and the hospital and can use appropriate channels of communication, (2) understand the philosophy and objectives of the nursing department and use these as a basis for giving quality patient care, (3) are acquainted with key hospital personnel in order to establish positive

**TABLE 6-1** Items Typically Covered by Organizations During Orientation Training

| *General Company Orientation* | *Specific Departmental Orientation* |
|---|---|
| The following items are among those typically included in this first phase: | The following items are typically covered in this phase: |

*General Company Orientation*

1. Overview of the organization—brief history, what the organization does (product/services), where it does it (branches, etc.), how it does it (nature of operations), structure (organization chart), etc.

2. Policies and procedures—work schedules, vacations, holidays, grievances, identification badges, uniforms, leaves of absence (sickness, educational, military, maternity/paternity, personal), promotion, transfers, training, etc.

3. Compensation—pay scale, overtime, holiday pay, shift differentials, when and how paid, time clock, etc.

4. Benefits—insurance, retirement, tax-sheltered annuities, credit union, employee discounts, suggestion system, recreational activities, etc.

5. Safety information—relevant policies and procedures, fire protection, first aid facilities, safety committee, etc.

6. Union—name, affiliation, officials, joining procedures, contract, etc.

7. Physical facilities—plant/office layout, employee entrance, parking, cafeteria, etc.

*Specific Departmental Orientation*

1. Department functions—explanation of the objectives, activities, and structure of the department, along with a description of how the department's activities relate to those of other departments and the overall company.

2. Job duties—a detailed explanation of the duties of the new employee's job (give him or her a copy of the job description) and how the job relates to the activities of the department.

3. Policies and procedures—those that are unique to the department, such as breaks, rest periods, lunch hour, use of time sheets, safety, etc.

4. Department tour—a complete familiarization with the departmental facilities, including lockers, equipment, emergency exits, supply room, etc.

5. Introduction to departmental employees.

*Source*: "Lets Not Forget About New Employee Orientation," by R. W. Hollman. Copyright © May, 1976. Reprinted with permission from *Personnel Journal*, Costa Mesa, CA. All Rights Reserved.

working relationships and are aware of proper resource persons available for assistance, (4) are familiar with procedures and policy manuals and other written resource materials available as aids in giving patient care, (5) know their role and legal responsibilities concerning administration of medications as outlined in the hospital's pharmacy policies, and (6) are familiar with the hospital's unique forms and its policies regarding nurses' responsibilities for documenting patient care.

Another example of good socialization by an organization involves an Ohio tire manufacturing plant. Their new employees receive an eight-hour orientation program. During the program, employees learn the customer's philosophy regarding such things as work rules, safety practices, quality control, and the importance of following engineering specifications. In addition, orientation sessions for spouses of newly hired employees are conducted. Besides providing a tour of plant facilities, the spouse program covers such items as filling out insurance claim forms; the company's policies on attendance, vacations, retirement, holidays, and employee discounts; a full explanation of all fringe benefits; and a discussion of the services provided by the company's credit unit.

New employees often have unrealistically high expectations about the amount of challenge and responsibility they will find in their first job. They are often assigned fairly undemanding entry-level positions and consequently experience discouragement and disillusionment. The result is job dissatisfaction, turnover, and low productivity. One solution to this problem is making entry-level jobs more challenging by giving new employees increased responsibility and authority and assigning them to supervisors who will set high standards. That is, instead of putting a new employee in any open job, some organizations give careful thought to job placement. These organizations realize that making first-year jobs more challenging not only reduces turnover, but also improves long-term career performance. Some organizations are currently training supervisors of new employees in the skills of job enrichment as a way of making initial assignments more challenging. These supervisors are trained to empower their new employees to deal directly with customers and clients (not just through them), do special projects and make recommendations, follow through and implement their recommendations, and continually assume added responsibility.

Where it is not possible to upgrade the demands of the first job, an alternative strategy is to provide realistic job previews (RJPs).[3] Your authors are aware of several organizations (e.g., Prudential Insurance Company, Texas Instruments, Southern New England Telephone, U.S. Military Academy) that employ realistic rather than traditional job previews to recruit outside individuals. The typical approach of many organizations is to make their organization appear very attractive, especially when the labor market is tight. In doing this, companies draw a lot of applicants and make the most efficient use of their selection systems, which function best when the number of applicants far exceeds the number of job openings. The RJP represents a different philosophy for recruiting new employees. It involves increasing the amount and accuracy of information given to job candidates in an attempt to maximize the quality of their organizational choices. Web sites, CD-ROMs, booklets, firms, plant visits, or talks are used to convey to the new employee not only the positive aspects of the job and the company, but the negative features as well (e.g., long hours, time pressures, excessive travel, limited upward mobility). The findings to date show that RJPs appear to lower new employee's expectations about the job and the organization, to increase the number of applicants who self-select themselves out from further consideration for a job, to somewhat increase initial levels of organizational commitment and job satisfaction, to increase job survival, and to improve job performance when audiovisual rather than just written information is provided.[4]

The socialization of new employees can be difficult because of their anxiety ("Will I be able to handle it?" "How will I get along with my boss?" "Where do I start?"). With these issues in mind, Texas Instruments conducted a classic experiment in which one group of new workers (control group) were given the normal first-day orientation, consisting of a two-hour briefing by the personnel department on hours of work, insurance, parking, and the like.[5] Then, as was customary, the new employee met a friendly but very busy supervisor, who provided further orientation and job instruction. A second (experimental) group received the same two-hour personnel department orientation followed by a six-hour anxiety reduction session. These individuals were told that there would be no work the first day, that they should relax, sit back, and use this time to get acquainted with the organization and each other and ask questions. The following points were emphasized during this phase: (1) the high probability of success on the job as evidenced by statistics disclosing that 99.6 percent of all new employees are successful on the job; (2) what new employees should expect in the way of hazing and unfounded rumors from older employees designed to intimidate them about their chances of success; (3) encouragement of new employees to take the initiative in asking their supervisors questions about their jobs; and (4) information about the specific personality of the supervisor to whom they would be assigned. This innovative orientation program had a remarkable impact: The experimental group exceeded the control group in terms of learning rate, units produced per hour, absentee rate, and tardiness. Although this research was conducted years ago, it clearly shows the beneficial effects of reducing the anxiety of new workers. Certainly, this research suggests that anxiety reduction of some sort should be included in all organizational orientation programs.

Since the manager or supervisor is an extremely important component of the socialization process, everything that this person expects of the new employee should be discussed openly during the orientation process: rest breaks, housekeeping, standards of performance, attendance, and so on. The better the supervisor is trained to explicate goals and expectations, the more confidence the employee will experience, and the quicker the employee will adapt to the organization.[6] Supervisors must be aware of the necessity of following the new employee's work progress by periodically checking how he or she is doing. Supervisors must know how important it is that the new employee has enough to do. Nothing is more frustrating to an individual full of enthusiasm about a new job than sitting around "stacking paper clips." We are happy to report that more organizations are beginning to train their supervisors in the subtle management of employee adjustment to jobs. Research indicates that newcomers rely not only on their supervisors for gathering information about the company, but their coworkers as well.[7] It appears that coworkers are important in the early stages of newcomer experience regarding their learning about intergroup relationships and group processes. In light of this, it can be recommended that training be directed as well at sensitizing coworkers to the important elements in the early socialization process. The effectiveness of orientation programs can be significantly increased if it is delivered via computers. Let's take a close look at innovations by Procter & Gamble (P&G) and Apple Computer.

Procter & Gamble's employee orientation program, known as "Experience the Journey," is targeted for every new P&G employee worldwide. The company uses both the Internet and intranet. The Internet conveys information using P&G's worldwide web that anyone can access. The intranet uses an internal server and has no connection to the Internet. It contains confidential information that can be accessed only after an employee is on board (e.g., information about pay practices). Four major online topics are covered: (1) About P&G, (2) Lingo, (3) Just for Me, and (4) Manager's Onboarding Essentials. "About P&G" gives the new employee information about such things as P&G's purpose, core values, principles, organization, products, press releases about products, what happened when, and how customers are served. New employees are encouraged to meet with their managers to discuss and compare their thoughts and observations. "Lingo" gives the new hire an understanding of the company's vocabulary. Terms such as AMJ (April, May, June), AD (Associate Director), BM (Brand Manager), and FYTD (Fiscal Year to Date) are listed alphabetically. "Just for Me" informs new employees what they will need to know and when they will need to know it to experience a smooth orientation and maximize their success. They are given a learning map that helps them before and during their first days and months on the job. They learn about such things as who their primary contact is and how to contact them, appropriate dress, available transportation, relocation procedures, and pay policies. They can click on the section "Other New Employees Say . . ." and read the tips offered by recent new hires. They can also read the information provided about the company's Career Center and its commitment to diversity. They are encouraged to share with their manager why they think a diverse workforce is good for P&G's business. The final section, "Manager's Onboarding Essentials," teaches managers how to make the onboard process a smooth experience for both themselves and their new employees. Managers are provided information about their specific responsibilities separated into those things that they need to do prior to new employees' arrival and during the employees' first days, first weeks, first month, and initial two to six months. The intranet also provides information to P&G managers about such things as relationship building, making connections, and providing feedback.

When classroom orientation is used, it is easy to ensure that new employees attend these sessions. Procter & Gamble does two things to build some accountability into their socializing and orientation of new employees. First, managers are trained that all their new employees are supposed to go through Experience the Journey. Second, new employees are expected to find three printed P&G Travelers Cheques that are embedded throughout these online training materials. All the new employee needs to do is to fill out the information, have their manager sign the cheques, and send them in to receive awards from P&G's "Duty-Free Shop." Experience the Journey attempts to give new employees a strong feeling of connection to the company by having, throughout the process, snapshots of company employees who give the whole story of their first assignment at Procter & Gamble. The company also feels that "navigation is critical" so that people don't get lost within their massive Experience the Journey. Reminders are provided at the top of each Web site page. Procter & Gamble is also committed to making their new employee orientation program "evergreen" by ensuring that it feels alive and is kept up to date so that employees want to come back to it.

Apple Training Support (ATS), a division of Apple Computer Inc. in Cupertino, California, has designed its own customized orientation. It is a computer-based program delivered via HyperCard, an Apple software product. Some of its main features that have contributed to its success and should be incorporated into other orientation programs include the following[8]:

- **It was based on a needs assessment.** Apple managers were questioned to determine their priorities for new employees. Current employees were interviewed about the confusions, questions, concerns, joys, and surprises they experienced during their first few weeks on the job.
- **It has an organizing framework.** The HyperCard program is based on the symbol of a building. Information of varying types (e.g., resources, technology, people) is stored on different floors. New employees maneuver from floor to floor by using an elevator.
- **Learners have control.** The software allows learners to browse through electronic material using their mouse to gain as much detailed information as they desire. For instance, in a screen that describes health benefits, the new employee might click on the phrase "more about the dental plan."
- **It is a process, not just a one-time event.** Since the orientation information serves as a database, employees can continue to access it even after they grow in experience.
- **It allows people and personalities to emerge.** People and their personalities are an important part of the orientation. For instance, new employees may choose to shadow a veteran employee by selecting a series of screens where the individual describes and talks about a typical workday.
- **It facilitates new employees' understanding of the company culture.** Apple's value statement is located on the fourth floor, while the mission statement for ATS and for each group can be found on floor three.
- **It is sensitive to the politics associated with orientations.** They have made sure that upper-level management is committed to the orientation effort, have sought out a wide array of opinions regarding its content, and have established a small committee that works together on its design and implementation.
- **It is amenable to revisions and updating.** The program is revised periodically to reflect new ATS policies, products, and technologies.
- **It provides new employees with a pleasant orientation experience.** The ATS orientation is interesting and enjoyable for new employees because it relies on graphics, interactivity, learner control, anecdotes, personalities, and digitalized images.

Now that we have covered the essentials of good socialization and orientation of new employees, let us move on to the topic OJT, which, quite often, comes next.

## ON-THE-JOB TRAINING

The most widely used training and development method involves assigning new employees to experienced workers or supervisors. Often, the experienced employee is told by a superior to "teach Chris your job" or "break Pat in." The trainee is expected to learn the job by observing the experienced employee and by working with the actual materials, personnel, and machinery that will comprise the job once formal training is completed. The experienced employee is expected to provide a favorable role model with whom the trainee can identify and to take time from regular job duties to provide instruction and guidance. In many cases, supervisors themselves assume responsibility for the OJT of their new employees.

On-the-job training has several positive features, one of which is its economy. Trainees learn while producing, thereby partially offsetting the cost of their instruction. For example, individuals in an automobile plant function as maintenance helpers while serving their two-year term as repair mechanic trainees. Moreover, there is no need to establish expensive off-site facilities such as classroom or equipment simulators, nor is there any need for outside trainers or members of the company's training staff. The method facilitates positive transfer of training (see Chapter 4), because the learning and actual job situations are identical. Ideally, the trainees learn by doing and receive immediate feedback regarding the correctness of their behaviors. This feedback can come from their performance on the job itself (i.e., intrinsic) as well as from their coworkers and supervisors (i.e., extrinsic).

Figure 6.1 shows that the major goal of OJT is to improve the job-related skills of employees by using primarily a behavioral (though also a cognitive) strategy. Although OJT can and often does work, it can also turn out to be a failure. This happens when organizations use it haphazardly. In these organizations, OJT is instituted simply by telling an individual to "train Pat," with little or no regard for the trainer's willingness or ability to do so. With these concerns in mind, we offer suggestions here for implementing effective OJT programs.

First, employees functioning as trainers must be convinced that training new employees in no way jeopardizes their own job security, pay level, seniority, or shift status. If for some reason they feel threatened, they will strongly resist training new people. For example, a large manufacturer of industrial boilers decided to institute a skilled trades program for developing their own first-class repair mechanics. Twenty-five experienced production workers were carefully chosen by the training staff to enter a three-year program that involved OJT and evening classes on such topics as blueprint reading, hydraulics, and safety procedures. Soon after the program began, it became evident that the tradesmen resented training the production workers. The tradesmen were concerned that many of the production workers had more plant seniority than they did and could, therefore, "bump them" if the company needed to lay off people. As one repair mechanic said, "Why should I spend my time training someone who could lay me off or bump me to the night shift if things get tight around here?" In order to get the program started, the company and the union had to agree that bumping would be based strictly upon seniority within the mechanical department.

Second, the individuals serving as trainers should realize that their added responsibility would be instrumental in obtaining rewards for them. If they do not, resistance will be encountered. For example, certain chicken producers employ nine-man work crews who are paid on a piece-rate basis as a group, based on the number of chickens they catch and load onto trucks each night. The crews catch the chickens by using special black lights in the chicken houses. Certain crew members bend down and grab seven chickens by their legs (three in one hand, four in the other) at one time. The chickens are then handed to someone at the door, who then passes them to other crew members stationed on the truck. These individuals place anywhere from 10 to 15 chickens into hauling cases. For years, the chicken catchers have been reluctant to train new people. They argue that this requires them to work too hard. They also resent the fact that the group makes less money for about four months during OJT because it cuts down on their crew's performance. They also feel inequity when they look at catchers on other crews making more money and not working as hard. One obvious solution to this problem is to provide special monetary bonuses to those crews who consent to provide OJT to new crew members.

Third, trainers and trainees should be carefully paired so as to minimize any differences in background, language, personality, attitudes, or age that may inhibit communication and understanding. For example, an older bookkeeper/secretary in a truck dealership was having difficulty keeping up with the pressures of her job. Management agreed to hire an assistant for her, whom she could train to assume some of her responsibilities. The trainee, an 18-year-old high school graduate, began learning the job. Within a few weeks, tension developed between these two individuals. One day, the office manager saw that the young woman was crying and approached the experienced employee to ask what had happened. She replied that she resented the younger person and refused to teach her what it had taken her 40 years to learn.

Fourth, the choice of trainers should be based on their ability to teach and their desire to take on this added responsibility. Trainers will not necessarily be the most competent and experienced employees. Job experience does not ensure that people have the ability to teach the job to somebody else. For instance, in a textile factory, management needed to identify those sewing machine operators inquiring about their willingness to serve in this role for three months. Next, this list of volunteers was sent out to all operators asking them to nominate the five operators who they expected would be the best teachers. Those individuals who received the highest number of peer nominations were chosen.

Fifth, those skilled workers chosen as trainers should be rigorously trained in the proper methods of instruction (i.e., use of reinforcement, knowledge of results, distributed practice). It has been found that only about 41 percent of companies that use OJT (i.e., primarily manufacturing firms) offer in-house classroom training or "train-the-trainer" programs on how to perform OJT.[9] Too often, these organizations rely solely on what is known as Job Instruction Training (JIT) for training supervisors and employees to instruct others. JIT was originally developed during World War II as an approach for helping supervisors feel confident in training employees. As shown in Figure 6.2, the approach consists of two major elements (i.e., how to get ready to instruct, how to instruct) and four basic steps (i.e., prepare the worker, present the operation, try out performance, follow-up). The information is usually printed on a wallet-sized card and carried about by prospective trainers. It is unlikely that this oversimplified cookbook approach to training trainers has much benefit. JIT does, however, serve as a reminder to trainers on how they can handle training situations more effectively than if they had been completely left on their own.

Sixth, it must be made clear to employees serving as trainers that their new assignment is by no means a chance to exploit others. For instance, a maintenance painter working in a large office building required his trainees to perform only those tasks that he disliked doing (e.g., cleaning paintbrushes,

**How to Get Ready to Instruct**
1. Have a timetable.
   —How much skill you expect and when.
2. Break down the job.
   —List the important steps.
   —Pick out the key points.
3. Have everything ready.
   —The right equipment, material, and supplies.
4. Have the workplace properly arranged.
   —As you would expect the worker to maintain it.

**How to Instruct**

STEP 1: *Prepare the Worker*
a. Put the worker at ease.
b. Find out what he or she knows.
c. Arouse interest.
d. Place the worker correctly.
(Ensure a learning situation.)

STEP 2: *Present the Operation*
a. Tell.
b. Show.
c. Explain.
d. Demonstrate.
(One point at a time. Stress key points.)

STEP 3: *Try Out Performance*
a. Have the worker perform the operation.
b. Have the worker explain the key points.
c. Correct errors.
d. Reinstruct as needed.
(Be sure he or she knows.)

STEP 4: *Follow-up*
a. Put the worker on his or her own.
b. Encourage questioning.
c. Check frequently.
d. Taper off assistance.
(Practice—key to performance.)

**FIGURE 6.2** Job Instruction Training (JIT)

removing rust from metals, cleaning grease and dirt from surfaces). He often said that he enjoyed being a trainer because he liked having his own helper! Unfortunately, those who worked with him learned little about constructing and repairing structural woodwork and equipment because of his abuse of his role as a trainer.

Seventh, the trainees should be rotated to compensate for weaker instruction by some trainers and to expose each trainee to the specific know-hows of various workers. For instance, many home realtors give their prospective real estate agents three months of OJT immediately after they pass their state examinations. Trainees are rotated from agent to agent every three to four weeks. This is done because some real estate agents are better at showing homes, others at writing contracts, and others at securing home listings.

Eighth, the organization must realize that there is a possibility that production may be slowed down, equipment damaged, and some defective products made. Learning must take precedence over production, especially during the early stages of training.

Ninth, the trainer must realize the importance of close supervision in order to avoid trainee injuries and the learning of incorrect procedures. Adequate evaluation of the trainee's progress needs to be secured periodically and fed back to the trainee using reliable and valid measures. For example, a cheese and specialty food retailing chain uses film cartridges to train their store salespeople. They offer slide presentations on such topics as customer relations, gift order forms, checkstand selling, cheddar cheese cutting, sampling and selling cheeses, and beefstick sampling and selling. After each film cartridge, trainees are asked to complete a review test similar to the one presented here for the gift order form segment of the program.

What sales step is missing?

1. Customer awareness
2. Greeting
3.
4. Qualifying
5. Closing

What is the guarantee delivery card?
What information must go on the back of the gift enclosure card?
When showing a customer our gift pack line, always start with the lowest price pack.

True ( ) False ( )

Check the proper gift pack sales approach.

—May I help you?
—What do you want?
—Is there a particular gift pack I can help you with today?
—You're just looking, aren't you?

Finally, OJT should be used in conjunction with other training approaches such as programmed instruction, lectures, operating manuals, videos, and TBT. It is good practice to supplement the skill learning derived on the job with factual (i.e., cognitive) knowledge. In this way, trainees can develop a better understanding of the principles, rationale, or theory underlying what they are being taught each day.

Sullivan and Miklas[10] described the design of an OJT program in a bank that is generic and useful for a wide range of training situations. For six months, assistant office manager trainees were given OJT in 13 distinct areas of the bank. Seven major steps were followed in the design of this highly successful program. First, the rationale and goals of the OJT program were presented to upper-level executives who, in turn, communicated their support for the program downward to their respective managers whose involvement and support would be essential to the program's success. The second step involved identifying the areas of the bank in which an assistant office manager needs training such as loans, customer credit, and collections. Next, job tasks were analyzed (see Chapter 3) so that lists of performance competencies (i.e., knowledge and skills) for each OJT area could be compiled and then rewritten as course objectives. Fourth, the training staff in collaboration with SMEs (subject-matter experts) began the task of scheduling trainees for their six-month OJT experience. This involved deciding on the length of time each trainee should spend in each OJT area. Next, before the management trainees arrived, they were each assigned to a mentor, an experienced office manager who volunteered to guide the trainee through the program. Sixth, a training manual was developed by the training staff and the SMEs that included such essential information as a description of each OJT area and the OJT manager, the schedule to be followed, the training specifications for each OJT area, and forms for trainees to report on their own performance in each area upon completion. The final step in the design of this OJT program involved the development of a reporting system. Upon a trainee's completion of each OJT area, the OJT manager submitted an assessment of the trainee's performance after discussing it with the trainee.

At General Motor's Saturn plant in Spring Hill, Tennessee, each new employee goes through one week of orientation training before he or she is placed on a team of 8 to 15 people on the floor. Each team has various "champions" chosen by the team to perform various functions such as training, quality, budgeting, safety, housekeeping, and materials management. New production employees work only part time during their first two or three months, dividing their time between classroom instruction and OJT from their team's training champion. Half their training time is spent learning various soft skills (e.g., conflict resolution, communication, problem solving, and presentation) and half learning the production processes.[11]

Up to now, we have given you the impression that OJT is used only with training *newly* hired employees. This is not so! Keep in mind that informal, just-in-time OJT occurs every day at work. For example, a coworker explains to an employee a more efficient way of operating a piece of equipment; a manager teaches a new accounting procedure; a sales manager instructs a salesperson on how to overcome customers' objections; and a team leader educates a team member about various safety procedures. Recent data gathered by the U.S. Bureau of Labor Statistics show that employees spend much more time in this type of informal, OJT program than they do in formal, employer-sponsored training programs. Specifically, the Bureau found that employees spend an average of 70 percent of their total training time in informal training activities.[12]

Perhaps, we have already given you the impression that those chosen as trainers are usually skilled coworkers. This, too, is not so. Surveys reveal that first-line supervisors have traditionally been primarily responsible for their employees' OJT.[13] However, OJT is increasingly being provided by other sources such as line managers,[14] a small group of one's coworkers,[15] training specialists,[16] and team associates.[17]

Closely related to OJT is the subject of apprenticeship training. Here, organizations are concerned with developing journeymen for various skilled trades. A large part of this training involves on-site instruction.

## APPRENTICESHIP TRAINING

Organizations that employ skilled tradespeople such as carpenters, plumbers, pipe fitters, electricians, cement masons, bricklayers, painters, roofers, sheet metal workers, and printers develop journeymen by instituting approved apprenticeship programs. According to the ASTD's 2000 *State of the Industry Report*, apprenticeship training occurs in 61 percent of organizations.[18] Apprenticeship programs are typically initiated by a committee composed of representatives from management and labor. The joint committee works together with the Department of Labor's Bureau of Apprenticeship and Training (BAT) in formulating a set of standards that specify the features of the particular program being established (e.g., curriculum, number of hours of classroom and workshop instruction, number of hours of on-the-job experience, affirmative action goals, schedule of wage advancements).

The official function of BAT, established by the National Apprenticeship Act of 1937, is to formulate and promote labor standards necessary to safeguard the welfare of apprentices, to bring together employers and laborers for the formulation of programs, and to cooperate with state agencies engaged in the formulation and promotion of standards of apprenticeship. Once the joint apprenticeship committee and BAT formulate standards, they are sent to a State Apprentice Council agency for review and possible modification. It gives the joint apprenticeship committee official approval to register their apprentices, and it issues certificates to trainees upon completion of their program.

Apprenticeship programs last anywhere from two to five years, with four years being the average length. They combine on-the-job instruction together with a minimum of 144 hours per year of classroom and shop instruction (a mixture of on-site and off-site training). The apprentice method involves the organization's delegating the responsibility for socialization of new employees to several of its skilled journeymen. Thus, the journeymen trainers are a critical component of this socialization process in that they serve as models to be emulated by the apprentices. Like OJT, apprenticeship training has skill development as its major goal. It, too, uses mainly a behavioral (in addition to a cognitive) change strategy.

The classroom and shop instruction is either held in the evenings at local high schools or community colleges or during regular working hours. Many large organizations send their apprentices to special half-day classes conducted by local trade schools specializing in apprenticeship instruction. Sometimes, it is advantageous for those large companies to hire instructors from these trade schools on a part-time basis to conduct their courses on company premises. Small companies located away from metropolitan areas often have to resort to correspondence courses in order to provide their apprentices with the requisite number of hours of "classroom" training.

During classroom and shop training, each apprentice is typically given a workbook consisting of materials to be read, problems to be solved, short tests to be taken, and reading assignments in other books. The workshop permits the trainees to work at their own individual pace. Many instructors use part of their class time for presenting lectures, giving demonstrations, conducting group discussions of actual work experiences, presenting films, inviting outside speakers, or providing skills practice. An example of what apprentices might be taught in this setting is as follows: A local of the Plumbers and Steamfitters Union established jointly with a manufacturer's association a four-year apprenticeship program for developing plumber/pipe fitters. Trainees are required to work 40 hours per week while attending evening classes six nights per month (four hours per evening). Their curriculum consists of the following topics:

**First Year:**
Basic math related to pipework
Beginning course in isometric drawing and blueprint reading
Use and care of tools
**Second Year:**
City, state, and national plumbing codes
Advanced blueprint reading and drawing
(Shop) Small piping projects
**Third Year:**
(Shop) Heating work on heating equipment
**Fourth Year:**
Occupational Safety and Health Regulations
Theory of refrigeration and air conditioning
(Shop) Welding

What are some of the factors that influence the number of apprentices trained each year? A major consideration is the amount of building construction in the country. Since the building trades are by far the largest employers of apprentices, their prosperity directly influences the need for such training. A second factor is labor and management attitudes toward the bureaucracy and paperwork involved in establishing formal apprenticeship programs to produce qualified journeymen. Organizations can use other channels to develop skilled tradespeople. These include the completion of informal, unregistered apprenticeship without an indenture and with little or no formal classroom training; learning the trade in a nonunion sector of the industry or a related industry; completion of a full-time course in a vocational school; and working one's way up from an unskilled or helper classification.

If organizations do not have to use apprenticeship programs, why then do they continue? Part of the reason is that they have had the support of unions. Union members look upon apprenticeship as a way of controlling entry into their trade, thereby preventing undue displacement of incumbents by trainees. Also, apprenticeships prevent poorly trained individuals from entering the craft and threatening the trade's sense of pride and status.

An on-site learning technique that is sometimes used in collaboration with OJT and with apprenticeship training is commonly referred to as a job aid. In the next section, we discuss the benefits of job aids and give several examples of their usefulness.

## JOB AIDS

A *job aid* can be described as instructional material that is located on the job to assist an employee in recalling information that was presented during training, or else it may be used in lieu of formal training. Job aids have a number of benefits: assisting employees in remembering precise or complex procedures and rules, helping to ensure that employees avoid committing critical errors, and guiding employees during a time when operating procedures are in the process of being changed.[19] They have been used since an early study conducted by the Air Force and Navy showed that they are capable of facilitating the learning process as well as reducing training time.[20] The goal of job aids is to teach job skills and to accomplish this by using a behavioral strategy (see Figure 6.1).

Job aids are particularly valuable when integrated into a training program, and then later used by employees to recall learning after they return to their jobs. For example, the Buick-Oldsmobile-Cadillac (B-O-C) Division of General Motors is committed to the concept of achieving continuous improvements through the ongoing development of B-O-C's greatest asset—its people. Consequently, the company developed and implemented a new personal development process called PDP (Personal Development Plan). All managers and supervisors within B-O-C were given extensive PDP training targeted on teaching each of them how to work with their people on bringing about continuous development and improvement. The job aid shown in Figure 6.3 was used to remind all managers, supervisors, and employees about the overall PDP process. It specified the five PDP steps as well as when during the introductory year each step should be implemented.

Like B-O-C, Domino's Pizza also makes good use of job aids. Directly above the pizza makeline, which is a sort of assembly line, pizzas are made with sauce, cheese, and additional toppings. There are large glossy pictures of exactly what the pizza should look like at successive stages along the pizza makeline. So, if the employee isn't sure whether he or she has added too much cheese, or whether the sausage and pepperoni were spread evenly enough, all the employee needs to do is compare the pie with a photo on the wall. The office tender, who is

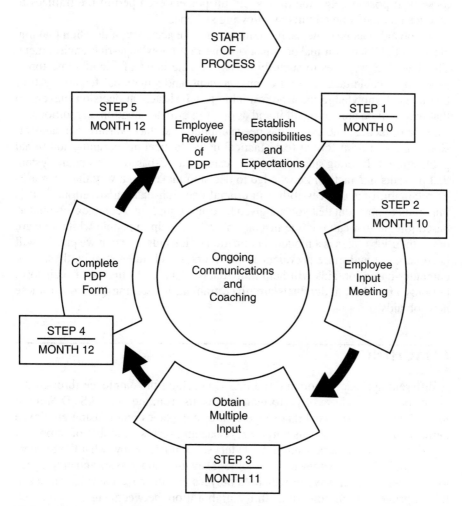

**FIGURE 6.3** B-O-C's PDP Process Schedule (Introductory Year)

responsible for slicing and boxing finished pizzas, also uses job aids. This employee uses two photos, one of the "perfect pizza," the other showing 10 common flaws, one in each slice. These imperfections include such things as bald spots, burned vegetables, bubbles, and soup bowl edges.[21]

Technical training is a large undertaking in the U.S. Navy. More than 7,000 courses are offered in Navy schools ranging from beginning orientation to Navy life during recruit training to highly advanced technical courses such as electronics and jet propulsion. At the naval school in Great Lakes, Illinois, various types of posters are used to aid apprentice electricians to apply what they have learned in their classrooms to their jobs. For instance, an AC and DC generator poster provides an overview of these two types of generally used generators. Some of these wall posters (e.g., the Series Circuit poster) even permit the trainees to practice manipulating circuits by throwing switches.[22]

Job aids can be quite useful in increasing the accuracy of decision making. Naval tactical decision makers must operate in a knowledge-rich environment. This knowledge relates to such things as characteristics of friendly and threat assets, applicable tactics, rules of engagement, and situational features. All of this tactical knowledge must be available to naval tactical decision makers so that they will be able to recall it and apply it in critical situations. Traditionally, the bulk of tactical knowledge has been supplied to surface warfare tactical decision makers in print format (e.g., tactical notes, tactical memoranda, additional publications). Training specialists have designed a PC-based, multimedia system that presents this tactical knowledge to decision makers in a way that increases its retainability and accessibility in crucial decision-making situations.[23] It is important to point out that you are given here an example of a complex, computer-based job aid that can provide instant, job-related help to people while they are doing their jobs. This is a modern application of job aids, one that we predict will become more and more prevalent in the years ahead. Interestingly, these new computer-based job aids will help individuals in the performance of their jobs, but only after these individuals are given training in learning how to use these new job aids.

# COACHING

A different approach to on-site training is coaching the employee through the use of periodic reviews of performance. Results from the 2000 ASTD *State of the Industry Report* reveal that 98 percent of companies report using employee performance reviews for this purpose.[24] Coaching serves a number of important functions within an organization. It (1) lets subordinates know what their supervisors think about how they do their jobs, (2) enables supervisors and employees to work together on ways in which employees can improve their performance, (3) improves communication and collaboration between supervisors and employees, and (4) provides a framework for establishing short- and long-term personal career goals. Unfortunately, in many organizations, problems may arise with these sessions that minimize or even eliminate their developmental benefits. Let us look first at some of the problems with this approach to employee development, and then discuss the ways that organizations can deal with them effectively.

Managers and supervisors often resist communicating appraisal information to their employees because they feel uncomfortable when put in the position of "playing God." This is especially true when they lack the skills needed for handling the coaching session itself and are reluctant to challenge or criticize the employee.

The manager's reluctance to use criticism is not completely unwarranted. In a seminal study conducted at General Electric, managerial attempts to develop an employee by pointing out performance deficiencies were often perceived by the individual as threatening to self-esteem and resulted in defensive behavior (e.g., denial of shortcomings, blaming others). This defensiveness, in turn, produced unfavorable attitudes toward the coaching program and a decline in subsequent job performance.

Some of these difficulties can be attributed to the fact that managers are fulfilling two conflicting roles: judge and helper. The manager is a judge when he or she is observing an employee's performance. As a helper, the manager attempts to work closely with the employee in order to improve the person's job performance.

The following suggestions should be used when conducting coaching sessions for motivational purposes (see Figure 6.1).

First, employees should have substantial participation in the developmental process.[25] Supervisors should do more listening than talking, ask questions that evoke lengthy rather than "yes" and "no" responses, and probe the employee's feelings and ideas. In general, the more the employee participates in the process, the more satisfied he or she will be with the coaching session, and the more likely it is that performance improvement goals will be accepted and met.[26] An exception to this suggestion is the finding that nonparticipative coaching works well with inexperienced or with new employees who have a need for a more directive approach from their supervisors or managers.[27]

Second, subsequent performance improves most when specific goals are established during the session. Setting specific performance improvement goals in the coaching session results in twice as much improvement in performance as does a discussion of general goals (e.g., "do your best" or "work harder") or criticisms without reference to specific goals.[28] An improvement plan should always be established that specifies areas in which the individual intends to change, the priority of areas needing change, and how the change will be accomplished.

Third, specific improvement goals should be mutually set by the manager or supervisor and the employee. This leads to higher goals being set than when the supervisor sets them unilaterally.[29] As mentioned previously in Chapter 4, hard goals result in higher levels of performance than easy goals.

Fourth, a helpful and constructive attitude on the part of the manger or supervisor is important. The more this individual displays supportive coaching behavior (e.g., giving recognition for good performance, assuming the role of helper, treating the employee as a fellow human being, showing tolerance), the more satisfied the employee will be with the session and with their supervisor,[30] and higher goals will be set.[31]

Fifth, criticism should be avoided unless it is used to justify disciplinary action. The key to effective coaching is to focus on what the trainee is doing right and, with the trainee, focus on the steps that need to be taken to advance the trainee's growth. The maxim is to emphasize the desired behavior (e.g., when making a forehand shot in tennis, keep your wrist stiff) rather than the undesired behavior (e.g., you are bending your wrist).

Sixth, a supervisor should provide feedback to the trainee on both behavior and results information. If, for example, the employee were a salesperson, the supervisor should tell her she is behaving effectively when dealing with customers and the effect of this in terms of dollar sales. This approach motivates the employee to engage in the appropriate behaviors that lead to the attainment of desired organizational outcomes.[32]

Seventh, from a motivational standpoint, coaching sessions conducted on a fixed-interval schedule (e.g., once or twice a year) are not as effective as those conducted on a variable-interval schedule.[33] Here, coaching takes the form of a pop quiz. However, daily coaching is more effective than using a variable-interval schedule when the trainee has yet to learn the requisite knowledge or skill.

Eighth, coaching is highly effective when the supervisor models the correct behaviors expected. When trainers fail to practice what they preach, the likelihood increases that the trainees will do what was done rather than what was said.

Finally, effective coaches are alert to situational constraints that might be interfering with the trainee's job performance.[34] For example, trainees who return to the job may find it difficult to demonstrate their newly acquired knowledge and skill due to inadequate tools, equipment, materials and supplies, or budgeting support. Trainees might also encounter a work environment that is adversely affected by too much noise, too little light, as well as too much or too little heat.

Behavioral criteria have been used by a division of Weyerhaeuser Company, a wood products business, to assist managers in improving the performance and potential for advancement of employees.[35] Weyerhaeuser's system incorporates many of the suggestions just described, and, for this reason, we briefly describe it here. Essentially, the system has three parts: appraisal instrument development, rater training, and goal setting. The system provides a step-by-step process for supervisors to follow when coaching their employees. This process consists of the following three steps:

1. The supervisor describes the employee's behavior by completing a Behavioral Observation Scale questionnaire (see Chapter 3). The supervisor is asked to indicate on a five-point scale the degree to which she or he has observed the employee behave in ways similar to those described in the questionnaire.

Taken together, the items represent a comprehensive picture of effective and ineffective performance in a given position at Weyerhaeuser (e.g., foreman, superintendent). In order to ensure that the evaluations are fair and accurate, the supervisors are given a four- to six-hour training program (a shortened version of the one described in Chapter 10) to eliminate rating errors.

2. After reviewing an employee's performance, the supervisor prepares for the coaching session by identifying the specific behavioral ratings that led to a low rating on a dimension indicating an area of weakness. Some supervisors ask employees to complete the appraisal on themselves in order to promote open and nondefensive discussion of their performance.

3. The supervisor and subordinate jointly formulate developmental plans and objectives. This process includes setting specific goals that the employee will seek to attain within a three- to six-month interval.

Many organizations today train their mangers and supervisors to conduct effective coaching sessions with their employees. The goal of such training is to increase employee motivation by giving them more open lines of communication with their boss, concrete feedback on areas needing improvement, positive reinforcement for what they do well, and specific goals for change. The strategy of this training is to ensure the effectiveness of the supervisor or manager who conducts coaching sessions. For example, Weyerhaeuser Company's training incorporates a series of modeling tapes, role-playing activities, and workbook exercises designed to teach such things as how to clarify the employee's job responsibilities, set mutually agreed upon goals, compare actual with targeted performance, analyze performance discrepancies, diagnose employee strengths and weaknesses, and pinpoint needed developmental efforts.

Another example of a systematical approach to coaching has been used successfully by such companies as Goodyear Tire & Rubber, Allstate Insurance, and Ohio Edison and is worth describing in some detail. Known as *ADEPT* (Appraising & Developing Employee Performance Training), this training program has five steps[36]: clarifying the employee's major responsibilities, developing performance standards, giving periodic performance feedback, diagnosing and coaching employee performance, and reviewing overall performance.

Now, let's look briefly at the seven learning modules that train managers and supervisors how to implement *ADEPT.*

### Module A: The Performance Appraisal

This video-based module shows a manager conducting a typical coaching session with an employee. The manager makes many of the common mistakes associated with employee coaching. After the video, the trainees are asked to evaluate and discuss this manager's coaching skills.

### Module B: Understanding Major Responsibilities (MRs) and Performance Standards (PSs)

This skill-building module teaches the participants how to establish performance expectations with their employees. Specifically, participants learn how to work with their employees on clarifying the 5 to 10 key functions of their employee's job. They also clarify the way the manager expects the work to be done and the bottom-line results that are to be attained.

### Module C: Clarifying Program Concepts With Employees

This video-based module teaches participants how to implement *ADEPT* back in their own departments. Role-plays give the trainees practice in developing these skills.

### Module D: Clarifying the Employee's MRs and PSs

Video scenes are used to teach participants how to sit down with their employees and generate MRs and PSs in a participatory manner. The object of this module is to eliminate role ambiguity on the part of employees (i.e., employees are not sure what their managers expect of them on their jobs). Vague job descriptions and weak communication between managers and employees often cause role ambiguity, which results in frustrated employees who are putting effort into doing things on their jobs that are relatively unimportant.

### Module E: Observing and Documenting
### Employee Performance

The trainees are given instructions and practice on the do's and don'ts of accurately observing and documenting (i.e., recording) employee job performance. They also learn how to eliminate various judgment errors (e.g., the tendency to be too lenient, stereotyping, prejudices) when coaching their employees.[37]

### Module F: Diagnosing and Coaching Employee Performance

Research has shown that most mangers and supervisors make incorrect attributions when diagnosing why an employee is having a performance problem and that these incorrect diagnoses hurt subsequent manager–employee communications.[38] Thus, this module focuses on teaching participants how to diagnose the causes of an employee's performance problems and how to reach agreement on the steps to be taken to solve these problems. The module also teaches participants how to give positive reinforcement to outstanding employees who deserve recognition for superior performance.

### Module G: Reviewing Overall Performance

This module teaches participants how to feed back performance information (e.g., quarterly or semiannually) in a manner that motivates their employees to improve, as well as how to establish an action plan for the next three- or six-month period.

## MENTORING

Related to the teaching of coaching is mentoring. The term dates back to Greek mythology where Odysseus asked his friend Mentor to teach his son Telemachus what could be learned from books, as well as the wiles of the world. Teaching newer and younger employees the wiles of the business world is what makes mentors so favorable and helpful. Mentors are typically people two or three levels higher in the organization than the trainee who want to help less experienced employees learn the roles in a nonthreatening, supportive relationship.[39] The goal of mentoring is the teaching of job skills (see Figure 6.1), and this is accomplished by means of a behavioral strategy. According to Kram,[40] a mentor is a manager who is experienced, productive, and able to relate well to a less experienced employee. The manager facilitates the personal development of the employee for the benefit of the individual and the organization. Typically, the mentor is about 8 to 15 years older than the protégé who is an up-and-coming professional with high career ambitions.[41] This mentoring relationship can be initiated by either party. Sometimes the protégé attracts the attention of the experienced manager by being an outstanding performer who shares common interests and values with the older manager. Other times, the protégé may seek an experienced manager who is able and willing to spend time answering questions about the organization and the protégé's job.

Most mentorships are informal, in that both people are interested in establishing and maintaining this relationship. However, formal mentoring programs in which organizations match up mentors and protégés are becoming prevalent in both the private and public sectors.[42] The 2000 ASTD *State of the Industry Report* examined the popularity of each of the different training practices. Interestingly, the only practice showing a significant increase between 1997 and 1998 among the Benchmarking Service participants was the mentoring program, which was used by 70 percent of organizations in 1998 versus only 65 percent the previous year.[43] One reason for the increased popularity of formal mentoring programs is probably the increasing number of women and minorities seeking management positions in the labor force and needing support from a mentor for understanding the culture of male-dominated business organizations.

What can be said about the effectiveness of formal mentoring programs? Through content analysis of detailed interviews, it has been found that mentors provide both career and psychosocial support.[44] Career support involves such things as providing protégés with coaching, protection, organizational visibility, and direct forms of sponsorship. Psychosocial support entails serving as a role model and counselor, as well as providing positive acceptance and recognition. It has also been shown that individuals who have experienced extensive mentoring relationships report receiving more promotions, getting higher incomes, and having greater satisfaction with their pay and benefits than individuals who have had less extensive mentoring relationships.[45]

What can training specialists do to make certain that all employees in an organization derive benefit from having a formal mentor? The purpose and goals of the mentoring program need to be clearly defined. Mentors also must be carefully selected based on their interpersonal skills and interests in developing employees. The organization should provide mentor training so that mentors know how to apply the principles of learning, engender trust, share information openly, and exhibit interpersonal skills tempered with a professional orientation.[46] Steps should be taken to ensure that mentors are accessible to protégés. For maximum effectiveness, mentoring should occur on a weekly basis.[47] It is interesting to point out that *informal* mentorships have been found to be more successful than formal mentoring programs. Apparently, protégés in *informal* mentorships tend to receive more career-related support from their mentors and higher salaries than do protégés in formal relationships. In light of this, those training specialists who manage formal mentoring programs need to instill a more informal climate in their programs by carefully outlining mentoring relationships and not promising specific benefits from participation or drawbacks for not participating. In addition, once people are identified who are truly interested in a formal mentorship, a great deal of care needs to be taken in matching each mentor and protégé so that mutual attraction exists between them.[48] Tyler[49] has offered several tips for increasing the success of mentoring programs beyond those we have already discussed, including:

- Participation should be voluntary because, if it is not, employees and managers will view the relationship as a burden and will perform their responsibility superficially.
- The duration of the mentoring relationship should be limited to about a year. Having a fixed period is less threatening because it allows the participants to make an easy exist later on, if they so desire.
- It is crucial to secure strong upper-management support by having them also serve as mentors.
- Mentors and their protégés need to get to know each other well by spending time in each other's work areas and setting specific objectives for their partnership.
- An evaluation system needs to be established by the training department to check on how well each mentor–protégé pair is doing so as to rescue those pairs in trouble.

It is important to keep in mind that mentoring can be a powerful developmental tool so long as it is implemented properly. The current practice followed by many organizations of randomly assigning protégés to mentors is analogous to blind dating where there is a lower probability of successful matching. Mentoring will be discussed again in Chapter 9 when we discuss management and executive development.

We will now turn our attention to the newest strategy for delivering learning—TBT. Today, using technologies such as the Internet, corporate intranets, and CD-ROMs enables employees from around the world to learn at a fraction of the time and cost and to learn more effectively.

## TECHNOLOGY-BASED TRAINING

Understanding what is and what is not TBT can be extremely confusing because of the profusion of terms that exist today to define the same thing. Other commonly used terms include computer-based training, instruction, or education; Web-based training; Internet- or intranet-based training; browser-based training;

instructional technology; computer-aided instruction; computer-supported learning resources; and distance learning.[50] We will use TBT to refer to training delivered by a number of different means such as the Internet, CD-ROMs, and floppy diskettes.

In 1999, the American Productivity and Quality Center (APQC) in Houston, Texas, conducted a multicompany benchmarking study to examine the best practices in the area of TBT. According to this report, good TBT can be characterized as customized, readily available, and just-in-time, and it gets trainees enthusiastic and involved in the process. The material is presented in a framework that makes sense for users with varied skill and knowledge levels, which is the reason why training specialists need to understand the benefits of each delivery method and how it affects the manner in which the material is presented to trainees.[51] For several years, the ASTD has conducted an annual *State of the Industry Report.* According to their 2000 report, companies are delivering less of their training in the classroom and more through TBT. Specifically, they found in their 1999 survey that 78.4 percent of training is delivered via classroom instruction while 8.5 percent is rendered through TBT. It is clear from their report that organizations are making large investments in TBT and that these investments will continue to grow in the future. In 1998, the average ASTD Benchmarking Service participant spent $101,538 on TBT hardware and software. By industry, those sectors reporting the highest use of TBT included nondurables manufacturing (13 percent of training time), trade (12.5 percent), and technology (11 percent). The lowest level (5 percent of training time) use of TBT was found to be in the health care sector. Predictably, the group that receives the most TBT, as measured by expenditures, is Instructional Technology staff members themselves, followed by administrative personnel and non-Instructional Technology professionals. The smallest portion of TBT dollars is directed at executives and senior-level managers.[52]

This entire book could be devoted to discussing all of the various TBT learning technologies that are now being used. It is interesting to note that the 2000 ASTD *State of the Industry Report* surveyed about 20 different methods. Let's look at those that are being used most frequently for training and developing employees.

## Floppy Disks

In the late 1980s and early 1990s, training programs were primarily delivered on floppy disks. Since the storage capacity is relatively small, TBT delivered via floppy disks is typically text-based with limited graphics. It is not that multimedia training cannot be delivered via floppy disks, but the problem is that it would take a very large number of floppies to hold even a relatively small multimedia program. For this reason, it will probably not be much longer before floppy disks become obsolete and are replaced by devices (e.g., Zip disks) that have much more storage capacity.[53] Nevertheless, one can still purchase many training programs that typically include three to nine diskettes. Among the topics covered are calming upset customers, coaching and counseling, telephone courtesy and customer service, ISO 9000—the worldwide quality standard, managing change at work, and empowerment.

## CD-ROM

CD-ROM, which stands for *compact-disc–read only memory,* is useful because it has a vast storage capacity. In fact, one CD-ROM can hold as many as 450 floppy disks. Due to their storage capacity, CD-ROMs constitute an easy and inexpensive way to distribute training programs involving text, audio, video clips, and/or complex animations. CD-ROMs are particularly good at creating realistic job simulations.[54] For example, sales trainees could be put face to face with irate customers, student nurses could be in front of simulated patients, and operator trainees in chemical plants could find themselves in a control room where an emergency is about to occur. Even people in the training field can learn about such things as Web-based training and TBT by purchasing CD-ROMs that accompany books on these sorts of subjects. These CD-ROMs provide individuals with such things as worksheets, job aids, documents, presentation templates, and links to the Web. You can purchase CD-ROMs focusing on a wide range of skills such as managing stress, organizing one's work space, and maintaining a healthy positive attitude at work.

The recent experience of a pharmaceutical company might forecast the fate of CD-ROMs. This company had been using CD-ROMs to deliver all their training materials. The company found that updating these CD-ROMs can be expensive and time consuming. By putting this information on the Internet, they did away with the expense of having to continually update the CD-ROMs and thereby increased the training department's ability to react more quickly.[55]

## DVD-ROM

DVD-ROM, which stands for *digital video disc–read only memory,* is basically bigger and faster than CD-ROM. Although they look like CD-ROMs, they are capable of holding as much as 2 hours and 13 minutes of full-screen digital video. DVD-ROMs, along with the Internet, are quickly replacing CD-ROMs. New computers are being equipped with DVD drives as standard equipment. They appear to be the new standard for providing training in business and education.[56]

### Electronic Performance Support Systems

According to Kruse and Keil,[57] Electronic Performance Support Systems (EPSSs) are designed to provide employees with the tool they need to perform a particular job task. In this sense, EPSS is the opposite of other forms of TBT in which trainees are taught something and later expected to use it; EPSS requires the learner to know when he or she needs help and to ask for it. Some examples of

EPSS would include such things as the steps involved in filling out an expense form, models of products available and prices, and the help feature built into Microsoft's Office applications.

## Internet and Intranet

Although the Internet can be traced back to 1969 when the Department of Defense needed a secure means of communication in the event of war, it was not until 1996 that it starting blossoming into what it is today. If you are not already familiar with and using the Internet, chances are that you will be in the near future. For many people, the Internet has become not only a big part of their personal lives, but more and more a part of their work lives as well. Internet-based training is becoming more popular each year because it allows training to be available on demand, to be delivered remotely, and to keep up with the rapid pace of change.[58]

Let us look at a few of the ways in which the Internet is currently being used for training purposes.

Microsoft's On-Line Institute (MOLI), accessible through the Microsoft Online Network, offers a host of computer-related courses from over 30 independent training providers. Microsoft contends that a classroom course that normally costs $2,800 can be offered on MOLI for $395.[59]

A *Fortune* 500 company described its private Web site as consisting of sales information, presentation materials, product data, and training information. The company reported that its Web site has been saving their salespeople five hours a week by cutting down on the time needed for researching, writing proposals, gathering information, devising sales materials, and dealing with difficult sales situations.[60]

A Maryland-based printing company suspended its practice of flying its salespeople to corporate headquarters semiannually to learn about new printing technology and products. Instead, a computer-based training program was placed in its Web site and downloaded to its salespeople scattered throughout the country, allowing salespeople to get new product information when they need it, to focus on only those aspects that are important to them, and to review it at their own pace.

Many companies are beginning to develop their own *"intranets"* for sharing in-house information. These are smaller, private networks that can only be accessed by company employees using special passwords. For example, Booz Allen & Hamilton, an international management and technology consulting firm, offers its employees 20 self-study courses through the company's intranet. At JCPenney, various company announcements and training materials are available to employees through its intranet. Eli Lilly, one of the largest pharmaceutical organizations, uses its intranet to provide not just needed information to employees (e.g., the employee handbook and job postings), but also outline help to computer users.[61]

## Multimedia

According to the 2000 ASTD *State of the Industry Report,* the most popular technology among the various TBT presentation methods is multimedia, which is used by 65 percent of the benchmarking companies. The decision to use multimedia (i.e., audio, visual, animations) in Web-based tutorials depends on the company's bandwidth (connection speed to the Internet or intranet) and number of plug-ins (small pieces of software that integrate with Web browsers to magnify their features). Those training departments that are fortunate enough to have high bandwidth and plug-ins can design Web-based programs that have the same full multimedia capability (i.e., large graphics, animations, text) as do CD-ROMs. With less bandwidth and/or plug-ins, smaller graphics, less audio, and less animation are possible.[62] Although multimedia training tends to cost more for development, it has been found to be 20 to 80 percent faster than instructor-led training, to result in greater trainee retention of the material, and to pique learners' curiosity while conveying information.[63]

## Virtual Reality

Today, state-of-the-art training programs exist that use virtual reality to immerse trainees wearing goggles and sensor gloves in a digitally created real-world environment. A few examples of the use of virtual reality include complex flight simulators, sales call simulations, surgery, and computer repairs. As Kruse and Keil[64] point out, the challenge in designing virtual reality TBT is to first identify those elements of a situation that can be controlled and must be mastered by the employee, and then put the trainee in control of these elements. Since virtual reality is really an off-site training method, we will discuss it later when we cover equipment simulators in the following chapter.

## TBT Best Practice

Now that we have described the TBT methods that best-practice companies are using, let's talk about the strategies that these companies are following when implementing them. The key findings derived from research conducted by APQC are as follows[65]:

1. TBT efforts at best-practice organizations are new initiatives usually designed and managed by a centralized group with dedicated funding. For instance, the Honeywell Technical Education Center is the only group within Honeywell that is providing significant TBT for learners. As the various business units within Honeywell begin to expand their horizons and move more toward TBT, the Tech Ed Center will function as the central area of expertise for implementing TBT solutions.

2. Best-practice organizations realize the critical importance of working collaboratively with the information technology (IT) function. For example, companies such as Buckman Laboratories in Memphis, Tennessee, have built their TBT functions by actually hiring people from within the IT department. These people provide insight for evaluating new training technologies, and it helps to ensure successful deployment and operations.

3. Best-practice organizations have a flexible head count that includes a core number of managers and designers and a network of supporting specialists on their teams. Additional resources are either hired temporarily from the outside or are borrowed from other internal functions. For instance, the Bank of Montreal's Distributed Learning and Performance Support group consists of 12 employees who manage another 50 on an as-needed basis. This is done to keep the organization responsive to the rapidly changing technology landscape.

4. Most of the best-practice companies "buy" rather than "build" their TBT inventories. They realize the benefit of filling gaps in their IT training by licensing extensive libraries of courses from several vendors and distributing them at a minimal cost through the internet or intranets. For instance, QUALCOMM Inc., a leading supplier of digital wireless communication products and technologies, tries to buy most of its training programs off the shelf.

5. Realizing that TBT is often delivered to a noncaptive audience, best-practice companies design programs only after conducting needs assessments (see Chapter 3) and listening to the demands of the grassroots organization. For example, before the Army introduces a new TBT course, the Army Research Institute evaluates a great deal of human factor issues such as quality of audio and video, opportunity to ask and responsiveness to questions, and the overall learning environment.

6. Best-practice organizations use a mix of TBT offerings and face-to-face training. These organizations acknowledge that some topics are best learned face to face. Typically, less than 25 percent of their courses are delivered solely through technology.

7. Best-practice organizations favor using asynchronous TBT delivery over synchronous because of its greater flexibility for the learner. Asynchronous delivery includes training experiences that can take place at different times/in the same place (e.g., taking a computer course at home over several occasions) or at different times/different places (e.g., taking a computer course on an airplane or at a hotel). With synchronous delivery, the learner and instructor experience is tightly coupled. This occurs with traditional classroom instruction (same time/same place solutions) or with broadcasts of lectures to multiple sites (same time/different place solutions).

8. Best-practice companies deliver "quick wins" through the use of simple technology solutions that deliver obvious value. In fact, most of them reuse templates. For instance, Honeywell discovered that internal systems tutorials could be put together and made available in only an afternoon via Lotus ScreenCam.

9. Best-practice companies realize that TBT solutions require some selling to learners and to traditional classroom instructors. They realize that it is important that learners see the personal advantage offered by many of these solutions and that classroom instructors need to be made a valuable part of the TBT initiative. For instance, the National Guard puts its classroom instructors through a train-the-trainer course that helps them to understand the capabilities of new TBT tools.

10. Best-practice organizations evaluate TBT more extensively than do their study counterparts. They have built-in learner assessment into their TBT offering, thereby making evaluation an integral part of the learning process. Typically, trainees are unable to move to the next skill-building exercise until they have mastered the current one.

## TBT and the Older Employee

Research has shown that a great many older employees possess computer anxiety and, therefore, are resistant to learning new TBT methods. Given the aging of the workforce, it is important to understand how to best train older adults to use computers. Following are several valuable tips based on various research findings[66]:

1. Feelings of anxiety can be reduced by training older staff members at their familiar place of work.
2. Since older employees prefer personal advice and care, people who are familiar and local training should be used.
3. Encouragement is needed from supervisors, particularly when older employees show signs of withdrawal.
4. It is advisable to visit a similar facility in which the same TBT system has already been installed.
5. The introduction of the new technology should be slow and gradual to give the older employee enough time to acquire competence at each stage before proceeding to the next.
6. The nature of the training given should be as simulating and active as possible.
7. Labeling the event as an opportunity will reduce anxiety, increase feelings of self-efficacy, and increase learning. It is encouraging to note that an introductory computer course was offered to adults age 60 years or older. A computer attitude survey was administered before and after the course. Contrary to widely held stereotypes, many of the older adults viewed computer technology positively and believed that they could benefit from the acquisition of basic computer skills. Essentially, all of this suggests that if more attention is devoted to understanding and accommodating the needs of older adults with regard to learning TBT, this problem can be solved.

The popularity of TBT in industry stems in part from the fact that it can reduce costs by cutting down on trainee travel and training time.[67] For instance, a large company can simply mail diskettes or CD-ROMs to several thousand trainees rather than flying these people to a centralized training center and then paying for hotel rooms and meals for several days. Furthermore, it is widely alleged that TBT can result in a 30 percent (sometimes, as high as 50 percent) reduction in training time and an 80 percent increase in retention of training content.[68]

Why might this training method be as good as its proponents claim? One answer is that the computer is sensitive to individual differences (see Chapter 4) in learning rates among trainees. Unlike human trainers, the computer does not become impatient or irritated with a slow learner. Equally important, the computer does not slow down the fast learner because of the presence of slow learners or a plodding trainer.

## CROSS-TRAINING OR JOB ROTATION

Participants in ASTD's Benchmarking Service reported extensive use of a variety of training practices designed to boost employee performance, one of the most popular being job cross-training or job rotation. Specifically, the Benchmarking Service found that 87 percent of companies use this on-site approach to training.[69] Cross-training involves giving trainees a series of job assignments in various parts of the organization for a specific period of time. Trainers may spend several days, months, or even years in different locations. The idea is to expose individuals to a number of environmental changes (see Figure 6.1) by rotating them through various key departments. In each department, trainees may assume an observational role or, preferably, take responsibility for training-specified results. It is important that they become personally involved in departmental operations. The best way to do this is to assign them full functional responsibility with ample opportunity to exercise judgment and make decisions. This responsibility should be supplemented with supportive coaching from an immediate supervisor in each job assignment.

With cross-training, trainees gain an overall perspective of the organization or their plant, as well as an understanding of the interrelationships among its various parts. In this way, trainees can become clearer about their career aspirations and their commitment to the organization (i.e., motivation: see Figure 6.1). Of course, at the same time, trainees increase their problem-solving and decision-making skills as well as their self-awareness.

Cross-training is an excellent method for preparing high-potential specialists for future general executive responsibilities. It compels people to broaden their perspective by acquainting them with various people, processes, and technologies. The method is also often used with college graduates and MBAs who have only a vague notion of where they want to be placed in the organization. Cross-training helps them crystallize their career plans before they commit themselves to any one career.

In order to be effective, however, cross-training must be tailored to the needs and capabilities of the individual trainee. It should not be a lockstep system in which all trainees proceed through the same departments in a standardized sequence. Instead, trainees' aptitude profiles and interest patterns should determine their particular pattern of assignments. The length of time trainees stay in a job should be determined by how fast they are learning, rather than how much time they have left to put in. Moreover, the trainees should only be placed in company locations where they will receive feedback, reinforcement, and monitoring of their performance by interested and competent supervisors.

An excellent example of the use of cross-training is the Squadron Program that has been used at Goodyear Tire & Rubber Company for training college graduates. Most college hires at Goodyear choose to become squadron members, as participants in cross-training were called. The objective of squadron training was to provide people with a wide range of experience in either technical, sales, production, or business management operations before they take their initial position in production or staff departments.

Each trainee's Squadron Program was individually tailored to match his or her experience, education, and vocational preference. Programs varied in length from 6 to 15 months, with trainees being rotated through various departments. When trainees completed their programs, they had a clearer notion of what they want to do. Also, the organization knew what each trainee can do. Specifically, the technical training program prepared college graduates for careers in such areas as research, development, machine design, project engineering, and plant planning methods.

Trainees began their program with three weeks in company orientation, becoming thoroughly acquainted with Goodyear. They studied the organization's structure, company objectives, basic manufacturing processes, and business communications. They also participated in a series of informal meetings with top company officials.

After an additional month of factory orientation, trainees discussed their career interests with the manager in charge of research and development squadrons. Each trainee selected up to six assignments to specific departments. These assignments, each approximately one month in length, helped to clarify the individual's career objectives. A chemical engineer graduate might choose to work in fabric development, chemical materials development, research, central process engineering, process development, or chemical production. A mechanical engineer might choose tire development, industrial rubber products development, central staff engineering, research, or special products development. Ultimately, trainees selected a specific job assignment as the starting point of their careers. This decision could be reached as early as the first departmental assignment or after experiencing several different departments.

Goodyear's domestic tire sales division has used job rotation for sales training. Sales trainees begin their training by spending two months at a company-owned tire store where they are exposed to basic selling practices at the retail level. They are then sent to corporate headquarters for three weeks of company orientation during which they learn about the production of auto, truck, farm, and earth-moving tires; curing; and final inspection operations. Following this are eight weeks of rotating assignments among corporate sales departments (e.g., budget sales, car and home merchandising, retail merchandising, petroleum sales, sales planning and promotion, retread tire sales and service, auto and truck tire sales). During this period of cross-training, trainees study principles of accounting, sales orientation, decision making, and computer concepts. They are asked to make written reports on each phase of their training, and their work is evaluated by training and sales department supervision. Field assignments are then provided. They include two months of training as a TBA (tires, batteries, accessories) merchandiser and two months as a credit sales manager trainee in a company retail store.

The whole area of career development is important both to the individual employee and to the organization. An employee's career represents an entire lifetime of work-related experiences and activities. The final section of this chapter deals with what organizations can do to aid their employees in handling career decisions.

## CAREER DEVELOPMENT

In today's world of work, it is unlikely that a person will remain with one job or organization for an entire lifetime. This widespread career mobility results from individuals' needs to "gain more responsibility," "find jobs in the same location as their working spouses," and so on. Related to this tendency toward greater mobility is a growing desire by employees for guidance in managing their career paths. Organizations, too, have become aware that effective management of human resource problems (e.g., minimizing turnover among recently hired employees, developing high-potential candidates for managerial positions) can be maximized through career-planning activities. In this section, we examine ways in which organizations are (or should be) attempting to improve the management of their employees' careers.

The primary goal of career development is to increase employees' awareness about themselves and their career goals by employing an information-based (i.e., cognitive) strategy (see Figure 6.1). Although career development workshops are sometimes conducted away from company premises, most career planning is conducted on site by the employees' supervisors or by members of the organization's training staff.

Certain organizations have designated a portion of their training staff as *career-planning specialists.* These individuals are often given special training in diagnostic testing in order to help employees understand their interests and abilities. Career specialists should be knowledgeable about jobs available in the organization as well as the skills required for successful performance in these positions. In this way, they can develop career paths that fit individual needs.

A career specialist can help an individual set realistic career objectives, plan a sequence of steps for obtaining them, and brainstorm ways of overcoming personal problems that may block goal attainment. For example, career-planning specialists at one of the nation's largest banks use Holland's theory of vocational choice when giving career guidance to employees.[70] This theory states that people fit into one of six categories: realistic, investigative, artistic, social, enterprising, or conventional. The realistic person prefers activities involving the systematic manipulation of machinery, tools, or animals. Investigative individuals tend to be analytical, curious, methodical, and precise. Artistic people tend to be expressive, nonconforming, original, and introspective. Individuals who are social enjoy working with and helping others but avoid ordered, systematic activities involving tools and machinery. Enterprising individuals enjoy those activities that entail manipulating others to attain organizational goals or economic gain, but they tend to avoid symbolic and systematic activities. Enterprising people often lack scientific ability. Finally, conventional individuals enjoy the systematic manipulation of data, filing records, or reproducing materials; they tend to avoid artistic activities. Listed here are typical occupations held by each of these six types of people:

1. *Realistic:* machinist, mechanic, electrician
2. *Investigative:* biologist, chemist, physicist
3. *Artistic:* decorator, musician, sculptor
4. *Social:* bartender, counselor, funeral director
5. *Enterprising:* lawyer, office manager, salesperson
6. *Conventional:* secretary, file clerk, financial expert

According to Holland's theory, there are also six environments (realistic, investigative, artistic, social, enterprising, conventional), and, for the most part, each environment is populated by individuals of the corresponding personality type. Further, individuals are more satisfied and work best in environments that will let them exercise their skills and abilities, express their attitudes and values, and take on agreeable problems and roles.

Congruence occurs when individuals work or live in an environment identical or similar to their personality type. The hexagon shown in Figure 6.4 is used by career specialists to portray the degree of congruence between an employee's personality type and environment. For instance, a perfect fit would occur in the case of a social type and a social environment. The next best fit would be represented by a personality type that is adjacent to an environment type, for example, an artistic person in a social environment. The least degree of congruence between person and environment occurs when a person's type and environment are at opposite points of the hexagon, for example, a social type in a realistic environment.

The career development staff at the bank we mentioned earlier also uses Holland's Vocational Preference Inventory (VPI) and Self-Directed Search (SDS). These instruments identify employees' preferences for a particular environment and several occupational alternatives they might consider when making an initial occupational choice, changing jobs, or considering added training. In addition to these two measures, the career development staff uses the Strong–Campbell Vocational Interest Blank, which provides bank employees with a computer printout of their interests, with appropriate job titles. Employees are also given an aptitude test battery that measures their potential in many areas (e.g., mechanical comprehension, spatial visualization, vocabulary, perceptual speed and accuracy, manual and finger dexterity, administrative, interpersonal).

For managers to become effective career counselors, they must be trained in conducting coaching sessions, establishing challenging work goals, helping employees plan for their next job in the organization, and obtaining and conveying up-to-date occupational information. It is also important that subordinate

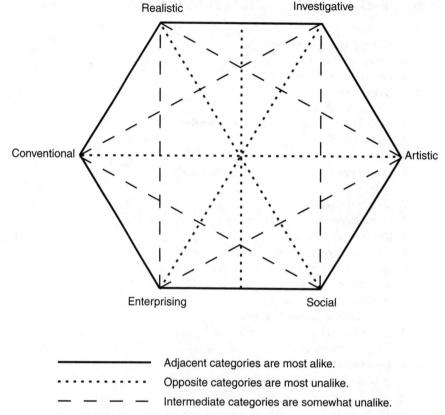

Adjacent categories are most alike.

Opposite categories are most unalike.

Intermediate categories are somewhat unalike.

**FIGURE 6.4**  The Psychological Resemblance Among Types

*Source:* Adapted from S. G. Weinrach, *Career Counseling: Theoretical and Practical Perspectives.* New York: McGraw-Hill, 1979. Reprinted by permission.

development be established by the organization as a bona fide aspect of the manager's job. For example, since 1970, General Electric has been successful in motivating its more than 26,000 managers to aid the career development of female and minority employees by linking each manager's compensation to his or her attainment of annual equal employment goals.

In order to better understand career development systems, it is important to explain that even though programs vary from organization to organization, there is a set of common tools and techniques that are usually used in most programs. As listed in Table 6.2, some of these techniques, such as self-assessment tools and individual counseling, are directed toward the employee and are designed to help the individual decide on a career strategy. Other techniques, such as career ladders and replacement/succession planning, focus more on organizational career management activities.[71]

| TABLE 6.2 Organizational Career Development Techniques |
| --- |

A. Self-assessment tools
   1. Career-planning workshops
   2. Career workbooks
   3. Preretirement workshops
B. Individual counseling
   1. Personnel staff
   2. Professional counselor (internal or external)
   3. Outplacement
   4. Supervisor or line manager
C. Internal labor market information/placement exchanges
   1. Job posting
   2. Skills inventories
   3. Career ladders/career path planning
   4. Career resource center
   5. Other career communication formats
D. Organizational potential assessment processes
   1. Assessment centers
   2. Promotability forecasts
   3. Replacement/succession planning
   4. Psychological testing
E. Development programs
   1. Job rotation
   2. In-house human resource development programs
   3. External seminars/workshops
   4. Tuition reimbursement/educational assistance
   5. Supervisory training in career counseling
   6. Dual-career programs
   7. Mentoring systems

*Source*: T. G. Gutteridge, "Organizational Career Development Systems: The State of the Practice," in D. T. Hall and Associates (eds.), *Career Develpopment in Organizations.* San Francisco: Jossey-Bass, 1986.

Now, let us briefly examine the current practices of three additional organizations to see how they apply some of these techniques in their career development programs.

The first setting is a fairly small organization of about 1,500 that is a certified Federal Aviation Administration (FAA) repair station. The company performs checks, modifications, refurbishments, and repairs on transport, corporate, and executive aircraft. The company consists of supervisors who manage clerical, professional, and skilled mechanics. A career development workshop, based on an assessment center approach (see Chapter 9) was used to help supervisors and potential supervisors to discover the challenge involved in interpersonal relations, leadership skills, and administrative complexities, as well as to provide them with an evaluation of their strengths and weaknesses in each of these competency areas. Each workshop is limited to six participants and three outside consultants who function as observers. The workshop requires about two days of each participant's time (a day for assessment and a day for career planning) and two days of the staff's time. The workshop includes a variety of activities designed to detect the participants' talents (e.g., structured interviews, leaderless group problem-solving discussions, psychological tests, role-plays, 360° ratings, and comments from coworkers).

By the end of the same week, each participant receives a comprehensive written report summarizing their strengths and weaknesses as judged by the staff, as well as a number of constructive recommendations for improvement. For instance, an individual who displays weak oral communication skills might be encouraged to take a public speaking course or join a local Toastmasters Club. The staff member who was responsible for writing the participant's report then meets with a participant to discuss the report and answer any questions the person might have. After this meeting, each participant's manager receives a copy of the report. During the same day, the participants are introduced to several career-planning concepts, given time to contemplate where they are now in their lives and careers, and encouraged to set career goals and test them on their workshop colleagues. Finally, each participant is encouraged to meet with their manager who is responsible for facilitating follow-through on the career goal setting and planning of the participants.

The National Aeronautics and Space Administration has established a Career Development Center (CDC) to help its employees deal with the question, "Where do I go from here?". Most of their employees are specialists and recognized as such, but they are perplexed about what direction to go in order to enhance their careers. Some are locked into dead-end positions and would like the chance to explore other options. To further complicate things, some are confused about what jobs are available and what kinds of skills and knowledge they require. To deal with this need, CDC has established a program called Career Counseling and Work Experience (CCWE), whereby employees are given the opportunity to function in short-term job assignments outside of their normal working area. In this way, they are given a mechanism for testing a new environment before making a career choice. Following is a description of one employee who participated in CCWE:

> This employee was a Grade 13 mathematician who applied for the work experience entitled "Development of improved computerized configuration change request status reporting system." The tasks performed included reviewing present configuration management systems, comparing their capabilities and making a recommendation for adaptation of a particular system. After completion of the work experience she was reassigned to a new area which makes use of her newly acquired skills and abilities. (Career Development Center, Goddard Space Flight Center)

In addition, CDC employs career specialists who are prepared to examine with employees the experience and education required to move through various career paths. They help the employees integrate these data into a realistic career plan. CDC also provides self-assessment techniques such as interest inventories, values clarification, and skills identification in order to aid the employees in carrying out their plans.

Another example of an approach to career development has been used by Disneyland in Anaheim, California. Their career development program included the following services:

- *Disneyland Intern Program:* Nonmanagerial employees selected for the program participate in a six-month development program involving weekly classes and on-the-job training. Upon completion of this program, employees are considered ready for promotion into managerial openings.
- *Employee Career Counseling:* Disneyland employs a full-time professional career counselor who offers counseling services to employees on request.
- *Career Planning Workshops:* The company offers a series of workshops intended to help employees formulate their career objectives and an individual career plan.
- *Career Resource Library:* This library includes such things as job descriptions, organizational charts, descriptions of available training programs, reports on occupational trends, and books on career and retirement planning.
- *Job Posting:* As positions become available, they are posted for all employees to see. This allows the company to fill about 85 percent of its salaried openings through its promotion-from-within policy.
- *Skills Inventory:* Disneyland has a computerized skills inventory system that contains valuable information (e.g., educational background, previous work experience, desired career interests, relocation preferences) on each employee who has used the services of the career planning department. When a job opening occurs, the skills inventory system generates the names of all employees who have been recommended by their manager for such positions and/or have expressed an interest in this functional area. These individuals are then interviewed.
- *Career Forum:* Disneyland schedules monthly forums in which interested employees hear company representatives discuss career opportunities within their area of expertise.[72]

Before ending this topic, we should pinpoint three groups of employees for whom career development is especially important: employees experiencing "career success and personal failure,"[73] employees whose careers have "plateaued,"[74] and employees whose "career motivation" has declined.[75]

Research on career success and personal failure is within the domain of career development because it pinpoints possible conditions associated with career dissatisfaction and frustration. A key feature of modern society has been an emphasis on career achievement and so-called success.[76] Most of us believe, either explicitly or implicitly, that success will lead to a better life. Yet, sometimes all is not as it should be. Successful people appear to be more satisfied in life than those who are not, but this relationship seems to be increasingly breaking down. Korman found that "career-successful" people are often unhappy with and alienated from others and from themselves. He attributed the emotional depression experienced by many successful people as being due to the fact that the so-called "success" these people have achieved does not meet the expectations they had for a better life (e.g., time for family life, good health, feelings of self-control and self-direction). In fact, many so-called successful people reported that they have *less* of what they had hoped for! One way of preventing this syndrome is to give new employees realistic expectations regarding the personal costs of striving for career success.

Many people are uncomfortable when they find themselves in the middle of their careers and simultaneously in the middle of their organization's hierarchy. They find that they are no longer receiving promotions. Their careers have plateaued. Unless managed correctly, these individuals can resist change and exhibit lowered performance, which can create problems for their organizations. Several ways of dealing effectively with these people have been suggested and are as follows[77]:

1. Exchange individuals laterally between existing jobs for varying time periods.
2. Redesign current jobs so that the new jobs require learning new knowledge and skills.
3. Create temporary work units to solve specific problems.
4. Reward such activities as the mentoring of younger employees and participating in community relations.
5. Use these people as internal consultants in other parts of the organization.

These steps maintain and enhance career motivation.[78] *Career motivation* has three principal components: career resilience, career insight, and career identity. Career resilience is the extent to which an individual resists career barriers or disruptions affecting their work. People high in career resilience see themselves as competent people who are able to control what happens to them. Career resilience influences a person's *persistence* in pursuing their career goals. Career insight is how realistic people are about themselves and their careers as well as how well they relate these perceptions to their career goals. They look for feedback about how well they are doing, use this information to set specific career goals, and formulate plans to achieve their goals. Their career insight affects the *degree* to which they pursue their career goals. Career identity is the extent to which people identify and define themselves in terms of their work. Individuals high in career identity are involved in their jobs and careers. Career identity reflects the *direction* of career goals—whether the individual wants to obtain a position of leadership, make a lot of money, have high status, or, perhaps, advance in their company.

How can career development techniques increase an individual's level of career motivation? Although career resilience starts early in life, it nevertheless can be changed. Supervisors can increase an employee's career resilience by giving them performance feedback, reinforcing them for what they do well, rewarding innovative behavior, and providing training to enhance their skills and knowledge and, thereby, build their self-confidence and desire to achieve.

Career insight can be increased by allowing employees to gain a better understanding of their strengths, weaknesses, and interests. This can be done through self-assessment tools, individual counseling, assessment centers, and psychological testing (see Table 6.2).

Career identity can be increased by giving employees an understanding of the rewards derived from alternative career pursuits. This can be accomplished through job rotation, external seminars/workshops, a career resource center, or other career communication formats (see Table 6.2). Organizations such as IBM, Xerox, and Polaroid offer their employees time off, with pay, to get involved in such things as community action projects, research projects, and government programs.[79]

## FINAL COMMENTS

There is a lack of formal evaluation studies in the professional literature concerning on-site training techniques. First, most of what is called evaluation is based on logical analysis and common sense. Training directors and their staffs are almost expected to take on faith the effectiveness of such techniques as OJT, apprenticeship training, and job rotation. Probably because these techniques are so closely linked to the job, there has been little empirical evaluation of their value with regard to improving employee learning, behavior, and results.

Second, very little is known at the present time about the factors that will ensure that our orientation, OJT, apprenticeship, job aids, coaching, mentoring, computer-based training, job rotation, or career development efforts will be successful. We need to know more about the proper design of these kinds of programs.

Third, although learning researchers have been at work for decades, there is not yet any science-based guide to tell us how to make accurate decisions about what training technique or combination of techniques to use in a particular organizational situation. Psychological research has provided a start in this direction. We do know, for example, that OJT can be an excellent method for teaching job-related skills because it allows for active practice, immediate feedback, positive transfer of learning, and so on. Until more evaluative research is conducted, however, Figure 6.1 should serve as a guide to the selection of on-site instructional techniques.

We feel that there is more potential in on-site training approaches than anywhere else in the training and development area. If more of an effort was made by managers and supervisors to develop their employees correctly on the job, organizations would not need to spend so much money on many of the off-site approaches we discuss in the next few chapters.

We see the Internet and intranets as continually having enormous potential for future on-site training and development efforts.

# ENDNOTES

1. D. P. McMurrer, M. E. Van Buren, and W. H. Woodwell Jr., "Making the Commitment," *Training & Development 54* (2000): 41–48.

2. R. E. Smith, "Employee Orientation: 10 Steps to Success," *Personnel Journal 63,* no. 12 (1984): 46–48.

3. J. P. Wanous, *Organizational Entry: Recruitment, Selection, and Socialization of Newcomers* (Reading, MA: Addison-Wesley, 1980).

4. S. L. Premack and J. P. Wanous, "A Meta-Analysis of Realistic Job Preview Experiments," *Journal of Applied Psychology 70* (1985): 706–19.

5. E. R. Gomersall and M. S. Myers, "Breakthrough in On-the-Job Training," *Harvard Business Review 44* (1966): 62–72.

6. C. Ostroff and S. W. J. Kozlowski, "Organizational Socialization as a Learning Process: The Role of Information Acquisition," *Personnel Psychology 45* (1992): 849–74.

7. Ibid.

8. J. Brechlin and A. Rosett, "Orienting New Employees," *Training,* April, 1991, 45–50.

9. W. J. Rothwell and H. C. Kazanas, "Planned OJT Is Productive OJT," *Training & Development Journal 44* (1990): 53–56.

10. R. F. Sullivan and D. C. Miklas, "On-the-Job Training That Works," *Training & Development Journal 39,* no. 5 (1985): 118–20.

11. B. Geber, "Saturn's Grand Experiment," *Training,* June 1992, 27–35.

12. G. Benson, "Informal Training Takes Off," *Training & Development 51* (1997): 93–94.

13. Rothwell and Kazanas, "Planned OJT Is Productive OJT."

14. P. Grace and C. Straub, "Managers as Training Assets," *Training & Development 45* (1991): 49–54.

15. E. E. Gordon, R. R. Morgan, and J. A. Ponticell, "The Individualized Training Alternative," *Training & Development,* September 1995, 52–60.

16. C. Harp, J. Satzinger, and S. Taylor, "Many Paths to Learning Software," *Training & Development 51* (1997): 81–84.

17. Geber, "Saturn's Grand Experiment."

18. McMurrer, Van Buren, and Woodwell, "Making the Commitment."

19. E. D. Pursell and J. S. Russell, "Employee Development," in K. N. Wexley (ed.), *Developing Human Resources* (ASPA/BNA Series, Washington, DC: Bureau of National Affairs, 1990).

20. C. S. Duncan, "The Job Aid Has a Future," in *Introduction to Performance Technology* (Washington, DC: National Society for Performance Instruction, 1986): 125–28.

21. D. Feur, "Domino's Pizza: Training for Fast Times" *Training 24* (July 1987): 25–30.

22. T. Sticht, J. Ellis, W. Montague, E. Quellmalz, and J. Slappy, "Combining Environmental Design and Computer Programs to Enhance Learning in Navy Technical Training," *Military Psychology 5* (1999): 63–75.

23. J. A. Cannon-Bowers, E. Salas, P. Duncan, and E. J. Halley Jr., "Application of Multi-Media Technology to Training for Knowledge-Rich Systems" (Proceedings of the 16th Annual Interservice/Industrial Training Systems Conference, Washington, DC: National Security Industrial Association, 1994).

24. McMurrer, Van Buren, and Woodwell, "Making the Commitment."

25. K. N. Wexley, J. P. Singh, and G. A. Yukl, "Subordinate Personality as a Moderator of the Effects of Participation in Three Types of Appraisal Interviews," *Journal of Applied Psychology 58* (1973): 543–60.

26. E. A. Locke and G. P. Latham, *A Theory of Goal Setting and Task Performance* (Upper Saddle River, NJ: Prentice Hall, 1984).

27. J. M. Hillery and K. N. Wexley, "Participation in Appraisal Interviews Conducted in a Training Situation," *Journal of Applied Psychology 59* (1974): 168–71.

28. R. J. Burke, W. Weitzel, and T. Weir, "Characteristics of Effective Employee Performance Review and Development Interviews: Replication and Extension," *Personnel Psychology 31* (1978): 903–19.

29. G. P. Latham and K. N. Wexley, *Increasing Productivity Through Performance Appraisal* (Reading, MA: Addison-Wesley, 1994).

30. W. F. Nemeroff and K. N. Wexley, "An Explanation of the Relationships Between Performance Feedback Interview Characteristics and Interview Outcomes as Perceived by Managers and Subordinates," *Journal of Occupational Psychology 52* (1979): 25–34.

31. G. P. Latham and L. M. Saari, "Application of Social-Learning Theory to Training Supervisors Through Behavioral Modeling," *Journal of Applied Psychology 64* (1979): 239–46.

32. Latham and Wexley, *Increasing Productivity Through Performance Appraisal.*

33. G. P. Latham, "Behavioral Approaches to the Training Process," in I. L. Goldstein and associates (eds.), *Training & Development in Organizations* (San Francisco: Jossey-Bass, 1989): 256–95.

34. G. P. Latham and S. R. Crandall, "Organizational and Social Influences Affecting Training Effectiveness," in J. E. Morrison (ed.), *Training for Performance* (Chichester, England: Wiley, 1991).

35. Latham and Wexley, *Increasing Productivity Through Performance Appraisal.*

36. S. B. Silverman, "Increasing Individual Development Through Performance Appraisal," in K. N. Wexley and J. R. Hinrichs (eds.), *Developing Human Resources* (ASPA/BNA Series, Washington, DC: Bureau of National Affairs, 1990).

37. G. P. Latham, K. N. Wexley, and E. D. Pursell, "Training Managers to Minimize Rating Errors in the Observation of Behavior," *Journal of Applied Psychology 60* (1975): 550–55.

38. K. W. Dugan, "Ability and Effort Attributions: Do They Affect How Managers Communicate Performance Feedback Information?" *Academy of Management Journal 32* (1989): 87–114; S. C. Freedman, "Attribution Theory and Management Education," *Training & Development Journal 38* (1984): 95–99; and S. A. Snell and K. N. Wexley, "Performance Diagnosis: Identifying the Causes for Poor Performance," *Personnel Administrator 30* (1985): 117–18, 123–25.

39. J. A. Wilson and L. M. Danes, "Is Mentoring Only for the Chosen Few?" *Executive Excellence 5* (1988): 8–9.

40. K. E. Kram, *Mentoring at Work: Developmental Relationships in Organizational Life* (Glenview, IL: Scott, Foresman, 1985).

41. D. M. Hunt and C. Michael, "Mentorship: A Career Training and Development Tool," *Academy of Management Review 8* (1983): 475–85.

42. R. A. Noe, "Women and Mentoring: A Review and Research Agenda," *Academy of Management Review 13* (1988): 65–78.

43. McMurrer, Van Buren, and Woodwell, "Making the Commitment."

44. Kram, *Mentoring at Work.*

45. G. F. Dreher and R. A. Ash, "A Comparative Study of Mentoring Among Men and Women in Managerial Professional, and Technical Positions," *Journal of Applied Psychology 75* (1990): 539–46.

46. Kram, *Mentoring at Work.*

47. Noe, "Women and Mentoring"; and R. A. Noe, "An Investigation of the Determinants of Successful Assigned Mentoring Relationships," *Personnel Psychology 41* (1988): 457–79.

48. G. T. Chao, P. M. Walz, and P. D. Gardner, "Formal and Informal Mentorships: A Comparison on Mentoring Functions and Contrast with Nonmentored Counterparts," *Personnel Psychology 45* (1992): 619–36.

49. K. Tyler, "Mentoring Programs Link Employees and Experienced Execs," *HR Magazine 43* (1998): 99–103.

50. K. Kruse and J. Keil, *Technology-Based Training: The Art and Science of Design, Development, and Delivery* (San Francisco, CA: Jossey-Bass/Pfeffer, 2000).

51. American Productivity & Quality Center, *Technology-Based Training: Global Strategies for Learning* (Houston, TX, 1999).

52. D. P. McMurrer, M. E. Van Buren, and W. H. Woodwell Jr., *The 2000 ASTD State of the Industry Report* (Alexandria, VA: American Society for Training and Development, 2000).

53. Kruse and Keil, *Technology-Based Training*.

54. Ibid.

55. D. Glener, "The Promise of Interest-Based Training," *Training & Development 50* (1996): 57–58.

56. Kruse and Keil, *Technology-Based Training*.

57. Ibid.

58. Glener, "The Promise of Interest-Based Training."

59. K. Wulf, "Training Via the Internet," *Training & Development 50* (1996): 50–55.

60. Glener, "The Promise of Interest-Based Training."

61. Wulf, "Training Via the Internet."

62. Kruse and Keil, *Technology-Based Training*.

63. B. Hall, "Easing into Multimedia," *Training & Development 50* (1996): 61–62; and J. J. Salopek, "Crank Up Your Coolness Quotient," *Training & Development,* November 1998, 21–34.

64. Kruse and Keil, *Technology-Based Training*.

65. Technology-Based Training—Global Strategies for Learning. Best Practices Report, American Productivity & Quality Center, Houston, TX, 1999.

66. C. L. Kelley and N. Charness, "Issues in Training Older Adults to Use Computers," *Behavior & Information Technology 14* (1995): 107–20; J. J. Martocchio, "Microcomputer Usage as an Opportunity: The Influence of Context in Employee Training," *Personnel Psychology 45* (1992): 529–51; and M. Staufer, "Technological Change and the Older Employee: Implications for Introduction and Training," *Behavior & Information Technology 11* (1992): 46–52.

67. D. J. Abernathy, "Thinking Outside the Evaluation Box," *Training & Development,* February 1996, 19–23.

68. J. Hassett and S. Dukes, "The New Employee Trainer: A Floppy Disk," *Psychology Today,* September 1986, 30–36.

69. McMurrer, Van Buren, and Woodwell, *The 2000 ASTD State of the Industry Report*.

70. J. L. Holland, *Making Vocational Choices: A Theory of Careers* (Upper Saddle River, NJ: Prentice Hall, 1973).

71. T. G. Gutteridge, "Organizational Career Development Systems: The State of the Practice," in D. T. Hall and Associates (eds.), *Career Development in Organizations* (San Francisco: Jossey-Bass, 1986): 50–94.

72. Ibid.

73. A. K. Korman, "Career Success and Personal Failure: Mid-to-Late-Career Feelings and Events," in M. London and E. M. Mone (eds.), *Career Growth and Human Resource Strategies* (Westport, CT: Quorum, 1988): 81–94.

74. D. T. Hall, "Project Work as an Antidote to Career Plateauing in a Declining Organization," *Human Resource Management 24* (1985): 271–92.

75. M. London, "Career Development," in K. N. Wexley and J. R. Hinrichs (eds.), *Developing Human Resources* (ASPA/BNA Series, Washington, DC: The Bureau of National Affairs, 1990).

76. Korman, "Career Success and Personal Failure."

77. J. Bardwick, *The Plateauing Trap* (New York: Amacom, 1986); and London, "Career Development."

78. M. London and E. Bassman, "Retraining Midcareer Workers for the Future Workplace," in I. L. Goldstein and Associates (eds.), *Training and Development in Organizations* (San Francisco: Jossey-Bass, 1989): 333–75.

79. London and Bassman, "Retraining Midcareer Workers for the Future Workplace."

# CHAPTER

# Off-Site Training Methods

In the previous chapter, we discussed on-site training methods that are frequently used in organizational settings. In this chapter, we review off-site training approaches. An obvious advantage of off-site training is that it allows the trainee to acquire skills and knowledge away from the day-to-day job pressures in settings such as company-operated training centers, hotels, conference centers, university/college facilities, or resorts. For instance, the building mechanic, assembly line worker, chemical plant operator, and senior vice president can each learn their jobs without worrying about a boiler explosion, the stoppage of an entire assembly line, the faulty generation of toxic gases, or the continual ringing of the telephone.

Another benefit of off-site training is the use of competent outside resource people who are trained trainers. Such people may include technicians, university faculty, and consultants. Trainees are thus exposed to individuals who not only have expertise in subject-matter areas, but who also are expert teachers. For instance, one manufacturer of conventional and nuclear boilers periodically sends its design engineers to special conferences held in hotels in New York City and Chicago. At these meetings, lectures are given by well-known power plant design engineers to familiarize conferees with the newest developments in fossil-generated power boiler design.

A potential limitation of off-site training can be the transfer of learning from the "classroom" to the job. Too often, trainees learn new facts and principles at lectures and special conferences with no idea about how to apply what they learn on the job. As you will see in this chapter, highly effective off-site procedures include those that simulate essential characteristics of the actual job, so that trainees learn to behave during training the way they will have to behave on the job.

In discussing off-site training methods, we again refer you back to the nine-cell framework (three goals × three strategies) presented originally in Figure 1.1. Specifically, five off-site methods are presented in this chapter: instructor-led classrooms, audiovisual techniques, video teleconferencing, cor-

**GOALS**

| | | *Self-Awareness* | *Job Skills* | *Motivation* |
|---|---|---|---|---|
| **STRATEGIES** | **Cognitive** | | Lecture<br>Audiovisual techniques<br>Programmed instruction<br>Teleconferencing<br>Corporate classrooms | |
| | **Behavioral** | | Computer-assisted instruction<br>Equipment simulators | |
| | **Environmental** | | | |

**FIGURE 7.1**    Off-Site Methods Classified According to Goals and Strategies

porate universities and institutes, and equipment and virtual reality simulators. Figure 7.1 shows these five methods classified by their particular goals (i.e., self-awareness, job skills, motivation) and strategies (i.e., cognitive, behavioral, environmental). All of the off-site techniques we discuss attempt to improve trainee skills. These skills may involve effective interviewing, active listening, more tactful handling of customer complaints, or the proper operation of machinery. Many of these skills are relevant to not only nonmanagerial employees, but managers and supervisors as well. The strategy used for teaching these skills varies depending on the particular technique chosen.

Instructor-led classrooms, audiovisual techniques, video teleconferencing, and corporate universities and institutes attempt to train employees by focusing primarily on their cognitions (i.e., thoughts and ideas). For instance, trainees may be informed about special features of products to be sold, safety procedures to be followed, more efficient ways to manage their time, or revised quality control standards. Even though lectures and audiovisuals can be equally useful in on-site situations, they are usually conducted in classrooms away from the workplace. Therefore, they are discussed here. Although equipment and virtual reality simulators also involve the presentation of cognitive information, they have been classified as a behavioral strategy because trainees are given considerable opportunity to practice their newly acquired behaviors in simulated, off-the-job settings.

## INSTRUCTOR-LED CLASSROOMS

According to the 2000 ASTD (American Society for Training and Development) *State of the Industry Report,* the average Benchmarking Service firm delivered 78.4 percent of its training in a classroom setting led by one or more instructors.[1] Despite the fact that business organizations are increasing their use of technology-based methods, instructor-led classroom instruction continues to be one of the two (i.e., along with on-the-job training) widely used training delivery methods.

In what ways do organizations make such wide use of instructor-led classrooms? First, most companies provide in-house training seminars for their employees. For example, at Procter & Gamble's Global Learning Center, employees come from around the world to attend various classroom courses in Cincinnati on topics such as Managing for Innovation, Sharpening Your Future Focus, and Leadership and the Business of Thinking. Even small organizations such as Whitmore Print & Imaging of Annapolis, Maryland, provide classroom instruction for its employees by inviting guest trainers to their facility or else encouraging their employees to attend special seminars by the Printing Industries of Maryland. Second, there exist several training resource companies that provide an incredibly large selection of seminars on timely topics led by professional trainers. These seminars are delivered in numerous cities throughout the United States, Canada, and the United Kingdom. For instance, one of these training resource companies offers as many as 85 seminars in such areas as communication skills, computer skills, conflict and stress management, customer service, design skills, management skills, skills for women, and professional development skills. Attendees from many different companies in the geographical area attend these one-day seminars at local hotels and conference centers. Third, the ASTD's annual look at training industry trends reveals that classroom training at community and technical colleges and in the corporate education departments of four-year colleges and universities is on the rise. Even though two-year community colleges have offered training programs to local businesses for years, more of them are jumping at the opportunity to form partnerships with companies. For instance, the American Association of Community Colleges estimates that the number of community colleges actively seeking to provide instructor-led classroom instruction to companies has increased dramatically from 50 percent in 1990 to 90 percent in the mid-1990s. For instance, Maricopa Community College developed a specialized curriculum of training courses to support Motorola's semiconductor manufacturing process in Phoenix. A joint Motorola–Maricopa curriculum committee designed these courses. Frequently, these courses are held at the local community college. A fourth important outside source of instructor-led training is provided by numerous professional and trade associations. These national associations deliver industry-specific classes at their local offices. For instance, the American Pharmaceutical Association offers its members AphA-developed educational programs in cooperation with various state-level pharmaceutical associations.

What can be concluded about the training effectiveness of instructor-led classrooms?

- Despite criticisms that this method involves one-way communication and it ignores differences in abilities among trainees by proceeding at a single rate, it gets high marks for both knowledge acquisition and trainee acceptance. When the basic instructional task involves the dissemination of information, instructor-led classrooms have a long history of being shown to be as good as other instructional methods such as programmed instruction, TV courses, and group discussion.[2]

- Its effectiveness is maximized when it is augmented by other training techniques that provide for learner participation and individualized feedback and reinforcement. For example, one of the authors conducted a one-day Effective Listening Program for salespeople, secretaries, and office staff. He made certain to combine the lectures on topics such as factors facilitating and impeding listening with audiotaped listening exercises. The advisability of augmenting instructor-led instruction with other techniques is confirmed by a meta-analytical research that integrated the findings from 70 different managerial training research studies. The researchers[3] examined the effectiveness of seven different training methods, three of which involved some lecturing—the lecture, the lecture plus group discussion, and the lecture plus group discussion plus role playing or practice. They found that each of these three lecturing approaches were surprisingly effective in improving on-the-job behavior as perceived by the trainees themselves, peers, and supervisors. Furthermore, their findings indicated that training that employs instructor-led classrooms is likely to generalize across situations.

- It can also be particularly beneficial when it introduces some new areas of content (e.g., the special features of some new product to be sold), it provides oral directions for learning a task that will eventually be developed through other instructional methods (e.g., the procedures for operating a piece of manufacturing equipment), it employs highly skilled lecturers, and the training materials are neither too abstract nor too complex for the trainees involved.

- Research evidence has shown that instructor-led classrooms are not as appropriate as role playing or the case study method (see Chapter 9) for modifying attitudes, developing problem-solving skills, or improving interpersonal competence.[4] Furthermore, comparisons made years ago between the lecture and conference discussion methods (see Chapter 9) for behavior change consistently favored the discussion approach.[5] It would not make sense to expect instructor-led classrooms to promote skill development as effectively as techniques that provide trainees with an opportunity for active participation, knowledge of results, and practice. For instance, we would obviously want to train machine operators in a pharmaceutical packaging plant using on-the-job training or equipment simulators rather than just lecturing them about the correct procedures to be followed.

In summary, the training objectives determine whether instructor-led classroom instruction is an appropriate training technique. If the primary goal is to convey information, particularly to large groups of trainees, this approach is effective and economical to use. Your authors have found it quite useful for orienting new employees, giving realistic job previews (see Chapter 6), instilling product knowledge, clarifying organizational policies and business plans, and educating employees about occupational safety. Its usefulness is maximized when the instructor's message can be delivered to several locations at one time through closed circuit TV or satellite programming, or the message can be reused as often as needed via videos and diskettes. For example, the Education and Training Directorate at Corning, Inc. (formerly Corning Glass Works), headquartered in Corning, New York, has made good use of the lecture approach in their farming out almost all training aimed at individual employees. For instance, they formed a partnership with the College Center of the Finger Lakes (CCFL), a nonprofit institution established to make college-level courses available to residents of the Corning, New York, area. This partnership with CCFL has allowed Corning to offer its employees as many as 1,000 different courses, via satellite programming, in areas such as accounting, management, computer science, and engineering.[6]

## AUDIOVISUAL TECHNIQUES

The effectiveness of any instructor-led classroom can be enhanced by using various audiovisual aids such as videos, TV, and presentation software. Let's start off by looking at how videos have been used to facilitate trainee learning:

- Weyerhaeuser Company has used videos of entertainment films such as *Bridge on the River Kwai* and *Twelve O'Clock High* as a basis for discussing interpersonal and social relationships in the organization's management school. These videos were chosen because they convey particular messages about effective ways of managing and handling other people.
- Videos have also been used by the authors for eliminating interpersonal judgment errors that usually plague managers when rating the performance of their employees and plague employment interviewers. We have found that judgment errors (e.g., first impressions, leniency, stereotyping) cannot be eliminated solely by lecturing trainees about them. Instead, videos are needed to provide trainees with the opportunity to view individuals on video, rate them, and discuss these ratings with one another and their instructor.[7]
- The Ford Motor Company has made use of videos in automobile dealer training sessions in order to simulate problems and reactions a dealer might face in handling various customer complaints. The technique involves filming the action as seen through the eyes of the central character in the role-playing situation, in this case the dealer, who is played by the trainee.
- Videos are an integral part of behavior-modeling training (see Chapter 4). Numerous organizations are now using behavior-modeling videos to teach their managers, supervisors, and employees how to improve various skills. Sometimes these videos are developed by the company's own training department and sometimes by outside consultants who specialize in the construction of video-based training materials. For instance, videos focus on such skills as orienting a new employee, delegating responsibility, terminating an employee, reducing tardiness, handling grievances, utilizing effective disciplinary action, and handling suspected substance abuse problems.
- Another interesting use of videos is in communications training. Certain organizations are sending their salespeople and customer service representatives to communication specialists in the hope that they will return as more confident, relaxed, and articulate speakers. By using videotaped feedback, trainees can pinpoint what they like and dislike about the way they communicate far better than any trainers can lecture them.

Another valuable audiovisual aid that can be used in instructor-led classroom settings is TV. The message can be delivered via closed-circuit TV or via satellite to multiple locations simultaneously. The TV may also have interactive capabilities. For instance, according to the 2000 ASTD *State of the Industry Report,* about 17.8 percent of organizations are using satellite TV and 14.6 percent are using interactive TV.

In recent years, new presentation software (e.g., Microsoft's PowerPoint 2000) has improved the clarity and the understandability of presentations given by trainers. Essentially, the software package helps trainers to create a series of slides that they can display electronically (using a computer) or in standard 35mm format (using a slide projector), or printed on overhead transparencies. In addition, printed handouts are prepared for the trainees that provide them with a copy of slides or transparencies along with a place to jot down notes. The software also prepares notes for the trainer that he or she can use for reference. If desired, trainers can augment their presentations by using various graphics such as clip art, sounds, pictures, and movies.

Audiovisual techniques offer unique advantages in the following situations:

1. When there is a need to illustrate how certain procedures should be followed over time. For instance, demonstrations of wire soldering, telephone repair, and welding can be facilitated with the use of TV or films. Stop action, instant replay, fast or slow motion, close-ups of equipment and manual techniques, and use of arrows to point out fine details are just a few options that are not available in live lectures.

2. When there is a need to expose trainees to events not easily demonstrable in live lectures (e.g., a visual tour of a factory, open heart surgery, childbirth). In training building mechanics, for instance, trainees can be shown a boiler gauge and a valve simultaneously by superimposing them both on videotape. The trainees can clearly see that as the gauge increases, steam begins to seep from the valve.

3. When the training is going to be used organizationwide and it is far too costly to ask the same trainers to travel from place to place or assemble everyone in one location. Instead, copies of the audiovisuals are mailed to all organizational units at one time and administered by local training staff members.

In the next section, we discuss teleconferencing. For companies such as Hewlett-Packard, Eastman Kodak, Xerox, FedEx, Domino's Pizza, and Aetna Life & Casualty, video teleconferencing has become a way of life. It is currently being used by 30 percent of business organizations[8] for teaching job skills using a cognitive strategy (see Figure 1.1).

# VIDEO TELECONFERENCING

Video teleconferencing is a method for simultaneously training individuals at multiple sites. It allows for the instantaneous exchange of audio, video, and text between two or more individuals or groups of individuals at two or more locations. A teleconferencing network basically consists of a central broadcasting facility (e.g., at a TV studio, hotel, corporate office, convention center), and a satellite service whose signal is delivered to satellite-receiving stations, which, in turn, transmit the signal to television projectors in either hotel ballrooms, meeting rooms, convention centers, civic auditoriums, or corporate headquarters.

Let us take a look now at some actual examples of its usefulness as a training strategy. According to the 2000 ASTD *State of the Industry Report,* 30 percent of companies are using video teleconferencing as one of their main learning technologies.[9]

Allstate Insurance Company links its headquarters in Barrington, Illinois, with its 28 regional offices throughout the company. The company contends that any material that can be presented in a classroom setting is appropriate for their two-way video, two-way audio, 24-hour teleconferencing system. If a trainer wants to pass out some instructional materials to the trainees, she puts it into a facsimile terminal and presses a button and it shows up in the teleconferencing rooms. If the trainer wants to show an object to the trainees, she puts it on a graphics table and it is projected on the screen. If trainees have questions, they press a button on a console in the room, their questions cue up in order of calls, and the trainer can answer them.

ComputerLand's major reason for using teleconferencing is that the store managers have a difficult time freeing their technical people to go to the Los Angeles or Boca Raton development centers for training on servicing new equipment. It is quicker and easier to use teleconferencing.

Hewlett-Packard Company has used teleconferencing to introduce a new business computer to most of its 84,000 employees all at once in 86 North American and 18 European offices.

Aetna's Television Network ties 235 field offices with Aetna Life & Casualty's home office. Most of the 17 hours of broadcasting each month are training related and focus on teaching Aetna's employees and field agents time-sensitive topics. This could involve introducing a new financial product, a new sales strategy, or information about a new governmental regulation affecting the insurance business.[10]

The costs of airtime and equipment have fallen quite a lot in recent years, and they will probably continue to drop. Even so, there are many companies that do not want to build their own facilities. Instead, they can rent facilities from various hotel chains such as Holiday Inn, Inc., and Hilton Hotel Corporation. When should an organization seriously consider either buying or renting a video teleconferencing network? A system is worth thinking about when your employees need to receive training immediately, the company does not have enough trainers to do the job, your company does not have sufficient facilities to accommodate all the trainees, and the company does not want to spend a large amount of money bringing people together. Additional advantages of teleconferencing include lower training costs due to lowered travel expenses, faster delivery of time-sensitive information, greater access to trainers with expertise in particular areas through online venues, and increased ability to train many individuals at global locations at one time.[11]

## CORPORATE UNIVERSITIES AND INSTITUTES

More and more large corporations have begun to build their own universities and institutes dedicated to the continuing education of their employees. There are currently over 1,600 such universities and institutes. The primary goal of corporate classrooms is to communicate the company's vision to all employees, to help employees understand the company's values and culture, to teach employees needed job skills, and to accomplish this by using mainly a cognitive strategy (see Figure 7.1).

Corporate campuses have features similar to traditional college campuses (e.g., classrooms, libraries, laboratories, residence halls). Moreover, these corporate learning centers are modern in that they use the most up-to-date instructional technology (e.g., teleconferencing, intranet, CD-ROM).

The ambience is very different from the typical collegiate setting because the students are older and hold full-time jobs in the company. The courses are company oriented and practical, with a time length that typically varies from a few days to a year depending on the concepts being taught. Despite the use of modern technology-based training, the teaching includes instructor-led classrooms, case studies, and team discussions and projects.

Among the best-known corporate universities and institutes are McDonald's Hamburger University in Oak Brook, Illinois; Xerox's Document University in Leesburg, Virginia; Motorola University in Shaumburg, Illinois; General Motors University located in Auburn Hills and Warren, Michigan; Chevron University in San Ramon, California; and the Caterpillar Training Institute in Peoria, Illinois. Corporate universities and institutes are not just restricted to large companies such as General Motors and Chevron. Managed Business Solution, a data processing consulting firm in Boulder, Colorado; GlobalNet, a global translations service in Pittsburgh; and Glen Raven Mills, Inc., a small textile company in Glen Raven, North Carolina, are three examples of smaller companies that have initiated corporate universities. For instance, Glen Raven Mills currently has what they call a "Lead Center" (Learning, Education, & Development) that provides training for its 3,500 employees. Executives as well as manufacturing associates are able to attend courses on such topics as business administration, computer resources, leadership development, safety and regulatory development, performance management, occupational/technical development, and professional development.

In order for you to better understand this off-site training method, let us look at one of the most famous corporate universities, Hamburger University (HU). HU is McDonald's worldwide management training center. It is designed exclusively to instruct people employed by McDonald's Corporation or employed by McDonald's Independent Francises in the various parts of the business. The year 2000 marked HU's 37th anniversary. During these years, the size of entering classes has grown from about 10 to more than 200 managers. Today, more than 50,000 managers in McDonald's restaurants have graduated from their university. It is now located in a state-of-the-art facility on McDonald's Home Office Campus and has a faculty of 30 resident professors who teach courses such as market evaluation, advanced operations, and employee motivation. Besides skills training, students learn about the company's espoused values, namely, quality, service, cleanliness, value, pride, and loyalty. As a result of MacDonald's international presence, translators and electronic equipment enable the professors to teach and communicate in 22 different languages at the same time. McDonald's also operates HU in England, Japan, Germany, and Australia.

The major advantage of corporate universities and classrooms is that trainees are from the same company and the material taught is targeted for that particular organization. The major disadvantage is the high cost of instituting and operating these types of facilities. Global organizations have to deal with the problem of language barriers among trainees and instructors.

Corporate universities and institutes can be particularly tricky to implement when the company is global, with multiple offices in various countries. Bain and Company, a Boston-based management consulting firm with 26 locations in 20 countries, has tackled this challenge by creating a virtual university on the Web. They report getting 50 hits per month per consultant. Their virtual university has more than 160 different training modules online, giving each consultant a virtual university on his or her desktop for easy access. The modules cover everything from strategic management tools to people development skills. Even with their virtual university, Bain and Company continues to put its employees through instructor-led classroom training as well.

In the next section, we will discuss equipment and virtual reality simulators, a very useful off-site training method whose goal is to teach job skills by means of a behavioral strategy.

## EQUIPMENT AND VIRTUAL REALITY SIMULATORS

Simulation is an excellent way to bring realism to off-site training situations. For some jobs (e.g., health care workers, pilots, truck drivers, machine operators), it is either too costly, inefficient, or dangerous to train workers on the equipment used to perform the job. In these cases, facsimiles or simulators of the equipment are designed and set up away from the actual work situation. Here, safety hazards are removed, time pressures for productivity are minimized, individualized feedback is increased, and opportunities for repeated practice are provided.

Simulators can be used in many different training situations for teaching job skills through a behavioral strategy (see Figure 1.1). They have generally been designed to represent tasks within the following five categories:

1. *Procedures.* In this category are the simulators designed primarily to train such things as cockpit procedures for pilots, as well as procedures for adjusting and calibrating complex electronic equipment.

2. *Motor skills.* A simulator may be used for teaching a motor skill such as climbing telephone poles, operating drilling rigs, and driving a mining truck.
3. *Conceptual tasks.* Activities requiring conceptual reasoning may be represented in simulators for equipment troubleshooting, aerial photo interpretation, and navigation.
4. *Identifications.* Simulators may represent such activities as the identification of safety hazards, terrain features, arrhythmia detection, and radar signals.
5. *Team functions.* Some complex simulators emphasize the coordination of effort among team members toward the achievement of a common goal (e.g., air defense system crews, missile launch teams, emergency room staff, air traffic control tower operators, astronauts).

In designing equipment and virtual reality simulators, it is important to maximize positive transfer of learning from the simulator to the actual work situation. This is accomplished by making certain that the simulator possesses both *physical* fidelity (representation of the essential physical components of the job) and, more importantly, *psychological* fidelity (representation of the essential behavioral and cognitive processes necessary to do the job).

Among the important responsibilities of the simulator designer is the careful analysis of the tasks involved in the job and the decision concerning which tasks should be simulated. This decision will depend on the specific training objectives of the simulator. Certain tasks will be omitted because the interactions between person and machine or between person and environment are relatively unimportant to the training objectives. Because simulators typically require a large investment of time and money to design up front, it is also important for the designer to get top management's support before the project is undertaken. One way of securing top management's backing is to show them a successful simulator in a similar business.[12]

Let's take a closer look at several examples of equipment and virtual reality simulators that are currently being used to train employees in various industries.

In the airline industry, simulators are used to train pilots. A flight simulator is a facsimile of the cockpit of a modern airliner, with functioning controls, lights, and instruments. The flight controls, instruments, lights, and warning signals are controlled by a computer that is programmed to respond to the pilot trainee's actions just as a regular airplane would. Not only can the trainee go through all the procedures involved in a number of normal flight maneuvers, but his or her trainer can call for all types of problems for the trainee to cope with (e.g., a 20-knot crosswind on landing, a fire in an engine, an emergency landing). Although the simulator cockpit is a fixed installation, it can move to imitate the effect of different aircraft maneuvers. The visual attachments to flight simulators allow the pilot trainee to see the airport and runway through the windshield. This makes it possible to provide simulator training in takeoff, landing, and instrument approach under widely different weather conditions and flight regimes.

In the petroleum and production industries, various types of simulators are used for training truck drivers and drilling operators. For instance, a company located in North Logan, Utah, has designed a mining truck simulator that provides a risk-free environment for training mining truck operators. By replicating physical system dynamics, trainees receive valuable operations experience and subsystem familiarization in areas such as engine, transmission, brake, steering, and truck dynamics. A virtual reality simulator is used that includes a full-scale driver's cab with the full array of controls and instrumentation, a wrap-around real-time photo-textured graphics system, a three-axis motion base, and a surround sound system.

In the health care industry, by taking a sensor-equipped simulator, a little black box (the communications interface module), and a computer, you have a virtual reality simulator of a full-scale emergency room at your fingertips. Trainees are taught such things as airway management, intravenous intervention, vital signs monitoring, cardioversion, external packing, implanted devices, and defibrillation. Also used are adult patient and newborn baby care simulators. Lifelike simulators provide nursing care trainees with authentic hands-on experiences.

Simulators are being used quite a lot in the electronic industry. For instance, Motorola, a company that manufactures various electronic products, has opened a lab to train production line workers throughout the country about automation so that they can program robots. Motorola's training department decided against using real industrial equipment during training because it was not conducive to learning, as well as being too costly, complex, and intimidating to trainees. The lab equipment was designed to resemble its industrial counterpart in form and function but is smaller and easier to operate.[13]

A highly sophisticated virtual reality simulator is currently being used to train emergency responders to handle various disasters (e.g., aircraft fires, hazardous materials skills, airline crashes, forest fires) that may need to be faced in the twenty-first century. Virtual reality simulators bring the emergency responder to the scene of an incident where he or she is forced to make decisions to mitigate the incident. Using vivid three-dimensional computer generated visual scenes, the trainee is virtually transported in to the emergency scene and called upon to use their skills to assess and respond to the incident at hand.

The Applied Physical Laboratory at Johns Hopkins University has designed a simulator for the Federal Bureau of Investigation (FBI) to enhance an agent's ability to detect truth and deception during an interview process. This PC-based training tool models human behavior using a computer-simulated person in a realistic setting. The training module facilitates an understanding and awareness of the psychology of human interaction through an interactive process. This self-paced multimedia courseware employs a sequence of questions and statements with a visual and audio response by an actor or actress to provide a realistic two-way conversational interview. Also, FBI trainees can observe their own improvement via critiques while developing their interview skills.

ASTD's 2000 *State of the Industry Report*[14] indicates that about 22 percent of the participating benchmarking companies use equipment simulators and about 3 percent use virtual reality simulators (i.e., three-dimensional learning experiences through fully, functional realistic models). Despite its expense to design, equipment and virtual reality simulation can be expected to increase steadily in the twenty-first century.

## FINAL COMMENTS

What can we conclude about the various off-site training methods? First, instructor-led classrooms have, over the years, been unduly criticized by us and authors of other training and development books. It can be a cost-effective technique for transmitting factual information to large groups of trainees. Further, positive results can be expected when dynamic, knowledgeable individuals are chosen as lecturers.

Second, we predict the continued rise in popularity of using various audiovisual techniques, particularly the use of software such as PowerPoint. Complex materials can be presented in a much more organized, clearer, and interesting manner.

Teleconferencing and corporate universities and institutes have also become popular as off-site training methods. We predict that the future belongs to video teleconferencing as well as corporate classrooms. Video teleconferencing is an excellent way of providing first-rate training to large numbers of individuals at multiple sites at a relatively low cost. Corporate universities and institutes allow individuals to receive training from others in their company using job-relevant materials.

Although equipment and virtual simulators are expensive to implement, there is something quite appealing about training people on a replica of the real thing, so as to ensure maximum positive transfer of learning. When the number of trainees is large enough to warrant the expense, organizations should invest in high-fidelity simulators.

## ENDNOTES

1. D. P. McMurrer, M. E. Van Buren, and W. H. Woodwell Jr., *The 2000 ASTD State of the Industry Report* (Alexandria, VA: American Society for Training and Development, 2000).

2. S. J. Carroll, F. T. Paine, and M. M. Ivancevich, "The Relative Effectiveness of Training Methods: Expert Opinion and Research," *Personnel Psychology 25* (1972): 495–509.

3. M. J. Burke and R. R. Day, "A Cumulative Study of the Effectiveness of Managerial Training," *Journal of Applied Psychology 71* (1986): 232–45.

4. Carroll, Paine, and Ivancevich, "The Relative Effectiveness of Training Methods."

5. J. Levine and J. Butler, "Lecture Versus Group Decision in Changing Behavior," *Journal of Applied Psychology 36* (1952): 29–33; and K. Lewin, "Group Decision and Social Change," in E. E. Maccoby, T. M. Newcombe, and E. L. Hartley (eds.), *Readings in Social Pscyhology* (New York: Henry Holt, 1958): 197–211.

6. S. Lang, "Corning's Blueprint for Training in the 90's," *Training,* July 1991, 33–36.

7. G. P. Latham, K. N. Wexley, and E. D. Pursell, "Training Managers to Minimize Rating Errors in the Observation of Behavior," *Journal of Applied Psychology 60* (1975): 550–55; and K. N. Wexley, R. E. Sanders, and G. A. Yukl, "Training Interviewers to Eliminate Contrast Effects in Employment Interviews," *Journal of Applied Psychology 57* (1973): 233–36.

8. McMurrer, Van Buren, and Woodwell, *The 2000 ASTD State of the Industry Report.*

9. Ibid.

10. K. W. Porter, "Tuning in to TV Training," *Training & Development Journal 44* (1990): 73–77.

11. P. D. Munger, "High-Tech Training Delivery Methods: When to Use Them," *Training & Development 51* (1997): 46–47; and E. C. Thach and K. L. Murphy, "Training Via Distance Learning," *Training & Development 49* (1995): 44–46.

12. B. Lierman, "How to Develop a Training Simulation," *Training & Development 48* (1994): 50–52.

13. A. F. Cheng, "Hands-On Learning at Motorola," *Training & Development 44* (1990): 34–35.

14. McMurrer, Van Buren, and Woodwell, *The 2000 ASTD State of the Industry Report.*

# CHAPTER

# Developing and Training Leaders: Theoretical Approaches

Peter Drucker, one of the most well-known writers on the effective practice of management, made an observation back in 1987 that in over 40 years of work as a consultant in a wide variety of organizations, he had never met a single "natural"—an executive who was born effective.[1] The underlying theme of this chapter supports Drucker's observation, namely, that people learn how to be effective leaders.

In this chapter, we present management development approaches that can be used to ensure quality leadership in our nation's organizations. These particular approaches are well grounded in theories of leadership and/or behavior change. In describing each management development approach, we explain what is done, how it is done, and why it is done.

We also examine evidence to see if the approach brings about a positive change in a manager's behavior. We answer the question, "Does the management development approach attain the objectives for which it was designed?" As in previous chapters, we again use the nine-cell conceptual scheme presented originally in Figure 1.1. Figure 8.1 displays the 11 theoretically based approaches discussed in this chapter. We begin our examination with a description of programs designed to promote managers' self-awareness of their leadership style.

## SELF-AWARENESS

Training programs designed to increase understanding of ourselves focus on role responsibility in the organization, recognizing differences between our managerial style versus our philosophy and practice, and improving interpersonal skills through awareness of how we are viewed by others. Two training approaches that use a cognitive strategy are managerial role theory and double-loop learning. Another approach, called leader match, uses primarily a behavioral strategy

223

**GOALS**

| | Self-Awareness | Job Skills | Motivation |
|---|---|---|---|
| **Cognitive** | Managerial role theory<br>Double-loop learning | Vroom–Yetton model | Role motivation<br>Need for achievement<br>Survey feedback |
| **Behavioral** | Leader match | Grid seminars<br>Leader–member exchange | Social learning theory<br>(behavior modeling) |
| **Environmental** | | | Behavior modification |

**STRATEGIES**

FIGURE 8.1     Goals and Strategies of Theoretically Based Approaches for Management Development

to teach people how to change the work environment in order to improve their managerial self-awareness.

## Managerial Role Theory: Henry Mintzberg

Management theorists have traditionally been content to point out that the primary job of a manager is to plan, organize, coordinate, and control resources (e.g., technological, capital, human). But these four functions, first introduced by the French industrialist Fayol in the early 1900s, tell us little about what managers actually do in their jobs. According to Mintzberg,[2] before we can develop effective managers, we need to have a clear understanding of the nature of their work. So, he developed a theoretical perspective of what managers (e.g., first-line supervisors, middle managers, chief executive officers) do in their jobs. Based on interviews and observations of managers, he found that managers do not have sufficient time to carefully plan, organize, coordinate, and control both their activities and those of their employees. Instead, today's manager must perform a large quantity of work at an unrelenting pace. In fact, Mintzberg observed that half of a manager's activities are completed in less than nine minutes, and only one-tenth of them take more than an hour to complete. In other words, the job of managing is often not conducive for reflective, systematic planning as was once thought. Rather, a manager must be a full-time responder to stimuli and must prefer "live" rather than delayed action.

In order to fully appreciate the implications of Mintzberg's writings for developing effective managers, it is important to understand the concept of role, since the crux of his theory is the notion of managerial roles. A *role* is an organized set of behaviors belonging to an identifiable office or position. An individual manager's personality can affect how, but not whether, a role is performed.

Based on systematic observations of five executives, Mintzberg concluded that all managerial positions can be defined in terms of the following 10 roles:

figurehead, leader, liaison, monitor, disseminator, spokesperson, entrepreneur, disturbance handler, resource allocator, and negotiator. Differences in managerial functions and levels affect only the relative importance of these 10 roles.

Management training based on role theory requires that the trainee become aware of a "contingency theory of managerial work." That is, the trainee needs to understand that the relative importance that should be given to each of their roles is affected by four basic variables: (1) the organization, the type of industry, the technology, and other factors in the environment; (2) the type of job itself, namely, its level in the organization and the function (e.g., marketing, quality control, or production) that the manager oversees; (3) the person in that job, that is, the effects of the individual's personality and leadership style; and (4) variations in the person's job caused by the situation, such as seasonal variations and temporary threats.

The primary purpose of a managerial training program is to teach managers how to shift their cognitive processes quickly, as they encounter different problems that need resolution. They are encouraged during the training to understand the actual nature of their managerial work. This is accomplished by encouraging them to ask themselves 14 sets of questions and/or receiving feedback from an objective third party who has spent days or weeks collecting answers to these questions by observing them. Shown below are two examples of these sets of questions:

> How do my subordinates react to my managerial style? Am I sufficiently sensitive to the powerful influence my actions have on them? Do I fully understand their reactions to my actions? Do I find an appropriate balance between encouragement and pressure? Do I stiffle their initiative?

> What information do I disseminate in my organization? How important is it that my subordinates get my information? Do I keep too much information to myself because dissemination of it is time consuming or inconvenient? How can I get more information to others so they can make better decisions?

After this self-study, the trainees are taught that there are several areas where they can concentrate their attention to improve their effectiveness. Briefly, these areas include:

1. *Sharing information:* The manager must give conscious attention to the dissemination of information to subordinates.
2. *Dealing consciously with superficiality:* The manager must deal consciously with the pressures that drive her or him to handle problems superficially.
3. *Sharing the job if information can be shared:* One way to deal with the heavy managerial workload, particularly at top corporate levels, is to share the job with a management team or task force.
4. *Making the most of obligations:* Managers should make a conscious effort to turn certain ceremonial duties and routine responsibilities to their own advantage. For example, the need to attend a routine meeting may present a chance to tap a new source of information.
5. *Freeing self from obligations:* Managers must free themselves from obligations that detract them from important issues.

6. *Emphasizing the role that fits the situation:* Although required to perform all 10 basic managerial roles, managers must pay attention to choosing which roles to emphasize in different situations.

7. *Seeing a comprehensive picture in terms of its details:* Though always working with small pieces of information, the manager must never forget to think about the whole organizational picture.

8. *Recognizing own influence in the organization:* Because subordinates are highly sensitive to the actions of their manager, managers must act with conscious recognition of the effects of their actions on employees.

9. *Dealing with a growing coalition:* Any organizational unit exists because certain people created it and are prepared to support it. One of the most important tasks of the effective manager is keeping this coalition of people together by ensuring that the benefits received by each of them is commensurate with their support of the unit.

10. *Using the behavioral scientist:* Clearly, the complexity of the problems that managers face, especially those at upper levels, will require that they turn more and more to behavioral scientists for help.

Research involving a survey of nearly 3,000 managers supports Mintzberg's role framework by showing that 6 of his 10 roles (i.e., entrepreneur, monitor, liaison, leader, spokesperson, resource allocator) are, in fact, measurable and meaningful for managers.[3] In addition, managers' perceptions of relative role importance across managerial levels and functions were found to be sufficiently similar to support Mintzberg's contention that managerial jobs are essentially alike. However, systematic variation was also found that supports his contention that there are differences in role emphasis across levels and functions.

Further support for Mintzberg's theory is provided in a study of over 1,000 managers at IBM.[4] The results suggested that a common approach to training and developing senior-level managers is both feasible and desirable. This is because the leadership positions in an organization involve essentially the same managerial roles. However, the relative emphasis that should be placed on training content for supervisors versus middle managers versus executives should differ.

Training for supervisors should focus on one-to-one skills such as motivation, career planning, and performance feedback. Training for middle-level managers needs to focus on the skills needed for designing and implementing effective groups and intergroup work and information systems, defining and monitoring group-level performance indicators, diagnosing and resolving problems within and among work groups, negotiating with peers and supervisors, and designing and implementing reward systems that support cooperative behavior. Training for executive positions, IBM found, should emphasize the external environment. The curriculum should focus on broadening the executive's understanding of the organization's competition, world economics, politics, and social trends. This approach to executive development will be elaborated on in Chapter 9.

To our knowledge, there is no empirical evidence that this self-study program actually increases a manager's self-awareness (see Figure 1.1) or managerial effectiveness per se. Frankly, much of the research to date supporting it is of an indirect nature. However, on a positive note, Mintzberg's realistic description of managerial work may help to reduce training costs. It may stop some people from entering managerial training programs to attain jobs for which they are really not interested or suited.

## Double-Loop Learning: Chris Argyris

Double-loop learning trains leaders to move from one set of behavioral strategies (termed Model I) to a presumably "better" set of behaviors (termed Model II). This is accomplished by making managers aware cognitively of the difference between what they actually do versus what they think they espouse they do when managing others. According to Argyris,[5] the vast majority (i.e., over 95 percent) of managers are programmed with "Model I theories-in-use." These managers strive to attain four primary values: (1) achieve purposes that they have defined for themselves, (2) win rather than lose, (3) suppress negative feelings, and (4) maximize rationality and minimize emotionality. To satisfy these values, people learn a set of action strategies that maximize their control over others. These action strategies result in other people becoming defensive and secretive about their activities. Problem solving in organizations tends to become ineffective, because the public testing of ideas (especially those issues that may be difficult and threatening) is all but forgotten, because everyone begins to "play it safe." Further, individuals are implicitly taught not to question the fundamental design, values, or goals of their organization. This phenomenon is called *single-loop* learning.

Argyris has argued that when single-loop learning exists in an organization, people have a tendency to deal with problems that are both difficult and threatening by compounding them instead of trying to truly solve them. In fact, these people create conditions within their organizations that inhibit the effective solution of these kinds of problems, and they also help to create an organizational culture that reinforces these limitations. Given this culture, over a period of time people begin to accept the idea that their organization is not a place for learning, and, consequently, they cease learning. In these kinds of organizations, people may accomplish their everyday jobs at increasing cost and organizational rigidity. The only way out, Argyris argued, is for top executives to first address these difficult underlying issues, and then work on converting from Model I (single-loop learning) to Model II behavior.

Model II strategies encourage the sharing of valid information, free and informed choice, and internal commitment among people. Like Model I, the action strategies required to satisfy these values emphasize that individuals articulate their goals and ideas and openly attempt to influence their environment. Model II, however, couples openness with an invitation to others to confront one's views and possibly alter them using valid information. That is, individuals who understand Model II become skilled at inviting double-loop learning (i.e., knowing how to articulate what one believes in and encouraging healthy inquiry and questioning of one's beliefs).

Argyris's training is designed to teach people to become aware of their espoused theories of action versus their theories-in-use. Espoused theories are those that people are aware of and would like to believe are the basis for their actions. Theories-in-use, on the other hand, are determined by observing an individual's actual behavior. Most people are not aware that the theories they espouse are incongruent with how they actually behave when dealing with others. This is true for two reasons. First, most people with Model I theories-in-use are so busy trying to win and control others, they do not have the ability to reflect accurately on their own behavior. Second, other people with Model I theories-in-use have been conditioned not to tell us when our behavior is incongruent with what we espouse.

The ultimate objective of double-loop training is to increase openness of communication and feedback among organizational members; increase willingness to openly communicate errors and failures, so that people will learn from this feedback; and consequently increase decision-making and policy-making effectiveness. The training program involves eight steps. First, the trainees read literature describing Models I and II in detail. Second, a group leader moderates discussion to ensure that trainees have mastered the key concepts in both models. Third, the trainees read or write a case study (see Chapter 9) and propose a solution to the problem.[6] The solution must include statements of what the trainees would do, plus their feelings and thoughts about their behavior. Fourth, a trainer analyzes the solutions to infer the degree to which they approximate Model I or Model II. Fifth, a trainer divides the trainees into small-groups. Each group examines one strategy or solution to the case that was typical of Model I solutions given by the trainees in step 3. Their task is to develop a Model II alternative strategy for the problem. Sixth, after 30 minutes of small-group discussion, the groups come together again. Each subgroup describes the intervention or solution that they developed. Seventh, one representative from each subgroup role plays the solution with a trainer. Eighth, the group provides feedback on the effectiveness of the feedback in adhering to Model II and solving the problem.

These steps are based on two basic principles of learning, namely, active participation and knowledge of results. However, a third variable, practice, apparently is not sufficiently provided during the training. Argyris reports that, despite these eight steps, people can only develop Model II solutions; they cannot behave in a manner congruent with Model II. Moreover, at the time that they are engaging in the behavior, they are unaware that they are still adhering to Model I. Thus, the training program appears to do well as defined by learning criteria (see Chapter 4), but it fails to do well on behavioral measures. Moreover, the program is extremely costly. Argyris illustrated this by describing that it took three years to help presidents of only six organizations move part way from Model I to Model II. As you will see later, this outcome is not surprising when the problem is viewed from an environmental rather than a cognitive strategy. When other people in the trainee's environment fail to reinforce Model II behavior on the job, it is unlikely that the newly acquired behavior will be maintained. The behavior that Argyris wishes to shape is especially difficult to approximate because Model I behavior has been well conditioned in most of us from an early age.

## The Leader Match Concept: Fred E. Fiedler

Leader match training teaches people how to change the situation so that it is favorable to them. It is classified here as an environmental strategy because the emphasis is training managers to change their situations to fit their own basic personality.

Leader match[7] is a training program based on a contingency model that has been developed over almost 40 years by Fred E. Fiedler and associates.[8] The theory states that the effectiveness of a leader depends on a proper match between the leader's primary motivational structure or style and the degree to which the situation in which the leader is working enables him or her to have control and influence over employees as well as the task itself. The training program is classified under the category of increasing one's self-awareness because it is designed to teach managers how to become aware of their primary motivation style, to diagnose the situation in which they are working, and to change the situation to fit their personality rather than the converse. Thus, the training differs from that designed by Argyris. Rather than focusing on the inadequacies of the leader and how these inadequacies must be corrected to overcome various situations, leader match focuses on teaching managers to understand the nature of the situation and how it can be changed so as to assist them in performing their jobs effectively. Managers become effective leaders when they change their situations to fit their leadership styles.[9]

The leader's primary motivational style is measured by an instrument known as the Least Preferred Co-Worker (LPC) Scale (see Table 8.1). Trainees are asked to think of the one person (e.g., manager, peer, employee) with whom they least preferred working. This person may be someone with whom the trainee works now or with whom the trainee has worked in the past. It does not have to be the person the trainee *liked* least well, but should be the person with whom the trainee had the most difficulty getting a job done. Each trainee describes this person on the LPC Scale by placing an "X" in the appropriate space. The scale consists of pairs of words that are opposite in meaning, such as pleasant and unpleasant. After giving a rank in each of the bipolar categories, add them up and come up with a total score. A total score of 64 or higher is considered to be a high score, while a total score of 57 or lower is a low score. These scores indicate what kind of leadership style a managerial trainee possesses. A high LPC score identifies leaders who are motivated primarily by the goal of having close interpersonal relations and group support. These high-LPC leaders are said to be primarily *relationship motivated*. Those who desire more tangible

**TABLE 8.1    The Least Preferred Co-Worker (LPC) Scale**

| | | | | | | | | | | *Scoring* |
|---|---|---|---|---|---|---|---|---|---|---|
| Pleasant | 8 | 7 | 6 | 5 | 4 | 3 | 2 | 1 | Unpleasant | _____ |
| Friendly | 8 | 7 | 6 | 5 | 4 | 3 | 2 | 1 | Unfriendly | _____ |
| Rejecting | 1 | 2 | 3 | 4 | 5 | 6 | 7 | 8 | Accepting | _____ |
| Tense | 1 | 2 | 3 | 4 | 5 | 6 | 7 | 8 | Relaxed | _____ |
| Distant | 1 | 2 | 3 | 4 | 5 | 6 | 7 | 8 | Close | _____ |
| Cold | 1 | 2 | 3 | 4 | 5 | 6 | 7 | 8 | Warm | _____ |
| Supportive | 8 | 7 | 6 | 5 | 4 | 3 | 2 | 1 | Hostile | _____ |
| Boring | 1 | 2 | 3 | 4 | 5 | 6 | 7 | 8 | Interesting | _____ |
| Quarrelsome | 1 | 2 | 3 | 4 | 5 | 6 | 7 | 8 | Harmonious | _____ |
| Gloomy | 1 | 2 | 3 | 4 | 5 | 6 | 7 | 8 | Cheerful | _____ |
| Open | 8 | 7 | 6 | 5 | 4 | 3 | 2 | 1 | Guarded | _____ |
| Backbiting | 1 | 2 | 3 | 4 | 5 | 6 | 7 | 8 | Loyal | _____ |
| Untrustworthy | 1 | 2 | 3 | 4 | 5 | 6 | 7 | 8 | Trustworthy | _____ |
| Considerate | 8 | 7 | 6 | 5 | 4 | 3 | 2 | 1 | Inconsiderate | _____ |
| Nasty | 1 | 2 | 3 | 4 | 5 | 6 | 7 | 8 | Nice | _____ |
| Agreeable | 8 | 7 | 6 | 5 | 4 | 3 | 2 | 1 | Disagreeable | _____ |
| Insincere | 1 | 2 | 3 | 4 | 5 | 6 | 7 | 8 | Sincere | _____ |
| Kind | 8 | 7 | 6 | 5 | 4 | 3 | 2 | 1 | Unkind | _____ |
| | | | | | | | | | Total | _____ |

*Source:* F. E. Fiedler, M. M. Chemers, and L. Mahar, *Improving Leadership Effectiveness: The Leader Match Concept.* New York: Wiley, 1976. Reprinted by permission of John Wiley and Sons, Inc.

evidence of their accomplishments, as indicated by successful task performance, are said to be primarily *task motivated* and are identified by low LPC scores. This is not to imply that some people are concerned *only* with satisfying task requirements or *only* with getting along with others. Everyone is concerned with the attainment of both goals. The theory states that, for some people, the concern for task accomplishment is dominant over the concern for good relations with others. As soon as the primary need is satisfied, the individual immediately becomes concerned with satisfying their secondary need.

A leader's "situational control" is determined by his or her organizational context in terms of three dimensions: (1) leader–member relations; (2) the degree of task structure; and (3) the leader's position power. Leader–member; relations refers to the manager's perception of the amount of loyalty, dependability, and support that he or she receives from subordinates; it is a measure of how well the manager perceives that he or she and the group get along with one another. Task structure relates to how clearly the employees' jobs (i.e., procedures, goals, evaluation criteria) are spelled out in the eyes of the manager. Position power concerns how much power or authority the manager perceives the organization has given him or her for the purpose of directing, rewarding, and disciplining employees when appropriate.

A situation is considered to be highly favorable for a manager when he or she has good leader–member relations, the tasks are highly structured, and the manager can easily reward and discipline employees. An example of a leader in a highly favorable situation is the well-liked commander of a military crew. On the other hand, the situation is unfavorable to the extent that there are poor leader–member relations, the tasks to be performed are highly unstructured, and the manager possesses limited authority. An example of this would be the disliked chairperson of a volunteer committee with an ambiguous problem that needed solving.

Research based on Fiedler's contingency model has shown that task-motivated (i.e., low-LPC) leaders perform well in situations that offer either a high or low degree of situational control. This is because, in highly unfavorable situations (e.g., the sinking Titanic), a take-charge person who is not all that concerned with the feelings or bruised egos of others is frequently effective in fulfilling job requirements (e.g., getting people immediately into lifeboats). Once the situation becomes highly favorable (i.e., people are rescued), this same leader does not need to be concerned as much with the task because things are going well. Therefore, that leader's attention can be turned to showing concern and giving support to others. Relationship-motivated (i.e., high-LPC) leaders, on the other hand, tend to perform best when situations are intermediate or moderate in favorability.

These findings suggest two major options for improving the quality of a manager's performance. In order to match manager's motivational pattern with the situation, one can either attempt to change their personality or their situational control. Attempting to change an individual's personality or motivational structure is an extremely difficult and uncertain undertaking with most managers (e.g., see the previous section on double-loop learning). Fiedler prefers to focus on training managers to modify their situational control to fit their personality structure in order to increase their job performance.

Leader match can be presented in the form of a self-administered workbook or through technology-based training (TBT) (see Chapter 6) in approximately 5 to 12 hours. It is recommended that the learning be spaced over two or three days in order to derive maximum benefit. Sometimes the training is augmented by lectures, discussions, and videos.

The training is divided into three major sections. The first section is concerned with helping trainees to identify their leadership style by completing the LPC Scale. The second section shows trainees how to diagnose their situational control by filling out scales measuring their perceptions of leader–member relations, task structure, and position power. Part three teaches trainees how to change their situation to maximize their effectiveness. They are given specific suggestions on how to change leader–member relations, task structure, and position power. For example, leader–member relations can be affected by increasing or decreasing one's accessibility to employees; task structure can be affected by spelling out in detail what is required of employees; and position power can be changed by taking away or giving more decision-making power to employees. Remember, the word *favorable* is not to be confused with the words *good* or *appropriate*. What is good or appropriate for the low-LPC person is not necessarily good or appropriate for the high-LPC person.

How well does the program work? There is considerable debate on the validity of the LPC Scale.[10] However, exhaustive reviews of the research literature suggest that the reliability and validity of the scale is satisfactory.[11] Moreover, Fiedler and associates have provided more evaluative evidence than just about any other management theorist, which satisfies the requirements set forth in Chapter 5 for evaluating training effectiveness (e.g., the use of a control group, multiple criteria, longitudinal measures, etc.). For example, Fiedler and Mahar[12] described 12 studies testing the effectiveness of leader match. Five studies were conducted in civilian organizations, and seven were conducted in military settings. The performance evaluations were collected from two to six months after training. The evaluations of 423 trained leaders were compared with those of 484 leaders who had been randomly assigned to control groups. All 12 studies yielded statistically significant results supporting leader match training. Fiedler and colleagues[13] also found that leader match training combined with behavior-modeling training was effective in decreasing accidents in silver mining and increasing productivity. A five-year follow-up evaluation showed that the combination of both types of training continued to have a beneficial effect on safety and productivity.[14] Burke and Day conducted a meta-analysis to examine the effectiveness of various managerial training methods.[15] The researchers concluded that, with respect to behavioral criteria (see Chapter 5), leader match is indeed effective.

On the other hand, not everything written about leader match has been positive. For instance, Frost[16] used a pretest–posttest control group design (see Chapter 5) and showed that experienced managers who received training not only changed their situational control, but also were able to do so in accordance with leader match prescriptions. Frost also compared the leader match training against an alternative training method and a control group. In the alternative training method, trainees were not informed of their LPC scores, but they were taught ways of changing their level of situational control. On-the-job behavior of the trainees was measured using a Behavior Observation Scale (see Chapter 5). Unfortunately, the results showed that performance in both training groups was basically the same as that of the control group. In commenting on these discouraging results, Frost reminded readers that most earlier evaluative studies on leader match involved supervisors who either joined new groups or else were new to their positions at the time of training. Based on these findings, Frost concluded that for experienced leaders in established situations, behavior modeling (Chapter 4) may be more effective than leader match for improving their performance. Moreover, in the Fiedler et al.[17] research mentioned previously, a comparison was made between "structured management training" (leader match + critical supervisory skills + motivation + action planning) versus an "organization development" intervention (team building + problem solving). This aspect of the research was conducted over a 42-month period in soda ash and silver–lead–zinc mines. The results indicated improvements in safety and productivity using either one of the interventions, compared with those mines where no training interventions had taken place. Unfortunately, none of this research tells us how much of the improvements in safety and productivity were due to leader match training by itself, the other training methods by themselves, or perhaps some combination. Future research should certainly be directed at ascertaining these additive and interactive effects.

Finally, it should be noted that leader match is cost effective and therefore is very appropriate for use in smaller organizations. Most leadership training programs require weeks, months, or even years, whereas leader match requires no more than 4 to 12 hours of training time and modest facilities. The program has recently been translated into several other languages. It has been used in such organizations as the U.S. Civil Service Commission, U.S. Military Academy at West Point, United Biscuits, Ltd. of Great Britain, Chase Manhattan Bank of Hong Kong, and various hotel chains (e.g., Western International Hotels).

## MANAGERIAL SKILLS

There are at least three theoretically based training approaches that have as their primary goal the improvement of managerial job skills. The Vroom–Yetton model employs a cognitive strategy to decision making. Specifically, it provides managers with a normative or prescriptive model to help them determine the extent to which they should share their decision-making power with their subordinates in different situations.

Grid seminars, popularized by Blake and Mouton, attempt to increase managerial skills by improving two basic components of a manager's behavior, namely, concern for production and concern for people. These two behavioral categories were originally identified during an extensive program of research on leadership behavior at Ohio State University during the 1950s and were labeled "initiating structure" and "consideration."[18]

Graen's Leader–Member Exchange (LMX) training focuses on improving managers' one-on-one relationships with their subordinates. LMX training improves managers' skills in such areas as active listening, exchanging mutual expectations, and practicing one-on-one interactions.

## Vroom–Yetton Model

This managerial training stems from the original leadership model proposed by Vroom and Yetton and later versions of it.[19] It focuses on one key aspect of leadership behavior, namely, how to manage employee involvement in leader decision making. The underlying assumption of this training approach is that a manager or executive should not always use a participative style of management in all situations, but rather should be taught how to diagnose a problem situation and determine the best decision-making style to use for the situation.

The validity of the model on which the training program is based was investigated in a study in which managers who were unfamiliar with the model reported one successful and one unsuccessful decision made in their managerial jobs. These managers then described the decision method they employed to solve each problem and the overall effectiveness, quality, and acceptance of the solution by subordinates. The results provided support for the model.[20]

To use the model shown in Figure 8.2, trainees are taught to ask themselves a series of key questions about the situations, such as: Is a superior solution required? Is more information needed? Do I know what information is needed and who has it? Is the commitment of others required? Will others commit without actively participating? Is there agreement about goals? Is there conflict about alternatives?[21] The answer to these important questions will determine whether a manager or executive can make the right decision alone or if others need to be involved and the extent of their involvement. Specifically, trainees are taught how to use a flowchart to determine the optimum decision process or processes (i.e., autocratic, consultative, participative) to use.

The training program is delivered in either one-day or two half-day formats (the half-day format is withoutout computer analysis of case study questions). It has been implemented successfully in numerous organizations such as Bristol-Myers, Hewlett-Packard, General Electric, and FedEx. Prior to the seminar, each participant is asked to make assessments of 30 computerized cases and to provide brief descriptions of their past and current job situations. At the seminar, trainees are taught a three-step process that will guide their behavior in the future:

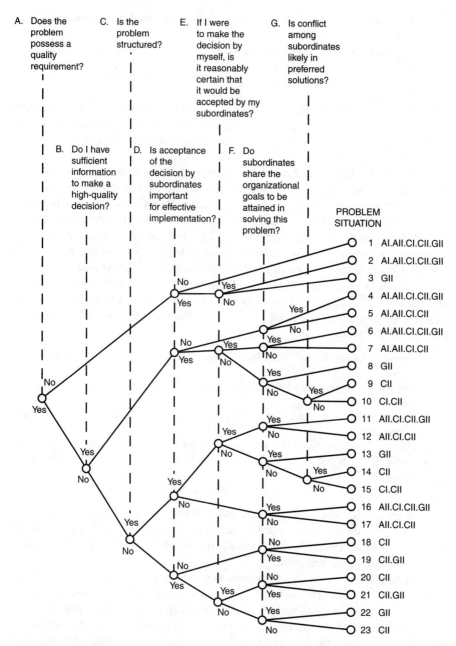

**FIGURE 8.2** The Vroom–Yetton Contingency Model of Leadership Behavior

*Source:* Reprinted by permission of the publisher from "Can Leaders Learn to Lead?," by Victor H. Vroom. *Organizationl Dynamics.* Winter 1976. Copyright © 1976 by AMACON, a division of American Management Associations, p. 19. All rights reserved.

1. *Defining the situation:* Describing the issue to be resolved and the end result to be achieved
2. *Assessing the variables:* Answering a series of questions about the situation
3. *Selecting the appropriate behavior:* Using a leadership tree to arrive at the appropriate behavior(s) for a given situation

The trainees also learn the characteristics of each leadership behavior and the skills (e.g., building consensus, setting group boundaries, handling conflict, managing meetings, active listening, questioning and analyzing) needed for carrying out each of the behaviors.[22]

The research that has been done suggests that managers and students who have been trained to use the model are better able to choose the appropriate participation level for their decision-making strategy than those who have not been trained.[23] More importantly, there is some evidence that training increases the overall effectiveness of managers on the job. For instance, a program called Managing Involvement, based on this model of leadership, was presented to 37 different organizations throughout the world involving 1,600 managers. This program was evaluated at three levels of analysis: participant reactions, learning, and behavior change (see Chapter 5). Two hundred sixteen managers from 13 different organizations used a self-report questionnaire to report the following benefits of the training:

- Seventy-two percent said they found some specific things they would do differently.
- Sixty-seven percent reported the program should help them generally in their current job.
- Thirty-five percent said the course should significantly increase their current job effectiveness.
- Fifty-one percent reported that the course should help in their career development.
- Two percent reported that the course was interesting but of no real value on the current job.
- No one reported that the course was a waste of time.

What happened on the job as a result of this training? Table 8.2 presents the results obtained from 91 participants 6 to 12 months after they had completed the course. These findings suggest that the course did affect the participants' subsequent job behavior.[24]

In another study, business students were randomly formed into four-person decision-making groups, and each group was asked to solve five decision-making problems using different decision-making processes prescribed in the model. Evidence for the validity of the model was found. Specifically, decisions made in line with the model were significantly more effective than decisions that were out of line with the model. Decision effectiveness was measured by asking an independent judge to rate the quality of each decision. In addition, two employees of each leader independently rated their degree of acceptance with their leader's decisions. Of the 105 decisions that were in line with the model, 51

**TABLE 8.2  6- to 12-Month Follow-Up of TELOS Training**

1. Which of the following skills are needed by managers in the organization?

2. How effectively does TELOS teach the following skills?

| % Needed | % Not Needed | % No Comment | | % Good | % Fair | % Not Applicable |
|---|---|---|---|---|---|---|
| 89 | 2 | 9 | a. More effective leadership techniques | 56 | 42 | 2 |
| 88 | 1 | 11 | b. Lead differently in different situations | 78 | 20 | 2 |
| 85 | 3 | 10 | c. Identify elements within a situation | 58 | 38 | 4 |
| 84 | 2 | 14 | d. Increase input from others to increase probability of success | 71 | 29 | 0 |
| 84 | 6 | 10 | e. Make decisions alone when information is adequate | 70 | 28 | 2 |
| 90 | 1 | 9 | f. Use participation as a development tool | 58 | 39 | 3 |

*Source:* B. B. Smith, "Evaluating a Leadership Training Program," Kepner-Tregoe, Inc., Princeton, New Jersey, 1980. Reprinted by permission.

were effective, whereas only 31 of the 87 out-of-line decisions were effective. Regarding the seven key questions asked, one of three quality questions and three of four acceptance questions worked as predicted by the model.[25]

Another investigation of the model involved 44 managers.[26] They were asked to report a recent situation that they faced and the process they used in arriving at a decision. When these self-reported managerial decisions are considered, the model was supported, yielding a differential advantage of 8 percent for decisions made according to the model's prescriptions. However, when the managers' employees were asked to rate these same exact decisions in terms of decision quality, the results did not support the model. Why was the validity of the model supported by manager data, but not by employee data? Managers and employees had different perspectives and, as Heilman and colleagues[27] showed, the role of the person is a crucial factor in the way that person evaluates the effectiveness of the leader's decision-making style.

In our opinion, this approach to management and executive development is a milestone because it resulted in empirical research that struck at one of organizational psychology's post–World War II's most cherished beliefs: Participative decision making is always good; anything other than participative decision making is not good. Vroom and his colleagues, Phillip Yetton and Art Jago, have made it clear that it is a mistake to assume that an effective leader always uses participative decision-making techniques. Rather, a manager or executive must learn how to diagnose a problem situation and determine which approach is best to use.

## Grid Seminars: Robert R. Blake and Jane S. Mouton

Blake and Mouton designed a six-phase program for organizations that lasts anywhere from three to five years. It begins by examining managerial behavior and style, and then systematically widens its focus to team and intergroup development, and finally to the total organization. We will focus only on Phase 1 of their intervention strategy, the Managerial Grid Seminar, which focuses its attention on the development of individual managers and executives.

Basic to the Managerial Grid Seminar is Blake and Mouton's[28] concept of effective leadership known as the *managerial grid.* As shown in Figure 8.3, there are two basic dimensions for describing managerial behavior: concern for production and concern for people. The horizontal axis of the grid reflects a manager's concern for production. This may include such considerations as the number of units of output, quality of service offered to customers, amount of scrap and waste produced, and the number of innovative suggestions developed. The vertical axis represents a manager's concern for people. This, too, can be exhibited in a number of ways, for example, concern for each employee's personal worth, establishment of good personal relationships with managers and peers, and the promotion of friendly and cohesive work groups. Figure 8.3 shows that concern for production and concern for people can range from low (1) to high (9), thereby yielding 81 (i.e., $9 \times 9$) possible managerial styles or orientations. For Blake and Mouton, the upper-right corner, the 9,9 position, is the soundest way to achieve leadership excellence. It is important to point out that they clearly recognized the need for 9,9 managers to choose specific forms of behavior appropriate for the particular situation in which they find themselves. Although they advocated a 9,9 pattern of leadership, they did not believe that a manager needs to respond reflexively with the same 9,9 behaviors in every situation.

There are two basic grid seminars available for management development. *Executive Grid Seminars* are for individuals engaged in the policy-making and planning functions at the top of their respective organizations. This seminar brings together persons whose position level permits them to exchange common interests and problems not shared by persons whose managerial job responsibilities are specialized. Typical attendees include presidents, directors, executive vice presidents, and managing partners. *Managerial Grid Seminars* are for persons from the middle and upper range of business and industry, government, and service organizations. Typical attendees include regional managers, plant managers, project managers, operations managers, and sales managers.

Since 1964, numerous individuals from companies such as Exxon, Procter & Gamble, and TRW have attended these seminars. In addition, exec-

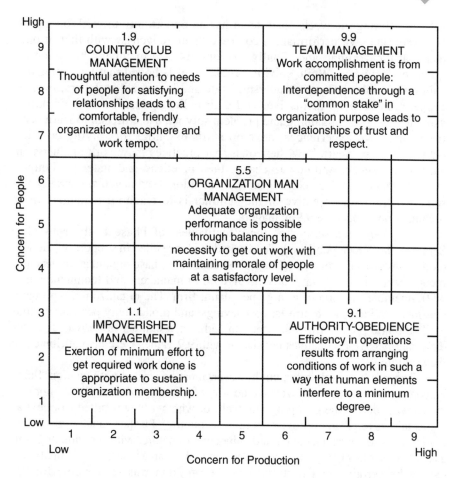

**FIGURE 8.3**  The Managerial Grid®

*Source:* The Managerial Grid Figure from *The Managerial Grid III: The Key to Leadership Excellence,* by Robert R. Blake and Jane Srygley Mouton. Houston: Gulf Publishing Company. Copyright ©1985, p. 12. Reproduced by permission.

utives from key branches of government including Congress, departments of Defense and Agriculture, and the Internal Revenue Service have utilized grid seminars. Currently, Managerial Grid Seminars are conducted in 23 countries around the world, and they have been translated into 17 languages. Each seminar lasts six days and is conducted either away from the organization by outside consultants or on an in-house basis by the organization's own top-level managers who have been trained in grid methodology. Six or more study teams are formed, each consisting of five to nine managers. Ideally, each team consists of members representing different departments, divisions, and levels within the organization. The teams participate in a series of team-learning activities during the week. Each team has an opportunity to work on a problem, score its own performance, compare its effectiveness with that of other teams at the seminar, and, finally, critique its own members' behavior and group performance. While solving problems, it is hoped that team members gain insight into their own leadership style and its impact on others, improve cooperation between themselves and their colleagues, increase their skill in using teamwork for planning and problem solving, use criticism to learn faster from their own experiences, develop skills essential for solving conflicts between groups, learn how their own past practices may work against standards of excellence and how to change their practices, and understand important differences between contingent (i.e., situational) management and 9,9 versatility. The main objective of the seminar is to teach all managers in an organization to become 9,9 managers.

No evaluative studies of the effectiveness of Phase 1 (the New Grid Seminar) have been published. The limited evidence cited in support of grid ideology comes from a study evaluating the entire six-phase organization development intervention.[29] That study involved 800 managers and technicians in a 4,000-member division of a large petroleum firm. The organization reported a considerable increase in profits, cost savings, and productivity per worker-hour while the grid program was in effect. In addition, a number of individual attitudinal and behavioral changes consistent with 9,9 values were also attributed to the program.

The results of this research, however, must be treated with caution. Since no control group was used, we have no way of knowing whether these improvements were due to the grid program itself, or whether they resulted from extraneous factors (e.g., an improvement in the economy). Further, much of the information obtained was anecdotal and subjective in nature, with individuals being asked to describe changes that had occurred more than a year earlier. Finally, we cannot be certain what portion(s) of the program was responsible for the reported changes in organizational outcomes. Therefore, considerably more evidence is needed before any definitive statements can be made about the effectiveness of grid seminars. On the positive side, attendees' comments about what happened in their organizations after Managerial Grid Seminars are encouraging. Sixty-two percent reported better communication between themselves and their employees, 61 percent reported improvements in working with other groups, 55 percent reported better relationships with colleagues, and 20 percent reported more openness to the ideas of others.

Blake and Mouton have argued that grid seminars have the same positive impact on organizational profitability. For instance, Figure 8.4 presents their comparison of the profitability of two matched organizations, Corporation A, which was involved in grid training, and Corporation B, where people did not receive grid training. The figure reflects the profits of these two corporations. The products of both corporations are identical, yet the profits of the corporation that received grid training are four times greater than those of Corporation B.

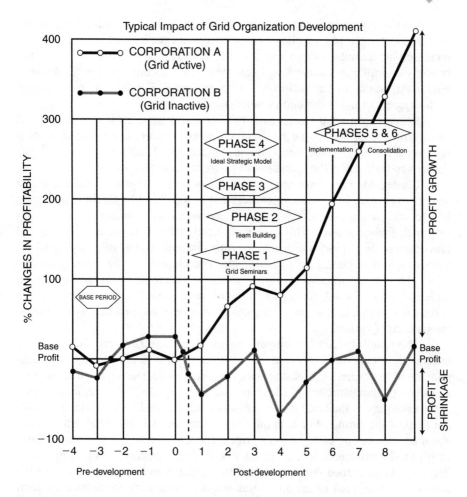

**FIGURE 8.4**  Comparison of the Profitability of Two Matched Corporations

*Source:* "Typical Impact of Grid Organization Development" figure from *The Versatile Manager: A Grid Profile,* by Robert R. Blake and Jane Srygley Mouton. Homewood, IL: Dow Jones-Irwin. Copyright © 1980, p. 194. Reproduced by permission.

## Leader–Member Exchange: George B. Graen

Another approach to dealing with the performance of employees is training in LMX. This training is based on research by Graen and colleagues on role making in leader–member dyads.[30] This research has shown that there is a consistent pattern to leader–member employee transactions. In exchange for positional resources from the leader, the employee commits him- or herself to a high level of involvement in the unit's functioning.

This source of influence can result in highly valued outcomes for both the leader and the employee. For example, a manager can offer outcomes of increased job latitude, influence in decision making, open communications, support of the employee's actions, and confidence in and consideration for the individual. An employee can reciprocate with greater availability and commitment to the success of the entire unit or organization.

Research on what Graen calls the vertical dyad (i.e., leader–employee) linkage model shows that a differentiation process occurs in a predictable manner over time, namely, the formation of low and high LMX relationships.[31] The consequence of this is the formation of in-groups and out-groups.

Leader–Member Exchange training is designed to enable and encourage leaders to correct those situations where out-groups exist by teaching managers how to analyze and act on major positive and negative elements of their relationship with each employee. This training typically takes place in an instructor-led classroom setting. It includes lectures, group discussions, and role playing where trainees alternate taking the role of leader and employee. The training usually takes place in six weekly two-hour sessions. The topics covered include an understanding of LMX theory and how to use it (two hours), active listening skills (two hours), exchanging resources (two hours), and practicing one-on-one interactions (four hours).

The main objective of this management training is to get each leader to analyze thoroughly and be prepared to act on major positive and negative components of his or her relationship with each employee. During the training sessions, the general structure of the conversations as well as the specific questions and techniques to facilitate the conversation are devised by the managers with the help of the trainer. For example, (1) the manager is to spend time asking about and discussing each person's gripes, concerns, and job expectations about their job, the manager's job, and their working relationship; (2) by using active listening skills learned during training, the leader is to be particularly attentive and sensitive to what issues are raised and how they were formulated by each employee; (3) the leader is to refrain from imposing his or her frame of reference on the issues raised; (4) the leader is to share his or her own job expectations about his or her own job, the employee's job, and their working relationship.

The actual treatment, following this training, usually involves a series of 20- to 30-minute conversations between the leaders and their employees. The goal of this follow-up treatment is to increase the level of reciprocal understanding and helpfulness within dyads regarding job issues and behaviors.

There has been a great deal of research in support of this training that meets the requirements outlined in Chapter 5. The quality of leader–member relations has been shown to directly affect both productivity and satisfaction,[32] as well as employee turnover.[33]

The effectiveness of LMX training was compared with a placebo control condition. The placebo training consisted of three two-hour sessions of general input on decision making, communicating performance evaluations, and job enrichment. The experimental design was the pretest–posttest discussed in Chapter 5 with random assignment of people to the training and control groups. An instrument measuring LMX was employed to measure the quality of exchange between supervisors and each of their employees. The employee form of the LMX contained seven items such as "How well do you feel your immediate supervisor understands your problems and needs" and "I have enough confidence in my immediate supervisor that I would defend and justify his or her decisions if he or she were not present to do so." The LMX training resulted in significant increases in the degree of manager support and member availability as perceived by the initial LMX out-group compared to the in-group. The outcome was an increase in both productivity (weekly output records) and job satisfaction.[34]

Graen and Scandura[35] have argued that managers and employees can be expected to collaborate on tasks that allow growth opportunities for the employee, if gain is desired by both parties. This is because the LMX model states that interdependence between a manager and an employee is necessary for both the offer and the acceptance of opportunities of growth on the job. To test this assertion, Graen et al.[36] manipulated growth opportunities by a vertical collaboration offer based on the LMX model. As predicted, only employees high in growth need strength (GNS) responded to the growth opportunity as defined behaviorally by actual collaboration over time on tasks by the employee with the manager. The result was an increase in quantity and quality of output on the part of high-GNS people.

The major criticism of this training program is similar to the criticism of Fiedler's leader match training. Both training approaches use a questionnaire (i.e., LPC and LMX) to explain their effectiveness, and both questionnaires have been attacked on psychometric grounds. Measurement issues aside, training theorists such as Graen are to be commended for not being content with simply showing that their training process is effective, but rather exploring the psychological variables that explain why training is effective. Keep in mind, too, the uniqueness of this theory in that it calls for training managers to focus on improving the quality of their dyadic relationship with *each* of their employees.

Graen's LMX plays an active role in today's executive coaching interventions. According to the 2000 ASTD (American Society for Training and Development) *State of the Industry Report,* a typical participant in the ASTD Benchmarking Service spent about $2 million on training in 1998, 3 percent of which was targeted at providing executive coaching for their senior-level managers.[37] Executive coaching involves a training specialist working one-on-one with a senior-level manager to understand: how they act, why they are motivated to act in this manner, the impact of their actions on others with whom they work, and how to adapt they behavior to bring about win–win outcomes with others. An important component of executive coaching involves helping the executive to understand and improve their dyadic relationship with particular individuals. For instance, in a recent executive coaching project at a medium-sized manufacturing firm, one of the authors worked with the senior vice president of marketing. This senior VP had five direct reports, two of whom were a lot younger than he. Based on a series of in-depth interviews with this executive, his manager, and each of his direct reports, it became evident that he had established healthy LMXs with each of his older direct reports, but not the younger, less experienced ones. One direct report described him as being "too intrusive, directive, and critical." The other felt that he was being "too condescending, verbally aggressive, impersonal, unfair." A significant amount of time and effort on this project involved helping this senior VP to improve his LMX with each of these individuals.

# MOTIVATION

Five training techniques deal with increasing the motivation level of managers: role motivation theory, training in need for achievement, and survey feedback employ cognitive strategies; behavior modification employs an environmental strategy; and social learning theory (or behavior modeling) uses cognitive, behavioral, and environmental strategies. The latter is classified in Figure 8.1 as a behavioral strategy because of its emphasis on changing behavior through practice. However, as we will see, it could easily have been designated as a cognitive and/or environmental approach to behavior change.

## Role Motivation Theory: John Miner

John Miner[38] found that certain key attitudes and motives affect an individual's choice of a managerial career, the success achieved in a given managerial position at any organizational level, and the speed of advancement up the managerial hierarchy. These key attitudes are described as follows:

1. *Favorable attitude toward authority:* Managers are expected to maintain a good relationship between themselves and their superiors. Managers should generally have a positive attitude toward individuals who hold positions of authority over them.

2. *Desire to compete:* With regard to peers, managerial work has a competitive element. Managers must be able to compete for available rewards for themselves and their work group and be favorably disposed toward engaging in such competition.

3. *Assertive motivation:* An individual in a managerial role should derive pleasure from taking charge, making decisions, taking disciplinary action as may be necessary, and protecting members of their work group.

4. *Desire to exercise power:* A manager must exercise power over subordinates and direct their behavior through the use of positive and negative sanctions. The manager should feel comfortable using such power and not find such behavior difficult.

5. *Desire for a distinctive position:* The managerial role requires that an individual act differently from the immediate subordinate group and do things that inevitably invite attention, discussion, and perhaps even criticism from subordinates.

6. *A sense of responsibility:* The individual should have a positive outlook toward routine administrative chores, such as serving on committees, filling out forms, and constructing budget estimates. The manager should gain some satisfaction from accomplishing these demands and not regard them with apprehension or dislike.

These six motives comprise what Miner calls *motivation to manage.* The concept of motivation to manage applies primarily to bureaucratic organizations. These organizations are typically large and use hierarchical control. The theory is likely to have less applicability in small organizational settings where there is little or no hierarchical or bureaucratic control. In one study, Berman and Miner[39] found that top executives who had risen up the managerial hierarchy in large, bureaucratic organizations had higher levels of managerial motivation than top executives in small family-owned businesses.

Managers who associate positive rather than negative feelings with the various role prescriptions just described will tend to meet existing organizational criteria of effectiveness. Those with predominantly negative reactions will be relatively ineffective. You must realize, of course, that these motivational factors are not the only ones affecting managerial performance. Factors such as job knowledge, verbal ability, and resistance to stress, among others, are also important. Nevertheless, the six motives of managerial role motivation theory have been found to be related to various criteria of managerial effectiveness.[40] And of these six motives, Miner[41] identified three that correlate most consistently with managerial success, namely, favorable attitude toward authority figures, desire to exercise power, and desire to compete with others. Desire for distinctive position and a sense of responsibility are less frequently associated with managerial success and are, therefore, slightly less important components of managerial motivation. Assertive motivation is the least useful key attitude for predicting success as a manager.

According to Miner's theory, organizations should develop managers by increasing their motivation to manage others. The training program utilizes conventional lecture and lecture–discussion teaching methods. These lectures are often supplemented with special guest lecturers, cases created by the trainees, videotaped scenes role-played by trainees, and selected books and articles. The two primary objectives of training are, first, to help managers deal more effectively with deficiencies in the work behavior of their subordinates, and, second, to develop all six components of managerial motivation. The training sessions are typically held once a week, with each session lasting approximately one hour. The program extends over a period of several months. Ten to 100 people can be trained at one time. The lectures focus on reasons why a subordinate might perform ineffectively and what a manager can do in such situations. The participants are requested to think of themselves as being in the managerial role and to feel the emotions associated with it. Toward the end of the training, these emotions are discussed, along with their implications for managerial effectiveness.[42]

The results obtained with this training approach are encouraging. Seventeen experimental (i.e., trained) groups and nine control (i.e., untrained) groups have been involved in evaluative studies of this program. Significant experimental group changes occurred in 16 out of 17 cases, and in all instances where a control was used, the changes were shown to be due to the training.

Interestingly, not all of these motives are influenced equally by the management development program. The strongest effects occur with assertive and power motivation. Further, increased favorable attitudes toward authority and willingness to perform administrative duties appear in over half of the studies. The desire to compete and the desire for a distinctive position are much less frequently influenced by the training. Nevertheless, all of the motives seem to be sufficiently affected by training to warrant their continued retention in the theory.

Thus far, the data suggest that people who are active and independent are more responsive to this training than those who are passive and dependent. Moreover, significant changes have been found among both female and male managerial trainees.[43]

## Achievement Motivation Theory: David McClelland

For over 40 years, David McClelland[44] and associates have been studying *need for achievement* (abbreviated NAch), a distinct human motive that can be defined as an "urge to improve" or as a "desire to exceed some standard of behavior." Thus, the overall objective of this program is to increase one's motivation level to excel in the job. This is done primarily by teaching people to think through the situations in which they are placed and to develop action plans to increase their effectiveness on the job. A unique aspect of the program is that it is designed primarily for entrepreners in small business settings.

People with high NAch seek challenging tasks, assume responsibility for individual achievement, persist in the attainment of achievement goals, enjoy surpassing previous achievements, and, generally, find goal attainment to be a satisfying experience. They function most successfully in situations in which there is moderate risk, in which they receive knowledge of their progress, and in which they have individual responsibility for the attainment of the goal. Because these kinds of situations are most frequently found in small business settings, achievement-motivated individuals tend to be attracted to entrepreneurial work situations. They have a burning desire to get things done, and they shun bureaucratic situations in which they are plagued by red tape. They make decisions, solve problems, and strive to accomplish the objectives of their organization. Simply put, they are doers; they are motivated to obtain results. It is important to point out that *high* NAch is not always an important motivator for managers in large organizations. Instead, NAch should be moderately high and supported with a strong need for power, so that a manager will express it to facilitate team performance rather than use it solely for his or her own success. If a manager were to have a very high level of NAch, he or she would try to accomplish everything alone, be reluctant to delegate responsibility to others, and not be able to develop a strong sense of commitment and responsibility among his or her subordinates.

McClelland estimated that only about 10 percent of the population is sufficiently high in achievement motivation. These individuals seem to be this way because of their early childhood experiences. Their parents expected and reinforced them to show independence between the ages of 6 and 8 with regard to making their own decisions and accomplishing things without help from others. Despite the importance of childhood experiences, McClelland is convinced that this motivation can be learned by businesspeople. Consequently, he designed a training course intended to increase achievement motivation.

His training approach is based on certain theoretical propositions that have evolved gradually over the years while developing NAch among businesspeople of various cultural backgrounds. For convenience, we will summarize these propositions under four main headings: the achievement syndrome, self-study, goal setting, and interpersonal support.[45]

### The Achievement Syndrome

The course participants are first taught how to recognize and produce achievement-related fantasies. They take a test known as the Thematic Apperception Test (TAT) in which they are asked to write imaginative stories about a series of ambiguous pictures that are shown to them. They then learn how to score what they have written according to a standard coding system for identifying NAch. With practice, they learn how to produce stories heavily loaded with achievement imagery. The object here is to strengthen their associative network or motive by eliciting and reinforcing it. This emphasis is primarily a cognitive strategy.

The next step in the course is to tie cognitions (thoughts) to action. As mentioned previously, high-NAch individuals behave in certain characteristic ways. They prefer work situations in which there is challenge (moderate risk), specific feedback, individual responsibility, and the chance to try new things. These action patterns are taught to the management trainees in connection with a business game. The game provides an opportunity to learn these action characteristics through practice and through observing other participants. Thus, the program incorporates two key principles of learning: active participation and practice.

So far, the course instruction has been abstract and removed from everyday work life. The next step is to illustrate how NAch thought and action can be applied to business activities. The training method used is the case study method (cognitive), popularized by the Harvard Business School (see Chapter 9). Participants analyze and discuss actual examples of the development of the careers of business leaders. They are also encouraged to bring in examples from their own business activities for analysis in motivational terms.

### Self-Study

Through outside reading, instructor-led classrooms, group discussion, and videos, the participants develop a clear understanding of the role that high-NAch persons must play in a business setting. By doing this, participants can decide for themselves whether they want to be that kind of person, and whether being more entrepreneurial is relevant to their career aspirations. During the course, participants are continually encouraged to think carefully about what information acquired during training means with respect to their own self-image and their current job responsibilities.

Next, the course focuses on an examination of the participants' value systems. A value analysis of the participants' cultures is conducted by analyzing children's stories, myths, popular religion, customs, and so on. The objective here is to identify possible conflicts between high NAch and a trainee's prevailing values. This is particularly important when facilitating entrepreneurship among culturally disadvantaged people or accelerating economic development in third-world countries.

### Goal Setting

A mainstay of this training is goal setting, namely, inculcating a trainee's NAch through "prestige suggestion." This means that reasons are given to trainees suggesting that each trainee's achievement-oriented behavior should and can change as a result of taking the course. This persuasive technique makes participants confident before entering the program that they will change their behavior to become more achievement oriented.

Toward the end of the course, each participant is asked to complete an achievement plan for the next two years. This is tantamount to setting specific performance goals. In addition, the trainees are asked every six months to report back to the trainers how well they are progressing toward attaining these goals.

### Interpersonal Support

The attitude assumed by the trainers can best be described as supportive, honest, and noncritical. The program is held at a retreat setting, away from everyday work, so that total concentration on the course objectives is possible.

The course attempts to heighten the participants' feelings that they are joining a new reference group. The new NAch coding system becomes almost a secret language that only those who have gone through the program can use intelligently. The retreat setting also fosters the feelings of alumni who have gone through it together and can thus look to one another for understanding and support.

What can be concluded about the effectiveness of achievement motivation training? One program was conducted at the Business School of Southern Methodist University (SMU). Through existing minority entrepreneur associations, 36 persons interested in business were recruited for the course; 23 were Mexican American and 13 were black. A second program was sponsored by the Small Business Administration (SBA) in eight cities. In all, 197 people attended the first weekend of the training, and 133 attended both weekends. One hundred seven of the former trainees and 86 of the latter were businesspeople. The third program was a special effort to aid mostly black business firms in Seattle that were not succeeding. This program, called Pep Up, involved 16 businesses.

For the SMU and SBA programs, financial data were available for both 18 months prior to and after the training. In the case of Pep Up, the data covered the 12 months before training and 12 months after training. The results showed that all three programs significantly improved small business profitability. Moreover, no one type of business (i.e., manufacturing, retail, service) seemed to benefit more than any other from the training. It has also been found to be effective for stimulating economic development among small businesspeople and managers from a depressed economic area in Washington, D.C.; a similarly depressed rural community in Oklahoma; and small cities in India.[46]

### General Conclusions

Taken together, studies on achievement motivation training suggest the following:

1. This development approach has mainly been implemented and shown to be effective in small business firms.
2. The type of business within this range does not seem to matter, because the training appears to be equally effective for all kinds of small organizations.
3. Businesspeople with power motivation higher than achievement motivation benefit less well from this training. High need for power among small businesspeople appears to interfere with their success, most likely because it results in too much risk taking.
4. This training has been shown to work not only with disadvantaged people in the United States, but also with small businesses in other countries as well.
5. Small business entrepreneurs appear to benefit from this type of training in the early stages of their careers.

## Survey Feedback: Rensis Likert

Survey feedback begins with a rigorous measurement of the way the total organization is presently functioning. Perceptions of behaviors and conditions related to organizational effectiveness are gathered by administering anonymous questionnaires to all organizational members. This information is carefully tabulated for every work group in the organization, for each combination of groups having responsibility of some sort, and for the total organization. Each supervisor and manager receives a tabulation of this information, based on the responses of her or his own immediate subordinates. A change agent, either from an outside consulting agency or from the organization's own staff, counsels the manager–recipient privately in order to maximize the individual's understanding of the survey feedback information. Afterward, the change agent attends a meeting between the manager and the subordinates for the purpose of examining the survey findings and discussing implications for corrective action. The agent's role is to help group members better understand the feedback information, set goals, and formulate action plans for the change effort.

This survey-guided technique was originated by Rensis Likert and a colleague of his, David Bowers, at the University of Michigan Institute for Social Research in Ann Arbor. The survey instrument they developed in 1965 was known as the Survey of Organizations (SOO). The instrument was developed to tap certain constructs contained in Likert's meta-theory of human organization management first outlined in his triple-award-winning 1961 book, *New Patterns of Management.*[47] Since 1965, the SOO has been under constant updating and fine-tuning.

Likert postulated three broad classes of organizational variables: causal, intervening, and end result. The *causal* variables are independent variables that influence the course of events within an organization and the results achieved. They include such things as the structure of the organization, managerial or supervisory leadership behavior, the flow of communication, and the decision-making practices. *Intervening* variables reflect the internal state of health of the organization, for example, motivation, attitudes, and loyalties of subordinates. The *end-result* variables are the dependent variables that reflect organizational results such as productivity, satisfaction, and earnings. The current 2000 version of the SOO taps major areas of Organizational Climate, Supervisory Leadership, and Peer Relationships, as well as several end results such as employee satisfaction. It contains 120 items along with the option of adding supplemental questions. For purposes of comparison, normative data are available by hierarchical level and by job function. It can now even be filled out on the World Wide Web. Shown below are two sample items from the 2000 SOO and the 5-point rating scale that is used in answering the items:

5 = to a very great extent,
4 = to a great extent,
3 = to some extent,
2 = to a little extent,
1 = to a very little extent:

To what extent does your supervisor encourage the persons who work in the group to work as a team?

| | | | | | |
|---|---|---|---|---|---|
| This is how it is now | 1 | 2 | 3 | 4 | 5 |
| This is how I'd like it to be | 1 | 2 | 3 | 4 | 5 |
| To what extent does your supervisor's attitude encourage participation and commitment from work group members? | 1 | 2 | 3 | 4 | 5 |

Although the survey admittedly does not tap all aspects of Likert's theory, it is reasonable to conclude that the content is representative of Likert's formulation. Numerous validation studies conducted over the years have shown that the SOO is related to such criteria as satisfaction, teamwork, job stress, and various "hard" measures (e.g., product quality, cost performance, safety) of performance. It is important to point out, however, that there are other survey instruments such as The Workforce Cultural Audit (WCA) that are currently being used too by training specialists because they yield additional measures not tapped by the 2000 SOO (e.g., diversity management; family, work, and life balance; organizational fairness and treatment of people).[48]

The effectiveness of the survey feedback can be found in research conducted as far back as 1973 up to the present time. Let's take a look at three of these studies.

A large-scale study was conducted, involving nearly 15,000 white- and blue-collar employees in 23 organizations. Survey feedback was compared to several other intervention strategies (sensitivity training and two varieties of process consultation) and two control groups in which there was no systematic change attempt. In general, the results showed survey feedback to be better than the other methods for improving leadership behavior, organizational climate, and job satisfaction.[49]

Additional research suggests that there are 17 distinct work group types common to both civilian and navy organizations, as measured by respondents' answers on the SOO. The impact of five intervention strategies (survey feedback, data handbook, sensitivity training, process consultation, interpersonal process consultation) on the different work group types was compared to determine their positive and negative effects.[50] Survey feedback was found to be the most positive across work group types, compared to the other four interventions.

Survey feedback was initiated in 1995 by the U.S. Coast Guard. One of the major goals of the project was to provide leadership and a working environment that enables all people in the Coast Guard to reach their full potential. The WCA was administered to 6,000 people representing a significant cross-section of the Coast Guard—military and civilian; female and male; all grades, ranks, and job types; and all cultural backgrounds. The WCA measured 23 topics and consisted of 319 questions. To better understand why people answered the questions as they did, the Coast Guard conducted 40 focus groups nationwide. Eight to 15 survey respondents participated in each focus group. Final analyses took place in 1997. During this phase, the WCA was used to identify the barriers to individual success, and the focus group results helped in understanding their root causes. These findings have led to 40 action items, many of which are management development initiatives, that are now under way.[51]

There are many large and small organizations in which survey feedback has been implemented. Here are just a few of them: the U.S. Department of Labor, the Canadian Postal System, Bristol Myers, Diamond-Star Motors, Douglas Aircraft, Brittania Sportswear Ltd., Ameritech, and Ontario Hydro.

## Behavior Modification: B. F. Skinner

Two theories underlie behaviorally based training programs, namely, behaviorism[52] and social training theory.[53] The latter theory is discussed in the next section of this chapter. At least two training techniques are based directly on the work of Skinner, namely, teaching machines that are forerunners to today's TBT techniques (see Chapter 6) and a set of procedures for shaping and modifying a person's behavior. This latter procedure is referred to by the scientific community as *operant conditioning* in recognition that the environment shapes the behaviors that operate on it. The more popular name given to these procedures is *behavior modification*. In this section, we focus on behavior modification as a training approach.

Behavior modification is based on the fundamental assumption that "behavior is a function of its consequences." This means that, if the consequences of behavior are aversive to an individual, the chances are reduced that the individual will repeat the behavior under similar conditions in the future. Conversely, if the outcomes are positive, the probability that the behavior will be repeated at some later time under similar conditions is increased. This process of inducing changes in frequency of behavior by changing the consequences of behavior is known variously among trainers as contingency management or behavior modification.

To better understand how this procedure works, let us briefly examine five strategies by which behavior can be strengthened, maintained, or weakened by making specific consequences contingent on specific behavior. The strategies include positive reinforcement, escape and avoidance learning, punishment, and extinction. The different strategies can be used singly or in various combinations.

According to Skinner,[54] a positive reinforcer is any stimulus that, when added to a situation, strengthens the probability that the behavior will be repeated. An organizational example includes the aspiring young executive who remains in the office at night because the outcome is immediate attention and praise from their manager. In using positive reinforcement, it is important to keep three things in mind.

First, any consequence of behavior (e.g., verbal praise, feelings of accomplishment, money) may be a positive reinforcer for one person, but not for another. One must make a careful evaluation of what is reinforcing for a given individual before beginning a program of positive reinforcement. Although it is possible to measure the importance of various positive reinforcers to an employee by asking them to fill out a self-report paper-and-pencil instrument, the best way to determine whether an agent is a positive reinforcer is to simply make its presentation immediately contingent upon engaging in a given behavior and seeing whether the response rates increase in frequency.

Second, it is necessary to design the reinforcement contingencies in such a way that the reinforcer follows directly from the desired behavior. This is a rule of reinforcement that is often violated. For example, too often in organizations, employees see little relationship between their job performance and how much money they earn. Regardless of the type of positive reinforcement used, it is essential that it be tied directly to effective performance.

Third, often an emitted behavior may not measure up to the behavior desired. For example, an employee may be submitting technical reports on time, but they are not clearly written. By systematically reinforcing closer and closer approximations to the desired product, the manager can shape the employee's writing behavior until it becomes acceptable. This process, known as *shaping,* is necessary whenever the response to be learned is either extremely complex or not within the trainee's immediate repertoire.

Two additional strategies for strengthening a desired behavior are called escape and avoidance learning. *Escape learning* refers to a contingency arrangement in which a desired response can terminate an already noxious stimulus impinging on the individual. For example, an engineer may learn to perform an unpleasant task assignment efficiently, so that he can move quickly to other assignments that he finds more enjoyable.

When an individual's behavior can prevent the onset of a noxious stimulus, the procedure is called *avoidance learning.* For example, a research chemist may remember to wear safety glasses when entering the research and development laboratory in order to avoid severe criticism from management. The important point to remember here is that both escape and avoidance learning increase the frequency of a response through the contingent termination or avoidance of an aversive condition by demonstrating a specific behavior.

One approach for reducing the occurrence of undesired behavior is punishment. In one type of punishment, an aversive or noxious consequence is presented immediately after an undesired response. Numerous examples of this pervade organizational life, such as being disciplined by a supervisor after engaging in some unsafe behavior. A second type of punishment involves the removal of a positive consequence after an undesired response. Examples include being demoted or even fired after performing one's job poorly. Interestingly, punishment is used quite frequently to control behavior in certain organizations. Its widespread popularity may be due to the immediate effects it has in stopping or preventing undesired behavior. In this sense, the trainer or manager administering the punishment is positively reinforced for punishing. An example of this might be a trainer who screams at a trainee who seems disinterested in learning, resulting in the trainee's immediately paying attention.

Despite its wide use, punishment may have unfortunate side effects. First, there is a high probability that the response will be reduced only when the punishing agent is present. Thus, the undesired response may reoccur at its initial rate whenever the trainer is away. Second, punishment may result in avoidance, hostility, or even counteraggression toward the punishing agent. This effect can be detrimental to the trainer who wants trainees to listen and accept what is being taught.

When positive reinforcement for a previously learned response is withheld, the behavior will eventually disappear. This decline in the probability of an undesired response by means of ignoring it is called *extinction.* This final strategy, when combined with positive reinforcement, is the procedure preferred by Skinner. From a training viewpoint, this combination allows for the elimination of undesired behavior without the unfortunate side effects of punishment or the use of any noxious stimuli. Moreover, it rewards trainees for their performance improvements in a positive way.

The effectiveness of positive reinforcement depends primarily on its scheduling. The two primary reinforcement schedules are continuous and intermittent. The continuous schedule is just that: Reinforcement follows every correct response. If a management trainee is praised every time she completes an assignment on time, that response is being continuously reinforced. With this schedule, behavior improves very rapidly and is maintained as long as reinforcement follows every response. However, the behavior stops being emitted shortly after the reinforcement ceases (extinction). With intermittent schedules, the reinforcer is not presented after every response, but rather varies the ratio of reinforcers to responses. Thus, from a training standpoint, trainers should initially provide trainees with continuous reinforcement. Once the desired response has been learned, an intermittent schedule should be used. Intermittent schedules of reinforcement have been shown for years to lead to higher performance levels than a continuous schedule in both lab and field settings.[55]

There are organizations that have used behavior modification programs in the area of employee training and performance improvement, for example, Emery Air Freight, Weyerhaeuser, General Electric, Michigan Bell, and Standard Oil of Ohio. These programs have been successful in improving attendance, safety, and production. For example, in one company, data were collected on store clerks daily for twelve weeks, on three different behaviors: remaining in the grocery store, assisting customers, and stocking merchandise. After 18 baseline observations, reinforcing consequences were administered for remaining in the grocery store. When this behavior increased (demonstrated over 24 observations), an intervention was made with regard to the second behavior (asking customers if they would like assistance). After the clerks were consistently in the store and consistently helping customers (demonstrated over 30 observations), an intervention was made with regard to the third behavior (stocking merchandise). Through this use of a multiple baseline design, the researchers were able to conclude that changes in the three behaviors were a function of the training intervention. The clerks' performance improved only after, and not before, the introduction of each intervention.[56]

The criticisms of this approach to training are at least twofold. The first is philosophical. Behavior modification is based on the philosophy of positivism, namely, that only social, objectively observable knowledge is valid. Thus, scientific data are restricted to the objective report of muscular movements or glandular secretions in time and space. Mental processes are said to be of little or no importance for scientific inquiry. This position has been attacked vehemently.[57] The second criticism focuses on the fact that some people regard behavior modification as being "manipulative." The truth is that people are using these five strategies every day with one another. The question is, "Why not use them systematically to facilitate managerial learning?" Let's turn now to a related topic, Albert Bandura's Social Learning Theory.

## Social Learning Theory: Albert Bandura

Social learning theory is a social cognitive theory. It explains human behavior in terms of continuous interplay among cognitive, behavioral, and environmental determinants. In the social learning view, people are neither driven by inner forces nor buffeted by environmental stimuli. Rather, psychological functioning is explained in terms of a continuous reciprocal interaction of personal and environmental determinants.[58] Implicit in this statement is the view that behavior is neither determined solely by its environmental consequences (i.e., reinforcer and punishers) nor by an individual's cognitions (i.e., conscious intentions and goals). Instead, social learning theory provides a theoretical structure that incorporates the views of both the behaviorists and the cognitivists. Thus, this theoretical approach to training managers is discussed at the end of this chapter because it encompasses cognitive, behavioral, and environmental strategies for increasing the motivation level of managers, and for improving their interpersonal skills in dealing with employees.

Social learning theory specifically acknowledges that most human behavior is learned observationally through modeling (see Chapter 4). Through the process of observing others, an individual forms an idea of how behaviors are performed and the effects they produce. This coded information serves as a guide for action. Because people can learn from example before actually performing the behaviors themselves, they are spared needless trial and error. This conception of the learning process is quite different from Skinner's theory, where learning by reinforcement is portrayed as a mechanistic process in which behaviors are shaped automatically and unconsciously by their immediate consequences. Social learning theory holds that people do not merely react to external influences, as if they were unthinking organisms, but actually select, organize, and transform stimuli that impinge upon them.

Both Skinnerian and social learning theorists agree that behavior is affected by its consequences, but the two theories differ with respect to the specific role of reinforcement. According to Skinner, a reinforcer strengthens preceding responses, even without awareness by the person of what is being reinforced. Social learning theorists argue that anticipatory capabilities enable individuals to be motivated by prospective consequences of their behavior.[59]

Laboratory experiments have shown that more effective learning is achieved when individuals are informed in advance of the consequences of performing a specific behavior, rather than waiting until the behavior is demonstrated and then receiving a reinforcer. This process is particularly true in observational learning, where anticipation of reinforcement influences what is attended to and how well it is remembered. Observer attention and retention processes are increased when the trainee knows that the consequences of a model's behavior will be effective in producing valued outcomes or in averting punishing ones. Unlike behaviorism, social learning theory also acknowledges that people can regulate their own actions by self-produced consequences.

Examples and goals impart standards of conduct that form the basis for self-reinforcing reactions. This process gives humans a capacity for self-direction.

Impressive empirical support for social learning theory has been obtained in well-controlled studies in experimental and clinical settings (see Bandura, 1986 [note 53] for a review of this literature). In addition, the theory has been embraced as a vehicle for changing employee behavior in organizations. Goldstein and Sorcher[60] were among the first to explain the potential value of behavior-modeling procedures for improving the interpersonal skills of first-line supervisors. Since then, several studies have presented results on the successful application of behavior-modeling procedures to industrial training programs.[61] These studies show that behavior-modeling training can be useful for improving the interpersonal and communications skills of managers and supervisors with employees.

### An Example of Behavior-Modeling Training

Behavior modeling was used to train supervisors how to interact effectively with their employees. Nine training modules focused on the following topics: (1) orienting a new employee, (2) giving recognition, (3) motivating a poor performer, (4) discussing poor work habits, (5) discussing potential disciplinary action, (6) reducing absenteeism, (7) handling a complaining employee, (8) reducing turnover, and (9) overcoming resistance to change. The training program was designed to include the components of effective modeling, namely, attentional processes, retentive processes, motor reproduction processes, and motivational processes.

The trainees met for two hours each week for nine weeks. Each training session followed a similar format:

1. Introduction of the topic by the trainers (attentional processes);
2. Presentation of a video that depicts a supervisor modeling effectively a situation based on a set of three to six learning points that were shown in a video immediately before and after the model was presented (retention processes);
3. Group discussion of the effectiveness of the model in exhibiting the desired behaviors (retention processes);
4. Actual practice in role playing the desired behaviors in front of the training class (retention processes; motor reproduction processes); and
5. Feedback from the training class on the effectiveness of each trainee in demonstrating the desired behaviors (motivational processes).

In each practice session, one trainee took the role of supervisor and the other trainee assumed the role of an employee. No set scripts were used. Instead, the two trainees were asked to recreate an incident relevant to the film topic for that week that had occurred to at least one of them within the past year.

The learning points in the video were posted in front of the trainee playing the role of supervisor. For example, the learning points for handling a complaining employee included (1) avoid responding with hostility or defensiveness, (2) ask for and listen openly to the employee's complaint, (3) restate the complaint for thorough understanding, (4) recognize and acknowledge his or her viewpoint, (5) if necessary, state your position nondefensively, and (6) set a specific date for a follow-up meeting. These learning points provided one of the key components of coding and retention.

At the end of each of the nine training sessions, the supervisors were given copies of the learning points for that session. They were asked to use the supervisory skills they had learned in class with one or more employees on the job within a week's time period. In this way, transfer of training from the classroom to the job was maximized. The supervisors were also asked to report their successes and failures to the training class the following week.

To further ensure that the supervisors would be reinforced for demonstrating on-the-job behaviors that were taught in class, their superintendents attended an accelerated program designed to teach them the importance of praising a supervisor, regardless of whether he or she was in the training or control group, whenever they saw him or her demonstrate a designated behavior. This procedure enhanced the motivational processes of the training.

An evaluation of this behavior-modeling training included four types of measures: reaction, learning, behavior, and performance criteria (see Chapter 5 for a complete discussion of these evaluation measures). The training program produced highly favorable trainee reactions, which were maintained over an eight-month period. Moreover, the performance of the trainees was significantly better than that of supervisors in a control group on a learning test administered six months after training and on performance ratings collected on the job one year after training.

The practical significance of this study is that it supports earlier applications of behavior modeling for training first-line supervisors. These studies taken together indicate that certain leadership skills can be taught, provided that the trainee is given a model to follow, a specific set of goals or learning points, an opportunity to perfect the skills, and feedback about the effectiveness of his or her behavior and is reinforced with verbal praise for applying the acquired skill on the job.[62]

Behavior-modeling training has been shown to improve sales performance. Salespeople who received this training increased their sales by an average of 7 percent during the ensuing six-month period; their counterparts in the control group showed a 3 percent decrease in average sales.[63] It has also been found to be effective in the training of appraisal skills. Specifically, a comparison was made of the effectiveness of (1) using TBT and (2) using TBT plus behavior modeling. The TBT alone was as effective as the TBT plus modeling in terms of performance on a multiple-choice test. However, the TBT plus modeling was found to improve significantly employee satisfaction with the way their managers conducted the appraisal discussions. The TBT was no more effective than the control group in this regard.[64]

A meta-analysis of 70 studies on the effectiveness of management training found that behavior modeling was among the most effective of all training techniques.[65] One reason for its superiority is that modeling affects trainees' feelings of self-efficacy as an intervening variable affecting their performance. However, different training methods may be needed for persons with high and low self-efficacy. In a study involving the use of computer software, it was found that modeling increased performance for people whose pretest self-efficacy was in the moderate-to-high range. For those with low self-efficacy, a one-on-one tutorial was more effective.[66] This is precisely why conducting person analyses (discussed in Chapter 3) is so important. It takes into account individual differences among trainees.

Bandura[67] identified four informational cues, which trainers can use to enhance a trainee's self-efficacy beliefs. In descending order of influence, they are enactive mastery, vicarious experience, persuasion, and emotional arousal.

The first strategy trainers can use to increase self-efficacy is to focus on the trainee's experiences with the particular task. Positive experiences and success with the task tend to increase self-efficacy; failures lead to a lowering of efficacy. For example, Bandura found that self-efficacy increases when one's experiences fail to validate one's fears and when the skills one acquires allow mastery over situations that the person once felt threatening. But, in the process of completing a task, if trainees encounter something that is unexpected and intimidating, or the experience highlights limitations in their present skills, self-efficacy decreases even if the person's performance was "successful." Only as people increase their ability to predict and manage threats do they develop a robust self-assurance that enables them to master subsequent challenges.[68] It would appear imperative that trainers arrange subject matter in such a way that trainees know in advance what they will be taught and that they experience success in that arena through active participation with the subject matter.

A second way self-efficacy can be increased is through vicarious experience, namely, modeling others' behavior. Observing others exhibit successful performance increases one's own self-efficacy, particularly when the model is someone with whom the trainee can identify.[69]

A third approach trainers can use to increase a trainee's self-efficacy is through verbal persuasion. This involves convincing the trainee of his or her competence on a particular task. For example, Gist[70] has argued that self-censorship can stifle creativity through the cognitive process of self-judgments (e.g., "my idea is no good"). Thus, she argued that cognitive modeling may be more appropriate than behavior modeling when the performance deficiency is due to inappropriate thought rather than overt behavior or skill.

Cognitive modeling is a self-instruction technique that involves visualizing one's thoughts as one performs an activity. The results of Gist's study in a federal research and development agency showed that subjects in the cognitive-modeling condition had significantly higher self-efficacy than their lecture-trained counterparts following training.[71] In addition, the cognitive-modeling subjects were superior to the lecture/practice group in generating divergent (i.e., creative) ideas.

The persuasive effect the trainer can have directly or indirectly on a trainee's self-efficacy and, hence, behavior was first mentioned in Chapter 2 when we discussed the *Pygmalion effect.* A study that provides further insight into the nature of the Pygmalion effect tested its influence when manipulated independently on the trainee as well as the trainer. Trainees in a clerical course in the Israeli Defense Force were randomly assigned to one of three conditions where the instructors were informed that trainees had either high potential for success or regular potential for success or that insufficient information prevented prediction of trainee success. The trainees in the insufficient information group, unbeknownst to the trainers, were then randomly assigned to two groups. Specifically, one group was told they had high potential for success; the other was told they had regular potential for success. Success in training was subsequently measured by instructor ratings as well as by an objective performance examination. The results of this study demonstrated significant Pygmalion effects for both the instructor-expectancy and trainee-expectancy conditions. Instructor expectancy accounted for 52 percent of the variance in mean instructor ratings, while trainee expectancy accounted for 35 percent. As for the objective performance exam, instructor expectancy accounted for 27 percent of the variance in scores, while trainee expectancy accounted for 30 percent. Interestingly, these results persisted despite a change midway through the training course to new instructors who were unaware of the Pygmalion manipulation. Thus, the effects of the initial expectancy condition carried over to the relief instructors whose expectations had not been experimentally manipulated.[72]

The results of this study show the powerful effect of trainer beliefs on trainee behavior. Trainers who have high expectations of trainees can communicate these expectations in a myriad of ways (e.g., attention given). Moreover, a trainee who believes that others think highly of his or her capabilities develops a strong sense of self-efficacy and thus exhibits high performance.

A fourth method of increasing self-efficacy is emotional arousal. Goal setting, discussed in Chapter 4, is an excellent way of accomplishing this.

*Self-management* is a second area of social learning theory. This training teaches people skills in self-management or self-regulation. The training has proven to be especially effective in increasing one's self-efficacy. The core of the training is goal setting.

Perhaps the most rigorously developed self-management program was that of Fred Kanfer, a clinical psychologist. Kanfer's training program was designed for obtaining commitment to, and the attainment of, self-generated goals. In brief, the training taught people to assess problems; to set specific hard goals in relation to those problems; to monitor ways in which the environment facilitates or hinders goal attainment; and to identify and administer reinforcers for working toward, and punishers for failing to work toward, goal attainment. In essence, this training taught people skills in self-observation, how to compare their behavior with the goals they set, and how to administer reinforcers and punishers to bring about and sustain goal commitment. The reinforcer or punisher is made contingent on the degree to which the behavior approximates the goal. Reinforcers and punishers are viewed in terms of informational as well as emotional feedback in order to take into account cognitive as well as motoric and autonomic effects. This training has proven to be especially effective in teaching people coping skills for overcoming alcoholism and substance abuse.[73]

A survey was conducted of salespeople to examine the extent to which self-regulatory activities take place in the absence of training. Self-regulation was operationalized in terms of three components: goal setting, self-monitoring, and self-rewarding/self-punishing contingent upon the magnitude of the discrepancy between one's behavior and one's goal. Interestingly, these data revealed that the salespeople did not regulate their own job performance. This demonstrates the need for this self-management training. The benefit of such training has been demonstrated in two field experiments.

In one study, Frayne and Latham[74] trained unionized state government employees to increase their attendance at the work site. The training consisted of goal setting, writing a behavioral contract, self-monitoring, and the selection and self-administration of rewards and punishments. Compared to a control condition, training in self-management gave employees the skills to manage personal and social obstacles to job attendance, and it increased their perceived self-efficacy. As a result, employee attendance was significantly higher in the training than in the control group. The higher the perceived self-efficacy, the better the subsequent job attendance. A follow-up study[75] showed that this increase in job attendance continued over nine months. The control group was then given the same training. Both self-efficacy and job attendance increased relative to that of the original experimental group.

Today, the number of managers in an organization is shrinking. A few years ago, an employee might have shared a manager with four or five other employees; today, as a result of company downsizing, that person may have to share that manager with as many as 30 people.[76] Because employees are expected to thrive despite less supervision, their self-management skills are more important now than ever before.

It can be said that behavior modeling is one of the most widely used management development approaches used today. One of the largest suppliers of this type of training reports that over the past 30 years, it has trained more than 6 million leaders in 8,000 organizations around the world. Its program involves nine modules targeted at improving managers' tactical skills (e.g., performance planning), and eight focused on developing managerial strategic skills (e.g., leading through vision and values, building a successful team). Once an organization has identified its training needs, it should select those modules it needs to build the particular skills its managers need. Each company can decide the delivery method (i.e., instructor-led classroom, classroom and self-study, self-study, online learning) that is best for it.

# FINAL COMMENTS

Related to the topic of organizational analysis (see Chapter 3) is the value, if any, that organizations place on psychological theory in developing training programs. The emphasis on theory has been the theme of this chapter. In our opinion, to the extent that theory is absent, there is a lack of understanding about why a training approach worked or failed to work. Consequently, the steps that can be taken to increase training effectiveness are often difficult to discern. Thus, in the absence of theory, it is not surprising that only an estimated 10 percent of the $2 million spent annually on training and development programs by companies in ASTD's Benchmarking Service results in enduring behavior changes.

Chapter 1 expressed the need to minimize fads in the field of training and explained why a reliance on systematic evaluation of training effectiveness is a forceful way of doing this. This chapter has illustrated the following points:

1. The scientific leadership literature is no longer dominated by fads. For example, applications of self-regulation techniques, leader match, role motivation theory, LMX, and double-loop learning have been systematically evaluated for more than three or four decades, and their evaluation is ongoing. The importance of this sentence is threefold. First, these management development approaches are grounded in theory; the training programs have been subjected to repeated investigation; and the training has been evaluated empirically. Many of the evaluations included follow-up data collected from three months to five years subsequent to the training. Moreover, the measures for evaluating the training programs included observable job behaviors.

2. Investigators have not been content simply to show the causal relationship between training and performance. Intervening variables such as self-efficacy, leadership style, motivation to manage, LMX/GNS, and a reduction in defensiveness have been studied to determine why these programs are effective.

3. The theories of training we reviewed in this chapter focus on what leaders do to be successful and on the psychological processes that make this "doing" a reality, not just merely of what they need to know. For example, role motivation focuses on what people need to do to increase their motivation to manage others. Self-management training focuses on what people need to do to regulate their own behavior. LMX focuses on what people need to do to prevent "we-they" behavioral patterns in dyadic situations. Leader match focuses on what people need to do to change the situation in which they are operating so that it is favorable to them. Double-loop learning teaches people what they need to do to minimize defensiveness.

4. Researchers are beginning to use combinations of training programs to form a treatment package to affect change. For example, the training based on Vroom and Yetton's model uses a combination of computerized diagnoses of one's leadership styles, instructor-led classes to clarify material, real-life case studies to promote understanding, and individual and team applications for practice. This treatment-package approach analogous to what is done in clinical psychological settings may be more appropriate than trying to tease out the additive or interactive effects of each, especially in light of the difficulty in making fair comparisons. The latter is

especially problematic if the components of the treatment package are designed to change different rather than the same target behaviors.

5. We believe that social learning theory will become increasingly useful as a theoretical framework for understanding and increasing training effectiveness in the twenty-first century. This theory posits reciprocal determinism among the person's cognitions, the environment, and overt behavior. In other words, behavior influences and is influenced by both cognitive thought processes and environmental (e.g., organizational) contingencies.

Training programs are often ineffective because they fail to take into account each of these three variables, or they fail to understand the interactions among them. Self-regulation plays an important role in social learning theory. Individuals regulate their behavior based on their performance goals, their belief about their ability to achieve these goals (self-efficacy), and their beliefs about the environmental consequences of their behavior (outcome expectancies). This self-regulation should be an important aspect of the training process. Training effectiveness is enhanced when the organization takes steps to ensure that trainees (1) are clear about the organization's goals, (2) develop a strong sense of self-efficacy regarding training content, (3) believe that effective performance on their part will lead to desired outcomes, and (4) believe their mastery of training content will enable them to overcome perceived environmental obstacles. Social learning theory takes these four considerations into account.

At the present time, the diversity in these different management development approaches allows training specialists a wide selection from which to choose. Figure 8.1 shows that these approaches differ not only in terms of the goals they are trying to achieve, but also in the strategies they use to attain these goals.

It might be helpful at this point to discuss where these approaches agree and disagree from one another by asking several key questions:

1. *Do the theorists mentioned in this chapter view effective leadership as being contingent on the nature of the situation?* Clearly, Mintzberg, Fiedler, and Vroom and Yetton would answer yes. Although Mintzberg holds that all managerial positions can be described in terms of 10 roles, he points out that the relative importance given to each of these roles should depend on the job itself, the environment, the person, and the situation. Fiedler argued that leadership effectiveness is contingent on a proper match between a manager's motivational structure or style (i.e., LPC) and the favorableness of the situation. According to Fiedler, certain situations call for relationship-motivated leaders. Vroom and Yetton's model takes into account a number of situational variables that a manager should take into consideration before deciding whether to permit subordinates to participate in a specific decision.

   Argyris (Model II), Blake and Mouton (9,9 management), Miner (six motives), and McClelland (high NAch) seem to advocate leadership prescriptions that would be good in all situations. Finally, it appears as though Likert, Bandura, and Skinner are not espousing a theory of leadership per se. Their theoretical approaches are concerned more with prescribing ways and means of getting leaders to behave effectively.

2. *Can managers learn to behave effectively?* Everyone would say yes. Fiedler contends, however, that it is easier to train managers to diagnose the particular leadership situation in which they find themselves, and then teach them to alter the situation to match their own individual leadership style.

3. *What are the costs in using each approach to improve a manager's effectiveness?* It seems as though the approaches of Argyris (Model II), Blake and Mouton (9,9 management), McClelland (high NAch), and Likert (survey feedback) involve relatively high costs. Argyris confirmed this by describing how three years of time and effort were required to help only six company presidents. Grid seminars last about a week and are either conducted away from the company by outside consultants or on an in-house basis by high-level executives who must be given training in grid methodology. Need-for-achievement training is a relatively long process involving achievement-related fantasizing, self-study, the use of interpersonal supports, goal setting, and follow-up of participants. With survey feedback, a consultant feeds back information to individual managers, typically starting at the top of the organization and proceeding down. Each manager then meets with his or her subordinates to interpret the information and decide on corrective action plans.

   The approaches advocated by Mintzberg (self-study questions), Fiedler (self-teaching guide), Miner (lectures), and Skinner (the strategic scheduling of positive reinforcement) involve fewer costs compared to the other approaches. The costs involved in the careful construction of behavior-modeling videotapes makes Bandura's approach moderately priced.

4. *What benefits can be obtained from using these approaches?* Despite the continued controversy over Fiedler's contingency model and the validity of his LPC Scale, the leader match program appears to bring about significant improvements in the performance ratings of managers in a variety of organizational settings. The major contribution of Fiedler's approach is the idea that, because it is extremely difficult to change an individual's leadership style, we should train managers to either adapt the situation to match their style or else choose to lead only in situations that fit their style. The main limitation of this notion, however, is that it may not be feasible for a manager to either change or avoid certain leadership situations.

Vroom and Yetton's approach deals with a more limited aspect of leadership than Fiedler's. However, like Fiedler, this model takes into account a number of situational variables that must be considered by a manager. Too often we have seen managers who are either "too participative" or "too autocratic" in dealing with their subordinates. The Vroom–Yetton model trains managers to decide whether to employ subordinate participation in decision making. Most of the evaluative research to date involves self-reported ratings; the results that do not do so are a bit discouraging.

Finally, all of the motivation approaches discussed have enormous potential for increasing the effectiveness of managers and the productivity of their work groups. Which one is used should depend on the results of one's needs analysis (see Chapter 2) and budget constraints.

# ENDNOTES

1. P. F. Drucker, "Managing for Business Effectiveness," *Harvard Business Review 65* (1987): 28.

2. H. Mintzberg, *Power in and Around Organizations* (Upper Saddle River, NJ: Prentice Hall, 1983).

3. M. W. McCall Jr. and C. A. Segrist, "In Pursuit of the Manager's Job: Building on Mintzberg," Technical Report No. 14, Center for Creative Leadership, Greensboro, NC, 1980.

4. A. I. Kraut, P. R. Pedigo, D. D. McKenna, and M. D. Dunnette, "The Role of the Manager: What's Really Important in Different Management Jobs," *Academy of Management Executive 4* (1989): 286–93.

5. C. Argyris, "Crafting a Theory of Practice: The Case of Organizational Paradoxes," in R. Quinn and K. Cameron (eds.), *Paradox and Transformation: Towards a Theory of Change in Organization and Management* (Boston: Pitman, 1987).

6. C. Argyris and D. A. Schon, "Reciprocal Integrity." Paper presented at the symposium on functioning of executive integrity. Weatherhand School of Management, Case Western Reserve University, October 1986.

7. F. E. Fiedler, M. M. Chemers, and L. Mahar, *Improving Leadership Effectiveness: The Leader Match Concept* (New York: Wiley, 1976).

8. F. E. Fiedler, "A Contingency Model of Leadership Effectiveness," in L. Berkowitz (ed.), *Advances in Experimental Social Psychology* (New York: Academic Press, 1964): 149–90; F. E. Fiedler, *A Theory of Leadership Effectiveness* (New York: McGraw-Hill, 1967); and F. E. Fiedler and M. M. Chemers, *Leadership and Effective Management* (New York: Scott, Foresman, 1974).

9. Fiedler, "A Theory of Leadership Effectiveness."

10. M. M. Chemers and F. E. Fiedler, "The Trouble with Assumptions: A Reply to Jago and Ragan," *Journal of Applied Psychology 71* (1986): 500–63; A. G. Jago and J. W. Ragan, "The Trouble with Leader Match Is That It Doesn't Match Fiedler's Contingency Model," *Journal of Applied Psychology 71* (1986): 555–59; and A. G. Jago and J. W. Ragan, "Some Assumptions Are More Troubling Than Others: Rejoinder in Chemers and Fiedler," *Journal of Applied Psychology 71* (1986): 564–65.

11. R. W. Rice, "Construct Validity of the Least Preferred Co-Worker (LPC) Score," *Psychological Bulletin 85* (1978): 1199–237; and R. W. Rice, "Reliability and Validity of the LPC Scale: A Reply," *Academy of Management Review 4* (1979): 291–94.

12. F. E. Fiedler and L. Mahar, "The Effectiveness of Contingency Model Training: A Review of the Validation of Leaders Match," *Personnel Psychology 32* (1979): 95–102.

13. F. E. Fiedler, C. H. Bell, M. Chemers, and D. Patrick, "Increasing Mine Productivity and Safety Through Management Training and Organization Development: A Comparative Study," *Basic and Applied Social Psychology 5* (1984): 1–18.

14. F. E. Fiedler, W. A. Wheeler, M. M. Chemers, and D. P. Patrick, "Structured Management Training in Underground Mining: Five Years Later," Technology Transfer Seminar, July 1987. *Bureau of Mines Information Circular No. 9145, 149–53.*

15. M. J. Burke and R. R. Day, "A Cumulative Study of the Effectiveness of Managerial Training," *Journal of Applied Psychology 71* (1986): 232–45.

16. D. E. Frost, "A Test of Situational Engineering for Training Leaders," *Psychological Reports 59* (1986): 771–82.

17. Fiedler, Bell, Chemers, and Patrick, "Increasing Mine Productivity and Safety Through Management Training and Organization Development."

18. E. A. Fleishman, "Factor Structure in Relation to Task Difficulty in Psychomotor Performance," *Educational and Psychological Measurement 17* (1957): 522–32; A. Halpin and B. Winer, "A Fractorial Study of the Leader Behavior Descriptions," in A. Coons (ed.), *Leader Behavior: Its Description and Measurement* (Columbus: Ohio State University, 1957); and J. K. Hemphill and A. E. Coons, "Development of the Leader Behavior Description Questionnaire," in R. M. Stogdill and A. E. Coons (eds.), *Leader Behavior: Its Description and Measurement* (Columbus: Bureau of Business Research, Ohio State University, 1957).

19. V. H. Vroom and P. W. Yetton, *Leadership and Decision-Making* (Pittsburgh: University of Pittsburgh Press, 1973); and V. H. Vroom and A. G. Jago, *The New Leadership: Managing Participation in Organizations* (Upper Saddle River, NJ: Prentice Hall, 1988).

20. V. H. Vroom and A. G. Jago, "On the Validity of the Vroom–Yetton Model," *Journal of Applied Psychology 63*, no. 2 (1978): 151–62.

21. C. H. Kepner and B. B. Tregoe, *The New National Manager* (Princeton, NJ: Princeton Research Press, 2000).

22. Ibid.

23. T. E. Hill and N. Schmitt, "Individual Differences in Leadership Decision Making," *Organizational Behavior and Human Performance 19*, no. 2 (1977): 353–67; and A. G. Jago and V. H. Vroom, "A Hierarchical Level and Leadership Style," *Organizational Behavior and Human Performance 18* (1977): 131–45.

24. P. B. Smith, "Controlled Studies of the Outcome of Sensitivity Training," *Psychological Bulletin 82* (1975): 597–622.

25. G. R. Field, "A Test of the Vroom–Yetton Normative Model of Leadership," *Journal of Applied Psychology 67* (1982): 523–32.

26. R. H. G. Field and R. J. House, "A Test of the Vroom–Yetton Model Using Manager and Subordinate Reports," *Journal of Applied Psychology 75* (1990): 362–66.

27. M. E. Heilman, H. A. Hornstein, J. H. Cage, and J. K. Herschlag, "Reactions to Prescribed Leader Behavior as a Function of Role Perspective: The Case of the Vroom–Yetton Model," *Journal of Applied Psychology 69* (1984): 50–60.

28. R. R. Blake and J. S. Mouton, *The New Managerial Grid* (Houston, TX: Gulf, 1978).

29. R. R. Blake, J. S. Mouton, L. B. Barnes, and L. E. Greiner, "Breakthrough in Organization Development," *Harvard Business Review 42* (1964): 133–55.

30. R. Liden and G. Graen, "Generalizability of the Vertical Dyad Linkage Model of Leadership," *Academy of Management Journal 23* (1980): 451–65; and G. B. Graen and T. A. Scandura, "Toward a Psychology of Dyadic Organizing," in B. M. Staw and L. L. Cummings (eds.), *Research in Organizational Behavior* (Greenwich, CT: JAI Press, 1987): 175–208.

31. F. Dansereau, G. Graen, and B. Haga, "A Vertical Dyad Linkage Approach to Leadership Within Formal Organizations: A Longitudinal Investigation of the Role Making Process," *Organizational Behavior and Human Performance 131* (1975): 46–78.

32. G. Graen, M. Novak, and P. Sommerkamp, "The Effects of Leader–Member Exchange and Job Design of Productivity and Satisfaction: Testing Manual Attachment Mode," *Organizational Behavior and Human Performance 30* (1982): 109–31.

33. G. Graen, R. Linden, and W. Hoel, "Role of Leadership in the Employee Withdrawal Process," *Journal of Applied Psychology 67* (1982): 868–72.

34. T. A. Scandura and G. B. Graen, "Moderating Effects of Initial Leader–Member Exchange Status on the Effects of a Leadership Intervention," *Journal of Applied Psychology 69* (1984): 428–36.

35. G. B. Graen, T. A. Scandura, and M. R. Graen, "A Field Experimental Test of the Moderating Effects of Growth Need Strength on Productivity," *Journal of Applied Psychology 71* (1986): 484–91.

36. Ibid.

37. D. P. McMurrer, M. E. Van Buren, and W. H. Woodwell Jr., "Making the Commitment," *Training & Development 54* (2000): 41–48.

38. J. B. Miner, *The Challenge of Managing* (Philadelphia: W. B. Saunders, 1975).

39. F. E. Berman and J. B. Miner, "Motivation to Manage at the Top Executive Level: A Test of the Hierarchic Rule—Motivation Theory," *Personnel Psychology 38* (1985): 377–91.

40. J. B. Miner, *The Management Process: Theory, Research, and Practice* (New York: Macmillan, 1978).

41. J. B. Miner, "Sentence Completion Measures in Personnel Research: The Development and Validation of the Miner Sentence Completion Scales," in H. J. Bernardin and D. A. Bownas (eds.), *Personality Assessment in Organizations* (New York: Praeger, 1985): 145–76.

42. J. B. Miner, *The Human Constraint: The Coming Shortage of Managerial Talent* (Washington, DC: BNA Books, 1974).

43. Miner, *The Management Process.*

44. D. C. McClelland, *The Achieving Society* (New York: Van Nostrand, 1961); and D. C. McClelland, "Towards a Theory of Motive Acquisition," *American Psychologist 20* (1965): 321–33.

45. D. C. McClelland and D. G. Winter, *Motivating Economic Achievement* (New York: Free Press, 1969).

46. Ibid.

47. R. Likert, *New Patterns of Management* (New York: McGraw-Hill, 1961).

48. H. Z. Wong, *The Workforce Cultural Audit* (Cambridge, MA: Herbert Z. Wong & Associates, 2000).

49. D. G. Bowers, "OD Techniques and Their Results in 23 Organizations: The Michigan ICL Study," *Journal of Applied Behavioral Science 9* (1973): 21–43.

50. D. G. Bowers and D. L. Hausser, "Work Group Types and Intervention Effects in Organizational Development," *Administrative Science Quarterly 22* (1977): 76–94.

51. Wong.

52. B. F. Skinner, "What Ever Happened to Psychology as the Science of Behavior?" *American Psychologist 42* (1987): 780–86.

53. A. Bandura, *Social Foundations of Thought and Action* (Upper Saddle River, NJ: Prentice Hall, 1986).

54. Skinner, "What Ever Happened to Psychology as the Science of Behavior?"

55. G. A. Yukl, G. P. Latham, and E. D. Pursell, "The Effectiveness of Performance Incentives Under Continuous and Variable Ratio Schedules of Reinforcement," *Personnel Psychology 29* (1976): 221–31; and G. Yukl, K. N. Wexley, and J. D. Seymore, "Effectiveness of Pay Incentives Under Variable Ratio and Continuous Reinforcement Schedules," *Journal of Applied Psychology 56* (1972): 19–23.

56. J. Komacki, W. M. Waddell, and M. G. Pearce, "The Applied Behavior Analysis Approach and Individual Employees: Improving Performance in Two Small Businesses," *Organizational Behavior and Human Performance 19* (1977): 337–52.

57. E. A. Locke, "Latham Versus Komaki: A Tale of Two Paradigms," *Journal of Applied Psychology 65* (1980): 16–23.

58. Bandura, *Social Foundations of Thought and Action.*

59. Ibid.; and G. P. Latham, "Behavioral Approaches to the Training Process," in I. L. Goldstein and Associates (eds.), *Training and Development in Organizations* (San Francisco: Jossey-Bass, 1989): 256–95.

60. A. P. Goldstein and M. Sorcher, *Changing Supervisor Behavior* (New York: Pergamon Press, 1974).

61. Burke and Day, "A Cumulative Study of the Effectiveness of Managerial Training"; B. L. Davis and M. K. Mount, "Effectiveness of Performance Appraisal Training Using Computer-Assisted Instruction and Behavior Modeling," *Personnel Psychology 37* (1984): 439–52; M. Gist, B. Rosen, and C. Schwoerer, "The Influence of Training Method and Trainee Age in the Acquisition of Computer Skills," *Personnel Psychology 41* (1988): 255–65; M. E. Gist, C. Schwoerer, and B. Rosen, "Modeling Versus Non-Modelings: The Impact of Self-Efficiency and Performance in Computer Training for Managers," *Academy of Management Best Paper Proceeding 47* (1987): 122–26; H. H. Meyer and M. S. Raich, "An Objective Evaluation of a Behavior Modeling Training Program," *Personnel Psychology 36* (1983): 755–62; J. I. Porras and B. Anderson, "Improving Managerial Effectiveness Through Modeling-Based Training," *Organizational Dynamics 9* (1981): 60–77; and M. Sorcher and R. Spence, "The Interface Project: Behavioral Modeling as a Social Technology in South Africa," *Personnel Psychology 35* (1982): 557–81.

62. G. P. Latham and L. M. Saari, "Application of Social-Learning Theory to Training Supervisors Through Behavioral Modeling," *Journal of Applied Psychology 64* (1979): 239–46.

63. Meyer and Raich, "An Objective Evaluation of a Behavior Modeling Training Program."

64. Davis and Mount, "Effectiveness of Performance Appraisal Training Using Computer-Assisted Instruction and Behavior Modeling."

65. Burke and Day, "A Cumulative Study of the Effectiveness of Managerial Training."

66. Gist, Schwoerer, and Rosen, "Modeling Versus Non-Modelings."

A. Bandura, "Self-Efficacy Mechanism in Human Agency," *American Psychologist 37* (1982): 122–47; and Bandura, *Social Foundations of Thought and Action.*

68. Bandura, "Self-Efficacy Mechanism in Human Agency."

69. Bandura, *Social Foundations of Thought and Action.*

70. M. E. Gist, "Minority in Media Imagery: A Social Cognitive Perspective on Journalistic Bias," *Newspaper Research Journal 11* (1990): 52.

71. Ibid.

72. D. Eden and G. Ravid, "Pygmalion v. Self-Expectancy Effects of Instructor and Self-Expectancy on Trainee Performance," *Organizational Behavior and Human Performance 30* (1982): 351–64.

73. F. H. Kanfer, "Self-Management Methods," in F. H. Kanfer and A. P. Goldstein (eds.), *Helping People Change: A Textbook of Methods,* 2nd ed. (New York: Pergamon Press, 1980): 334–89.

74. C. A. Frayne and G. P. Latham, "Application of Social Learning Theory to Employee Self-Management of Attendance," *Journal of Applied Psychology 72* (1987): 387–92.

75. G. P. Latham and C. A. Frayne, "Increasing Job Attendance Through Training in Self-Management: A Review of Two Studies," *Journal of Applied Psychology 74* (1989): 411–16.

76. K. N. Wexley and S. B. Silverman, *Working Scared: Achieving Success in Trying Times* (San Francisco: Jossey-Bass, 1993).

# C H A P T E R

# *Management and Executive Development*

This chapter discusses management and executive development methods. We have chosen those techniques that are most prevalent and represent the range of training methods currently being used. In reviewing these techniques, we have again categorized them according to the scheme presented in Figure 1.1 (see Figure 9.1).

Each technique is described together with its advantages and disadvantages and any research evidence bearing on its effectiveness. Like the training methods reviewed in Chapter 8, we hope to see more evaluative research on these management and executive development approaches in the near future. At the present time, it is difficult to know with assurance which approach is the best to use for various purposes. We begin by discussing three approaches designed primarily to increase a manager's or executive's self-awareness.

|  | | **GOALS** | |
| --- | --- | --- | --- |
| | *Self-Awareness* | *Job Skills* | *Motivation* |
| **Cognitive** | Sensitivity training<br>Transactional analysis<br>Self-directed<br>  management<br>  development | Seminars and workshops<br>Corporate classrooms<br>The incident process<br>Case study | |
| **Behavioral** | Interactive skills<br>  training | Rational manager training<br>Conference (discussion)<br>Assessment centers<br>Role playing<br>Management games<br>Junior board<br>Understudy assignments | |
| **Environmental** | | | |

**STRATEGIES** (vertical label on left axis)

FIGURE 9.1    Goals and Strategies of Additional Management Development Techniques

# SELF-AWARENESS

Self-awareness involves learning about ourselves. It involves understanding how our behavior is viewed by others, identifying the interpersonal games being played around us and the ones we are playing ourselves, and understanding our own managerial capabilities and limitations. Training techniques that embrace one or more of these objectives by changing the way managers think include T-group training, self-directed management development, and 360° Feedback.

## T-Group Training

T-group training is a unique and popular approach to increasing people's awareness of how their behavior is perceived by and affects others. Pioneered over 50 years ago by the NTL Institute for Applied Behavioral Science, a T-group or Training-group is a type of experience-based learning approach. Participants work together in a small group of about 10 to 13 people over an extended period of time. The duration varies according to the specific needs of the trainees, but most groups meet for about 30 to 40 hours. Each T-group is facilitated by a trainer whose function is to assist the group in maximizing its learning, to encourage communication, and to encourage each group member to understand member interactions and group dynamics. The T-group experience involves not only intense discussions among the participants, but intergroup exercises, role playing, and/or other experience-based activities as well.

Its popularity stems largely from the discouragement some organizations have experienced when attempting to improve the interpersonal skills of their managers and executives by more conventional informational presentation techniques such as instructor-led seminars and conferences. These organizations will opt to send their managers and executives to either NTL, university institutes, or various management consulting firms.

To better understand this approach to training, let's look at the goals of NTL's programs for developing managers and for developing senior executives. Their Management Work Conference is targeted at managers in both line and staff positions. NTL claims that by the end of the conference, managers will:

- Increase self-awareness
- Improve their understanding of group process
- Identify the range of perceptions of behavior
- Expand leadership skills
- Develop and increase problem-solving and decision-making skills
- Enhance interpersonal communication skills
- Increase understanding of management style on group effectiveness
- Increase understanding of the issues of racism, sexism, age, and cultural differences and how these affect human relationships

NTL's Senior Executives' Challenge is designed for presidents, vice presidents, general managers, and comparable high-level administrators. It is claimed that by the end of this program, executives will be given:

- Greater awareness of their leadership and decision-making styles
- A better understanding of the impact of their behavior on others
- An awareness of the effect of others' behavior on them
- Increased skill in achieving group effectiveness and understanding of group process
- Deeper self-insight
- An opportunity to practice new skills in interpersonal competence
- Increased understanding of the issues of racism, sexism, age, and the like

The following excerpt should give you a good description of the procedures followed in a typical T-group session:

At the fifth meeting the group's feelings about its own progress became the initial focus of discussion. The "talkers" participated as usual, conversation shifting rapidly from one point to another. Dissatisfaction was mounting, expressed through loud, snide remarks by some and through apathy by others.

George Franklin appeared particularly disturbed. Finally pounding the table, he exclaimed, "I don't know what is going on here! I should be paid for listening to this drivel! I'm getting just a bit sick of wasting my time here. If the profs don't put out—I quit!" George was pleased; he was angry, and he had said so. As he sat back in his chair, he felt he had the group behind him. He felt he had the guts to say what most of the others were thinking! Some members of the group applauded loudly, but others showed obvious disapproval. They wondered why George was excited over so insignificant an issue, why he hadn't done something constructive rather than just sounding off as usual. Why, they wondered, did he say their comments were "drivel?"

George Franklin became the focus of discussion. "What do you mean, George, by saying this nonsense?" "What do you expect, a neat set of rules to meet all your problems?" George was getting uncomfortable. These were questions difficult for him to answer. Gradually he began to realize that a large part of the group disagreed with him; then he began to wonder why. He was learning something about people he hadn't known before. . . . "How does it feel, George, to have people disagree with you when you thought you had them behind you?. . ."

Bob White was first annoyed with George and now with the discussion. He was getting tense, a bit shaky perhaps. Bob didn't like anybody to get a raw deal, and he felt that George was getting it. At first Bob tried to minimize George's outburst, and then he suggested that the group get on to the real issues, but the group continued to focus on George. Finally Bob said, "Why don't you leave George alone and stop picking on him. We're not getting anywhere this way."

With the help of the leaders, the group focused on Bob. "What do you mean, 'picking' on him?" "Why, Bob, have you tried to change the discussion?" "Why are you so protective of George?" Bob began to realize that the group wanted to focus on George; he also saw that George didn't think he was being picked on, but felt he was learning something about himself and how others reacted to him. "Why do I always get upset," Bob began to wonder, "when people start to look at each other? Why do I feel sort of sick when people get angry at each other?". . . Now Bob was learning something about how people saw him, while gaining some insight into his own behavior.[1]

What conclusions can be reached about the effectiveness of T-group training? First, it is clearly effective on the basis of reaction criteria. Many individuals report significant changes and impact of the training on their lives as managers and executives, family members, and citizens. Second, there is some research evidence that T-groups can bring about changes in trainees' job behavior. Unfortunately, this evidence is tainted by the fact that trainees in these studies nominated their own observers who reported on the trainees' behavior changes or, worse yet, the studies used trainees' self-reported improvements.[2] Third, NTL contends that roughly two-thirds of the managers and executives who have attended their T-group programs are more likely to improve their skills than those who do not (as reported by their peers, managers, and employees). Finally, the incidence of serious stress and mental disturbance during training is difficult to assess, but it is estimated by NTL to be less than 1 percent in participants and, in almost all cases, in individuals with a history of prior disturbances.

## Self-Directed Management Development

The underlying assumption of self-directed management development is that the best way to help supervisors and managers improve themselves is to encourage them to become actively involved in thinking about and setting goals for their own development and career growth. The starting point in this process is for them to assess their own supervisory and managerial capabilities and gain an understanding of the skills they must acquire to become effective managers. Through self-assessment, individuals decide for themselves whether they possess the motivation and potential to manage others effectively. Further, individuals are taught that they must assume primary responsibility for their own development. This entails preparing personal development plans to acquire the experience, knowledge, and skills needed to increase their supervisory or managerial talents, or to pursue another career of their choice.

Careers in Management is an example of a management development system incorporating the concepts of self-assessment and self-directed development. This system is comprised of three series. Each series is designed to meet the needs of employees at different levels within the organization. Series 1 is directed at premanagement employees, that is, those individuals interested in a possible career in supervision or management. Series 2 is designed to assist current supervisors and managers assume primary responsibilities for their own development. The third series is intended to help upper-level managers increase their effectiveness in developing the supervisors and managers who report to them. Although these programs have been designed as an integrated system, they can be used independently for personnel in each of these three hierarchical levels. Table 9.1 lists the program objectives for the participants in each of the three series. The instructional technique used in all three series is called the situation-response method. With this method, a group watches a series of typical supervisory situations on videocassettes. Each cassette is stopped at a critical point where the supervisor or manager on the videocassette must decide how to handle a particular problem. However, before the participant is shown what happens, a trainer interrupts the program to ask each participant to describe how he or she would handle that particular situation. After each participant indicates his or her intended course of action in a Viewer's Guide, a group discussion takes place. Each member of the group has an opportunity to interact with other participants and defend his or her point of view. After the group discussion, the participants view the video program to learn how the supervisor in the program actually handled the situation. The group is then shown another situation. A module is made up of several situations. At the end of each module, the participants use the materials in the Viewer's Guide to evaluate their own effectiveness, reassess their own capabilities and development needs, and think about their motivation to manage.

**TABLE 9.1    Program Objectives for "Careers in Management" Series**

**Series 1 (premanagement employees)**

Assess their supervisory and managerial capabilities and potential;

Evaluate the amount of satisfaction they would get from supervising the work of others;

Decide whether they really want to pursue a career in management or supervision;

Identify the capabilities they need in order to become effective supervisors or managers; and

Prepare personal development plans.

**Series 2 (supervisors and managers)**

Assess their capabilities and supervisory practices;

Identify the knowledge and skills they need to acquire to improve their performance on the job and to increase their potential for future assignments;

Define the development objectives they wish to achieve in order to attain their performance objectives and career goals; and

Prepare "Action Plans" that identify the steps they must take to achieve their development objectives and to increase their supervisory or managerial effectiveness.

**Series 3 (upper-level managers)**

Identify and evaluate their development practices and their development "styles";

Identify opportunities to increase their skill in helping others to develop their capabilities;

Increase their effectiveness in coaching and counseling their subordinates; and

Prepare "Action Plans" to improve the productivity of their organizations by assisting the supervisors and managers who report to them to develop the capabilities they, in turn, need to improve their performance and potential for future assignments.

*Source:* Adapted from "Careers in Management: A Video-Based Self-Directed Management Development System," Sterling Institute, Washington, DC, 1976.

When the modules in the series have been completed, the participants analyze their supervisory style profiles, compare their style with that of other members of their discussion group, and consider ways to change their style to improve their managerial effectiveness. In the final segment of the program, each participant generates a developmental action plan and then "reality-tests" his or her plan with the other trainees.

At the present time, there is no scientific evidence on the effectiveness of this training. However, it is based on four key learning principles that have been shown to be effective in bringing about desirable behavior change: observing a model handle interpersonal situations, active participation, feedback, and group discussion on action steps. Because of this, self-directed management development has become quite popular. It has been used by such organizations as General Motors; Ford Motor Company; Coca-Cola; General Tire; and the U.S. Department of Health, Education, and Welfare.

Closely related to self-directed management development is the general notion of self-leadership, which is the process of influencing oneself so as to generate the self-direction and self-motivation needed to perform one's job effectively. This is accomplished by controlling one's thoughts through the application of various cognitive strategies such as self-dialogue and mental imagery.[3] According to Manz and Sims,[4] leaders can become superleaders by developing not only their own self-leadership skills, but those of their employees as well. This, Manz and Sims contend, is the path to generating self-leading teams.

Before ending this section, however, two cautions are in order: First, those organizations using Series 1 should be careful about generating unrealistically high expectations on the part of premanagement trainees. Participants in this series should be informed if there are not enough supervisory positions open to satisfy all those who may want to be supervisors. Second, self-directed learning apparently does not work with everyone. For instance, in a recent study, it was found that self-leadership training did not work as well with those trainees who described themselves as highly conscientious employees perhaps because they were already engaged prior to training in these self-directed behaviors.[5]

## 360° Feedback

Both private and public sector organizations are adopting 360° Feedback systems to develop managers and executives by giving them a better understanding of how they are perceived by others, and then using this self-awareness to formulate individual development plans. Among the first companies to implement 360° Feedback were Disney, Monsanto, FedEx, McDonnell-Douglas, Du Pont, Westinghouse, Motorola, Florida Power & Light, and the U.S. Department of Energy. Today, according to the 2000 ASTD (American Society for Training and Development) *State of the Industry Report,* 50 percent of the companies in their benchmarking survey use some type of peer review or 360° Feedback system.[6]

The 360° approach incorporates two distinct areas of human resource management: survey feedback (see Chapter 8) and performance appraisal (see Chapter 3). It refers to the assessment of a focal manager or executive from different perspectives and the use of that information as feedback to the individual as a guide for personal development planning.[7] For each focal person, self-ratings are collected along with ratings from one's manager, peers, employees, and, sometimes, customers. With the exception of the manager's ratings, all the other ratings are anonymous. All that the respondents are asked to do is to indicate on the 360° questionnaire whether they are the focal person's manager, peer, employee, or customer. Anonymity is assured because several respondents are involved from each of these four rating sources.

Let's take a closer look at a typical 360° management development process currently used by one of the authors. The process consists of four main tools:

- **The 360° Development Instrument** is the questionnaire provided to the multiple rating sources (i.e., the individual manager himself/herself, their manager, direct reports, peers, customers) to assess their level of effectiveness on 13 skill dimensions, such as: Leadership and Vision Relationships, Strategic Thinking and Planning, Developing Associates Business Acumen, Change Agent, and Building a Team Culture. The instrument consists of a large number of items that comprise these skills dimensions.
- **The 360° Feedback Report** provides the results of the self-ratings and ratings given by their manager, direct reports, and others on the 13 skill dimensions and on individual items that comprise the dimensions. The report also provides the manager with the summary information needed to diagnose strengths and areas for developmental focus.

  Two pages from a typical feedback report are shown in Figures 9.2 and 9.3. Figure 9.2 provides feedback at the dimension level, while Figure 9.3 gives feedback at the item level. The ratings provided by the focal person, their boss, and others are indicated by the "i" symbol. That is, the triangle represents either a self-rating; a boss rating; or the average of the ratings provided by their direct reports, peers, and customers ("other"). The shaded area portrays the middle 50 percent of responses (25th percentile to 75th percentile) for one's company. So, not only can the focal manager or executive see their absolute ratings, but their ratings can be compared to the company as a whole. For instance, one could see where one's self-ratings fall compared to the self-ratings of other managers in their company. Also, one can compare the ratings given by direct reports, peers, and customers to the ratings given to other managers by their direct reports, peers, and customers. Similar comparisons can be made for boss ratings.
- **The 360° Development Workbook** guides the individual through a series of activities to help investigate and better understand the results of their Feedback Report and to establish a developmental action plan. For instance, the workbook helps the manager assess how the skill dimensions relate to their major responsibilities and career growth, how to analyze their report to identify their strengths and areas for improvement, how to discuss their results with their manager and others, how to select areas for developmental focus, and how to develop and implement a developmental action plan.[8]

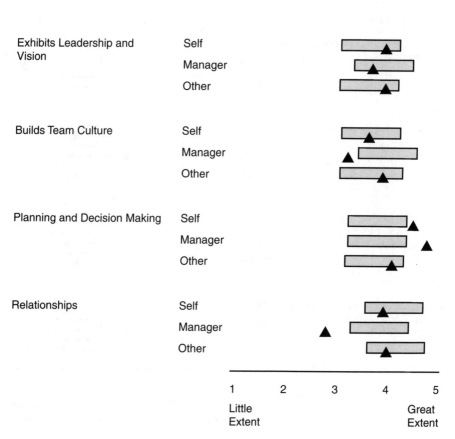

**FIGURE 9.2**    360° Survey Feedback Results

- **The 360° Development Guide** provides many recommended activities and readings for developing the specific skill dimensions. Managers refer to the guide often. In the guide, they are offered many options so they can be selective with regard to their own professional goals and developmental needs.

There are several reasons why 360° Feedback has gained so much popularity in recent years. First, years ago, a typical manager or executive supervised fewer employees than they do today. Within the last decade or so, the average number of employees reporting to a manager at such organizations as Xerox Corporation and General Electric has doubled. The reason for this trend is that many organizations are stripping away middle-level management layers.[9] As a result, it is unrealistic to expect any manager's boss by themselves to provide

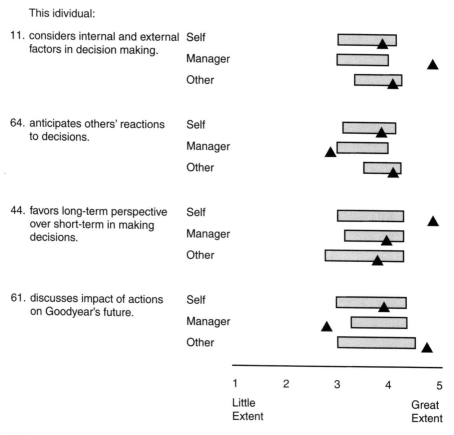

FIGURE 9.3   360° Survey Feedback Results

meaningful feedback when they lack the opportunity to observe very many employee actions. Only through the addition of other sources can companies hope to observe a focal manager's or executive's full range of behaviors. Second, with the increases in technological complexity, it is often unrealistic to expect bosses to have sufficient expert knowledge to provide credible feedback to focal managers and executives in highly specialized fields. Third, the use of 360° Feedback provides information from many different sources, which is great because research has shown that these sources do, in fact, see the manager or executive from unique perspectives. Fourth, unlike performance appraisals, everyone views 360° information as being used primarily for developmental purposes. Fifth, the role of the manager has changed in recent years. Even though the individual is expected to manage more people, he or she is also responsible for their job and career development. Sixth, certain organizations such as Monsanto and Florida Power & Light prefer to use a 360° Feedback system because individuals work in matrix or project management situations, in which they report to more than one boss during a project.[10] Last, but not least, many companies are making the implementation of 360° Feedback easier by making it accessible via the Internet and the company's intranet.[11]

Evaluation surveys of 360° Feedback conducted by companies such as Meridian Oil, Intel, and Du Pont reveal that 78 percent or more users perceive it as providing useful information and being time efficient. The year after a 360° Feedback system was initiated at Westinghouse's Steam Turbine Generator Division in Orlando, Florida, productivity increased 28 percent at the plant. At Chemetals, Inc., a Baltimore manufacturer of manganese, customer satisfaction was found to have increased from an average of 7 to 8.6 (on a 10-point scale) as a result of providing 360° Feedback to their salespeople.[12] Evaluative studies are needed in the future where control groups are used. Without having a control group, we can't be sure how much of the improvement in productivity or customer satisfaction was due to the 360° Feedback itself or a result of other things taking place at the plants at the time. However, we can say with assuredness that the vast majority of trainees have favorable reactions to 360° Feedback. Let's turn our attention now to discussing approaches that are focused on increasing a manager's or executive's job skills.

## JOB SKILLS

Nine training approaches will be presented that are designed to increase managerial and executive skills. Seminars, workshops, plus conferences; case study; managerial and executive mentoring; and rational manager training employ primarily cognitive strategies. The remaining three (outdoor experiential learning (OET), developmental assessment centers, action learning) use mainly a behavioral strategy to increase managerial and executive effectiveness. Let's begin by discussing seminars, workshops, and conferences.

### Seminars, Workshops, and Conferences

According to the 2000 ASTD *State of the Industry Report,* 501 benchmarking service organizations, on the average, spend $2 million or 2 percent of their payroll on training activities. These expenditures provide 29 hours of training per employee a year.[13] Many of these training hours are spent attending a plethora of available managerial seminars, workshops, and conferences. Approximately 73 percent of these seminars, workshops, and conferences are conducted "in-house"; the remainder are delivered through outside providers such as consulting firms, professional organizations, four-year colleges, and community colleges. The following list is a sampling of the diversity of topics that are covered in these seminars and workshops:

- Managing and working with difficult people
- Effective managerial coaching and counseling
- Finance for the nonfinancial manager
- Executive communication
- Project management
- Leading creativity
- Leadership and high-performance teams
- Managing international joint ventures
- Effective sales management
- Strategy: formulation and implementation

These seminars and workshops typically last anywhere from one to five days. They are held at a local hotel, the company's conference room or training facility, or at a college or university's executive education center. These programs are usually conducted by in-house instructors or outside consultants or faculty members.

In-house seminars and workshops are preferred by organizations that have a large enough training department and trainee population to make them cost effective. These programs are developed by in-house training specialists, conducted by company trainers (occasionally supplemented by outside speakers), and tailor-made to fit the company's unique needs. Sometimes, however, it makes more sense for an organization to simply purchase commercially available programs. The effectiveness of these seminars and workshops vary enormously, depending on the particular program leader(s) as well as the organizational relevance of the content for the attendees. Quite frankly, these outside seminars and workshops are sometimes enjoyed by the participants with little or no positive transfer of what they have learned (see Chapter 4) back to their managerial and executive positions. One approach for increasing positive transfer is to conduct rigorous personal analyses to ensure that the managers and executives who are asked to attend these seminars and workshops do, in fact, really need them (see Chapter 3).

The 2000 ASTD *State of the Industry Report* indicated that 71 percent and 60 percent of companies provide training through four-year colleges or universities and community or junior colleges, respectively. Despite this widespread use, evaluation has been notably absent regarding these types of executive education programs. In an attempt to fill this void, a study was conducted of Harvard's Advanced Management Program (AMP) to determine what was actually learned and whether that knowledge brought about an enduring change in the attendees' behavior. These data were collected through questionnaires and interviews with managers and executives who had attended the program two to six years earlier. In addition, spouses completed a questionnaire. It was found that attendance at Harvard's AMP brought about the following lasting changes in behavior: broader perspective, strategic thinking, self-confidence, ability to make executive decisions, and interpersonal skill. The responses from spouses corroborated the findings regarding an increase in self-confidence and taking a broader perspective. We turn now to one of the newest and most popular forms of management and executive development—case study.

# Case Study

The case study method was pioneered at the Harvard Business School. It involves presenting a trainee with a written description of an organizational problem. Each trainee is given an opportunity to read the case in private, diagnose the underlying issues, and exercise judgment in deciding what should be done in the situation described. Then the individual meets with other trainees and, as a small group, they discuss the various diagnoses and proposed solutions.

The trainer's role is primarily that of a catalyst. The trainer provides information sources when appropriate, maintains the direction of the discussion by posing appropriate questions, and encourages the participation of trainees who have difficulty expressing themselves. Thus, the primary purpose of the trainer is to facilitate the group's learning process by providing a climate for group discussion. No attempt is made to lecture the participants; the trainer merely helps them discover for themselves the managerial concepts and principles underlying the case, how the problem might have been avoided, what can be done to prevent this problem from recurring, and so on.

The problems described in the cases vary in length and complexity, depending on the experience level of the trainees involved and the purpose of the case. Most cases deal with solving specific organizational problems, rather than examining theoretical issues.

The use of the case studies can be found in three main settings. Many of today's corporate universities and institutes (see Chapter 7) such as Motorola University, AT&T's School of Business Technology, and IBM's Advanced Business Institute Advocates make extensive use of this method in educating their managers and executives. For instance, one of the major components of the curriculum at Sears University is a business case study that is followed from the first class to the last. It helps Sears's middle managers gain skills such as client relationships management, staff development, and confidence to make judgment calls. Case studies are also used by various management consulting firms such as McKinsey & Company, Bain & Company, Anderson Consulting, and the Center for Creative Leadership. Frequently, they develop tailored cases for clients that teach participants how to better address organziation-specific issues and business situations. Finally, case studies continue to be an integral component of many of the premier MBA programs, such as the Harvard Business School, the Wharton School at the University of Pennsylvania, the Darden School at the University of Virginia, and Stanford University's Graduate School of Business.

Advocates of the use of the case study method contend that it teaches executives and managers to identify and analyze complex problems and to formulate their own decisions. It exposes them to a wide variety of approaches, interpretations, and personalities. In doing so, it shows them that there is seldom a pat solution to most business problems. It also allows managers and executives to derive principles from the cases that they can later apply in solving on-the-job problems.

Critics of the method point to its inability to teach general principles and its lack of control over the inferences that trainees draw from their case discussions. Its advocates reply that this lack of structure is precisely its strong point; trainees learn better and retain more of what they have learned when they discover general principles for themselves.

Unfortunately, the research evidence on the effectiveness of the case study method as a management and executive development approach is minimal. One study based on observations and tape recordings taken during a three-week management development program uncovered certain limitations of the case study method.[14] First, most trainers dominate the classroom interactions by advocating positions, asking questions, and making connections between responses so as to maintain control of the learning process. This often increases participants' dependence on the trainer and ignores issues that might be important to the participants. Second, trainers often act to save face for the participants as well as for themselves, thus discouraging a confrontational atmosphere and the candid generation of ideas and approaches. Third, participants observe that the trainers' behavior is often incongruent with what they espouse. Some examples of this inconsistency include:

1a. There are no right or wrong answers; yet
1b. Some trainers do take positions and give answers.
2a. There are many different views possible; yet
2b. Trainers seem to select viewpoints and organize them on the board in a way to suggest that they have a preferred route.

Finally, very few trainers attempt to relate the participants' behavior in the classroom to their behavior on the job. To improve this method, Argyris argued that participants should read cases from their own organizations (if possible) and that trainers should be less dominating and more willing to allow participants to discuss how to apply their new ideas to their situations back home.

For the case study method to be beneficial, it must simulate as closely as possible situations that trainees are likely to encounter on the job. If the case is fabricated, the trainers are likely to find themselves in the uncomfortable position of having to "invent" facts. As soon as the trainees realize that this is happening, they will lose confidence in the trainer's credibility. Fortunately, many of the new instructional technologies discussed in Chapter 6 (e.g., DVD-ROMs and Web-based training) allow trainers to create a wide range of more realistic case study materials.

## Managerial and Executive Mentoring

Although mentoring was discussed in Chapter 6, it is important to talk about it again as it relates specifically to management and executive development. Numerous organizations such as Ernst & Young, Texas Instruments, 3M Company, IBM Corporation, The Boeing Company, and Merck & Company are currrently using mentoring for developing their managers and executives. Their training and development departments have three types of mentoring programs from which to choose: one-on-one, group mentoring (i.e., one senior executive mentors a group of four to six managers), and team-to-team (i.e., junior teams of mentees interact with senior teams) mentoring.[15] Research has shown that managerial trainees who have had mentors learn more about organizational issues and practices than those without mentors.[16] Moreover, they receive more promotions, have higher incomes, and are more satisfied with their pay and benefits than are managers who have received less extensive mentoring.[17]

Mentoring programs also offer women the opportunities to learn from more seasoned executives. In fact, 91 percent of female executives surveyed reported that they had a mentor at some time in their careers, and 81 percent perceived their mentor as being either critical or fairly important in their career progress. In this same survey, 44 percent of chief executive officers listed mentoring as one of the three most effective strategies for providing women with the knowledge and skills to move into senior management.[18]

## Rational Manager Training

Rational manager training was initiated 40 years ago based on the extensive research of Kepner and Tregoe.[19] They developed a conscious, step-by-step process by which information, judgment, and experience are organized to solve problems and to make sensible decisions in order to achieve specific business results. For Kepner and Tregoe, being a rational manager involves having the following four fundamental cognitive skills:

**Situational Appraisal**
Looking at the whole picture by identifying and evaluating overall concerns, breaking down the concerns into manageable issues, prioritizing them, and then developing a plan for the effective resolution of the issues.

**Problem Analysis**
Resolving problems by first defining the problems in detail, identifying possible causes, and then testing against the problem definition.

**Decision Analysis**
Clarifying the purpose of the decision and forming clear objectives, evaluating possible courses of action, and assessing related risks prior to making a decision.

**Potential Problem and Opportunity Analysis**
Anticipating potential problems and opportunities and their likely causes by developing preventive plans and implementing the appropriate contingent actions, if needed.

The primary purpose of this training is to make managers aware of aids to good decision making and problem solving, give them practice in applying these aids, and then provide them with feedback as to the results of their performance. The program lasts anywhere from three to five days, depending on the management or executive level involved. In this time period, a group of approximately 15 managers grapple with the problems and decisions of a simulated organization. Before each session, the managers or executives discuss the concepts and methods involved with the course instructor. The participants receive materials explaining what has happened recently in this hypothetical company with respect to a given problem. Data are provided in the form of memos, policy directives, financial statements, production and sales records, and so on. During each exercise, each manager is assigned a specific role (e.g., production manager, sales manager). Trainees have their own offices, talk to one another on the telephone, and conduct group meetings to solve the problems at hand (this is why we classify the program with those that use a behavioral strategy).

When the group of trainees has used the time allotted (regardless of whether they solved the problem), they return to the conference room for a critical evaluation of their performance. In this time period, they examine any assumptions they made and the manner in which they used the information available to them. These feedback sessions try to make them aware of inadequate methods of problem analysis and decision making and to show them where they could have improved if they had followed the systematic procedures prescribed by the course instructor.

Rational manager training's learning objectives include:

1. Understanding the basic steps of situation appraisal, problem analysis, decision analysis, and potential problem and opportunity analysis;
2. Questioning and listening intently to access relevant information;
3. Interacting more effectively as a team through use of a common approach and language;
4. Recognizing when participation from others is needed to create commitment or enhance the quality of a solution;
5. Understanding the technique for managing conflict and reaching group consensus; and
6. Applying the concepts to work-related concerns in order to achieve organizational results.[20]

To date, nearly two million people in both private and public organizations have been exposed to this type of training. The program incorporates many of the learning constructs (e.g., case practice, on-the-job application, videos, simulation) that have already been presented in previous chapters. Most of the evidence supporting its effectiveness can be found in the types of case studies described below[21]:

- Twenty-six cross-functional teams were initiated at Ricoh Corporation to streamline operations across the organization. Out of the 26 teams, the risk management team was the only one able to bring about tangible results. This team used the four-step rational process to uncover a hidden opportunity to save $1.3 million in insurance premiums without reducing staff or disrupting the organization.

- Alberta Agriculture, Government of Alberta (Canada), used the rational processes to analyze the causes of low grain prices throughout the world and recommend a new approach to paying income supports to farmers. Tens of millions of dollars were redistributed based on these recommendations.

Although these case studies are quite interesting and encouraging, we still can cite only one study that systematically examined the effectiveness of this managerial/executive training. This study, conducted by the NASA Manned Spacecraft Center, involved the use of self-report questionnaires completed by 125 participants. The results indicated that 85 percent of the NASA-MSC managers felt that the course was valuable to them for performing thorough analyses, planning and asking better questions, and making and evaluating recommendations. The average increase in job performance attributed to the course by the NASA managers was 10 percent, with no managers reporting any negative effect on their performance. Almost 40 percent of the managers, however, felt that the most frequent barriers for applying the concepts to their jobs were "not enough time" and "other people not familiar with the course of concepts."[22]

## Outdoor Experiential Training

We are fascinated by the national captivation with OET programs, known variously as outdoor challenge training, adventure learning, executive challenge, outdoor management training, and personal growth training.[23] They are generally used to improve the effectiveness of managers and executives in such soft-skill areas as teamwork, problem solving, risk taking, self-esteem, and interpersonal communication.[24] Although the programs can take on a variety of forms, they can be categorized into three basic types[25]: the wilderness experience, the high-ropes courses, and the low-ropes courses. Wilderness experiences typically involve participants living outdoors and engaging in such activities as sailing trips, backpacking, whitewater rafting, canoeing, extended camping, and mountain climbing. High-ropes courses are shorter-term activities than wilderness experiences, but they too involve a high degree of risk taking. Examples include rock climbing, rappelling, and crossing canyons by rope. Low-ropes courses approximate many of the learning situations in the high-ropes courses but are perceived to be safer by participants because they take place closer to the ground. Examples here include such activities as backpacking, desert treking, sea kayaking, and low-ropes crossings.[26]

Suppliers that offer OET programs find that their businesses are booming. Given their popularity, what can be said about their effectiveness? Studies so far have focused almost exclusively on evaluating the low-ropes programs. These studies suggest that low-ropes OET programs significantly improve the overall functioning of work groups, particularly those groups that are intact (i.e., interact at work on a regular basis). These improvements in group behaviors have been confirmed by supervisors as much as 15 months after the OET program, and by top managers as much as 18 months later. It has also been found that OET's effectiveness is *not* contingent on whether participants volunteer or not, whether their immediate supervisor is present, or the amount of days spent outdoors during training. Despite its effectiveness for improving group processes, OET has been found to have little or no impact on the growth and change of individuals.[27] Two essential components of any OET program are the development of action plans to ensure positive transfer of learning of the participants back to the work setting and follow-up on the success of these efforts by trainers.[28]

Considering the widespread use of this management and executive development approach, more rigorous evaluative research is needed regarding its effectiveness on bringing about lasting behavior changes back on the job. This research needs to focus on all three OET approaches, not just the low-ropes approach.

## Developmental Assessment Centers

The term *assessment center* (AC) refers to a comprehensive, standardized procedure in which multiple assessment techniques and job simulations (e.g., business games, group discussions, interviews, presentations) are used to evaluate individual managers and executives for various purposes. A number of trained management assessors, who are not in a direct supervisory capacity over the participants, assess each participant on a number of managerial competencies.[29] Originally, the AC method was used primarily for selection and promotion purposes. Recent surveys, however, show that ACs are increasingly used for developmental purposes.[30] The objectives of these ACs vary from personal analysis, to formulation of a personalized developmental action plan, to skill development on the basis of immediate feedback and on-site practice.[31]

How many and what particular managerial or executive competencies are focused on during developmental ACs? Participants are assessed on anywhere from 15 to 25 competencies that have been identified (see Chapter 2) as being important for success in a particular managerial or executive job and particular company. The number of competencies identified should be an important factor in influencing the length of the developmental AC, which can vary from one to three days. Listed below are a few examples of the types of competencies that are measured at the managerial and executive levels:

| Managerial Level | Executive Level |
|---|---|
| Empowering others | Strategic overview |
| Managing resources | Business acumen |
| Interpersonal relations | Global perspective |
| Communications | Seasoned judgment |
| Team building | Visionary thinking |
| Adaptability | Driving execution |
| Problem analysis and solving | Entrepreneurial risk taking |
| Determination to succeed | Cross-functional capability |

What has research shown about the effectiveness of developmental ACs? In one study, the researchers interviewed recent participants to determine their reactions to being evaluated by the AC. They found differences of opinion between the high and low scorers with respect to the accuracy of the assessors' evaluations, the value of the developmental recommendations they received, and the benefits to their careers of participating in it. As one might expect, the low scorers were more negative on each of these points. Based on their interviews, the researchers offered the following recommendations for maximizing the developmental value of the AC process[32]:

1. Feedback interviews should be conducted within two weeks after assessment.
2. Assessors should explain fully the bases for their evaluations.
3. A follow-up interview should be held between the immediate manager and the individual to review the strengths and weaknesses identified at the center.
4. The immediate manager and the individual should discuss and agree on future actions to capitalize on the individual's strengths and correct weaknesses.

In another study, it was found that 41 managers who received feedback after an AC experience and who had engaged in subsequent developmental activities were rated higher on several competencies than a comparable group of 35 managers who had not been put through this developmental process. These training effects were still measurable three months later.[33]

In a comprehensive review of the literature on this topic, Lievens and Klimoski[34] cited research that casts some doubt on the effectiveness of developmental ACs. In one study, a lack of difference in career advancement was found between managers who went through a developmental AC and a naturally occurring control group.[35] A follow-up study attempted to explain these disappointing findings.[36] Several factors were identified that interfered with the subsequent developmental activities: perceived time constraints, lack of social support for development, and low managerial self-efficacy.

Let's look more closely at how a developmental AC, known as the MDP (Management Development Process), has been implemented by one of the authors. It involves the following seven steps:

### Step 1: Orient Participants and Participants' Managers

A two-hour session is conducted with all the participants and their managers to describe the MDP, explain its benefits, distribute 360° materials to the managers, and give a self-rating form and a personal bio sheet to the participants.

### Step 2: Collect Coworker Ratings and Comments

Ratings and comments are collected anonymously on each participant from at least five coworkers who have had an opportunity to directly observe the participant at work. These ratings and comments are sent directly to the MDP staff prior to the session.

### Step 3: Conduct the Half-Day or One-Day MDP Session

Three to six participants are put through tailor-made simulated situations (i.e., group discussions, role-plays), personal interviews, and paper-and-pencil development instruments. Their interactions are observed and recorded by trained assessors who are company managers and/or outside consultants.

### Step 4: Prepare Development Reports

Two days after participating in the MDP session, participants receive a written report highlighting their strengths and development needs on the key competencies. An important feature is the quickness of the developmental feedback. Rather than the assessors leaving and taking a week or so to write long-winded reports, it is advisable to achieve same-week delivery of reports that are clear and concise.

### Step 5: Individual Feedback Meeting

Upon receiving the reports, a feedback meeting is held by one of the assessors with each of the participants to discuss the contents of their report, answer questions about it, and explain how to work collaboratively with their immediate manager on using the written report to generate a developmental action plan to remedy the development needs and to capitalize on the managerial strengths.

### Step 6: Train Participants' Managers

Immediately after the participants have their feedback meeting with the assessor, their managers are brought together for a three-hour meeting at which time they read their participant's report and have their questions answered about it by the assessor. They then are given training on how to work collaboratively with the participant on generating a development action plan.

### Step 7: Follow-Up

Six months and twelve months after the MDP, the 360° rating forms are readministered to each participant's coworkers. These 360° ratings serve two purposes: to evaluate the success of the MDP, and to provide continual developmental feedback to the participants.

The MDP has been found to bring about substantial improvements in managerial behaviors only when: (1) participants follow through on their development plans; (2) the organization is willing to spend the money to provide participants with the needed seminars, videos, and online training called for in their development plans; (3) the human resource department provides a training specialist who can suggest the most appropriate training materials for each participant; and (4) the company's performance appraisal system recognizes and rewards financially those superiors who make the effort to develop the managers reporting to them.

## Role Playing

Instead of simply presenting a problem for discussion, as is done in the case study and the conference (discussion) methods, role playing requires trainees to actually respond to specific problems that they encounter in their everyday organizational roles. The technique makes it possible for them to learn by doing, rather than by merely talking about ways to handle a problem.

Role playing is frequently used in management and executive development programs for teaching such skills as interviewing, handling grievances, conducting performance reviews, changing one's leadership style and its impact on others, conducting team meetings, dealing with direct reports who are having performance problems, and making effective presentations. Regardless of its use, role playing incorporates the following four approaches to learning:

1. *Active participation:* Role playing provides the opportunity for practice, experimentation, and trial-and-error learning.
2. *Modeling:* Trainees can observe how other trainees handle problems, and can then imitate their successful behaviors.
3. *Knowledge of results:* Participants can learn about their personal strengths and weaknesses by receiving constructive feedback from other trainees who are observing their behavior.
4. *Practice:* Repeated experience with a series of role-play problems allows trainees to begin to conceptualize the principles being taught.

Participants are told to imagine themselves in the situations presented by the trainer. The situation may be imaginary and designed solely for training purposes, or it may be an actual problem that the managers or executives are currently experiencing. Trainees are free to try out different behaviors and reactions as long as they stay "in role" throughout the session. Typically, not all members of a training group role play at the same time. Instead, part of the group acts as observers while others act as participants. Before the session ends, all the trainees role play at least once. In this way, they not only receive the benefits of the role-playing exercise, but they also get practice in observing and analyzing the behavior of others. A discussion follows immediately after each role play. Here, the issues and problems that developed during the enactment are examined, so that both the role players and the observers understand the underlying principles that were demonstrated and their organizational implications.

The appropriateness of using role playing depends on the objectives of the training. For instance, to give participants greater insight into their own behavior and the behavior of others, a role reversal may be used. Here, managers or executives in the session who are experiencing interpersonal conflict and misunderstandings might be asked to exchange roles in a role-play problem. For example, managers from quality control and from production might change roles, in order to give them a feel for the other manager's viewpoint. Hopefully, differences of opinion will be minimized as a result of each person's acquiring an understanding of the other person's perspective.

*Multiple role playing* is a method that is particularly appropriate when trainers desire to demonstrate the effects of varying organizational factors on the conclusions and decisions reached by groups. With this method, a large number of managerial trainees (e.g., 20 to 30) are divided into smaller groups of five or six people. The trainer presents a problem that each group is asked to role play. After the role playing has taken place within each subgroup, the entire group of trainees reassembles to share their experiences. Often, the various subgroups are given different instructions (not known to them) so that the effects of these factors can be dramatically demonstrated during the final discussion session. For example, we know of one organization in which different leadership styles (i.e., autocratic, democratic, consultative) are established in each of the subgroups. This results in differences in member satisfaction and performance effectiveness between subgroups becoming evident to the trainees, resulting in their understanding of the impact of different leadership styles on their own employees.

Finally, if the training objective is skill development (e.g., sales strategies, interviewing, conducting performance reviews), videotape playback and/or freeze framing may be useful for demonstrating to the trainees certain effective and ineffective behaviors that were exhibited during the role play. *Role rotation* is another form of role playing that we have found to be extremely useful for teaching interpersonal skills to managers and executives. One trainee plays a role, usually that of an employee who has a problem or is somehow responsible for creating one. Several participants attempt, one by one, to apply their skills in handling the situation. During the final discussion session, the participants can compare the relative effectiveness of their individual approaches. *Freeze framing* is useful for training negotiation and conflict management skills. At timely moments, the trainer instructs the trainee and the auxillary person(s) to freeze their action. Then, the trainer asks the trainee to critique his or her own performance and to suggest other strategies that might have been tried. The rest of the trainees are given the opportunity to provide input.[37]

Unfortunately, the 2000 ASTD *State of the Industry Report* did not report any survey statistics on the current use of role playing. Moreover, your authors can find little evaluative information about it. This paucity of evaluative information, we believe, is probably due to the fact that role playing is rarely used by itself. Instead, it is typically employed in conjunction with other methods of management and executive development such as developmental ACs, managerial behavior modeling, and corporate universities and institutes. Fortunately, its value was examined in a meta-analytical study in which the effectiveness of several different managerial training methods were examined across 70 studies.[38] Some of these evaluate studies used lecture/group discussion combined with role playing. The researchers concluded that the lecture/group discussion with role playing was effective in terms of reaction, learning, and behavioral measures (see Chapter 5). To date, we are unable to cite any evaluative studies in which results measures have been used to evaluate the impact of role playing on managers or executive trainees.

## Management Computer Simulations

Unlike role playing, where participants are assigned roles and are asked to react to one another in terms of their roles in the exercise, management games ask participants to play themselves. This approach to training is currently enjoying a great deal of popularity in both management and executive development programs. Some management simulations are quite complex because they attempt to model the major components of a total organizational system (e.g., a company, a city, a medical center). They focus on teaching general management principles such as long-range planning, financial policy, communications, and marketing. Others are focused on teaching specific managerial skills such as team building, project management, and problem solving.

The popularity of management computer simulations can be traced to several sources. One of the more important is the increasing expertise and sophistication in the computer simulation area. Today, programmers are able to capture various aspects of real-life organizations with much of their complex interrelationships. Second, there has been an increasing interest in understanding organizations from a systems viewpoint. These simulations allow managers and executives to manipulate various components of a system, to better understand how the components interrelate, as well as the system's relationship with its external environment. Third, the development of decision making as a scientific discipline has supported management simulations because they tend to focus attention on the decision-making processes of managers and the effects of their decisions on their organization's effectiveness. Fourth, they are able to compress time so that trainees can derive years of on-the-job managerial or executive experience in just a few days. Finally, the simulations are often intrinsically interesting for the participants because of their realism, their competitive nature, and the immediacy and objectivity of the feedback.

It might be helpful at this point to look at three examples of these management simulations. First, the Looking Glass Experience is a one-day business simulation that closely parallels managerial life. The simulation plunges 10 to 15 middle-, upper-, and executive-level managers into a high-pressure management role at a fictional company where they have to struggle with choices, pressures, and crises. During the simulation, trainers observe and document participants' behaviors. Along with other participants, they provide feedback later during debriefing sessions.[39] A second example involves one of the major airlines. They set out to introduce their new Nexus system of gate-boarding, hardware, software, and practices. These new tools were designed to provide more efficient and effective gate and board processes, reduce the burden currently endured by agents, and increase the accuracy and timeliness of information to both customers and gate agents. They created and used various simulations to teach managers and agents about implementing the new system: a question-and-answer game to increase knowledge of the hardware and software, a drill-and-practice game to increase proficiency in using Nexus's function, and a simulation experience mirroring the events of a typical day.[40] Third, a corporate simulation is used as a four-day program to help upper-level managers and executives learn how to better guide their organizations toward strategic goals. The participants take on a senior leadership role in a simulated global company where they interact with other regions and develop long-range goals, budgets, and strategies.[41] A computer simulation is used at the core of a program that teaches leadership to technical managers. The simulation emphasizes the importance of teamwork and decisions needed to bring a new product to the marketplace. The simulation was designed to capture the challenges of project management in a multidisciplinary environment.[42]

It is important to realize that computer simulation also has some limitations. Sometimes participants become so engrossed in beating the system that they fail to grasp the underlying management principles being taught. This problem can be minimized by combining the simulation with instructor-led classrooms and discussion periods. The method may also stifle highly innovative managers by penalizing them financially during the simulation for their unorthodox strategies. Finally, little evaluation of management simulations has been done. The existing research has been limited primarily to showing that games increase managers' enthusiasm and enjoyment for the learning process.[43] Consequently, it is not possible to conclude today with any assurance exactly what management computer simulations accomplish regarding on-the-job performance. In fact, based on a review of 39 fairly rigorous studies conducted between 1973 and 1983, it was concluded that it is still difficult to make clear statements about the positive effects, if any, of games regarding performance on the job.[44] At the present time, there is little evidence that management games result in long-term improvements in managerial effectiveness. Most of its appeal stems from its face validity and the persuasiveness of its advocates. The final method aimed at increasing managerial and executive job skill incorporates the old adage "learn by doing."

## Action Learning

Action learning was first introduced by Reg Revans,[45] a Cambridge physicist, who conceived of the learning process as being: $L = P + Q$. P, programmed knowledge, is what is stored in books, videotapes, and computer files. It dominates our formative school years with facts, figures, dates, and formulae. It is the knowledge that is communicated during technical training programs. Q, however, is at the heart of action learning. Q is the ability to ask the right questions when everything is uncertain and nobody is clear about what to do next. Revans argued that while P is the domain of experts, Q is the domain of leaders who need to drive a project by seeking answers.[46]

The last decade has seen the emergence of action learning as a training approach for developing managerial talent and producing innovative solutions to organizational problems. Action learning programs bring small groups of managers or executives together (known as a "set") that meet regularly to take action on solving critical, real problems while explicitly seeking learning from having taken that action. The learning aspect is facilitated by a learning "set advisor" (trainer) who is skilled in using the collective experience of the participants to create learning opportunities.[47]

Action learning is another experiential-based learning approach that is in the same domain as OET, role playing, and management games. It differs from these other experienced-based approaches in one very important respect: action learning uses real problems. As the trainees work through solving these problems, they receive specific technical knowledge (P) from experts on a just-in-time basis. Q, asking the right questions and finding the answers, involves an immense range of learning opportunities for trainees such as going into other departments to seek out information, discussing operational and strategic issues with their senior managers, making presentations, and implementing solutions.[48]

Although this approach seems to be a logical way to develop managers and executives, it may encounter resistance in various parts of an organization where managers are accustomed to instructor-led classrooms and more structured learning.[49] Instead, both types of learning have their proper places, particularly when you consider that people come to training having different dominant learning styles (see Chapter 4).

Action learning's success hinges on the sponsorship by a key individual or group within the organization and having a strategic mandate; selecting a "set" of managers who will be successful both as a learning community and as a problem-solving team[50]; and a set advisor who may come from within the organization's training department or else be an external consultant who has built up an expertise in facilitating action learning programs. This management and executive development approach has been used by companies as diverse as Exxon, General Electric, Arthur Andersen, and British Airways.

Action learning can be implemented successfully in small companies. For instance, Bentley Woolston, a 10-person marketing firm, was having financial difficulties and decided to use action learning to give its managers a deeper understanding of how the business works as well as a heightened awareness of their strengths and weaknesses. The action learning program also resulted in improved profitability, quality, and teamwork.[51] There are case studies that describe its effectiveness in large organizations as well. For example, at Citibank, several action learning teams were able to break down barriers among various functions and business that were thwarting company growth and profitability. Let's turn now and look at two approaches that impact primarily managerial and executive motivation, but improve job skills as well.

## MOTIVATION

### Special Job Assignments

In a survey of 611 companies of various sizes and types, it was found that 80 percent of respondents reported using special projects and task forces for developing their managers and executives.[52] Even though we found little empirical evidence supporting the effectiveness of this approach for developing managers, the fact is that the use of special job assignments is quite popular.

There are five types of special job assignments that managers and executives report facilitated their development, namely: (1) managing an operation of significant scope, (2) making an organizational switch from a line to staff position, (3) assignments that entailed starting somewhere from scratch, (4) receiving fix-it assignments, and (5) being assigned to various project teams or task forces.[53] Besides being encouraging and motivating, these special assignments increase managers' and executives' self-confidence, tolerance of ambiguity and stress, ability to act and stand alone, and willingness to direct others.[54] Special assignments are particularly useful for developing global managers. Multinational companies such as Coca-Cola, Du Pont, and Weyerhaeuser encourage people to become internal managers and executives by giving them various special assignments abroad.[55]

Apparently, special job assignments can be excellent vehicles for increasing the enthusiasm and skills of managers and executives, but only when certain key organizational factors are present: (1) the organization is willing and able to withstand less-than-perfect performance for a while[56]; (2) the assignments are long enough to provide managers with ample opportunity to learn, but not last more than about three years[57]; and (3) organizational units are not running so lean that unit managers resent letting any of their people leave.[58]

## Real-Time Coaching

Real-time coaching involves providing managers and executives with individualized performance feedback and professional coaching by an internal training specialist or an external human resource consultant.[59] The coach "shadows" the manager on the job for one or more days, breaking frequently to discuss the individual's management style and to suggest new strategies.[60] Managers and executives claim that they benefit greatly from the close attention to detail and the personal attention that they receive from the coach. Based on our experiences, we have found that real-time coaching can be successful only when:

- The manager or executive (i.e., learner) is really willing to change.
- There is a high level of mutual trust and respect between the coach and the learner.
- What occurs between the trainer and learner is confidential.
- The coach solicits periodic input from the learner's coworkers regarding improvements and regressions that are fed back to the learner.
- There is understanding by all concerned that this improvement process will take time.
- The newly acquired behaviors are supported and rewarded by the learner's coworkers.

Although this approach is quite costly, it is obvious why it has so much potential for increasing managerial motivation and skills. No other management development approach described in Chapters 8 and 9 provide the individual support, feedback, and goal setting that this affords. Despite all these accolades, we look forward to seeing some rigorous research evaluating its effectiveness at the learning, behavior, results, and utility levels.

## FINAL COMMENTS

Most evaluations of management development programs ask participants if they thought the program was beneficial. With this approach, few participants will indicate that the program was a waste of time, even though they may privately think so. The reason for this is that, in many organizations, program participation is a sign that the trainees are "fast trackers" or "comers" who will soon be promoted. Thus, these people are not likely to criticize publicly a program that will help them move upward in the organization. This is why the evaluation procedures presented in Chapter 5 must be thoroughly understood by training specialists.

Obviously, not all management and executive development programs use just one technique to improve effectiveness. On the contrary, organizations frequently embark on long-term management and executive development efforts that involve several techniques. Today, evaluative research comparing the combined effects of two or more techniques are too few to warrant any definitive conclusions. Hopefully, we will see more effort in this direction in the near future.

Most of the management development techniques we presented in Chapters 8 and 9 were aimed at the individual manager. Yet an organization's competence depends greatly on the ability of its managers to work effectively with one another. This is particularly true today as organizations deal with more complex technological problems that cannot be handled by an individual manager. Thus, we see the increasing need for establishing special groups of managers (i.e., task forces, ad hoc committees) to tackle specific problems. Consequently, team-building programs are being used by certain organizations to clarify role expectations and obligations of team members; improve problem solving, decision making, and planning activities; and reduce interpersonal conflict. For instance, Phases 2 and 3 of grid seminars (see Chapter 8) are employed by some organizations to improve teams as well as intergroup relations. Training in team building is among the subjects we will discuss in Chapter 10.

We now turn our attention to societal concerns of the training and development staff. This final chapter illustrates how many of the ideas and strategies described in the first nine chapters can be brought to bear on challenging contemporary issues.

## ENDNOTES

1. R. Tannenbaum, I. R. Weschler, and F. Massarik, *Leadership and Organization: A Behavioral Science Approach* (New York: McGraw-Hill, 1961).
2. M. J. Burke and R. R. Day, "A Cumulative Study of the Effectiveness of Managerial Training," *Journal of Applied Psychology 71* (1986): 232–45.
3. C. P. Neck and C. C. Manz, "Thought Self-Leadership: The Influence of Self-Talk and Mental Imagery on Performance." Unpublished manuscript: Arizona State University, 1992.
4. C. C. Manz and H. P. Sims, "Super Leadership: Beyond the Myth of Heroic Leadership," *Organizational Dynamics 20* (1991): 18–35.
5. G. L. Stewart, K. P. Carson, and R. L. Cardy, "The Joint Effects of Conscientiousness and Self-Leadership Training on Employee Self-Directed Behavior in a Service Setting," *Personnel Psychology 49* (1996): 143–64.
6. D. P. McMurrer, M. E. Van Buren, and W. H. Woodwell Jr., *The 2000 ASTD State of the Industry Report* (Alexandria, VA: American Society for Training and Development, 2000).
7. S. Brutus, J. W. Fleenor, and S. Taylor, "Methodological Issues in 360-Degree Feedback Research." Paper presented at the Meeting of the Society for Industrial and Organizational Psychology, San Diego, CA, April 1996.
8. S. B. Silverman, "Goodyear 360° Development Workbook." Akron, OH, 1994.
9. K. N. Wexley and S. B. Silverman, *Working Scared: Achieving Success in Trying Times* (San Francisco: Jossey-Bass, 1993).
10. M. R. Edwards and A. J. Ewen, *360° Feedback: The Powerful New Model for Employee Assessment and Performance Improvement* (New York: AMACOM, 1996).
11. G. D. Huet-Cox, T. M. Nielsen, and E. Sundstrom, "Get the Most from 360-Degree Feedback: Put It on the Internet," *HR Magazine 44* (1999): 92–103.
12. Edwards and Ewen, *360° Feedback.*
13. McMurrer, Van Buren, and Woodwell, *The 2000 ASTD State of the Industry Report.*
14. C. Argyris, "Some Limitations of the Case Method: Experiences in a Management Development Program," *Academy of Management Review 5* (1980): 291–98.
15. K. Tyler, "Mentoring Programs Link Employees and Experienced Execs," *HR Magazine 43* (1998): 99–103.
16. C. Ostroff and S. W. J. Kozlowski, "Organizational Socialization as a Learning Process: The Role of Information Acquisition," *Personnel Psychology 45* (1992): 849–74.
17. G. F. Dreher and R. A. Ash, "A Comparative Study of Mentoring Among Men and Women in Managerial, Professional, and Technical Positions," *Journal of Applied Psychology 75* (1990): 539–46.
18. G. Holmes, *Personal Communication* (Bloomington, MN: Menttium Corporation, 2000).
19. C. H. Kepner and B. B. Tregoe, *The Rational Manager: A Systematic Approach to Problem Solving and Decision Making* (New York: McGraw-Hill, 1975).
20. Ibid.
21. C. H. Kepner and B. B. Tregoe, "The Spring Salon: Showcase for Project Excellence," *Forum Magazine* (1999).
22. S. Goldstein, J. Gorman, and B. B. Smith, "A Partnership in Evaluation," *Training & Development Journal, 27,* no. 4 (1973): 10–14.
23. J. A. Conger, "Personal Growth Training: Snake Oil or Pathway to Leadership?" *Organizational Dynamics 22* (1993): 19–30; and G. M. Tarullo, "Making Outdoor Experiential Training Work," *Training,* August 1992, 47–52.
24. C. Clements, R. J. Wagner, and C. C. Roland, "The Ins and Outs of Experiential Training," *Training & Development 49* (1995): 52–56.
25. B. L. Thompson, "Training In the Great Outdoors," *Training,* May 1991, 46–52.
26. Clements, Wagner, and Roland, "The Ins and Outs of Experiential Training."

27. R. J. Wagner and C. C. Roland, "How Effective Is Outdoor Training?" *Training & Development,* July 1992, 61–66.

28. T. T. Baldwin and M. Y. Padgett, "Management Development: A Review and Commentary," *International Review of Industrial/Organizational Psychology* (1993); and A. L. Gall, "You Can Take the Manger Out of the Woods, but . . . ," *Training & Development 41* (1987): 54–61.

29. G. C. Thornton and W. C. Byham, *Assessment Centers and Managerial Performance* (New York: Academic Press, 1982).

30. A. C. Spychalski, M. A. Quinones, B. B. Gaugler, and K. A. Pohley, "A Survey of Assessment Center Practices in Organizations in the United States," *Personnel Psychology 50* (1997): 71–90.

31. J. D. Kudisch, R. T. Ladd, and G. H. Dobbins, "New Evidence on the Construct Validity of Diagnostic Assessment Centers: The Findings May Not Be So Troubling After All," *Journal of Social Behavior & Personality 12* (1997): 129–44.

32. K. S. Teel and H. DuBois, "Participants' Reactions to Assessment Centers," *Personnel Administrator 28* (1983): 85–91.

33. A. S. Engelbrecht and A. H. Fischer, "The Management Performance Implications of a Developmental Assessment Center Process," *Human Relations 48* (1995): 387–404.

34. P. Lievens and R. J. Klimoski, "Understanding the Assessment Centre Process: Where Are We Now?" in Cary L. Cooper and Ivan T. Robertson (eds.), *International Review of Industrial and Organizational Psychology 16* (2001): 245–86.

35. R. G. Jones and M. D. Whitmore, "Evaluating Developmental Assessment Centers as Interventions," *Personnel Psychology 48* (1995): 377–88.

36. D. R. D. Mitchell and T. J. Maurer, "Assessment Center Feedback in Relation to Subsequent Human Resource Development Activity." Paper presented at annual meeting of the Academy of Management, San Diego, CA, 1998.

37. D. F. Swink, "Role-Play Your Way to Learning," *Training & Development 47* (1993): 91–97.

38. Burke and Day, "A Cumulative Study of the Effectiveness of Managerial Training."

39. Center for Creative Leadership, *Programs 2001.* Center for Creative Leadership. Greensboro, NC.

40. K. Kruse and J. Keil, *Technology-Based Training: The Art and Science of Design, Development, and Delivery* (San Francisco, CA: Jossey-Bass/Pfeffer, 2000).

41. Center for Creative Leadership, *Programs 2001.* Center for Creative Leadership. Greensboro, NC.

42. Ibid.

43. P. Ernest, "Games: A Rationale for Their Use in the Teaching of Mathematics in School," *Mathematics in School 8* (1986): 2–5; and C. Wesson, R. Wilson, and L. H. Mandlebau, "Learning Games for Active Student Responding," *Teaching Exceptional Children 5* (1988): 12–14.

44. J. Gordon, "Games Managers Play," *Training 22* (1985): 30–47.

45. R. W. Revans, *Active Learning* (London: Blond & Briggs, 1982).

46. S. Inglis, *Making the Most Out of Action Learning* (Brookfield, VT: Gower Publishing Limited, 1994).

47. L. Yorks, "The Emergence of Action Learning," *Training & Development 54* (1998): 56.

48. Inglis, *Making the Most Out of Action Learning.*

49. Yorks, "The Emergence of Action Learning."

50. Inglis, *Making the Most Out of Action Learning.*

51. Ibid.

52. L. Saari, T. R. Johnson, S. D. McLaughlin, and D. M. Fimmerle, "A Survey of Management Training and Education Practices in U.S. Companies," *Personnel Psychology 41* (1988): 731–44.

53. E. Lindsey, V. Holmes, and M. W. McCall Jr., "Key Events in Executive Lives" (Tech. Report No. 32). Greensboro, NC: Center for Creative Leadership, 1987.

54. M. W. McCall, M. M. Lombardo, and A. M Morrison, *The Lessons of Experience: How Successful Executives Develop on the Job* (Lexington, MA: Lexington Books, 1989).

55. Wexley and Silverman, *Working Scared.*

56. Baldwin and Padgett, "Management Development."

57. J. J. Gabarro, *The Dynamics of Taking Courses* (Boston: Harvard Business School Press, 1987).

58. D. T. Hall and F. K. Foulkes, "Senior Executive Development as a Competitive Advantage," *Advances in Applied Business Strategy 2* (1991): 183–203.

59. M. Olesen, "Coaching Today's Executives," *Training & Development 50* (1996): 22–29.

60. K. L. Rancourt, "Real-Time Coaching Boosts Performance," *Training & Development 49* (1995): 53–56.

# CHAPTER

# 10

# *Societal Concerns*

In the four previous chapters, we discussed training and development methods for improving the performance of both managers and their employees. This chapter reviews recent efforts aimed at dealing with special concerns within our society requiring training and development.

The distinguishing feature of this chapter is its contemporariness. The topics covered reflect not only current social issues affecting society, but issues that will likely receive significant emphasis in the future. The first part of the chapter is concerned with basic skills training, training English as a second language, training disabled, training older workers, and training teleworkers. The second part focuses on training managers and professionals to improve their skills in rating others accurately, working effectively in foreign cultures, preventing technical obsolescence, dealing with personal problems and substance abuse, and, finally, managing their own stress and time effectively.

The final section focuses on concerns that are, and will remain, particularly crucial during the start of the future: training for the prevention of sexual and, racial harassment, diversity training, wellness training, safety training, customer service training, and team skills training. Lets start off by focusing on some special issues and target groups.

## Special Issues and Groups

### Basic Skills Training

Basic skills are the reading, writing, speaking, and math abilities required to function in society and to perform one's job effectively. Basic skills includes such activities as reading directions, locating information on a table, filling out a log book, explaining a work-related problem to a coworker, and computing sales tax. The most recent National Adult Literacy Survey conducted in 1992 by the U.S. Department of Education's National Center for Education Statistics estimated that about 21 percent of the adult population—more than 40 million over the age of 16—have only rudimentary reading and writing skills. Most adults in this category can pick out key facts in a brief newspaper article, for example, but cannot draft a letter explaining a mistake on their credit card bill. The survey also showed that the highest math skill for 22 percent of adults in the United States is simple arithmetic. They can add 6 plus 6 if the problem is put into a mathematical format such as, $6 + 6 = ?$. They cannot, however, solve math problems such as, "You have 4 oranges, Betty gives you 5, and John gives you 3 more. How many oranges do you now have?" According to the National Institute for Literacy (NIFL), a federal institute located in Washington, D.C., American businesses are losing $60 million in productivity each year due to their employees' lack of basic skills. Even so, an NIFL survey of more than 300 executives found that while 71 percent of them believed that written communication training was critical for meeting the challenging demands of their jobs, only 26 percent of organizations provide this type of training. Further, although 47 percent of these executives saw a need for workers to improve their basic math skills, just 5 percent of companies offer such training.[1]

In light of this situation, more and more business organizations are slowly being forced to take on this added responsibility of teaching their employees basic skills. After all, as more sophisticated technologies are being developed, employees can no longer get by without having certain basic skills. In addition, low employment rates have forced companies to promote more from within, thereby making it necessary for them to provide remedial education programs to ensure the future promotability of their current employees.

Before designing and implementing basic skills training programs, training specialists must undertake task and person analyses (see Chapter 3). The purpose of the task analysis is to determine the types and levels of basic skills employees need to perform their jobs. This involves assembling a panel of incumbents who are quite knowledgeable about their job and asking them to provide samples of such things as the types of computations that they need to make, the document materials they read, as well as the memos, logs, and letters they need to write. The purpose of the person analysis is to ascertain which of the employees need basic skills training, and what specifically each needs. The person analysis should be accomplished by using both a formal and informal assessment. The formal assessment involves designing a battery of job-related basic skills tests and administering them to all employees in the job. As you might expect, formal assessment is not easy to do since certain employees will be reluctant to take these tests for fear that they will somehow be used to get rid of them. Employees must be reassured that the testing is solely for training needs analyses. It is also crucial that the test items be geared closely to their jobs. One would never want any employee to leave the testing session saying, "that test didn't have anything to do with what I do on my job." An informal assessment entails asking supervisors which of their employees have been having difficulty doing such things as speaking, listening, reading, writing, and solving problems using arithmetic or math. Supervisors should be given a behavioral checklist that lists key behaviors that suggest that an employee is having difficulty in these skills areas. Examples of these behaviors include: does not follow written safety rules, fills out all forms at home, refuses to take written phone messages, fails to listen and understand verbal instructions, and makes repeated calculation errors.

Most organizations make participation in basic skills training programs voluntary, realizing that an employee who is forced to attend probably will not get much benefit from it. They also give their employees release time during work hours to attend classes that meet two or three times a week for two to three hours each time.[2] Basic skills training programs are being conducted in a variety of settings such as corporate classrooms and universities, local community colleges, and nonprofit literary organizations. Various private training firms now have Web sites where one first fills out a self-assessment questionnaire and, depending on the score, can order courses via CD-ROMs, workbooks, and online courses.

School-to-Work programs offer companies the opportunity to not only do something for their local communities, but also develop the skilled workforce that they need now and in the future. In 1994, the School-to-Work Opportunity Act was passed in the United States, which provides seed money to states and localities to develop programs to help students successfully make the transition from school to work. The act recognized the fact that only about one-third of high school graduates go on to college and that the remaining two-thirds are poorly prepared to succeed in the workplace, particularly with respect to reading and math skills. The act leaves the actual developing of the training systems in state hands, to qualify for federal funds newly created and existing training programs must include three essential elements: work-based learning, school-based learning, and connecting activities. Let's take a closer look at a few examples of these programs. UPS has developed an alliance with five colleges and high schools in Maryland to help high-risk students stay in school. These students learn workplace readiness skills, gain work experience, and learn about career opportunities. Bell Atlantic has set up, in cooperation with the International Brotherhood of Electric Workers, a program that prepares students, as well as people reentering the job market, for technology-related jobs in the telecommunication industry in New Jersey. At Eli Lilly and Company in Indianapolis, engineers give minority students experience in computer science and engineering. These students and Lilly engineers meet two Saturdays each month for activities that include hands-on exercises and computer presentations.[3]

It is crucial that basic skills training programs be evaluated in terms of employee reaction, learning, job behaviors, and bottom-line results. It is not enough to just review the course content and assume that the program will solve the problem. The results of a recent survey conducted jointly by the National Institute for Literacy and the Conference Board are encouraging. They examined the benefits gained through basic skills training programs at various organizations. Listed below are these benefits and the percentage of employers reporting them[4]:

| | |
|---|---|
| Improved employee morale/self-esteem | 87% |
| Increased quality of work | 82% |
| Improved capacity to solve problems | 82% |
| Better team performance | 82% |
| Improved capacity to cope with change in the workplace | 75% |
| Improved capacity to use new technology | 75% |
| Higher success rate for promoting employees within the organization | 71% |
| Increased output of products and services | 65% |
| Increased profitability | 56% |
| Reduced time per task | 56% |
| Reduced error rate | 53% |
| Better health and safety record | 51% |
| Reduced waste in production of products and services | 49% |
| Increased customer retention | 42% |
| Increased employee retention | 33% |
| Employers reporting at least one benefit gained | 98% |

Closely related to the training of basic skills is the need to provide certain employees with English language training.

### English as a Second Language

In more and more U.S. firms, the immigrant population is the engine that is driving the organization's productivity level. As a result, these companies are providing English as a Second Language (ESL) training to these employees. For example, Tommaso Fresh Pasta, a pasta manufacturer located in Dallas, started its ESL training in 1995. Since then, more than 85 percent of its employees have participated, resulting in reduced rework, increased productivity, improved employee relations, and higher employee loyalty. An additional benefit of ESL classes has been realized at Uncle Wally's, a muffin manufacturer located in Hauppage, New York. Offering ESL classes has helped them to broaden their hiring pool on Long Island where it is normally quite difficult to find qualified manufacturing people. Relatives and friends of employees hear about the ESL training and recognize that the company is concerned about its employees' welfare. As with basic skills training, ESL is conducted in a variety of settings such as universities, community colleges, corporate classrooms, private training firms, and nonprofit volunteer literacy programs. It is important not to underestimate the importance of gaining middle-management support before initiating an ESL program. Too often, language classes start out full, but attendance starts dropping off as a result of backlash from trainees' supervisors who do not see the benefits of this type of training and resent time taken away from regular job duties to attend. To avoid this problem, training specialists need to involve supervisors in both the design of ESL programs (e.g., incorporating job-related materials) and the identification of those employees who are experiencing difficulty, frustration, or anxiety due to a lack of English.[5]

Perhaps you are among many students today who have voiced the same complaint regarding the frustration of trying to learn from non–native-speaking professors and teaching assistants, particularly in math, science, and engineering courses. Too often, students drop courses, avoid lectures, and suffer through unintelligible hours with sophisticated scholars whose accents and halting speech frequently defies understanding. Fortunately, more and more colleges and universities are following the lead of the College Park and Baltimore County campuses of the University of Maryland as well as Baltimore's Johns Hopkins University. On these campuses, teaching assistants must take oral language tests before being cleared to teach. If these individuals are unable to pass these tests, the schools offer ESL training and culture instruction.

Millions of workers in North America suffer from various forms of disabilities. We discuss in the next section what is being done to provide training for them.

### The Disabled

There are two major pieces of legislation that affect individuals with disabilities: (1) the Vocational Rehabilitation Act, and (2) the Americans with Disabilities Act. The Vocational Rehabilitation Act of 1973 requires employers holding federal contracts of $2,500 or more to take affirmative action in hiring qualified individuals with disabilities. The act requires organizations to take proactive steps (e.g., special training programs, redesign of tools and machinery, wheelchair ramps) to accommodate workers with disabilities. A disabled person is defined broadly as any person who has a physical or mental impairment that substantially limits one or more major life activities. This classification includes not only those individuals traditionally classified as disabled (e.g., paraplegic, deaf, blind), but also those with high blood pressure, arthritis, epilepsy, or diabetes. It also includes people with a former history of severe illness (e.g., cancer, emotional breakdown, heart attack) who are no longer suffering from their disability. Although this act was clearly a historic breakthrough in protecting Americans with disabilities, it nevertheless applies to only a small portion of the workforce because it applies primarily to those organizations doing business with the federal government. As mentioned in Chapter 2, the Americans with Disabilities Act of 1990 was a sweeping piece of legislation that affects an estimated 43.6 million Americans with disabilities. This act makes it illegal to discriminate against a disabled job applicant who is otherwise capable of doing the job. These disabilities and the number of people who have them, according to the Congressional Research Service, are as follows[6]:

| | |
|---|---|
| Absence of extremities | 1.0 million |
| Deformity/orthopedic | 12.8 million |
| Hearing impairment | 4.3 million |
| Paralysis (complete or partial) | 0.4 million |
| Speech impairment | 1.1 million |
| Visual impairment | 4.3 million |

| | |
|---|---|
| Other impairments | 3.7 million |
| Two or more impairments | 9.9 million |

As a result of this legislation, employers need to review their human resource policies to determine whether their present procedures assure careful and thorough consideration of the job qualifications of disabled applicants and employees for training opportunities. Moreover, employers must make reasonable accommodations to the physical and mental limitations of employees during training unless the employee can show that such an accommodation (e.g., modifying a piece of equipment, getting special help from coworkers, receiving extra supervision) would impose an undue hardship on the conduct of their business. Employers are also encouraged to arrange for career counseling for known disabled employees. Finally, all personnel involved in the recruitment, selection, promotion, disciplinary, and related processes should be trained to ensure their commitment and understanding of the organization's affirmative action efforts regarding disabled persons.

Let us take a look at what several organizations are doing today to accommodate individuals with disabilities during training. Our first example focuses on using an innovative training approach to accommodate workers with mental disabilities. It takes place at NEC America's Oregon plant. This plant employs about 625 employees, and it manufactures fiber optic transmission systems, digital microwave radio systems, cellular telephones, data modems, and very small aperture terminals. Department supervisors carefully select certain of their employees to learn procedures for training newly hired employees having moderate to severe mental retardation. The employee/trainers are put through a two-day seminar that focuses on training them how to provide the right type and amount of assistance at various times, how to measure how a trainee is progressing, and how to apply reinforcement to strengthen the learning that took place. Everyone is organized into teams, each consisting of an employer/trainer and an employee with mental disabilities. NEC America's positive findings clearly demonstrate that companies can voluntarily accommodate certain employees with mental disabilities by teaching coworkers basic training strategies.[7] Our second example focuses on those companies that are now making computers accessible to people during training who are so severely paralyzed that they can move nothing but their eyes. A small device is placed beneath a monitor that fires an infrared beam at the trainee's cornea that then bounces back onto the computer screen. A red dot appears on the screen informing the trainee where their eyes are looking. Using this red dot, the trainee can use the movement of their eyes to operate the computer so as to learn at their own pace. We know of a pet store chain that hires and trains mentally disabled individuals to feed and care for the animals at their pet stores. The instructions from the training manuals have been rewritten in the form of easy-to-understand checklists. An insurance company had no difficulty training deaf people for positions as data entry operators. Written, rather than oral, instructions were provided during the two-month period of on-the-job training. A bank provided amplified telephones for hard-of-hearing bank teller trainees.

We are quite optimistic regarding the future success of training individuals with disabilities thanks to technology-based training (TBT). For instance, computer keyboards are now available that can be modified to accommodate trainees with mobility impairments so that they can type combinations of keys using only one finger. Visually impaired trainees can now use computers that read aloud to them whatever documents appear on their screens. They are also able to use braille keyboards, about the size of a brick and consisting of just eight keys, that allow them to download their training notes to a computer. Just as encouraging, hearing-impaired trainees can now answer phones by typing a message on their computer, and a voice synthesizer reads it to the caller. The caller can likewise type messages across the phone lines using letters associated with the numbers on the keyboard of a touch-tone phone.[8]

**Older Workers**

If one noticed that more and more of their coworkers are a little gray around the temples and are now eligible for senior discounts at local retailers, one has observed an important trend that greatly impacts the field of training and development. Older workers are remaining in, and are reentering, the workforce. According to the U.S. Department of Labor:

- The number of workers 55 and older is projected to reach 2.2 million, or 25 percent of the workforce, by 2005.
- More than a million seniors between the ages of 55 and 64 have returned to the workplace since 1994.
- Older Americans account for 22 percent of the country's job growth since 1995.
- Approximately 15 percent of Americans 65 and older (about 4.7 million) are working full or part time.
- About one-third of the employed seniors work 40 hours or more per week, while 46 percent work 20 hours or less.

Why is this trend occurring? First, thanks to the current labor shortage, many older persons who have the opportunity to return to the workforce are jumping at the chance either because they find that their fixed incomes aren't sufficient or because they are not really interested in early retirement.[9] Second, two well-known facts are that the workforce is aging as a result of the baby boomers' growing older and that the relative proportion of young people entering the workforce is expected to decline in the next few decades.

As with other groups who have experienced discrimination, there are a number of stereotypes that limit the participation of older workers in the labor force. Employers and employees alike need to be made aware of research findings in order to change their current attitudes about what older workers can't or won't do. The following is a summary of pertinent findings on senior workers[10]:

1. It is often assumed that as a worker's age increases, the capacity to perform physical tasks declines so much as to seriously impede the person's ability to perform a job. Actually, in most jobs today, the physical demands are well below the abilities of most normal aging workers.

2. The major obstacle for some older workers is not the physical heaviness of the work, but rather the stresses of a machine or work group to maintain a high rate of productivity. If job performance is being affected, a small change in the design of the task can usually return it to the capability of the older worker.

3. For over 60 years, there has been sufficient research evidence to argue that anyone over 60 can learn about as well as they ever could. Although IQ declines with age, it occurs much later than most people have thought. When it does become critical to work performance, most people are already retired and in their late 70s or 80s.

4. Several large-scale studies conducted by the National Council on Aging and the Department of Labor have shown that differences in output rates among age groups are insignificant. In addition, it appears as though supervisors consider a majority of their workers aged 60 and over to be as good as, or better than, younger employees with respect to such job dimensions as absenteeism, dependability, work quality, and work volume.

5. Older workers are generally more satisfied with their jobs, have longer job tenure, and have fewer psychiatric symptoms than younger workers.

In light of these facts, organizations should do several things when designing training programs for these older workers. First, a critical feature of successful training programs for older employees is that basic skills are mastered before training progresses to more complex components. By lowering the chances of failure, older trainees' feelings of self-confidence can be enhanced, which, in turn, maximizes their learning. The most direct way to do this is to establish performance criteria so that progression can be regulated from one level of training to the next. If this is not done, any gains at one level can be compromised by the premature introduction of information from higher levels.

For example, underground train guards in London are given six weeks of training before entering passenger service. The program has been sequenced so as to reduce the resignation rates of older trainees, who are less likely to leave their jobs once they have passed the training period. In the first week of service, the trainee studies the basic operation of the railway, the signaling system, and emergency procedures. Practical experience is gained through three days of action work as a stationperson. During the second week, the trainee learns about the rules governing operations, safety, emergency procedures, and the guard's responsibilities. A tour of several train stations provides the practical component. In the third week, the trainee studies the equipment found on a train, the brakes, safety devices, procedures in the event of mechanical or electrical failure, door operation, and so on. For practical experience, there is a visit to the main depot to examine a train and its equipment with a trainman's inspector. The remaining three weeks involve primarily on-the-job training. The key element of this program is that each trainee must show satisfactory performance before moving on to the next step in the training sequence.

Second, it is important that the pace of training be relaxed. If the pressure to produce is lowered somewhat during training, older workers will be able to learn the tasks correctly, and subsequently be able to cope with time pressures on their jobs. For instance, the effectiveness of computer training for older employees can be substantially increased by slowing it down. If pressure from above dictates that training fit into a compressed time schedule, the company will pay for speed now in higher turnover and lower productivity later.[11]

Third, older adults in particular learn better when the training involves activity rather than rote memorization and passive listening. Conventional means of instruction such as instructor-led classrooms and large seminars need to be deemphasized and replaced by more active learning methods. For example, memorization cannot be completely eliminated in the learning demands of the underground train guard. A detailed knowledge of the braking system, for instance, is important. Rather than requiring older workers to sit passively during lectures, the training should rely on presentation methods using multimedia, interactive TV, equipment simulators, and teleconferencing.

Fourth, older workers sometimes develop their own unique methods of organizing information, which can clash with the requirements of the training program.[12] To avoid this problem, self-paced training works better with older trainees than the classroom because it gives them more control over the speed with which the material comes at them.

Fifth, trainers need to adapt their instructional style to the needs of the older audience. For example, computer training for older employees seems to work best when they are taught in small groups of 6 to 10 trainees where they can look at other trainees' screens and help one another. Because seniors are often collaborative learners, it makes sense to move their computer stations closer together to take advantage of this learning style.

Sixth, it is important during training that the future transferability of the training experience be emphasized to the trainees and that the training materials be job relevant and customized. Most older workers want to be assured that their efforts are not a waste of time and that what they are learning is worthwhile.

Finally, some older workers feel intimidated by the material, particularly when it involves computers or other high-tech equipment. There are several ways to alleviate these fears such as using mature instructors who are close in age to the trainees, training seniors in classes with other seniors, and making needed software and hardware adjustments. For instance, simple software adjustments can make a mouse a little easier to use, and changing the height and tilt of a monitor can make it easier to read for trainees wearing bifocals.[13]

Many states are committed to promoting the employment of older employees. For instance, Maryland has the Senior Employment Program, which is available to men and women, ages 55 years and older, who meet established low-income guidelines and who desire an opportunity for training and employment. Individuals are given a training assignment that most closely matches their personal goals for employment. These training assignments are coordinated with nonprofit or government agencies and are 20 hours per week, at the established minimum wage hourly rate. Participants are hired by a variety of "host agencies" including schools, health care agencies, hospitals, retail merchants, administrative and management offices, and technology companies. The Senior Employment Program provides subsidized training and employment for up to two years. The goal of this program, authorized under Title V of the Older Americans Act, is to help older workers to develop workplace skills that will enable them to attain permanent, unsubsidized employment, either with their host agencies or with other nonprofit, government, or private sector employers.

Before we leave this topic, it is important to point out that older employees need financial information long before retirement. Although preretirement seminars are becoming more and more prevalent, less than 25 percent of U.S. companies currently offer this form of training for their older employees. One exception is Coca-Cola USA, which has been conducting three-day preretirement training sessions for its employees, 45 years old and above, since the 1970s. The program focuses on various psychosocial issues surrounding retirement as well as estate and financial planning. We hope to see more organizations offering this type of training in the years ahead, especially as the large number of baby boomers starts getting ready to retire.

In the next section, we will discuss one of the most important pieces of legislation affecting the training of workers today—the Workforce Investment Act.

**Adults, Dislocated Workers, and Youth**
Starting in July 2000, the 1983 Job Training Partnership Act was replaced by the 1998 Workforce Investment Act (WIA). The most important aspect of the act is its focus on meeting the needs of U.S. businesses for skilled workers *and* the training, education, and employment needs of three groups of individuals: adults, dislocated workers, and youth. Key components of the act enable customers to easily access the information and services they need through a "One-Stop" system, empower adults to obtain the training they find most appropriate through individual training accounts, and ensure that all state and local programs meet customer expectations.

Each state is required to establish both state and local workforce investment boards. The state board helps the governor develop a five-year strategic plan describing statewide workforce development activities, explaining how the requirements of the act will be implemented and outlining how the special populations will be serviced. Local workforce investment boards, in partnership with local elected officials, plan and oversee the local system.

Most services for adults and dislocated workers (e.g., those who have lost their jobs because of permanent layoffs or plant closings) are provided through the One-Stop system. Through this system, information about and access to a wide array of job training, education, and employment services are available for customers at a single neighborhood location. Adults and dislocated workers are able to easily: (1) receive a preliminary assessment of their skill levels, aptitudes, abilities, and support services needs; (2) obtain information on a full array of employment-related services, including information about local education and training service providers; (3) receive help evaluating their eligibility for job training and education programs; (4) receive career counseling; and (5) have access to up-to-date labor market information that identifies job vacancies, skills necessary for in-demand jobs, and information about local, regional, and national employment trends.

Provisions of the act promote individual responsibility and personal decision making through the use of "individual training accounts," which allow adults and displaced workers to "purchase" the training they determine is best for them. This market-driven system enables customers to get the skills and credentials they need to succeed in their local labor markets. WIA recognizes that good customer choice requires quality information. Therefore, the One-Stop system provides customers with a list of eligible training providers and information about how well those providers perform. The act also provides that training providers must meet certain requirements in order to receive the adult or dislocated worker funds. The training providers are held accountable for completion rates, the percentage of participants who obtain unsubsidized jobs, and their wages at placement. They must also provide information about the cost of their programs.

Most services for adults and dislocated workers are provided through the One-Stop system, and most customers use their individual training accounts to determine which training program and training provider best fit their needs. Two types of services are provided: (1) core services, and (2) intensive services. Core services are available to all adults *with no eligibility requirements.* Core services include such things as job search and placement assistance, career counseling, labor market information, initial assessment of skills and needs, information about available training services, and follow-up services to help customers keep their jobs once they are placed. Intensive services are for unemployed individuals who are not eligible to find jobs through core services alone. In some cases, the intensive services are available to employed workers who need more help to find or keep a job. Intensive services include more comprehensive assessments, development of individual employment plans, group and individual counseling, and short prevocational services. In those cases where qualified customers receive intensive services, but are still unable to find jobs, they receive training services that are directly linked to job opportunities in their local area.

WIA, which is administered by the U.S. Department of Labor, is also targeted at eligible youth who are typically low income and 14 through 21 years of age. These young customers also must be facing one or more of the following challenges to successful workforce entry: (1) school dropout; (2) basic literacy skills deficiency; (3) homeless, runaway, or foster child; (4) pregnant or a parent; (5) an offender; or (6) need help completing an educational program or securing and holding a job. These youth are prepared for postsecondary educational opportunities or employment. These youth programs must link academic and occupational learning. Moreover, all service providers must have strong ties with employers. All programs have to include tutoring; study skills training and instruction leading to completion of secondary school (including dropout prevention); alternative school services; mentoring by appropriate adults; paid and unpaid experience (e.g., internships and job shadowing); occupational skills training; leadership development; and appropriate supportive services. Youth participants also receive guidance and counseling and follow-up services for at least one year, as appropriate. Youth councils are established as a subgroup of the local workforce investment board to develop parts of the local plan relating to youth, recommend providers of youth services, and coordinate local youth programs and initiatives.

In the following section, we discuss one of the most interesting trends affecting the workplace today—the increasing use of telecommuting.

## Telecommuting Training

Telecommuting involves bringing the work to the worker by substituting telecommuting technology for transportation. Telecommuters typically have company-provided workspace, but also work in a remote work location, such as their home, on an as-needed basis.[14] According to the International Telework Association and Council, a nonprofit organization dedicated to promoting the benefits of teleworking, more than 19.6 million people in the United States reported working as telecommuters in 1999, up 10 percent from 1998.[15] Several factors are contributing to its increased popularity: (1) the impact of the Internet; (2) employees are realizing more than ever that they have work/life choices; (3) employers realize that they can save $10,000 per teleworker in reduced absenteeism and costs, plus attain productivity gains equating to about $685 per teleworker annually; (4) applicants are conditioning their acceptance of new job offers on approval from prospective employers to telecommute; and (5) new technology (e.g., cell phones, fax machines, notebook computers) is allowing employees to communicate with coworkers and customers from anywhere.

Despite all these advances, the transition to telecommuting is often unnerving for everyone involved because it affects the interactions among teleworkers, their managers, and their coworkers back in the office. In fact, experience has shown many organizations that telecommuting programs will not work effectively unless telecommuting training is factored in from the program's conception. Teleworker training should involve the following components[16]:

- A short overview on telecommuting followed by presentations from employees who have already experienced it
- A short self-scoring questionnaire to help participants identify how likely they are to succeed as telecommuters
- The development of the self-management skills that are needed to be productive away from one's workplace

- How to do handle the lack of quality face time with one's manager by clarifying with one's manager how productivity will be evaluated through the completion of assignments and projects, rather than hours spent in the office
- How to enhance communications with coworkers in the office so as not to stifle motivation and creativity
- How to set up a home office, create a work schedule, and deal with family, friends, and neighbors who see telecommuters as always available because they work at home

At Merrill Lynch, telecommuting trainees get a realistic preview of what it will be like to work from their homes through a "simulation lab." The lab is a large room that contains stations where telecommuters work for two weeks without any face-to-face contact with their supervisors or coworkers. According to this New York–based brokerage firm, this simulation lab has proven to be an excellent way of dealing with the problem of unmet expectations that often beset telecommuters.[17]

Supervisors of teleworkers also need to receive training for telecommuting to be successful. Among the topics that need to be covered are[18]:

- How to clarify performance goals, expectations, and productivity measures with teleworkers
- Understanding that telecommuting is not going to make their jobs nonessential to the organization
- Shifting from activity-based management to result-based management (i.e., managing projects rather than time)
- How to maintain a high level of communication with teleworkers through alternate (e.g., phone, e-mail) means
- How to keep teleworkers involved in what is going on in the office
- How to handle employees who are left in the office, stop their jealousy, help them to be supportive of the teleworkers, and communicate with them about what the teleworkers are doing and not doing

Arthur Andersen Performance and Learning (AAPL) in St. Charles, Illinois, has seen firsthand that this type of supervisor training makes a big difference in the success of telecommuting programs. AAPL's training covers topics similar to those listed above. They emphasize the business case so that their supervisors understand what AAPL is trying to achieve with the program. They also focus on training supervisors on how to communicate effectively with remote employees and teams.

It is not enough to just have separate training sessions with teleworkers and their supervisors. At some point, these two groups have to be brought together to understand what the supervisors' problems are going to be and vice versa. Merrill Lynch uses these joint sessions to iron out how this arrangement is actually going to work. Supervisors talk about when they expect their employees to be available and what kinds of communications will be used. Employees bring up issues such as how many days a week they are going to telecommute, the accessibility of their supervisors, and their working relationships with other teleworkers and coworkers in the office.[19]

Two other groups of people, besides teleworkers and their supervisors, need training. All coworkers of telecommuters need training and education to familiarize them with the telecommuting program—how it works, how and why certain people were selected to participate in it, and what is expected of them. Finally, executive training is equally important for ensuring the program's success. Vice presidents and middle-level managers also need to understand how the program will work and its expected benefits, so that they support it. They need to be brought into the process six months later to be shown the success of the program using reaction, behavior, and results measures (see Chapter 5).

# THE MANAGER AND PROFESSIONAL

We now turn our attention to six concerns affecting today's managers and professionals and some of the training efforts designed to alleviate them. First, the current trend to improve the accuracy of managers' evaluations of their subordinates stems largely from governmental pressures to increase fairness in personnel decisions such as promotions, transfers, and layoffs. Second, the fact that more and more organizations are building their offices and plants in foreign countries and transferring their managers to these locations has necessitated the smooth assimilation of these people into other cultures. Third, the rapid and dynamic knowledge explosion in our modern technological society has accelerated the problem of obsolescence. Fourth, problems of substance abuse continue to plague North American industry. Finally, the abilities to handle stress and to manage time remain as two areas of vital concern to today's managers and professionals.

## Training to Improve Rating Accuracy

Many of the most critical decisions in their organizations surround the recruitment, hiring, promotions, appraisals, and discharges of individual employees. Yet, these decisions are plagued by various judgment errors (e.g., first impressions, prejudices, leniency, stereotyping, similarity/dissimilarity) that individuals are susceptible to regardless of their experience, education, or level within the organization. Research has shown that these errors cannot be eliminated by merely warning or lecturing people about them. If this approach is tried, people are either not sure that they themselves fall victim to these errors or they feel that they do not commit them.[20] Subsequent research has shown that the only way to eliminate these judgment errors is to use a workshop program, which includes the following essential components[21]:

- Viewing employees on videotape
- Having an opportunity to rate their performance
- Comparing and discussing one's ratings with other participants
- Learning for oneself the kinds of judgment errors one commits
- Learning solutions for eliminating these judgment errors when selecting, promoting, appraising, and interacting with others

This type of training has been conducted with over 50,000 managers and supervisors. Accuracy training is a one-half-day program that has been implemented by itself or used in conjunction with other leadership and management development programs. It has been used to train over 50,000 managers and supervisors in numerous organizations such as Bridgestone/Firestone, Boise Cascade, Weyerhaeuser, Merck & Company, and Allstate Insurance.

## Cross-Cultural Training

As more and more managers are working overseas for multinational corporations, the training they receive in adjusting to their host culture is increasing in importance. This is especially so, given the following facts[22]:

- U.S. companies spend between $150,000 and $250,000 per year for each manager sent abroad.
- Approximately 20 percent of all U.S. expatriates return home before completing their overseas assignments, which is about double the rate experienced by Japanese and European firms.
- Failures in overseas assignments are not due to technical incompetence, but instead to the manager's inability to adapt to a new and different culture.
- About 20 percent of all U.S. expatriates quit their jobs within a year of returning to the United States, thereby resulting in significant human resource losses for their employers.
- Research indicates a strong linkage between cross-cultural training and managerial success overseas.
- Only about 35 percent of U.S. firms conduct any predeparture training of a cross-cultural nature, much less than firms in other industrialized countries.

Let's look at the variety of cross-cultural training that these particular multinational corporations are providing for their managers.

Managers employed by a large U.S. manufacturer of electronic products were given intercultural training in preparation for their assignments in Seoul, Korea, for three months. Some of these managers received *Didactic-Information Training* in the form of written materials that compared the United States and South Korea in terms of such general areas as politics, economics, religion, and history as well as specific aspects of Korea such as food, relationships between males and females, and culturally appropriate gestures. Other managers were given an *Intercultural Experiential Workshop,* which involved several role-playing and experiential exercises designed to increase their awareness of the South Korean culture and their openness to unfamiliar modes of behavior and value systems. It was found that both methods were effective in preparing managers to work in a different culture.[23] Specifically, before the trainees returned to the United States, they were rated by their supervisors in South Korea. These ratings were significantly higher than those received by a nontrained (i.e., control) group of managers with respect to job performance and getting along with others.

Another approach to intercultural training is an adaptation of sensitivity training (see Chapter 9). The purpose here is to give trainees an opportunity to explore their own interpersonal styles and their basic values and attributions. An example of this approach is a two-week program, developed in Great Britain, that combines a multicultural group of participants, an international group of trainers, and multinational training materials.[24] The program was designed to generate a true cross-cultural situation, in which participants can directly experience cultural differences and learn through them. The participants are confronted with actual organizational cases involving intercultural conflicts and decision making. The trainers serve as resource persons for the trainees in their process of discovering for themselves alternative ways to deal with themselves and others in intercultural situations. Unlike other cross-cultural training techniques that involve the imparting of technical knowledge, this approach attempts to increase a trainee's awareness of the cultural bases of behavior and, through this awareness, to improve trainee sensitivity to self and to the environment.

Many companies, such as Coca-Cola, Dow Chemical, Glaxo Wellcome, Motorola, Shell, and Hewlett-Packard, provide a predeparture orientation program for personnel being transferred abroad. The orientation may be as extensive as teaching a basic level of proficiency in the host country's language, allowing managers and their spouses to visit the prospective country for a few weeks, and encouraging them to talk with managers and their families who have already lived in the host country. General Motors (GM) is an example of a company that provides excellent predeparture training. The GM program is designed for both employees and their spouses. It includes such things as an explanation of all personnel policies (e.g., taxes, medical insurance, payroll) and relocation expenses. The entire family is given three to six weeks of language training and three days of culture training. If GM does not have in-house people who are knowledgeable about a country's culture, it will call on American University in Washington, D.C., to provide the needed training.[25]

It is not enough to provide employees and their families with only predeparture training. The success of any cross-cultural training effort can be appreciably increased by providing continued training once the employee and his or her family arrive overseas. This postarrival training should include continued language instruction as well as additional culture training. It should also involve the company providing a mentor—someone who knows the ropes, who greets employees and their families upon arrival, and who is available to them thereafter. It is also important that employees and their families be helped to readjust upon reentry. This can involve providing specially prepared written materials, individual or family counseling, and/or support groups of people who are going through a similar adjustment period. Reentry training is important because it has a huge impact on the future of recruitment of employees for cross-cultural assignments and employees' productivity once they have returned home.[26] Failure to provide such repatriation training can be an expensive mistake if it results in repats taking what they have gained from their experience and bringing it to a competitor.[27]

Today, with global markets expanding rapidly, U.S. employees need to develop basic language skills to be able to communicate with colleagues and customers in foreign countries. According to a survey conducted by the Alaska Pacific University, just under 4 percent of American multinational corporations require additional language capabilities in their international employees. For some reason, most U.S. companies do not see the link between their profitability and their employees' linguistic skills. Fortunately, there are some organizations that are realizing that multilingualism makes good business sense. 3M, which earns more than $7 billion in annual sales overseas, sponsors an in-house language society that organizes lunchtime classes for more than 1,000 employees in 17 different languages. These classes use audiocassettes as their primary instruction tool. The success of the language society is evident from the fact that its utilization has grown 15 to 20 percent annually as 3M has become more global. United Airlines has 22,000 flight attendants and is working to help most of them become bilingual. The airline uses self-instructional methods combined with instructor-led classrooms.[28]

Training at Diamond-Star Motors, a joint venture between Mitsubishi and Chrysler, exemplifies an innovative use of cross-cultural training. Diamond-Star developed a program for its Japanese managers who are being transferred to the United States. The purpose of the program was to provide insight and information on American employee attitudes, values, work-setting needs, and related subjects relevant to the Diamond-Star setting. The program was designed to enable Japanese to work effectively with Americans by providing them understanding and knowledge about what motivates and demotivates Americans. Among the topics covered are motivational influences, work-related values, factors that promote trust and cooperation, educational influences, as well as American views on working with the Japanese.

The training of individuals to manage international teams is another important new component of cross-cultural training. The objective of these training initiatives is to develop the skills needed to manage international teams that are separated by distance, culture, time, and technology. Among the topics that are typically covered in these one- to three-day programs are[29]:

- Understanding what is different about leading international teams in areas such as building relationships, attracting loyalty, clarifying goals, managing high levels of travel, managing performance issues, teamwork, and transfer of learning
- Knowing how to coach remotely over the telephone and explore the implications for appraisal and performance evaluation
- Enabling understanding of cultural differences and developing the skills to reconcile these differences into effective business solutions
- Learning how to apply influence across cultures and through technology
- Developing a global culture and international business processes

With such rapid changes in technology occurring today, it is no wonder that the prevention of professional obsolescence is a major challenge for training specialists. Let's look at what they are doing to combat this problem.

## Professional Obsolescence

Today's professional (e.g., engineer, manager, chemist, physician, accountant) faces the danger of becoming obsolete. *Obsolescence* can be described as a reduction in one's professional competence resulting from a lack of knowledge of new techniques and technologies that have developed since the acquisition of the individual's education. Technological changes such as computer-aided design, "just-in-time" manufacturing, e-mail, the World Wide Web, and high-performance work teams have created dramatic changes in people's jobs and, therefore, in the need for continual retraining during their careers. A useful measure for estimating the extent of obsolescence in various professions is the concept of *half-life,* a term borrowed from nuclear physics. For instance, it has been asserted that an engineer's education today has a half-life of five years (i.e., half of what he or she learns in college becomes obsolete in five years) as compared with a half-life of 12 years in 1940. Due to the rapid addition of data and knowledge in many professions, organizations are finding that the performance of their "knowledge workers" (those who apply ideas, concepts, and information) tends to peak in their middle to late 30s and falls steadily thereafter until retirement.

An important part of the process of successful updating of knowledge is to increase the professional's own desire for continued lifelong education. A person's decision to expend a certain amount of effort for self-development is a function of the individual's perceptions of the organizational rewards that will accrue from engaging in such behavior. Thus, organizations must reward (e.g., better salaries and assignments) their people equitably for expending effort to prevent professional obsolescence.

Organizations should make updating behavior an important component of their performance review system and remove constraints from employees (e.g., lack of training opportunities, weak supervisors, outdated equipment) that keep them from advancing their knowledge and skills. For instance, organizations concerned with avoiding professional obsolescence should encourage their managers to formulate mutually agreed upon updating goals with their employees and make pay increases and promotions contingent on the accomplishment of these goals. These organizations should also encourage their employees to access the company's intranet, attend professional meetings, purchase or rent CD-ROMs and DVD-ROMs, read technical journals and reports, publish their own findings, and so on.

Several professions take proactive steps to cope with obsolescence. For example, in the medical profession, the American Board of Internal Medicine has accepted the recommendation that periodic recertification of its diplomas be undertaken. The board administers examinations dealing with significant new developments in internal medicine and subspecialties at 10-year intervals. The examination is administered to approximately 11,000 candidates once a year at 50 test centers in the United States, Canada, and Puerto Rico. The exam covers a wide range of content areas such as cardiovascular disease (CVD), medical oncology, neurology, and gastroenterology. A second example is the Human Resource Certification Institute (HRCI), which is the credentialing body for human resource professionals. It is affiliated with the Society for Human Resource Management (SHRM), the world's largest organization dedicated exclusively to the human resource professional. Certification as a human resource professional clearly demonstrates a commitment to personal excellence and to the human resource profession. To become certified, an applicant must pass a comprehensive examination and demonstrate a strong background of professional human resource experience.

It is a given that today's companies must keep new products and services coming and be flexible enough to respond quickly to changing customer demands. To keep their competitive edge, these organizations have to make sure that their knowledge professionals (i.e., engineers, scientists, lawyers, programmers, researchers) do not become professionally obsolescent. AT&T's Bell Laboratories believed that defining the difference between top and average performers is essential for maintaining the productivity level of their professionals. For the past several years, their research has focused on the engineers and computer scientists at Bell Labs. The research, for instance, identified nine work strategies (i.e., taking initiative, networking, self-management, teamwork effectiveness, leadership, followership, seeing one's job in its larger context and taking on other viewpoints, presenting ideas in writing and oral form, organizational saavy) that differentiated their "star" engineers from their "average" engineers. Based on this research, Bell Labs created a detailed curriculum for each of the nine work strategies. Each piece of that curriculum includes frank discussions, work-related exercises, self-assessments using work strategy checklists, specific case studies and exercises, discussions and disagreements among participants, and homework that requires participants to practice while they learn. Since 1989, many of the 5,000 engineers at Bell Labs have participated in this professional training. The company has found that the productivity of participants improves twice as much as nonparticipants over an eight-month period. Moreover, engineers who receive training improve in seven areas, including spotting and fixing problems, getting work done on time with high quality, pleasing customers, and working well with other departments. In addition, they found that star performers are not alone in benefiting from this training; star and average performers improved at similar rates.[30] Many organizations are using their intranet to help professionals and others stay abreast of the latest developments in their fields. For instance, at Procter & Gamble (P&G), employees worldwide can access *"Socrates,"* where they can keep abreast of such things as new hardware and software skills, the changing P&G culture, and P&G's Success Actions for Winning. Employees can also click on *"P&G University"* and do such things as build and maintain libraries of knowledge, collaborate with others, chat with experts, purchase and deploy off-the-shelf training, participate in live distance training, and keep abreast about P&G's global business units and corporate functions.

Research has long shown that the degree of technical challenge experienced by professionals early in their careers relates positively to their competence level in subsequent years. If a professional's early work is extremely challenging in terms of using knowledge and skills to the fullest, the individual is more likely to be stimulated to demonstrate good performance and competence throughout his or her career.[31] Many organizations are capitalizing on these findings by providing maximum challenge and stimulation during their professionals' early years.

In the next two sections, we will discuss how organizations are training their employees to handle the problems and stresses that come about through their work and their personal lives.

## Employee Assistance Programs

In recent years, many organizations have established special programs to aid employees at all job levels who have alcohol-related, drug-related, or emotional problems that affect their job performance. The vast majority of large companies (about 90 percent) and about a third of companies with less than 100 employees have some form of assistance program for their employees.[32]

How do these employee assistance programs (EAPs) work? The vast majority involve an independent agency that provides counseling services to one or more client organizations. Usually, training sessions are given by this agency to all employees, labor representatives, and managers of their client organizations to inform them about the service and how they might take advantage of it. They are told that they and their family members may use the service as often as needed. There is no charge because the service is typically paid for by their company. Most often, employees and their family members contact the service on their own because of marital problems, emotional stress, financial difficulties, alcoholism, or drug abuse. Sometimes, however, an employee's supervisor or union representative might refer the employee to the program due to a documentable decline in job performance. To do this, supervisors must receive training in their approach to employees whose job performance, attendance, or relationship with other employees has recently deteriorated for some unknown reason. Managers and supervisors are taught to be alert to changes in the work patterns of their employees. They are trained to interview the troubled employee and present all the facts regarding declining performance. Their role is simply to advise the employee that outside professional services are available on a confidential basis.

There is no need for the supervisor to know the causes of the employee's problems. The supervisors are taught that they are not qualified to give advice on how to deal with the problem. They are not to be judgmental or moralistic, but simply to show concern and firmness about the employee's declining performance. If the employee refuses help, and performance continues to decline, the supervisors are instructed to give the individual a choice between seeking professional assistance or accepting dismissal.

What other types of training programs are typically involved for supervisors and for employees when first-rate EAPs are implemented? Supervisors receive training in such areas as drug and alcohol education, coping with change, conflict resolution, respectful workplace, and violence in the workplace. Employees are given training in such topics as balancing work and family, taking care of the caretaker, improving interpersonal communication, and handling financial concerns.[33]

Years ago, the only vehicles available for employee assistance were office visits, telephone calls, and instructor-led classrooms. Today, employees are able to download educational materials of their choice at no cost from their employers' Web site. Moreover, the Internet and intranet are providing employees with support through locked chat rooms under the guidance of qualified counselors, who are qualified to correct misinformation and direct discussion.[34]

How well do EAPs work? Evaluation studies of EAPs have clearly shown their effectiveness. For example, McDonnell-Douglas Corporation estimated that it saved $4 for every $1 that it spent on its EAP, which served 100,000 employees and 250,000 dependents. Employees treated for alcohol or drug dependence missed 44 percent fewer days of work after participating in the EAP, compared with pre-EAP years. McDonnell-Douglas was also able to reduce turnover among these employees from 40 percent to 8 percent after their EAP had been in existence for four years. The Campbell Soup Company found in 1992 a one-year reduction of 28 percent in mental health care costs at their plants where their initial EAPs were implemented, with costs dropping from $261 to $188 per employee. As a result of this pilot project, Campbell Soup has expanded their EAPs to 50,000 workers and their dependents at more than 40 different locations. Finally, NCR Corporation derived clear benefits from their EAP by offering their employees financial incentives to use their EAP before seeking mental health care or substance abuse treatment elsewhere. After one year, 80 percent of the cases were resolved without using more expensive health care benefits.[35]

## Stress Management

Although many individuals experience stress as a normal part of their job, some employees experience stress more severely than others, to the extent that they become ill and need time away from work. According to the The American Institute of Stress, a nonprofit organization founded in 1978 to serve as a clearinghouse for information on all stress-related subjects, stress is America's number 1 health problem. Their surveys and research reports conducted over the past two decades reveal that:

- Job stress is estimated to cost U.S. industry $300 billion annually, as assessed by absenteeism, diminished productivity, employee turnover, legal and insurance fees, and so on.
- An estimated 1 million workers are absent on an average workday because of stress-related complaints. Stress is said to be responsible for more than half of the 550,000 workdays lost annually due to absenteeism.

- Nearly half of all American workers suffer from symptoms of burnout, a disabling reaction to stress on the job.
- Forty percent of employee turnover is due to job stress. The Xerox Corporation estimates that it costs approximately $1 to $1.5 million to replace a top executive, and average employee turnover costs between $2,000 to $13,000 per individual.
- Workplace violence is rampant. There are almost 2 million reported instances of homicide, aggravated assault, rape, or sexual assaults. Homicide is the second leading cause of fatal occupational injury and the leading cause of death for working women.

According to a survey conducted by the U.S. Bureau of Labor Statistics, there were 3,418 cases of occupational stress in 1997. The median absence from work for these cases was 23 days, more than four times the median absence for all nonfatal occupational injuries and illnesses.[36]

What are organizations doing to counterattack these problems. It has been estimated that about $11.41 billion was spent in 1999 on stress management programs, products, and services.[37] A review of company stress management programs reveals that:

1. Most efforts consist primarily of educational programs designed to acquaint employees with the role of stress in health and illness, sources of stress, and the nature of stress-related symptoms.
2. Most commercial programs provide trainees with individual stress profiles based on their answers to self-report questionnaires or standardized psychological instruments.
3. Most stress management programs teach participants one or more physiologic techniques (e.g., muscular relaxation, deep breathing, meditation).
4. Various behavioral techniques such as assertiveness training, time management, and reduction of type A coronary-prone behaviors are used in programs to reduce inappropriate or exaggerated responses to stress.
5. Physical fitness is definitely the most popular method used to cope with stress in the workplace. This includes a wide variety of activities such as company-sponsored exercise and aerobic classes, weight reduction programs, in-house fitness facilities, and programs to help employees quit smoking.

To help you to truly understand the nature of these stress management training programs, we are going to look at one of them closely. This program has been applied to such diverse population members as social welfare case workers, university administrators, bankers, business executives, test-anxious college students, heavy social drinkers, and athletes. It has been evaluated using both time-series designs and pre- and postmeasure designs (see Chapter 5) with random assignment of individuals to either the control group or the group to whom the training is given.[38] The conceptual model of stress that underlies the training is similar to Bandura's[39] Social Learning Theory (see Chapter 8) in that it emphasizes reciprocal relationships among the situation, the individual's cognitive appraisal processes of what is occurring to him or her, affective arousal, and instrumental behaviors.

The program involves five phases. First, there is *pretreatment assessment.* Interviews and questionnaires are used to identify the trainee's behavioral and cognitive skills as well as deficiencies so that the program can be tailored to the person's special needs. For example, the trainer determines how well the person can voluntarily relax and how aware the person is of the cognitive processes that elicit emotional responses and impair performance.

In short, the trainer tries to build on the trainee's strengths and help him or her acquire new coping skills in deficit areas. Thus, the training program for a person who already has fairly good relaxation skills, but who has little control over self-defeating thought processes, will tend to focus on developing stress-reducing, stress-preventing, and performance-enhancing cognitive skills. Conversely, a primary focus on the development of relaxation and self-instructional skills may be the preferred approach for an intellectually dull and chronically tense person.

Second is the *conceptualization phase* or treatment rationale, which is designed to help trainees understand the nature of their stress response. This step is of crucial importance in obtaining trainee commitment. Thus, care is taken to ensure that the conceptualization is understandable and plausible. The person is asked to describe his or her stress responses. Questions such as "When did it happen?" "What was it like?" and "What were your thoughts at the time?" are usually sufficient to elicit descriptions of situational, physiological, and cognitive elements. Answers to these questions provide an entrée to the necessity for training that will allow the person to acquire specific cognitive and behavioral coping skills.

Two important points are made during the conceptualization phase. One is that the program is not psychotherapy; it is an educational program. It is emphasized that the basic difference between people who are negatively affected by stress and those who cope successfully is that the latter group has been fortunate in having previous life experiences that enable them to learn the kinds of coping skills taught in this program. The second point is that it is a program in self-control, and the coping abilities that result from the training are a function of how much effort the person devotes to the acquisition of them.

*Skill acquisition,* the third phase, is directed toward the development of an integrated coping response having both relaxation and cognitive elements. The skill acquisition phase consists of the learning of muscular relaxation coupled with an analysis of thought processes. Stress-eliciting self-statements are replaced with specific cognitions designed to reduce stress and improve performance.

Training in voluntary muscle relaxation begins immediately. Individual muscle groups are tensed, slowly relaxed halfway, and then slowly relaxed completely. The procedure is designed to enhance discrimination of slight changes in muscle tension. As training proceeds, increasingly larger groups of muscles are combined until the entire body is relaxed as a unit. Although some of the relaxation is led by the trainer, much of it is accomplished on a daily basis in the form of homework assignments.

Special emphasis is placed on the use of deep breathing to facilitate relaxation. The person is asked to breathe slowly and deeply and to say repeatedly the mental command "relax" during exhalation. The command is thus repeatedly paired with the relaxation that occurs with exhalation, so that in time the command becomes an eliciting cue for inducing relaxation.

Training in cognitive coping skills begins with a didactic description and the reading of written materials on the manner in which emotional responses are elicited by internal sentences. The trainees are given daily homework forms on which they list a situation that upsets them, the emotion they experienced, what they must have told themselves about the situation in order to have been upset, and what they might have told themselves instead in order to have prevented their distress. These exercises, discussions with the trainer, and written materials form the basis for an antistress log in which the trainees list their habitual stress-producing self-statements (usually five or fewer) and an antistress substitute for each. The latter form the basis for further practice and rehearsal. In analyzing their stress-eliciting thoughts, trainees are shown how the beliefs underlying their self-statements are often irrational (e.g., "I must always be successful in order to be worthwhile"). Replacing irrational statements with comments such as "I can do no more than give 100 percent" and "I'm still the same person whether I succeed or not" provides the person with a potential tool for preventing or reducing self-induced stress responses.

The approach just described is a form of cognitive restructuring because its objective is to evaluate and replace irrational beliefs that cause stress. However, in addition to cognitive restructuring is self-instructional training. The focus of this approach, as the name implies, is on the development of specific task-relevant self-commands. Examples of such commands are "One step at a time" and "Take a deep breath and relax."

*Skill rehearsal* is the fourth phase of this training. Stress coping skills are no different than any other kind of skill. To be most effective, they must be rehearsed and practiced under conditions that approximate the real-life situations in which they will eventually be employed. The feature that most clearly differentiates this training from other stress management programs is the use of *induced affect* during the rehearsal phase after the development of cognitive and physical coping skills.

Induced affect, the fifth phase, is used to generate high levels of emotional arousal, which are then reduced by the trainee, using the coping responses acquired in the preceding phase of training. The trainee is asked to imagine as vividly as possible a stressful situation. The person is then asked to focus on the feeling that the situation elicited. The trainer states that as the trainee focuses on it, it will begin to grow and to become stronger and stronger. The suggestions continue as the trainee begins to respond to them with increasing emotional arousal. Physical indications of arousal are verbally reinforced by the trainer ("That's good," "Let that feeling grow," "It's okay to let it come, because in a minute you'll see how easily you can turn it off"). At intervals during the arousal phase, the trainer asks the trainee what kinds of thoughts are occurring, and this information is used to elaborate on the arousal. It also provides information on the nature of the cognitions that accompany the arousal.

After a high level of arousal is achieved, the trainee is told to "turn it off" with his or her coping responses. Initially, relaxation alone is used as the coping skill. Then self-statements alone are used. Then, the two types of coping responses are combined into an integrated coping response that ties both the self-statements and the relaxation response into the breathing cycle. As the trainee inhales, he or she emits a stress-reducing self-statement. At the peak of inhalation, the trainee says the word "so" and while slowly exhaling gives the command to "relax" and induces muscular relaxation.

It should be noted that during relaxation training, exhalation, the mental command to relax, and voluntarily relaxing are repeatedly combined with one another. The introduction of the self-statement during inhalation results in the integration of cognitive and physiological coping responses within the breathing cycle.

What can be concluded about the impact of other stress management programs being used today in organizations? Due to their heterogeneity, the imprecise measures of efficacy used, and the lack of control groups, proof of the success of these programs is difficult to confirm. However, there are some reasons for feeling optimistic about this training endeavor. First, research conducted with Navy technical school personnel suggests that the beneficial effects of stress training appears to generalize from one stressor to others, and from one task to others. In other words, the effects of training that address one type of stressor (time pressure) will generalize to other stressors (e.g., noise, interruptions). Likewise, the beneficial effects of stress training on one type of computer task (e.g., a spatial orientation task) appear to generalize to other tasks (e.g., a computer task involving memory). This research is encouraging because it suggests that the development of stress training procedures has application for a wide range of situations.[40] Second, the military has been successful in using training to reduce stress in combat performance by incorporating two basic strategies in its training endeavors: providing realistic preexposure to the stress environment by means of high-fidelity simulations, and ensuring ritualistic or highly drilled responses.[41] Finally, team performance under stressful conditions has been empirically tied with the effectiveness shown by the team leader in both military and nonmilitary environments. Fortunately, as a result of research that has examined the behaviors exhibited by team leaders under stress, training specialists now understand the specific knowledge and skills that need to be taught team leaders to enhance their performance in stressful situations. Examples of the knowledge and skills needed include: (1) remove obstacles that may inhibit team member motivation, (2) relay information pertaining to performance of team member tasks, (3) communicate the effects of team interaction on team performance, (4) communicate information pertaining to issues that affect team performance, and (5) double-check team member performance and provide feedback.[42]

Another way to minimize stress in the workplace is to manage one's time effectively. We discuss this important training topic next.

## Time Management

All of the downsizing that occurred in the 1980s and 1990s has created the situation in which employees now have to work harder and smarter than ever before.[43] As a result of this, the topic of managing one's time effectively takes on special importance in today's times. The underlying theme of time management is goal setting. As noted in Chapter 4, goal-setting theory states that specific hard goals lead to higher productivity than generalized goals or the setting of no goals at all.

Hard goals lead to higher performance than easy goals. Time limits increase productivity to the extent that they lead to the setting of specific hard goals. Support for this contention was found years ago in both laboratory studies and in field settings. Let's take a closer look at two of these studies.

In a well-controlled laboratory study, it was found that if the time available to complete a task is longer than needed, the pace will be slowed to fill the allotted time. On the other hand, if the time allotted is minimal, the pace will be adjusted in order to complete the task before the deadline. This occurred because people with shorter time limits set harder goals than those with longer time limits.[44] In a field setting, logging crews showed a significantly higher rate of output when they were allowed to sell wood to forest products companies only one or two days a week rather than five. Because the crews were paid on a piece-rate basis, there was an incentive for them to maximize production early when the buying restrictions were operative. When the mills restricted the amount of wood they purchased to fewer days per week, they were implicitly urging a higher production goal (per employee hour) on the logging crews. To minimize income loss, the crews tried to harvest as much wood in one or two days as they formerly harvested in five days.[45]

In summary, time limits can affect one's work pace through goal setting—hence the growing interest in the management of time through goal setting. Although the number of books written on time management is too numerous to mention, a synthesis of their ideas is given in the following goal-setting steps:

1. Establish a daily "things to do" list.
2. Categorize your things to do as either (a) top priority, (b) medium priority, or (c) low priority.
3. Rank order the items that fall in the category of top priority.
   a. Tackle only top-priority items. An item of top priority that will require an extensive amount of time should be broken down into meaningful subparts. Rank order the subparts and work on the most important first.
   b. Ignore items that are of medium priority until there is a follow-up request.
   c. Ignore items of low priority until all top-priority and medium-priority items are completed. Do not work on items that fall in these latter two categories because your time limits are such that you can complete one of them more easily than

you can complete a top-priority item. The principle of setting subgoals by breaking a top-priority item into a number of different tasks is to keep you working on top-priority items. Adherence to this principle is also necessary to keep you from feeling reinforced for the successful completion of many low-priority tasks while top-priority items remain untouched.

4. Don't overschedule. The goals set for the day should be difficult but attainable.

The well-known practice of management writer, Peter Drucker, offered a slightly different approach to mastering time management. Step 1 for Drucker is the admonishment that planning does not come first. This is because even the best-intentioned plan is doomed unless managers first diagnose exactly how they are spending their time. Only when they take an audit of where their time is going can they hope to cut back on all the unproductive demands that inevitably interfere with their ability to accomplish their high-priority tasks. To uncover time wasters, Drucker suggests the following question: "What would be happening if I didn't do this, or if someone else did it?" If the answer is "nothing," then discard or reassign the task.

Step 2 is to consolidate blocks of time. Larger blocks of time should be assigned to major tasks. Trying to cope with projects in dribs and drabs is a sheer waste of time. Nowhere is the need for continuous and uninterrupted time blocks more vital, contends Drucker, than in dealing with people issues. Managers who attempt to direct or improve the performance of a subordinate in 20 minutes are deceiving themselves and doing a disservice to their employees. It pays to invest time in those things that matter.

Step 3, argues Drucker, is to concentrate one's effort. Too many executives and managers try to do several things at once. As a result, they dissipate their powers of concentration. Single-minded concentration on one task at a time is as close to a "secret" of effectiveness as you will find.[46]

# INTO THE TWENTY-FIRST CENTURY

In the remainder of this chapter, we discuss six issues that are relevant to all employees in the twenty-first century: (1) training for the prevention of sexual and racial harassment, (2) diversity training, (3) wellness training, (4) safety training, (5) customer service training, and (6) team skills training.

## Training for the Prevention of Sexual and Racial Harassment

Whether it occurs because of someone's sex or race, harassment is a form of discrimination and is therefore prohibited by federal law in both the United States and Canada. Violations of this law can be quite costly for organizations as shown by recent gender- and race-discrimination cases such as the sex-discrimination settlement of $508 by the U.S. federal government in 2000 and a $176 million race-discrimination settlement by Texaco in 1996. In light of these potential costs, most human resource departments develop a strongly worded statement against harassment in their employee handbooks. Even better are those companies that supplement these written statements with comprehensive training programs so that everyone in the organization clearly understands the legal basis preventing harassment, how to differentiate illegal and legal behaviors, whose conduct creates liability, additional situations creating liability (e.g., unequal conditions of employment, style of dress, making jokes), as well as recommendations for preventing harassment and avoiding liability.

Training programs designed to prevent sexual harassment are currently being conducted by many different organizations such as Sony, Chase Manhattan Bank, First Bank of Chicago, U.S. Office of Personnel Management, and the Government of Saskatchewan. These programs typically involve one or more training methods such as mini-lectures, small and large group discussions, case studies, role playing, and videos. The modules cover a range of topics for management personnel and/or nonsupervisory employees such as how to: recognize and prevent harassment, manage sexual harassment investigations, resolve harassment situations, and manage the healing process.

It has been more than 35 years since the passage of the Civil Rights Act of 1964. To be sure, there have been many encouraging developments. For example, in 1964, there was not a single *Fortune* 500 company headed up by a black in the United States, today, there are three (i.e., Avis Rent-a-Car, Maytag Corporation, and Fannie Mae), and even more in the pipeline. However, even with these high-profile examples, the overall statistics are sobering in that blacks and Hispanics combined still account for less than 2 percent of executive positions in the United States. Moreover, according to data from the U.S. Bureau of Labor Statistics, African Americans still have not attained financial parity with whites. For instance, for every dollar a white man earned in 1979 (the first year for which data are available), a black man earned, on average, 76 cents. Two decades later, that figure has increased, but to only 64 cents on the dollar. Why haven't blacks and other minorities fared better in the workplace, despite the passage of legislation that was passed years ago? Some say that, despite the Civil Rights Act of 1964, discrimination and prejudice remain in the workplace, although in subtle forms.[47] Fortunately, many companies are training their employees to create and maintain a respectful workplace. Typically, the topics covered include: examples of unacceptable and unlawful behaviors, effects of disrespectful behavior on the individual and the work group, how to intervene to stop racial discrimination situations before there is a formal complaint, equal employment opportunity and the law, and management's liabilities. In addition to the efforts to prevent sexual and racial harassment discussed in this section, some organizations have been providing diversity training programs for their employees. Let's take a closer look at this training effort.

## Diversity Training

The United States has a highly diverse workforce. It consists of people of different sexes, races, religions, cultures, and ethnic origins. Let's took a closer look at a few interesting statistics[48]:

- The populations of Hispanics/Latinos are growing fives times as fast as the general population.
- The U.S. Census Bureau estimates that Asians and Latinos will represent more than half of the population growth each year for the next 50 years.
- Sometime during this century, whites will become the minority in the U.S. population.
- The increase in the proportion of women working or looking for work that began after World War II has been one of the most significant social and economic trends in modern U.S. history. In 1940, 28 percent of American women were in the workforce. This figure rose to 40 percent in 1966, 51 percent in 1979, and 60 percent in 1998. This trend is expected to continue in the twenty-first century.
- By 2050, immigration is expected to increase the U.S. population by 80 million people; two-thirds of the projected U.S. population increase will be due to net immigration.

To help organizations retain productive workers, maintain high employee morale, and foster cooperation and harmony among culturally diverse employees, diversity training programs are being implemented by many organizations such as NASA, IBM Canada, Merrill Lynch, Sony Pictures, Visa USA, Carrier, and Black & Decker. For instance, a major human resource consulting firm reported that three-quarters of companies today either have or plan to have training programs to deal with diversity issues.[49] Before we discuss the factors associated with the adoption of diversity training and its perceived success, let's take a closer look at some diversity training programs that are now being used in the public and private sectors:

- Wisconsin Power and Light (WP&L) has one of its vice presidents or managers open each one-day training session supporting the importance of valuing diversity. The trainer then explains the benefits of diversity for WP&L, explains the company's expectations of employees, and helps them to recognize supportive and nonsupportive behaviors. Participants become actively involved during the training rather than sitting passively listening to lectures. Positive transfer of learning is facilitated by asking the participants for specific actions that they will take back on their jobs to support diversity. They are also asked to help create a list of diversity ground rules or "norms" specific to how their work group is run and how employees should interact.[50]
- The Federal Aviation Administration (FAA) Southwest Region has provided diversity training for about 740 of its managers and supervisors. The objectives of the training are to: (1) explore the primary dimensions of diversity; (2) analyze the effect of assimilation on the ability of others to succeed; (3) explore participants' personal values, stereotypes, and prejudices; (4) discuss the effect of destructive "ism" on others; (5) assess participants' readiness to value diversity; (6) identify current barriers that could interfere with cultural change; and (7) analyze ways to

prevent sexual harassment in their work environment. FAA managers and supervisors from Oklahoma, Texas, Louisiana, New Mexico, and Arkansas are exposed to real FAA incidents using simulations, case scenarios, videos, and group discussions.[51]

- UPS has taken about 800 upper- and middle-level managers off their jobs for one month to participate in its "Community Internship Program." The purpose of the program is to put them through an experience that will sensitize them to people who live in very different circumstances such as some of their employees and customers.[52] Rather than sitting in a classroom, the participants find themselves serving meals to the homeless, helping migrant workers build temporary houses and schools, and helping to rid urban ghettos of drugs. The main message that the company wants them to transfer to their jobs is that poor and disadvantaged people are not really as different from them as they once thought.

- Asians, African Americans, Hispanics/Latinos, and Native Americans are finding new opportunities that were closed to them in the past. Nevertheless, many members of these groups find that their education and experiences have not prepared them adequately to deal with subtle racial and cultural dynamics that still exist in many organizations. In light of this, minority self-development programs are being conducted in-house and by various consulting firms to increase their self-awareness and their motivation to deal with barriers they may encounter in the workplace in a constructive manner.[53]

These examples should give you an appreciation of the range of diversity programs! Despite the popularity and the expense involved in designing and implementing these programs, there is very little empirical research examining the factors associated with their effectiveness. Fortunately, a survey was completed by 785 human resource professionals that shed light about the adoption, characteristics, and perceived success of diversity training.[54] The researchers found that both training adoption and perceived training success was strongly associated with top-management support for diversity. Moreover, training adoption was associated with large organizational size, high strategic priority of diversity compared with other organizational objectives, the existence of a diversity manager, and a relatively large number of formalized policies (e.g., flexible work schedules, subsidized day care benefits, mentor programs for minorities) that support diversity. Perceived training success was associated with mandatory attendance of all managers, managerial rewards for increasing diversity, and a company definition of diversity that encompasses a broad range of diverse individuals according to their special needs and talents. These findings, together with the following guidelines, should help training specialists in the adoption and implementation of successful diversity training programs[55]:

- Incorporate both *education* (building awareness and understanding) and *training* (building usable skills) diversity initiatives.
- Position training as a part of an overall strategy for managing diversity, not as an end in itself. In the absence of other changes in the culture, systems, and practices of the organization, changes in employees' behavior are usually short lived.

- Do not start training prematurely simply to meet the need to "do something quickly." It is a mistake to simply turn to some diversity videos or a charismatic "sensitivity trainer" as the answer. Instead, programs need to be customized to meet each organization's specific needs based the same types of analyses (see Chapter 3) as would be used with any other training initiatives.
- Seek out diversity in the design process so as to ensure that the program responds to their concerns.
- Given the sensitive or even volatile nature of issues covered in diversity training, it is advisable to test the program thoroughly before rollout to reduce risk and generate enthusiasm. It isn't all that rare to have an angry participant stomp out of the room after taking offense at the meeting dialogue. News of such an episode spreads quickly to future trainees, thereby lessening the program's effectiveness.
- Incorporate diversity training and education into the core curriculum so that it becomes an organizational way of life, rather than just a One-Shot program. It should be blended into existing programs of orientation, supervisory skills, sales training, executive and management development, and so on.

Now, let's move on to another important training topic that is closely related to EAPs and stress management training—wellness training.

## Wellness Training

Organizations are beginning to realize that it is less costly to prevent the onset of disease and injury than it is to allow their occurrence and subsequent treatment. By spending modest amounts of money on teaching their employees ways of reducing health risks for major diseases, these organizations can expect to spend less in the future on corporate health care expenses. Let us take, for example, the case of CVD, which is responsible for the largest part of the nation's health care expenses. The known risk factors for CVD are smoking, high levels of serum cholesterol, family history of CVD, sedentary lifestyle, the type A behavior pattern, high blood pressure, and obesity. Note that all of these risk factors, with the exception of family history, have behavioral components. For this reason, wellness programs have focused on teaching employees the importance of health-oriented behaviors such as eating properly, getting regular exercise, and keeping one's weight down.

Let's take a look at Johnson & Johnson's "Health & Wellness" strategy, which serves as an example of an outstanding corporate wellness program. Created in 1995, Health & Wellness focuses on prevention and education with an emphasis placed on lifestyle modification and assisting employees to be better educated consumers of health care services. Listed below are several of Health & Wellness's major components[56]:

- *Occupational Injury/Illness Prevention:* Health and Wellness professionals work in collaboration with operating company management and other health and safety professionals in developing, implementing, maintaining, and continuously improving the health and safety initiatives in the workplace.

- *Medical Case Management:* Although the major focus is on injury/illness prevention, medical case management plays an important part in complex cases to positively address employee health needs, ensure a safe and proper return to work, and improve morale while minimizing lost productivity.
- *Encouraging Healthy Lifestyles:* Johnson & Johnson has a health education/health promotion program that began in the early 1980s and has evolved over the years into a sophisticated program with the following key features: increased focus on education, self-care, behavioral changes, and disease prevention and delivery of lifestyle modification interventions.
- *Drug-Free Workplace:* In support of a drug-free workplace, Johnson & Johnson has alcohol and drug training for its sales force, supervisory training providing information on identification of behaviors indicative of substance abuse, drug testing procedures, and substance abuse treatment coverage through the health plans offered to employees.
- *Ergonomics:* The company initiated egonomics programs in the early 1980s to determine root causes of certain types of injury/illness related to repetitive motion and excessive strain conditions in an effort to develop corrective action and preventive solutions for these problems. During 1998, the training of Health & Wellness occupational health nurses was completed.
- *Managing Disabilities Through Return to Wellness:* Begun in 1997, the Return to Wellness Program aims to support an employee's return to work as well as return to wellness. It also involves tailoring work assignments to match an employee's capabilities and providing the training needed to handle these modified jobs.

Most companies, particularly smaller ones, do not have wellness programs that are as sophisticated as Johnson & Johnson's Health & Wellness initiative. Instead, they typically provide their employees with customized corporate wellness educational seminars. Although the majority of these seminars continue to be delivered via instructor-led seminars, we see more and more companies putting them on their intranets or on CD- or DVD-ROMs. The health and wellness issues that are covered vary tremendously as you can see from the samples we have listed below:

- How to Help Someone Who's Depressed
- Low Back Pain Prevention and Treatment
- AIDS and HIV: An Update for Employees
- Diet and Nutrition
- Effective Parenting
- Getting Your Financial Life in Shape
- Diabetes Management and Exercise
- Smoking Cessation
- Coping with an Elderly Parent
- Effective Parenting of Adolescents
- Coping as Adult Children of Alcoholics

With the advancing age of the post–World War II baby-boom generation as well as the growth of managed care, we predict that the overall health of employees will become a major issue as we enter the twenty-first century, as will the next societal concern we will discuss—ensuring the safety of individuals at work.

## Safety Training

The importance of safety training to prevent occupational injuries can easily been seen through the following facts: (1) The cost of work-related injuries and fatalities is estimated to be greater than $121 billion annually; (2) from 1980 to 1992, more than 77,000 workers died as a result of work-related injuries, and more than 17,000 were injured; and (3) the leading causes of occupational injuries are motor vehicles, machines, falls, electrocutions, and falling objects.[57] In light of these statistics, it is not at all surprising that the 2000 ASTD (American Society for Training and Development) *State of the Industry Report* found that 9 percent of training expenditures are aimed at occupational safety programs.[58]

In addition to these facts, the amount spent on safety training is also a result of various government regulations. Since the early 1970s, the government has been working to ensure safe and healthy working conditions. As part of its program, it has established certain training standards that various industries are required to follow.

In 1970, the Occupational Safety and Health Administration (OSHA) was established as a federal agency to ensure the safe and healthy working conditions of American workers. Violations of standards may result in citations, fines, or court cases initiated by OSHA personnel who conduct compliance visits to workplaces.

Although OSHA does not certify or approve training programs per se, its compliance officers look for evidence that employers have met certain "training standards" related to their industry. The following is an example of the training standards for pulpwood logging:

> Chain saw operators shall be instructed to daily inspect the saws . . . follow manufacturer's instructions as to operation and adjustment . . . fuel the saw only in safe areas and not under conditions conducive to fire . . . hold the saw with both hands during operation . . . start the saw at least 10 feet from fueling areas . . . start the saw only on the ground or when otherwise firmly supported. (Training Requirements of the Occupational Safety and Health Standards, U.S. Department of Labor, Occupational Safety and Health Administration)

Employers must be able to produce records indicating that their employees have received training in the areas identified in the standards. Moreover, the employers must be able to show the compliance officer that the training program is based on an analysis of the tasks performed by the employee. The task analysis must identify, at a minimum, the actual and potential hazards the employee will encounter on the job and the equipment and practices the employee should follow to minimize the risk of injury to self or others. Finally, employers must be able to demonstrate that the training gives special attention to the conditions and practices most likely to result in injury and illness.

Goodyear Tire & Rubber Company, in accordance with OSHA standards, has established special programs in their tire plants to inform employees of possible health hazards due to carcinogens (e.g., vinylchloride, benzene, acrylonitrile). During these sessions, trainees are informed of such things as the atmospheric monitoring devices that have been used in the plant and the results obtained; possible consequences if one exceeds the action level (i.e., one-half the permissible exposure level); possible diseases that might occur and their symptoms; and the medical examinations associated with the particular job.

A large farm machinery manufacturing plant had a much higher accident rate than that reported by the National Safety Council for similar organizations. The effects of a safety training program was evaluated using a multiple-baseline design across three departments (Raw Material Prep, Parts, Final Assembly) using a total of four phases: (1) baseline, (2) training only, (3) training and goal setting, and (4) training, goal setting, and knowledge of results.[59] The results of their evaluation replicate those of previous research demonstrating that goal setting is effective by itself, but far more effective when combined with feedback[60] in modifying job behaviors.

We discussed equipment simulators and virtual reality in Chapter 7. We mention it again in this section on safety training because *accident simulation* is quite popular in many of today's safety training programs. It involves the use of devices that duplicate particular dangers while allowing trainees to act safely or unsafely. The most obvious example, of course, is the use of flight simulators for pilot training. Other examples include Aetna Life & Casualty Company's driver education program, which involves automobile simulators used in conjunction with videos to portray various highway conditions. This program stresses safe driving procedures and covers such topics as timing maneuvers to the actions of other highway users, coping with emergencies resulting from vehicle malfunctions, encountering motorcycles in traffic, and executing appropriate evasive actions when only split seconds are available. Goodyear has established Performance-Based Training Centers in their tire plants for new hires and transfers. These centers consist of equipment simulators (e.g., mills, fabric cutting units, tire-building machines) as well as permanent training staffs. Trainees are shown the potential hazards that can result from performing each step of their jobs incorrectly, as well as how to do it correctly. The company has found at their Danville Center in Virginia, for instance, that there has been a substantial reduction in the total number of OSHA reportable accidents and lost-time days. Babcock & Wilcox, an organization that manufactures nuclear boilers, uses simulators in Lynchburg, Virginia. Their equipment simulates the operation of nuclear power plants similar to the one located at Three Mile Island in Pennsylvania. It trains nuclear power operators by simulating temperature, pressure, and flow readings on their instruments, allowing them to react, and providing them with immediate feedback regarding the consequences of their actions. Our final example focuses on using an accident simulator for submarine ship control training. The U.S. Navy has had the Applied Physics Laboratory, a research division of

Johns Hopkins University, design a PC multimedia and simulation-based training tool that instructs Navy personnel on the principles of submerged ship handling. The key component is an interactive submarine simulation that incorporates interactive control panel replicas and uses sound, animation, and a three-dimensional rendering of the submarine to create a virtual environment that allows trainees to respond to various scenarios. Besides learning how to properly moor and get a submarine under way with tug boats, trainees can practice driving a submerged submarine through various casualty-laden events.

Most employees receive safety training via either full-length videos, five-to seven-minute videos, digital safety videos, interactive CD-ROMs, and online training. There are literally hundreds of full-length training videos that vary in length from 15 to 20 minutes. They cover a wide range of safety topics such as back injury prevention, ladder safety, taking the right steps, hazardous spills, benzene safety, and machine guarding. The concise five- to seven-minute videos serve as excellent supplements to, and refreshers for, the full-length videos. All of these videos are typically also available in DSV format, which eliminates the need for bulky video players by allowing employees to play the videos right on their desktop computers. Interactive CD-ROMs provide full-screen videos that have high-impact graphics and allow trainees to receive interactive training that can be customizable by adding video, text, quizzes, and other materials. CD-ROMs are used to teach many safety topics such as fire prevention, equipment lockout and tagout procedures, accident investigation, forklift safety, and asbestos maintenance. Increasingly, companies are moving from using CD-ROMs to using online safety training. If a company wanted to have 100 training stations, it would have to install one CD-ROM at every station. Moreover, if the safety training material needed to be updated, all of these CD-ROMs would need to be replaced. However, when safety training is delivered over the World Wide Web or over the company's intranet, or LAN (a local area network), or a WAN (wide area network), only one installation is required and the materials can easily be updated. The popularity of these TBT methods is evident from the 2000 ASTD *State of the Industry Report*.[61] Specifically, the percentage of companies using them are as follows: CD-ROM (56.3 percent), World Wide Web (19.8 percent), intranet (32.2 percent), LAN (40.2 percent), and WAN (13.95 percent). Examples of safety topics delivered online are driver safety, office ergonomics, and hazard communications.

To our knowledge, no effort to address the problems of safety and health equals that of GM. Since the UAW-GM Health and Safety Training Center opened in 1985, more than 2,000 trainers have received training in safety programs at their home plants designed to reduce the number of accidents and injuries on the job. Located in Auburn Hills, Michigan, the center offers numerous training programs on fork truck safety, robotic safety, rigging safety, mobile crane safety, and the potential hazards of handling six categories of chemicals used by GM. All of these training programs use state-of-the-art training methods. For instance, the hands-on workshop for the mobile crane safety program involves an obstacle course that has been set up at the center. Working in pairs (i.e., an operator and a signalman), trainees navigate their way through the obstacle course using techniques that they learned through TBT.

Besides using training to ensure safe work habits, some progressive organizations have begun to give their employees training in the prevention of ill health and disease. Some organizations call their efforts wellness programs; others refer to them as workplace health promotion programs.

The next topic is an extremely important one because without satisfied customers, no organization can be effective and survive.

## Customer Service Training

"Focus on the customer" has become a corporate mandate in numerous organizations striving for excellence. This is because customer satisfaction results in repeat business and enduring business relationships, which increase profitability. According to the 2000 ASTD *State of the Industry Report,* customer service training accounts for 7 percent of training expenditures annually or, on average, $833 per employee. Moreover, 8 percent of the spending on TBT is directed at customer service employees.[62]

Who needs customer service training? Certainly, the employees who have direct contact with customers. But these frontline people are not the only ones who should receive training. Every individual in an organization should be familiar with the company's customer service philosophy and understand how their job, regardless of how far removed it may be from customers, has an impact on service. Moreover, customer service training should not be looked at as a one-time or even an annual event. Instead, it is an ongoing training process that should be incorporated into the organization's culture and way of doing business.[63]

One service provider that has been using employee training to increase the satisfaction level of their customers is the Radisson Hotel Corporation. Their training program, known as "Yes I Can," is the direct result of a Radisson study demonstrating that a friendly, helpful staff is the most important element of their customers' hotel experience. The Yes I Can training consists of two parts. Part I teaches Radisson employees about the corporation's commitment to the finest in customer service, the various components of top-quality service, how to better understand guests and their needs, as well as techniques based on a positive attitude that can enhance a guest's experience. The first part of the program also consists of an "Inform and Explore Session" in which new ideas and skills are introduced and examined and a "Review and Practice Session," where the newly acquired skills are perfected and applied. The second part of the training follows graduation from Part I. During follow-up sessions, supervisors encourage employees to review what they have learned, apply their new skills on their jobs, and look for new ways of improving customer service. Monthly meetings help maintain the flow of ideas and innovations.

The Educational Institute of the American Hotel and Motel Association has a guest relations training program known as "The Spirit of Hospitality" available for its members. Thousands of hospitality industry employees have already been through this program that was designed to sensitize all employees to guests' needs and expectations, increase communications (between staff and guests, staff and staff, staff and management), create a spirit of teamwork, promote positive guest relations, provide opportunities for recognition, and motivate employees to take pride in their jobs.

Numerous service organizations in the energy (i.e., electric and gas utilities), financial (banks and savings and loans), and telecommunications (telephone companies) industries have instituted training programs to enhance, at all levels, employees' skills and attitudes toward serving customers. These service organizations will frequently hire a consulting firm that specializes in improving customer service that will first help senior executives in establishing a plan and timetable that recognizes their company's situation, the extent of their team's commitment to becoming customer focused, and their visions for the future of their organization. Once senior-level management is committed to cultivating service excellence, everyone in the company is trained in creating satisfied customers. It makes no difference whether the employee interacts with external customers (i.e., the public) or internal customers (i.e., employees in other departments that one's department services). Trainees are taught how to recognize the difficult customer, manage customer expectations, reduce stress, build rapport, and create positive outcomes. For example, IBM conducted a survey of 13,000 IBM customers and found that their single biggest complaint was poor call handling when they telephoned an IBM office. After carefully determining the specific reasons customers were dissatisfied with call handling as well as how much IBM employees knew about the telephone system, two audiences were targeted for training: intensive users (e.g., secretaries, information operators) and casual users (engineers, managers) of the system. Separate training programs were designed for each group of user groups. The intensive users training package includes a videotape and workbook, a mainframe CBT package, instructional pamphlets, and job aids. The casual users training package consists of a videotape package, an audiotape, a short mainframe CBT package, and a series of job aids. After completing the design of the two programs, IBM performed the traditional "make versus buy" analysis and decided to contract with outside suppliers for the majority of the self-study materials. These customer service training programs have increased customer satisfaction with IBM's telephone responsiveness from 74 percent to 82 percent.[64]

The single most effective training approach that fosters customer focus is the modeling of that focus by senior-level management. Sam Walton, the founder of the Wal-Mart retail chain, exemplified this approach to training. His personal attention to merchandising and customer service modeled what he expected from his employees. Failure to maintain these standards is considered both a personal defeat as well as a shortfall in mutual obligations between upper management and the Wal-Mart employees.

We have been talking about increasing customer service by providing training to company employees. Customer service can also be improved by companies' training their customers. Here are two examples[65]:

- Fisher Controls of Marshalltown, Iowa, is a manufacturer of control valves as well as regulated and automated control systems. Fisher Controls has been training employees of utilities, chemical plants, and other large users of its products for many years. The instructors are Fisher technicians and engineers who have been given training in needs assessment and instructional techniques.
- Armstrong World Industries prints an 800 number on the surface of its no-wax floors. Printing on the flooring tells customers to call the 800 number to find out how to remove the message. While Armstrong has customers on the phone, they give them tips on how to care for the floors correctly, thereby lowering the many complaints that Armstrong received from customers because they didn't know how to take care of these floors properly.

The final section of this chapter focuses on one of the most important trends affecting the world of work, namely, the increased use of teams.

## Team Skills Training

According the 2000 ASTD *State of the Industry Report,* participants in the Benchmarking Service reported extensive use of a wide variety of work practices designed to boost employee and organizational performance. Two of the most widely used work practices were task forces and problem-solving teams or quality circles. Moreover, these uses of teams registered the largest year-to-year gains: from 78 percent in 1997 to 98 percent in 1998. As a result of this, there is a concern in organizations with improving the effectiveness of various types of work teams (e.g., departments, committees, management teams, task forces, project teams).

Let us take a brief look at what various companies and the military are currently doing in the way of team skills training. We have carefully chosen these examples to illustrate the wide range of approaches that are currently being used for team training.

In our first example, S. B. Thomas, Inc., one of the largest producers of English muffins in the United States, relies primarily on *individual performance feedback* for team building. At one of their plants in Schaumburg, Illinois, workers (or, as they are called, associates) are organized into teams, or action groups, according to their function. For instance, associates assigned to muffin production are members of the process action group; those working in the packaging area belong to the pack action group. Once the applicants are hired and appear on the bakery's production floor, they receive weekly reports during their 60-day probationary period that give them specific feedback on both their interpersonal behavior as a team member as well as on technical aspects of their work performance.[66]

Our next example exemplifies the use of *understanding of oneself and others* as the primary vehicle for team member training. Numerous organizations approach team skills training by using assessment techniques that help team members gain a better understanding of their own personal behavioral styles and how their styles are compatible or incompatible with other team members' styles. For instance, a mid-Michigan professional liability insurance company had difficulty in the teamwork among their staff of underwriters. Clearly, both cooperation and communication among the underwriters were suffering terribly. This lack of teamwork was primarily caused by misunderstandings and misperceptions among the individuals involved. To help everyone understand themselves and others better, each underwriter was asked to take a battery of tests that assessed their personality traits, values, and interpersonal styles. Next, a skillful trainer met individually with each underwriter to examine and discuss their test scores with them in private so as to help them to gain a better understanding of their own behaviors. Once this was accomplished, the trainer met several times with the whole team of 10 underwriters. At these team-building meetings, each underwriter presented *some* of the things that they learned about themselves to the others. Each underwriter's presentation about themselves generated quite a lot of further discussion within the team. The trainer was always present to ensure that others' reactions did not become malicious or hateful. The improvement of the underwriting team did not occur overnight. Instead, it took several months for the team members to improve the cooperation and communication among themselves.

Employee *cross-training* using positional rotation as a team training technique has received a growing amount of attention.[67] This technique can be conceptualized as a form of job rotation (see Chapter 6) among team members. It provides each team member with a basic understanding of the knowledge needed to perform the duties of other team members. It also gives each team member an overview of the team task and how their role is important to the team's success.[68] The basic objective of cross-training is to foster in team members a shared mental model of the task and how to accomplish it, the equipment being used, the role each plays in the task, as well as the roles of other team members.[69] Research results have shown that cross-training is an important determinant of effective teamwork process, communication, and performance.[70] For instance, the Navy has enhanced team performance through cross-training of individual combat information center (CIC) team members. Initial interviews with CIC team members revealed that they had multiple mental models regarding the equipment, individual tasks, CIC team performance, the ship, and how the ship fits within a battergroup context. As a result, the Team Model Training (TMT) was designed by the Navy, a low-cost, off-the-shelf, PC-based training device. By way of description, a training session with the TMT starts with learning about any of the six tasks and/or team-related knowledge domains, and then participating in a scenario simulation where the various knowledge domains can be applied and practiced. Individual team member participation in the scenario simulation can occur in one of two ways. The team member can choose to either observe a 30-minute anti–air warfare scenario where they experience an expert team identify air traffic and take actions in line with the rules of engagement or else carry out the duties and responsibilities of a watch station by listening to teammates, making reports, and entering data into the system.[71] TMT's success illustrates that complex team interactions can be demonstrated, practiced, and learned using a low-cost, PC-based system.

A number of organizations are using *360° Feedback* (see Chapter 9) as a vehicle for improving team performance. For instance, job analyses were conducted for a group of first-line supervisors and for a vice president and his immediate staff by one of the authors. Two Behavioral Observation Scales (BOSs) were developed for each respective group (see Chapter 3). Each person was then evaluated anonymously on the BOS by his or her peers.

The advantage of using a BOS, as the 360° instrument, was that the individual employee was involved in the job analysis that was the basis for developing the yardstick (BOS) on which he or she is assessed. Thus, the BOS was developed by the employee for the employee. The results proved to be highly beneficial in terms of inducing and sustaining behavior change. The mechanisms were straightforward. The feedback was based on job-related items, and specific goals were set regarding job-related items. It was difficult for an employee to downplay the importance of these job-related items because the items were identified as important to job success by the employee and his or her peers. It was also difficult for the employee to say that the BOS did not provide a comprehensive measure of what is required of him or her as a team player because everyone in the group participated in its development. More importantly, it was more difficult to discredit the observations of a group of people, namely, one's fellow team members, than it is to discredit the observations of one person, namely, one's supervisor. The employee cannot risk the condemnation of the team for failing to work toward the attainment of the goals agreed upon during the appraisal but could enjoy the reinforcement for working toward and attaining these goals on an ongoing basis on the job.

Another team-building approach has focused on *increasing the skills of individual team members,* regardless of the particular task facing the team. Typically, team members are given training in such skills as team decision making, listening, mutual supportiveness, sharing information, managing conflict, assertiveness, and problem solving. Team leaders receive training in such areas as effective team leadership, discipline in the team, facilitating team activities, managing individual and team performance, team problem solving, and methods of job instruction.[72] These individual skills are important to team success, particularly when the plan is to create teams that will eventually be self-managing.[73] Nevertheless, research had shown that these individual skills are a necessary but not sufficient condition for good team performance. Apparently, the magnitude of the relationship between the average skill level of individual team members and team effectiveness is small. It appears that enhancing team performance is often a more complex interactive undertaking than solely improving the skills of individual team members.[74]

Another team-building approach that some organizations use is *simulation*. This approach is adopted when organizations need to be particularly concerned with the fidelity of the training environment to operational task conditions. This occurs particularly when conditions are stressful and there is a critical need for coordination among team members. Simulation has been used successfully in training for developing effective military, surgical, astronaut, fire fighting, and aviation teams.[75]

A final approach for increasing team effectiveness focuses on increasing *role clarification*. This approach is based on the assumption that a team is a combination of overlapping roles and that much of a team's behaviors can be accounted for by team members' perceptions of their own and others' roles.[76] Role clarification is often brought about through an intervention known as Role Analysis Technique (RAT). One of the authors recently used RAT to increase team effectiveness in a small restaurant chain. He had a structured series of meetings in which each person listed the specific responsibilities and duties of their job with the help of coworkers, listed what is expected from others, learned what others expected of them, and left the RAT session with a written summary of their complete role. Role Analysis Technique resulted in an increase in role clarity, team cohesiveness, and service as reported by a random sampling of customers.

What can be said about the effectiveness of team skills training? First, the overall magnitude of the effect of team building on performance is actually quite modest. Only about 2.2 percent of the variability in a team's performance can be accounted for by knowing whether or not the team had gone through team training. Second, team-building interventions that have focused on increasing role clarification have been found to have the greatest impact on team performance.[77] Third, team-buliding interventions tend to show a stronger effect on team member attitudes and perceptions than on performance. Finally, it is important to keep in mind that team training may not be the answer to a team's performance problems. Team training will fail when a team's real problems stem from motivational problems, resource problems, management problems, and/or task design problems.[78] For example, one of the authors was recently consulting with a small, newly formed, high-tech dot-com company. Although management professed its desire to create "high performance work teams" throughout the company, starting with them, this was found to be impossible due to their oversized egos.

# FINAL COMMENTS

There is no reason to be complacent over the quality of scientific research on training and development, nor is there reason for despair. Fads do not dominate the scientific literature on training and development; advancement in theory and empirical research is ongoing. What troubles some people is the extent to which practitioners and practitioner journals appear to be unaffected by these advancements. Overcoming this problem is certainly an area for research. One solution may be simply to translate scientific articles for a lay audience. This has been one of the main objectives of this book.

The success of any training and development program in organizations depends on three basic elements: (1) systematic determination of training needs, (2) careful design to facilitate learning and transfer back to the job, and (3) systematic evaluation of the training program.

If training is to become respected as a science of behavior, we cannot retreat from the crucial task of specifying what it is that trainees are supposed to learn. We need to specify exactly what trainees are expected to know and do differently as a result of participating in the training program. Course objectives cannot be properly generated through armchair speculation and wishful thinking. Instead, they must be determined through a painstaking identification of each of the tasks involved in performing a job.

Unfortunately, at the present time, not enough is known about the principles of learning to ensure that learning will take place with every trainee. However, there are aptitude measuring instruments today to select individuals who have the ability to learn what is being taught. Also, enough is now known about human motivation to design programs so that individuals will remain interested in learning. Further, it is clear that psychomotor learning should include some combination of goal setting + modeling + practice + feedback, whereas, for factual learning, goal setting + meaningfulness + practice + feedback are important components of learning and transfer.

Evaluation should not be viewed as a simple yes/no decision about continuing training. Programs are seldom all good or all bad. Rather, evaluation studies should be part of a continuous feedback process for the training staff. When an evaluation study has been completed, the training staff needs to consider whether and/or how the training should be modified. It is a costly mistake for trainers to let their emotional reactions cloud their thinking about improving their programs. It is important that they carefully think through why certain course objectives were not attained and how they can improve their program the next time it is administered.

In conclusion, note the following four important suggestions for future efforts in the field of training:

1. It is important to further understand how differences among trainees moderate the effectiveness of different training techniques. More research is needed to examine aptitude-treatment interactions (see Chapter 4). If this is done, instructional programs will be designed that best suit each trainee.

2. It is important to understand how different organizational variables (e.g., technology, motivational conditions, unionization) affect training efforts. Training specialists have to become more cognizant of, and knowledgeable about, the "macro" variables that affect trainees in their organizations. It is no longer appropriate to assume that training exists independent of its organizational context.

3. There is a need for rigorous evaluation studies that examine the usefulness of individual training approaches as well as different combinations of training and devel-

opment approaches. Too many of the training methods currently in use fall far short of the standards we have discussed in this book.

4. The impact of training and development activities will be maximized when they take place in the right culture, a "learning organization."[79] This is an organization whose members at all levels spontaneously learn and innovate,[80] whose employees are allowed to use their brains to implement their own ideas,[81] and whose members are continually learning how to learn together.[82]

# ENDNOTES

1. K. Tyler, "Mentoring Programs Link Employees and Experienced Execs," *HR Magazine 43* (1999): 99–103.
2. Ibid.
3. Overman, 1999.
4. Tyler, "Mentoring Programs Link Employees and Experienced Execs."
5. Ibid.
6. C. Robertson, *Hire Right Fire Right* (New York: McGraw-Hill, 1992).
7. D. Mank, J. Oorthuys, L. Rhodes, D. Sandow, and T. Weyer, "Accomodating Workers with Mental Disabilities," *Training & Development 46* (1992): 49–52.
8. B. Filipczak, "Adaptive Technology for the Disabled," *Training,* March 1993, 23–29.
9. B. Filipczak, "Old Dogs, New Tricks," *Training,* May 1998, 50–57.
10. Ibid.
11. Filipczak, "Old Dogs, New Tricks."
12. H. L. Sterns and D. Doverspike, "Aging and the Training and Learning Process," in I. L. Goldstein and Associates (eds.), *Training and Development in Organizations* (San Francisco: Jossey-Bass, 1989): 229–329.
13. Filipczak, "Old Dogs, New Tricks."
14. MATAC "What Is Telecommuting?" The Metro Atlanta Telecommuting Advisory Council. Atlanta, GA, 2000.
15. International Telework Association & Council. Telework America Online Curriculum, 1999. Washington, DC.
16. L. Grensing-Pophal, "Training Employees to Telecommute: A Recipe for Success," *HR Magazine,* December 1998, 76–82.
17. Ibid.
18. L. Grensing-Pophal, "Training Supervisors to Manage Teleworkers," *HR Magazine,* January 1999. 67–72.
19. Ibid.
20. K. N. Wexley, R. E. Sanders, and G. A. Yukl, "Training Interviewers to Eliminate Contrast Effects in Employment Interviews," *Journal of Applied Psychology 57* (1973): 233–36.
21. G. P. Latham, K. N. Wexley, and E. D. Pursell, "Training Managers to Minimize Rating Errors in the Observation of Behavior," *Journal of Applied Psychology 60* (1975): 550–55.
22. Intercultural Training Institute, Office of International Programs, University of North Carolina, Charlotte, NC, 2000.
23. C. Earley, "Intercultural Training for Managers: A Comparison of Documentary and Interpersonal Methods," *Academy of Management Journal 30* (1987): 685–98.
24. S. Ronen, "Training the International Assignee," in I. L. Goldstein and Associates (eds.), *Training and Development in Organizations* (San Francisco: Jossey-Bass, 1989): 417–54.
25. K. N. Wexley and S. B. Silverman, *Working Scared: Achieving Success in Trying Times* (San Francisco: Jossey-Bass, 1993).

26. Ibid.

27. A. C. Poe, "Welcome Back," *HR Magazine,* March 2000, 94–96.

28. J. Freivalds, "Self-Study Programs Aid Language Learning," *HR Magazine,* January 1997, 57–63.

29. Global Integration, *Training People Who Work Internationally.* Portland, OR, 2000.

30. R. Kelley and J. Caplan, "How Bell Labs Creates Star Performers," *Harvard Business Review,* July–August 1993, 128–39.

31. D. E. Berlew and D. T. Hall, "The Socialization of Managers: Effects of Expectations on Performance," *Administrative Science Quarterly 11* (1966): 207–23.

32. J. Robinet, "Employee Assistance Programs Gain Popularity as Benefit," *Pittsburgh Business Times,* November 11, 1996; and Dr. Wilson, "How to Implement an Employee Assistance Program," *B. C. Solutions Magazine,* May 1998, 1–3.

33. National Employee Assistance Services, "NEAS: Training Programs," *www.neas.com* (2000).

34. Wilson, "How to Implement an Employee Assistance Program."

35. N. Seppa, "EAPs Offer Quality Care and Cost-Effectiveness," in the *APA Monitor.* March 1997, 1–3.

36. T. Webster and B. Bergman, "Occupational Stress: Counts and Rates," *Compensation and Working Conditions Online 4* (1999): 1–4.

37. *AIS: Dedicated to Advancing Our Knowledge of the Role of Stress in Health and Disease* (Washington, DC: American Institute for Stress, 2000).

38. R. E. Smith, "A Cognitive-Affective Approach to Stress Management Training for Athletes," in C. H. Hadeau, W. Holliwell, K. M. Newell, and G. C. Roberts (eds.), *Skillfulness in Movement: Psychology of Motor Behavior and Sport* (Champaign, IL: Human Kinetics, 1980).

39. A. Bandura, *Social Foundations of Thought and Action* (Upper Saddle River, NJ: Prentice Hall, 1986).

40. J. E. Driskell, E. Salas, and J. Johnson, "Is Stressing Training Generalizable to Novel Situations?" Paper presented at the Annual Conference of the Society for Industrial and Organizational Psychology. Orlando, FL, 1995.

41. J. E. Driskell and E. Salas, "Overcoming the Effects of Stress on Military Performance: Human Factors, Training and Selection Strategies," in R. Gal and A. D. Mangelsdorff (eds.), *Handbook of Military Psychology* (Chichester: John Wiley & Sons, 1991): 183–93.

42. K. A. Burgess, E. Salas, J. A. Cannon-Bowers, and J. Hall, "Training Guidelines for Team Leaders Under Stress." Paper presented at the Annual Meeting of the Human Factors Society. Atlanta, GA, 1992.

43. Wexley and Silverman, *Working Scared.*

44. J. F. Bryan and E. A. Locke, "Parkinson's Law as a Goal-Setting Phenomenon," *Organizational Behavior and Human Performance 2* (1967): 258–75.

45. G. P. Latham and E. A. Locke, "Increasing Productivity with Decreasing Time Limits: A Field Replication of Parkinson's Law," *Journal of Applied Psychology 60* (1975): 524–26.

46. P. F. Drucker, "Managing for Business Effectiveness," *Harvard Business Review 65* (1987): 28.

47. R. J. Grossman, "Race in the Workplace," *HR Magazine,* March 2000, 41–50.

48. *The U.S. Population Is Becoming Larger and More Diverse* (Washington, DC: U.S. Department of Labor, 2000).

49. Towers Perrin, "Companies Train Managers to Prevent Harassment," *The Monitor 127* (1992): 1, 3–5.

50. N. L. Mueller, "Wisconsin Power and Light's Model Diversity Program," *Training & Development,* March 1996, 57–60.

51. Ibid.

52. B. Filipczak, "What Employers Teach," *Training,* October 1992, 43–55.

53. Pope & Associates, Inc., *Management Skills for the Diverse Work Forces* (Cincinnati, OH, 2000).

54. S. Rynes and B. Rosen, "A Field Survey of Factors Affecting the Adoption and Perceived Success of Diversity Training," *Personnel Psychology 48* (1995): 247–70.

55. A. P. Delatte and L. Baytos, "Guidelines for Successful Diversity Training," *Training,* January 1993, 55–60.

56. Johnson & Johnson, *Environmental, Health, and Safety Report* (New Brunswick, NJ: Johnson & Johnson Corporation, 1998).

57. Centers for Disease Control and Prevention, *Centers for Disease Control and Prevention: Training and Employment Opportunities* (2000).

58. D. P. McMurrer, M. E. Van Buren, and W. H. Woodwell Jr., *The 2000 ASTD State of the Industry Report* (Alexandria, VA: American Society for Training and Development, 2000).

59. R. A. Reber, J. A. Wallin, and J. S. Chhokar, "Improving Safety Performance with Goal Setting and Feedback," *Human Performance 3* (1990): 51–61.

60. E. A. Locke, K. N. Shaw, L. M. Saari, and G. P. Latham, "Goal Setting and Task Performance," *Psychological Bulletin 90* (1981): 125–52.

61. McMurrer, Van Buren, and Woodwell, *The 2000 ASTD State of the Industry Report.*

62. Ibid.

63. Grensing-Pophal, "Training Supervisors to Manage Teleworkers."

64. M. Estabrooke and N. F. Foy, "Answering the Call of 'Tailored Training,'" *Training,* October 1992, 85–88; and K. N. Wexley and W. F. Nemeroff, "Effectiveness of Positive Reinforcement and Goal Setting as Methods of Management Development," *Journal of Applied Psychology 60* (1975): 446–50.

65. B. Filipczak, "Customer Education (Some Assembly Required)," *Training,* December 1991, 31–35.

66. N. Rubin, "Training in a Team Environment: S. B. Thomas, Inc.," in J. Casner-Lotto and Associates (eds.), *Successful Training Strategies* (San Francisco: Jossey-Bass, 1988): 142–56.

67. K. K. Travillian, C. E. Volpe, J. A. Cannon-Bowers, and E. Salas, "Cross-Training Highly Interdependent Teams: Effects on Team Process and Team Performance." Proceedings of the 37th Annual Human Factors and Ergonomics Society Conference (Santa Monica, CA: Human Factors Society, 1993): 1243–47.

68. E. Salas, J. A. Cannon-Bowers, and E. L. Blickensderfer, "Team Performance and Training Research: Emerging Principles," *Journal of the Washington Academy of Sciences 83* (1993): 81–106.

69. J. A. Cannon-Bowers, E. Salas, and S. A. Converse, "Shared Mental Models in Expert Team Decision Making," in N. J. Castellan Jr. (ed.), *Current Issues in Individual and Group Decision Making* (Hillsdale, NJ: Lawrence Erlbaum, 1993) 221–46.

70. P. C. Duncan, J. A. Cannon-Bowers, J. Johnston, and E. Salas, "Using a Simulated Team to Model Teamwork Skills: The Team Model Trainer." Unpublished manuscript, 1994; and C. E. Volpe, J. A. Cannon-Bowers, E. Salas, and P. Spector, "The Impact of Cross-Training on Team Functioning: An Empirical Examination," *Human Factors 38* (1993): 87–100.

71. E. Salas, J. A. Cannon-Bowers, and J. H. Johnston, "How Can You Turn a Team of Experts into an Expert Team? Emerging Training Strategies," in C. Zsambok and G. Klein (eds.), *Naturalistic Decision Making* (Hillsdale, NJ: LEA, 1997): 359–70.

72. K. A. Smith and E. Salas, "Training Assertiveness: The Importance of Active Participation." Paper presented at the 37th Annual Meeting of Southeastern Psychological Association, New Orleans, LA, 1991; and S. I. Tannenbaum, R. L. Beard, and E. Salas, "Team Building and Its Influence on Team Developments," *Issues, Theory and Research in Psychology* (Amsterdam: Elsevier, 1992): 117–53.

73. A. Harper and B. Harper, *Skill-Building for Self-Directed Team Members* (New York: MW Corporation, 1993).

74. E. Salas, T. L. Dickinson, S. A. Converse, and S. I. Tannenbaum, "Toward an Understanding of Team Performance and Training," in R. Swezey and E. Salas (eds.), *Teams: Their Training and Performance* (Norwood, NJ: Ablex, 1992): 3–29.

75. J. A. Cannon-Bowers, E. Salas, and J. D. Grossman, "Improving Tactical Decision Making Under Stress: Research Directions and Applied Implications." Paper presented at the International Applied Military Psychology Symposium. Stockholm, Sweden, 1991; and J. K. Hall, D. J. Dwyer, J. A. Cannon-Bowers, E. Salas, and C. E. Volpe, "Toward Assessing Team Tactical Decision Making Under Stress: The Development of a Methodology for Structuring Team Training Scenarios." Proceedings of the 15th Annual Interservice/Industry Training Systems Conference. Washington, DC: National Security Industrial Association, 1993, 87–98.

76. Tannenbaum, Beard, and Salas, "Team Building and Its Influence on Team Developments."

77. E. Salas, B. Mullen, D. Rozell, and J. E. Driskel, "The Effects of Team Building on Performance: An Integration." Presented at the Annual Conference of the Society for Industrial and Organizational Psychology. St. Louis, MO, 1997.

78. Tannenbaum, Beard, and Salas, "Team Building and Its Influence on Team Developments."

79. P. M. Senge, *The Fifth Discipline: The Art and Practice of the Learning Organization* (New York: Currency Doubleday, 1990).

80. T. Kramlinger, "Training's Role in a Learning Organization," *Training,* July 1992, 46–50.

81. L. Honold, "The Power of Learning at Johnsonville Foods," *Training,* April 1991, 55–58.

82. D. A. Garvin, "Building a Learning Organization," *Harvard Business Review,* July–August 1993, 78–91.

# Author Index

# Subject Index